Experience & Jewish Education

Edited by David Bryfman

Torah Aura Producitons

ISBN 10: 1-934527-75-7

ISBN 13: 978-1-934527-75-0

Torah Aura Productions • 4423 Fruitland Avenue, Los Angeles, CA 90058
(800) BE-Torah • (800) 238-6724 • (323) 585-7312 • fax (323) 585-0327
E-MAIL <misrad@torahaura.com> • Visit the Torah Aura website at www.torahaura.com

MANUFACTURED IN THE USA

Dedication

To Jonah and Abby

Children are not the people of tomorrow, but people today.
They are entitled to be taken seriously. They have a right to be
treated by adults with tenderness and respect, as equals. They should
be allowed to grow into whoever they were meant to be—
the unknown person inside each of them is the hope for the future.

Janusz Korczak

Without apologetics or defensiveness, the articles in *Experience & Jewish Education* explore charged questions that vex and inspire the field of experiential Jewish education. The authors tackle philosophical, practical, and even ontological dilemmas, including: if the field exists or should exist apart from simply "good education;" and if so, what the field should be called; how serious playful learning is not an oxymoron; why effective is not the same as efficient education; why assessment is neither intimidating nor optional; and perhaps most important of all, why successful experiential Jewish education is not about having experiences, but about carefully designed opportunities to reflect upon them. Together, Bryfman and the contributors of his stimulating anthology offer a range of generative heuristic definitions that are at once specific and concrete enough to propel the conversation forward, while also flexible enough to allow the field to be a thoughtful work in progress. Nothing could be more refreshing or timely for Experiential Jewish Education than gathering a group of rigorous voices who embrace its major tensions, criticisms and achievements. There are already a number of Jewish experiential education courses and programs taught at various levels around the country, and more continue to sprout. *Experience & Jewish Education* should be on all of those required reading list, but also taught across the nation's schools of Jewish education. Through these bold explorations, *Experience & Jewish Education* just might help rescue academics and educators from a tediously polarized discourse that has limited us long enough.

Tali Zelkowicz, Assistant Professor and Sara S. Lee Chair for an Emerging Scholar in Jewish Education, Rhea Hirsch School of Jewish Education, Hebrew Union College-Jewish Institute of Religion, Los Angeles, CA.

In an era of so much destabilizing change in all aspects of our complex lives, we must have enchanting cultural, spiritual and social horizons. As we remake Jewish life we keenly need concepts and practices that can forge a flourishing Jewish education fit for our times. Educators, rabbis, and cultural arts programmers should pause to ponder the nuggets of insight explored in this invaluable collection. Kudos to the authors.

Yonatan Ariel, Executive Director of Makom: the Israel Education Lab

Experiential Jewish education matters, and it will only continue to matter. The complexity of our post-modern world — and our post-modern selves — intertwine what were once dichotomies: organic and organized, personal and communal, affective and cognitive learning. In response, if learning in the 20th century can be seen as the transmission of cold facts, Jewish learning in the 21st must be the helping of students to develop ways of thinking and feeling, habits of mind and heart, about those facts, so that organized, cognitive, communal learning takes into consideration the organic, personal, and affective experiences that students bring to education. It is only through the blending of experiential education and what have been typical classroom techniques that we will help to build Jewish actors and thinkers who can build Jewish vitality. And it is only through close study and active conversation that we will understand the complexity of experiential education, of the blending of affective and cognitive learning through doing.

Experiential Jewish education has lacked core texts to establish its key principles and ideas. David Bryfman has assembled leading practitioners and scholars — blending, appropriately, voices, backgrounds, and approaches — to create such a core text. Bryfman's introduction and the book's essays provide equally a set of fundamental definitions, a skeleton on which to build the practice, as well as conceptual questions, textured ideas, and even debates, opportunities for educators to sharpen their practice through additional discussion and thought. The book provides a foundation on which not just this field but our growing understandings of the hows of Jewish learning in a post-modern era can be built.

Beth Cousens, Principal, Beth Cousens Consulting

Over the past decade, "experiential education" has garnered growing attention from policy makers and funders as perhaps our best hope for engaging and inspiring the next generation of Jews. Venues for Jewish experiential learning have expanded, new training programs have been launched, and the approaches that characterize experiential education have increasingly found their way into Jewish schools and other so-called "formal" settings. Now, this movement also has its "Bible" in *Experience & Jewish Education*, edited by David Bryfman. Bringing together chapters written by leaders in the field, this volume offers both rich conceptual frameworks for understanding what experiential Jewish education is and why it is so important and effective in the context of 21st century Jewish life and practical reflections on how to build an encompassing system that can provide dynamic, high quality learning experiences from early childhood into adulthood. Bryfman and his colleagues have brought the documentation and analysis of experiential Jewish education to an entirely new level. Educators and policy-makers alike will benefit enormously from the insights and clear-headed guidance this book provides, and American Jewish life as a whole will be immensely richer and more secure as the ideas detailed herein become the framework for educational practice in a wide array of settings.

Dr. Jonathan Woocher, President, Lippman Kanfer Foundation for Living Torah

CONTENTS

ACKNOWLEDGEMENTS

Attempting to credit the origins of this book turned out to be a more difficult task than I anticipated. Definitely not a linear path, there have been several pivotal episodes in my own journey that have contributed to the publishing of this anthology that I hope serves as a milestone in the evolution of experiential Jewish education.

To an external observer my Jewish education may have appeared to be delivered in Jewish day schools. Indeed several teachers were pivotal figures in my Jewish learning journey. One was a modern Orthodox fourth grade teacher in a secular Jewish day school who drew stick figures on the blackboard to recount Jewish history. He also left an indelible impression on me when he volunteered to stay back after school for several weeks to teach me and a few of my friends the *Birkhat ha-Mazon* (Grace after Meals) so that we wouldn't be embarrassed when we attend the bar mitzvah ceremonies of our friends from more traditional backgrounds.

In a moment of reflection I can identify one Saturday afternoon when my father dropped off a rather energetic eight-year-old boy at the youth hall of our local synagogue in Melbourne, Australia. I am fairly certain that leaving me there for a couple of hours was a way to get me out of the house and for me to release some energy. I don't think anyone, especially the *madrikhim*, at this *Habonim Dror* gathering ever imagined the impact they would have on my life, and especially that three decades later this volume would emerge.

What perhaps began as a refuge for my parents, the journey through *Habo*, ultimately laid the foundations for this book. Now it is true, nothing happens by coincidence. My parents were also graduates of *Habonim Dror*, as are many of their friends even to this day, and so one could argue that this journey was always in my blood; but the topic of whether educators are born or made is one for another chapter.

After graduating high school I spent a year in Israel with some of my closest friends. Studying (amongst other things) at the *Mahon le Madrikhei Hutz l'Aretz* (Institute for Youth Leaders from Abroad) opened up, for the first time in my life, the possibility that this type of learning that I had experienced, and by now the types of educating that I was involved with, could become a career and a way of life. To those educators who motivated, inspired and at times chided me during that year, this journey and this book's publication are largely because of you.

Fast forward several years. After teaching and working as an informal Jewish educator at Mt. Scopus in Melbourne, I found myself in the back of a classroom atop Mt. Scopus in Jerusalem. It was in this classroom, and later in the faculty lounge, that I first met John Dewey, read Yehuda Amichai poetry and became acquainted with baseball and Dockers jeans. Such was the mix that Professor Barry Chazan brought into his classroom. A course on informal Jewish education, at Hebrew University, confirmed for me that informal Jewish education had the capacity to achieve even more than I had been exposed to. Most importantly I learned that informal Jewish education was a philosophy, and indeed a worldview, and not just pedagogy. As often happens on life journeys, Barry and I met up again almost ten years later, this time at New York University, where he provided the framework, ironically in the most formal of academic settings, for me to continue along this path.

There is one other episode in this journey necessary to convey in order to acknowledge and complete the broad strokes of my life that led to the emergence of this book. In 2002 I was living in St. Louis after completing a stint in Sydney as a Hillel director. My boss (and later colleague and friend) Jeffrey Lasday opened me up to the possibilities of American Jewish education. Through some connection or other I enrolled in the Brandeis University Institute for Informal Jewish Education, where I experienced many wonderful educators and met colleagues, many of whom I am still in contact with. Under the direction of Professor Joseph Reimer, this program was a major turning point in my professional trajectory. And it was at the conclusion of the seminar in 2005 that the conversation took place among a few of us that would begin the quest to change the name of the field from "informal" to "experiential" Jewish education.

Journeys like this are made possible only with the support of many more individuals and entities than just those mentioned above. To the Wexner Heritage Foundation I am grateful for the support they gave me throughout gradate school; they saw in me a capacity to emerge as a leader in this community. I am privileged to currently work at The Jewish Education Project whose leadership continually gives me space to dream and push boundaries. And to Joel Grishaver and team at Torah Aura Productions I am thankful for recognizing that this was a book whose time had come.

For someone who is usually reticent about personal disclosure, opening this book with the sharing of the trajectory that has brought it to fruition is, I believe, both important and instructive. The sum of our education is often the accumulation of these episodes, and perhaps the unusual step of publicly naming some these influential figures in my life is an acknowledgment of their untold influence. I also recognize that there are many more people I could have named along this journey who have and inspired and challenged me and who continue to do so.

In terms of influence there has been no greater factor than family in this journey. To a mother and father who never failed to provide, to a sister who has always supported and been there for me, to a Buba who has always inspired, and grandparents whose legacy I have always tried to live up to—the journey that has led me to here is due only to you. To Mirm, who has been my champion, cheerleader, partner and support over the last decade, I will always be grateful. With you has also come the extended support of Reva, Abe (z"l), Lara and Alex, which has ensured that family is never too far away. And to Abby and Jonah, thank you both for the wonder and amazement that you expose me to every day. My hope for you is that you may only know the joys of learning, exploration and challenge that are described throughout this book.

And finally, to the friends, colleagues and complete strangers who have experienced the wonder of experiential Jewish education, this book belongs to all of us.

INTRODUCTION
EXPERIENCE AND JEWISH EDUCATION

Dr. David Bryfman

For many years I found myself defending the "other" type of Jewish education. Compared to Jewish day schools, everything else was deemed by many as inferior and hardly as effective. Summer camps, youth groups and Israel trips were all too often seen as being "worthwhile" but never quite packing the same punch as the more formal settings of schools or universities, at least when it came to the development of Jewish identity. Sometimes the detractors would be subtle in their dismissiveness. They would say things like, "there is no such thing as informal Jewish education—it's all good education." Some people were more blunt and would relegate informal Jewish education into the "warm and fuzzy" buckets of experiences, leaving the *real deal* to the more traditional institutions of Jewish learning. But to someone who is a product of all of these settings, these distinctions, at least in terms of the impact they have had on my life and the lives of so many of my peers, have never made much sense.

It has been a while since I have had one of those discussions that challenged the credibility of informal Jewish education. It's not because I'm avoiding these discussions or that the naysayers are necessarily avoiding me. If anything, many of my colleagues and I are being called upon by more formal settings to introduce informal experiences into traditional settings of Jewish learning—perhaps more than ever before.

What has happened in the last few years that has changed this discourse? What has led to the explosion of young Jews from the diaspora traveling to Israel on organized trips? What has transpired to bring the community to the realization that Jewish summer camps are pivotal in the development of identity? What has triggered the expanding investment in Jewish youth and college-age programming, which were once the forgotten children of Jewish philanthropy? What has brought us to the point where I am able to assemble twenty-two authors to contribute to this book, eleven of whom are in doctoral programs, engaged in research related to this area of study? Although no single answer exists to these and related questions, this book does position itself as a stake in the ground, suggesting that, albeit still in its nascent stages, informal Jewish education has cemented itself into Jewish communal life.

Among other things, this book sets out to explore why it is that today anyone with a finger on the pulse of twenty-first-century Jewish education and communal life knows the potency of experiential education and understands that for the Jewish community to thrive, multiple and varied modes of Jewish learning, both formal and informal (and everything in between), need to be on our collective menu.

I should be very clear from the outset that what we are describing in this book is a philosophical approach to Jewish learning that has been somewhat present, although perhaps not dominant, in our collective history for millennia.

"We will do and (then) we will hear" (Exodus 24:7).

"Educate a child in the way he should go, and when he is old he will not depart from it" (Proverbs 22:6).

"In each and every generation a person is obligated to see himself as if he had gone out of Egypt" (Passover Haggadah).

I also need to reiterate that although this book suggests that the field of experiential Jewish education is emerging, the phenomenon itself has been part of Jewish communal life across geographic boundaries for centuries. From the origins of youth movements in nineteenth-century Europe and Palestine to the first Jewish summer camps in the early twentieth-century America, and to the scores of Jews across time who have traveled together with educators to learn about their culture and history, these are all practices of experiential Jewish learning. But only relatively recently has the effort been made to identify the commonalities among these settings and to develop the philosophy and pedagogy that binds them together.

Knowing full well that a single book cannot cater to everyone, the intended readership for this anthology is still a varied one. In keeping with this idea, I assembled an eclectic array of authors and gave them permission to express themselves in ways that felt most natural for them. The result is an anthology with deliberate variations in format, style and resonance. Some chapters in this collection will speak to different people, and the compilation in its entirety may speak to relatively few. But it is my contention that because of the attention that experiential Jewish learning is currently receiving and the anticipated growth that I continue to foresee for this field, this book will speak at times to Jewish communal leaders, educators, students and funders alike. The book's breadth and depth provides a good grounding for both those reading about its subject for the first time and those more familiar with experiential Jewish education. In particular, authors were encouraged to blend the theoretical and the practical to ensure that readers could both conceptualize the bigger picture and make connections that could be applied in any number of ways to contemporary Jewish living and learning. Perhaps what the book does more than anything else is to offer a broader context for those of us who have been inspired by the likes of summer camp or youth group and equip us with a framework and language that empower us to spread the reach and impact of experiential Jewish education.

LANGUAGE MATTERS

On my first day of graduate school the question was posed to our class, "What constitutes a field of study?" Then the discussion drew on the literature from general academic studies to deconstruct whether Jewish education was indeed a field, a discipline or a subset of something larger. Such are the discussions in academia that on day one of a doctoral journey were more overwhelming than helpful. Yet even from that haunting first day, one message continued to resonate. For any area of study/field/discipline to be taken seriously, it needed a literature so that it could be studied, heralded and dissected. When discussing informal Jewish education this message reverberated many times over for me. Where was the literature, and de facto the language, that articulated what informal Jewish education was? It seemed in the absence of this literature that the phenomenon would continue to be defined as what it was not rather than what it was.

As you can already see in this introduction, language can be confusing when not precise and consistent. For a long time I didn't really think that such nuances mattered. Now I can attest that language really does matter, if for no other reason than that it is very difficult to advance a cause without having some common terminology. Several of the chapters in this book (particularly in the first section) address a variety of language distinctions head-on, but to make matters more complex, the authors don't always agree with one another. But in the interest of moving forward, or at best not getting mired in battles over lexicon, I want to posit the following working definitions from the outset to advance our conversation. These stipulative definitions have their basis in the world of general education and have been expanded upon in prior writing undertaken by myself, and in part co-authored with Professor Joseph Reimer.

Formal learning commonly takes place in educational settings that are defined by specific parameters, including assessment, teacher qualifications and government regulations and standards, all of which are critical, usually to the obtaining of recognized diplomas and qualifications that allow students to advance either in professional life or in further academic settings (Livingstone, 2006).

Non-formal learning takes place alongside the mainstream systems of education and training and does not typically lead to formalized certificates. It is most commonly provided in the workplace and through the activities of civil society organizations and groups (such as in youth organizations, trades unions and political parties) (Husén and Postlethwaite, 1994).

Informal learning is a natural accompaniment to everyday life. It encompasses any activity involving the pursuit of understanding, knowledge or skill that occurs without the presence of externally imposed curricula criteria. Unlike formal and non-formal learning, informal learning is usually not intentional learning, and so may well not be recognized even by individuals themselves as contributing to their knowledge and skills (Husén and Postlethwaite, 1994; Smith, 1996).

It is necessary, albeit perhaps confusing, to highlight that much of what has been referred to as *informal* education in the Jewish educational sphere to date would most closely align with the definition of *non-formal* education derived from the general education world.

Experiential education is an educational philosophy that focuses on a process of learning between teacher and learner that integrates direct experiences with the learning environment and content. Despite its roots within progressive education, today the term is most commonly used in relation to outdoor or challenge education.

Experiential Learning is a subset of experiential education that refers specifically to the methodologies (or pedagogies) employed in experiential education.

FROM INFORMAL TO EXPERIENTIAL

And now to the big distinction, at least in terms of this book—the difference between informal Jewish education and experiential Jewish education. On this issue of the language itself, the transition from *informal Jewish education* to *experiential Jewish education* has been a very deliberate one. The mission to change the terminology over the last few years was one devised by a few people, ironically connected to a program run by the Institute for Informal Jewish Education at Brandeis University.

The discussions would follow a similar trajectory.

> By calling it "informal" we are defining something by what it is not, and when the "not" (i.e., formal education) is a vague term this becomes even more problematic. It's no longer enough to define informal education as anything that takes place outside of the classroom; we must be steadfast in describing precisely what it is. Furthermore, despite the difference between the various settings in which so-called informal Jewish education is taking place (i.e., camps, youth groups, trips), there is enough in common in these domains that the term "experiential Jewish education" makes the most sense. The philosophy, the pedagogies, the "curriculum," the educators all hold similar qualities and attributes that coalesce under this banner.

And so a story can be told of how experiential Jewish education is now regarded in many circles as the more descriptive terminology that binds the field. But this abridged version of the change in nomenclature is not a full account of how the current terminology has emerged. The true story starts many years prior, and for brevity's sake I use as my starting point the publication of the third iteration of Barry Chazan's "The Philosophy of Informal Jewish Education" in 2003. It is no coincidence that this book begins with the fourth edition of Chazan's updated seminal piece, both to celebrate its influence and to build upon its significance.

Chazan writes:

> Informal Jewish education is aimed at the personal growth of Jews of all ages. It happens through the individual's actively experiencing a diversity of Jewish moments and values that

are regarded as worthwhile. It works by creating venues, by developing a total educational culture and by co-opting the social context. It is based on a curriculum of Jewish values and experiences that is presented in a dynamic and flexible manner. As an activity, it does not call for any one venue but may happen in a variety of settings. It evokes fun in the present, pleasurable feelings and warm memories. It requires Jewishly literate educators with a "teaching" style that is highly interactive and participatory, who are willing to make maximal use of self and personal lifestyle in their educational work.

In combining Chazan's articulation with the literature of experiential education, a definition of experiential Jewish education emerges. Experiential Jewish education might best be understood as

A philosophy and pedagogy that purposefully engages learners in direct experiences and focused reflection within settings inspired by Jewish values, traditions and texts, in order to create knowledge, develop skills, clarify values and develop the individuals' capacities to contribute to their communities.

Again it should be emphasized that this term is not interchangeable with experiential Jewish learning—a subset of experiential Jewish education that refers specifically to the methodologies that it employs.

THE "JEWISH" IN EXPERIENTIAL JEWISH EDUCATION

Collectively the authors who contributed to this book give insights and share outstanding wisdom, particularly related to experiential education. Although each addresses the "Jewish" component of this term in their own way, it still remains the most difficult of the three words—experiential, Jewish and education—to adequately define and certainly to achieve any consensus. There is something about adding the "Jewish" to "experiential education" that does more than just create a subset of a broader field. I offer three distinct possibilities for framing the "Jewish" that also reflect the way in which this book was ultimately organized—the why, the who, and the where of experiential Jewish education.[1]

One way of defining the *Jewish* in experiential Jewish education is by its intention, the why. For the learning to be considered Jewish the experience must be infused with certain values. Here I loosely use the term "values" to cover varying aspects of Jewish tradition, including text, ritual and culture. The Jewish element of what is taking place is sometimes a cognitive overlay of the experience. It could be the inclusion of a text study within the broader learning experience, or the use of Hebrew language or viewing of a movie with Jewish themes. It could also be a behavioral or affective aspect of the experience, such as the performance of a Jewish practice or a song session with incredible *ruach* (spirit). The methodologies are endless, but importantly the learning experience has intentionally been constructed as a Jewish experience. Section one of this book looks at the why of experiential Jewish education from various vantage points, beginning with Chazan's "A Philosophy of Informal Jewish Education." Joseph Reimer builds upon Chazan's core principles by examining what transpires when educators deliberately infuse greater levels of risk and challenge within experiential Jewish education. Shuki Taylor approaches the conversation from an identity perspective by considering what the desired outcomes of experiential Jewish education should be. In what I imagine could be a source of tension for strict adherents of John Dewey, Taylor pushes readers to acknowledge that the destination in Jewish education, and even in experiential Jewish education, is paramount. Scott Sokol applies a neuroscientific framework to better understand why experiential Jewish education is so in tune with brain development. The section concludes with Robyn Faintich exploring the "curriculum" of experiential Jewish education and Bradley Solmsen looking at how we measure the success of this learning. By looking at curriculum and evaluation, both chapters further uncover issues related to the intentionality necessary in experiential Jewish education.

Section two of this book looks specifically at the who of experiential Jewish education, focusing mainly on the educator, and by extension often the learners engaged in these experiences. The educator, central to almost any learning experience, has the capacity to make any experience a Jewish one. In most cases

---

[1] The why, the who and the where strongly reflect Joseph Schwab's four commonplaces of education, the teacher and student being the who, the where being what he describes as the milieu, and the why being a manifestation of his notion of curriculum. Rather than forcing this categorization on this anthology, I have chosen to go with the why, who and where of experiential Jewish education.

this is most obvious when the educator responsible is Jewish. In cases where educators are not Jewish, it is often their respect, if not reverence, for Jewish life and learning that is most impactful.

This section looks at the who of experiential Jewish education, dealing with themes ranging from the qualities of an experiential Jewish educator, explored by Daniel Held, to the training that experiential educators could be undertaking, discussed by Jeff Kress, Mark Young and Abby Uhrman and in a further chapter authored by Jacob Cytryn. Throughout the book many authors focus on reflection as core to experiential Jewish learning, and two chapters look exclusively at this topic. Culminating this section, Clare Goldwater looks at the role that coaching and mentoring currently play and how they could be further expanded to advance the growth of experiential Jewish educators.

The third and final section of this book looks at the where or, as Joseph Schwab would suggest, the milieu of experiential Jewish education. Here I have taken both a demographic and a geographic approach to looking at the various settings. While in the past most attention was paid to the younger years, we have found that today experiential Jewish learning spans the ages. Collectively we examine three distinct age groups. Lisa Samick explores early childhood, Deborah Meyer focuses on adolescents and Scott Aaron and Josh Feigelson discuss emerging adulthood.

This section also looks at the physical geography, or where experiential Jewish education takes place, and raises several questions in doing so. In some instances this is as obvious as walking into a building that is identifiably Jewish. When one enters a synagogue or JCC one understands that this is going to be a Jewish experience. But this isn't always the case. There is nothing intrinsically Jewish about a campsite—not the trees, the dining room or the lake. And yet when you walk into a Jewish summer camp you know that it is a Jewish setting. With intention the site has been curated into a Jewish space, whether through signage, posters, flags or other non-physical elements, including being greeted by an Israeli, the wearing of Jewish T-shirts or being served falafel for lunch. There is very little Jewish going on in hurricane-ravaged New Orleans or amidst the desert towns of Rwanda, and as Brent Spodek explores, many providers of service learning opportunities are able to create very Jewish spaces in these and other destinations. And consider for a moment cyberspace, by definition a neutral and all-encompassing space, but one that separate chapters by Deborah Nageler and Owen Gottlieb explore as the locus of much experiential Jewish learning.

The Jewish of experiential Jewish education is in many ways defined cumulatively by the impact of its why, who and where. However, in the final week before submitting this book to the publisher, I was reminded about why this topic was so important, and in the process perhaps why this breakdown of why, who and where was possibly too clinical a categorization. With great humility and pride I have included an amended version of Molly Wernick's address to the Foundation for Jewish Camp. It serves as a powerful reminder that at its core there is something that transcends these categories and permeates all aspects of experiential Jewish education. It's difficult to label, although some attempt do so by referring to it as "magic." Molly reminds us of the amazement and wonder of experiential Jewish education and ultimately of the timeliness of the publication of this book.

This book stands as a tribute to a decade of work since Chazan published his piece on informal Jewish education. While it has taken ten years for this book to come to fruition, I know that the next volume is already being considered. Such is the growth of experiential Jewish education, and such is the optimism that the field will continue to develop and expand in ensuing years.

BIBLIOGRAPHY

Husén, T., & Postlethwaite, T. N. (1994). *The International Encyclopedia of Education* (2nd ed.). Oxford, New York,: Pergamon.

Livingstone, D. W. (2006). Informal Learning: Conceptual Distinctions and Preliminary Findings. In Z. Bekerman, N. C. Burbules & Silberman-Keller (Eds.), *Learning in Places: The Informal Education Reader*. New York: Peter Lang Publishing.

Smith, M. K. (1996). Non-formal education [Electronic Version]. Retrieved January 20, 2009, from http://www.infed.org/biblio/b-nonfor.htm

MY 10,000 HOURS AT CAMP

By Molly Wernick

(Speech delivered at the Foundation for Jewish Camp Funder's Summit—Dec 5, 2012)

According to Malcolm Gladwell's 2008 book *Outliers*, it takes 10,000 hours to master a skill or a trade. It was at the end of my first summer on staff at *Habonim Dror* Camp *Galil* that I completed my 10,000th hour at camp. Master of Jewish Camp can look like a million different things. It depends on how those hours were filled.

But here's the thing—I remember many of those hours with the same clarity I have from my trip yesterday from Philadelphia to New York City. I remember the smells, the feelings and the lyrics of every song we sang by heart. I remember so many nights lying down on the basketball court, with the concrete still warm from the day's sun, looking at the sky and knowing exactly where to find the Little Dipper. I remember being so small and tripping over my own feet to learn the steps of Israeli folk dancing on Friday nights.

I remember the hours of my first morning waking up at camp. Like many ten-year-olds, I woke up just before the sun, put on my cleanest newest shirt and my overall shorts, brushed my teeth—without my parents telling me I had to—and set out for the soccer field, where I found three boys in my age group kicking around a soccer ball. When I asked if I could join them, one of them stopped the ball with his foot, looked at me and said, "Fine. But it's you versus the three of us." Those guys didn't even stand a chance. And all of a sudden the same little girl who was too often reprimanded in social studies for being outspoken and had too much chutzpah for Hebrew school teachers to tolerate had realized that she—that I—found the place where I was allowed to become myself for the first time.

Standardized tests told me year after year that I just average. But camp, camp told me I could be a coach and an educator, a chef and a party planner, a blogger and a community organizer, a choreographer and a storyteller, a graphic designer, a super villain and a superhero ... or maybe become counselor, a counselor-in-training director, a director of education or even a camp director at age twenty-three.

Guess whose "standards" landed me a scholarship for leadership development at Ithaca College and whose planning and executing skills gave me the experience to work for a Jewish nonprofit that holds 150 events a year for young adults in the Philadelphia Jewish community. I will give you a hint: Its letters don't include SAT.

My 10,000 hours at camp taught me that I *could*—because if I listened to the outside world telling me I was just average, I would eventually start to believe it and soon be it. Average wouldn't have learned all of those dance steps, and average wouldn't have made hundreds of decorative signs for special programming days. Average wouldn't have taken me to live in Israel for a year before I started college, and average wouldn't have gotten me hired to run four years of Hillel programming once I got there. Average wouldn't have connected me with the Foundation for Jewish Camp and wouldn't have landed me here in front of you today.

When I was finally on staff and I had campers of my own, I made sure that they could kick butt in soccer or Israeli dancing or anything they loved, and I would be there cheering on the sidelines or showing them the steps—that I could have them learn and believe that they were anything but average. My kids are in college now and have kids of their own, kids who have now empowered the next generation to be allowed to become themselves for the first time.

That year I spent in Israel with *Habonim Dror* North America's Workshop 56 was the year that connected this cycle for me. It was when I learned about my kin in the *Habonim Dror* movement of the past, which spoke to my life as an educator in the present. First my kin from *Habonim* brought forth my love for Israel as our homeland as I heard firsthand from the <u>H</u>alutzim, the pioneers, who left their homes to build a state in a faraway land from scratch. Their legacy solidifies my passion for being a Jewish educator. And second, my kin from *Dror* allowed me to soak up every ounce of history in the Ghetto Fighters' kibbutz in the Galilee to inspire my relationship with my campers at home—to teach that love, trust and knowledge are the good that conquer the most horrific evil the world has seen. The latter brings me back to camp, the community built upon that very same love and trust and knowledge.

Therefore every kid who has the opportunity to go to camp adds a stone to the foundation of the Jewish future. It made us all feel we were part of something before we could vote or donate or apply to anything—that we had a voice that mattered and an entire community to validate that voice. Now that I do vote and do donate and will likely one day apply to be an accredited master of something, I keep my camp "well-beyond-average" standards close to heart, because really, every one of those 10,000 at *Habonim Dror* Camp *Galil* added another stone to the foundation of my future. Without that confidence or those skills or that validation, or that love and trust and knowledge, I would have never believed that I could do anything to make a difference in the world around me.

Because those hours taught me that I could make that difference, I now aim to live out the legacy of every ghetto fighter from *Dror* to ensure the strength of the Jewish future, every pioneer from *Habonim* who built the Jewish state, every camp counselor who taught the importance of a child knowing that somebody believes he or she can make difference in the world and every little girl who found the place she was allowed to become herself for the very first time.

SECTION 1:
WHAT IS EXPERIENTIAL JEWISH EDUCATION?

THE PHILOSOPHY OF INFORMAL JEWISH EDUCATION

Barry Chazan

BEYOND SCHOOL: A NEW ERA IN JEWISH EDUCATION

What happened to education?

As we enter the second decade of the twenty-first century we are witness to significant changes about what education is and where it happens. Traditional notions about where people learn are constantly being re-examined, and some dramatically new and unlikely milieus and venues have emerged. The new settings join the traditional venues of education—elementary schools, secondary schools and universities—as vibrant partners in the process of education—and sometimes they even challenge traditional hegemonies.[1]

The Jewish world has exhibited great excitement about this kingdom of "beyond school" frameworks, which encompass camping, Israel programs, travel to other Jewish sites, retreats, youth movements and youth organizations, adult programming and the internet, among others. The territory of education beyond schools has come to popularly be denoted as "informal" or "experiential" education. In addition to diverse programs the field has been characterized by a growing body of articles and research,[2] university courses, training programs, increased funding and heightened lay interest. Spearheaded specifically by demonstrated achievements in camping and Israel educational travel, Jewish policy-makers, donors, professionals and lay people often view informal education as the exciting new arena for the amelioration of Jewish life. Indeed, there is a kind of frenzied excitement in which informal education is sometimes seen as the panacea for Jewish life.

MEANINGS OF 'INFORMAL EDUCATION"

The emergence of a distinct term to denote "out of school" education was initially driven by the linguistic need for a term to denote this "other" kind of education.

In the early part of the twentieth century in America this non-school phenomenon was frequently denoted as 'recreational education".[3] In Austria and Germany a group of educationally minded colleagues of Sigmund Freud called this kind of education "indirect education".[4] By the late 1950s this "other" kind of education was increasingly denoted as either "informal" or "non-formal" education.[5]

In Jewish education, the "Benderly Boys" spoke about a "total environment educational strategy" that encompassed camping, music, arts and culture.[6] The term "experiential Jewish education" was introduced into the lexicon in the 1970s by our late colleague and teacher Bernard Reisman of Brandeis University. The word "experiential" seemed to have been chosen to imply a connection to John Dewey's

---

[1] D. Rushkoff, Playing the Future: What We Can Learn From Digital Kids (New York: HarperCollins1996).

[2] See articles on informal or experiential Jewish education in: Roberta Goodman, Paul Flexner, Linda Bloomberg (editors). *What We Now Know About Jewish Education* (Los Angeles: Torah Aura, 2008); and Helena Miller, Alex Pomson, and Lisa Grant, (editors). *The International Handbook of Jewish Education* (Heidelberg: Springer, 2011); *the Journal of Jewish Education* and this volume.

[3] Rolland G. Paulston, Non-Formal Education: An Annotated International Bibliography (New York: Praeger, 1972).

[4] Eran Rolnick. Freud in Zion: Psychoanalysis and the Making of Modern Jewish Identity (London: Karnac, 2012).

[5] Paulston, op.cit., p. x ("non-formal education" is structured, systematic non-school educational and training activities of relatively short duration in which the sponsoring agencies seek concrete behavioral changes in fairly distinct target populations, and "informal education" is "learning in a nonsystematic manner from generally non-structured exposure to cultural facilities".

[6] Jonathan D. Krasner. The Benderly Boys and American Jewish Education. (Waltham, MA: Brandeis University Press, 2011), pp. 185–322.

notion of experience and education.[7] My colleagues Joseph Reimer and David Bryfman have made an important contribution to the emergence of the term "experiential Jewish education" as common parlance in twenty-first-century Jewish life.[8] Generally, in the literature of general education, "informal education" has had two different emphases. The first direction has looked at "informal education" organizationally, viewing it as educational activities that take place outside of "schools".[9] According to this approach, "formal education" refers to "schools" and "informal education" refers to "out-of-school educational activities". This approach is rooted in a structural or institutional delineation that focuses on venues or places in which education is delivered. This "definition" is concise, clear and certainly convenient. At the same time, this approach doesn't hold up in all or even many cases. There are many activities that take place in "schools"—clubs, sports, extracurricular activities—that, while occurring in a school building, are generally still regarded as "informal". Moreover, there are some out-of-school frameworks—a boot camp, specialized sports programs—that are outside of school but, in terms of practice and approach, seem not to be "informal" at all. Another problem with this approach is that it doesn't tell us what "informal education" is; it only tells us what it is not. So-called negative definitions are not very helpful in describing a phenomenon in an operative way. Ultimately this approach does not help the educator who wants to know exactly what "informal education" is so that he or she may be able to do it in practice.

The second emphasis in general literature has focused on the voluntary nature of informal education.[10] This approach says that informal education's main characteristic is that one chooses to participate in it, whereas schooling is a required type of education. There is some validity to this voluntary notion, but in terms of Jewish life it is ultimately neither precise nor particularly helpful. In contradistinction to public school that is legally mandated, ultimately all of Jewish education is voluntary. Families are not legally required to provide any Jewish education to their young—and all of Jewish life is, in a sense, a matter of choice. In addition, the notion of "voluntary", when related to youth, is somewhat precarious; the young don't have total choice over their out-of-school choices. They may express strong preferences or even have right of approval or refusal, but ultimately families decide whether or not to send a youngster to camp or a trip or a club. While "voluntary" may be a sociologically interesting concept, in terms of helping us understand what "informal Jewish education" is, it is ultimately not practically helpful.

Some colleagues have asked the legitimate question, "Why bother with all this?"[11] Some even suggest that the distinction between "formal" and "informal" sets up a false dichotomy and does damage to Jewish education. Rather than attempting to separate, why don't we just talk about "Jewish education"?

There is something tempting in this argument. However, for decades I have continued to be preoccupied with understanding what "informal Jewish education" is, not out of stubbornness but out of curiosity. I feel and believe that there is something out there called "informal (or 'experiential') education". I believe it is useful to try to understand the essence of the "thing out there" because it can help us do it better and it might improve the overall work we do in Jewish education. I do not necessarily defend the division that exists (indeed, as the reader will see at the end, I propose a much greater interaction between the two), but rather I believe that words are important and that understanding them is not semantics but useful conceptual clarification. Therefore the subject of this monograph—and the ones before[12]—is the explication of the meaning of the concept "informal Jewish education"[13].

---

[7] Bernard Reisman. The Jewish Experiential Book (New York: Ktav Publishing, 1979), pp. 18–36.

[8] Joseph Reimer. "Informal Education: The Decisive: How Informal Jewish Education Was Transformed in Its Relationship with Jewish Philanthropy" in The International Handbook of Jewish Education, op.cit, pp. 805–824; Joseph Reimer, "Beyond More Jews Doing Jewish: Clarifying the Goals of Informal Jewish Education" in The Journal of Jewish Education (Vol. 73, 2007), pp.5–23; Joseph Reimer and David Bryfman, "Jewish Experiential Education" in What We Now Know About Jewish Education, op.cit,,Reimer (Journal of Jewish Education).

[9] Paulston, Ibid, pp.9–14.

[10] Reuven Kahane. The Origins of Postmodern Youth: Informal Youth Movements in a Comparative Perspective. (Berlin: Walter de Gruyter, 1997).

[11] Sheldon Dorff. "Informal Education? Let's Not Go Back There Again". Journal of Jewish Education (Vol. 73; No. 2, Winter, 2007); pp. 119–120; Journal of Jewish Education; Jacob Cytryn. "Getting Beyond "Formal vs. Informal: Good Education Is Good Education,".Hayidion: The RAVSAK Journal. (Winter, 2011), pp. 18–20, 57.

[12] This is my fourth iteration of this attempt. The previous three versions were in 1981 ("What is Informal Education?" Philosophy of Education, 1981. Carbondale, IL: Philosophy of Education Society); 1991 "What is Informal Jewish Education?" Journal of Jewish Communal Service 67, no. 4 (summer 1991); and 2003 "The Philosophy of Informal Jewish Education," The Encyclopedia of Informal Education, www.infed.org/informal education/informaljewisheducation.htm. Each new iteration has been fueled by 1) new questions that I pondered, 2) reservations by myself and others about previous versions, 3) new literature on education and the nature of mind that I have read, 4) attempts to be more precise and 5) dialogue and discussion with a small group of colleagues interested in this subject.

[13] In this paper I use the terms "informal education" and "experiential education" to refer to the same phenomenon, except in instances where I suggest some distinct differences.

GENERIC TYPE ANALYSIS AND DEFINING INFORMAL JEWISH EDUCATION

Over the years I have utilized a methodology of analytic philosophy of education to attempt to arrive at an understanding of the tern "informal Jewish education". This approach (known in educational philosophy as *generic type analysis*[14]) presents a number of examples of activities that are often denoted in common language by the use of this term and, on the basis of analysis of these terms, extracts what seem to be a group of common (or "generic") characteristics that are shared by most or all phenomena denoted as "informal Jewish education" (this approach is similar to explicating what a "car" is by looking at a Toyota Corolla , a Hyundai Sonata, a Fiat 500 and others and then attempting to see what elements they have in common that could qualify as defining a "car").

So let us look at some popular examples of "things" called "informal Jewish education". One of the most prominent activities today referred to as "informal Jewish education" is camping. Jewish camps are educational settings where (generally young) Jews spend blocks of time with peers (often in the summer) in a diverse range of activities, including education, sports, recreation, social pastimes and Jewish living.[15] Camps (and their related "sibling", the retreat) are particularly effective in creating an intense Jewish milieu. The Hebrew-speaking summer camp made Hebrew language and culture come alive twenty-four hours a day. The weekend "Shabbaton" affords a full experiencing of Shabbat—preparation, *kabbalat Shabbat,* Shabbat meals, singing *zmirot,* study, singing and dancing and *havdalah*—that many young people have never before encountered. Camps and retreats are effective at developing a sense of "togetherness" and group loyalty. The "bunk" (which refers as much to a social network as to a building) or camp as a whole often becomes a close-knit community that is united by shared songs, experiences, activities, shirts and memories. In camps all elements of the schedule—waking up, sports, nature, evenings, meals, free time—can be co-opted for educational purposes[16]. Every moment in camp or at the retreat is potentially a time for education, and the overall setting is a "classroom" and "campus" for learning. Finally, the experience of going to camp or to a retreat has an aura of great engagement and fun about it.

Jewish travel is today regarded as a very important form of informal education (major travel venues include Israel, Eastern Europe and Jewish sites in America). Jewish travel refers to organized educational programs that take young people and adults to various places in the world of Jewish interest. This kind of education involves directly experiencing sites, events and people. The trip to Prague or Venice presents a living "museum" of exciting historical settings of creative interactions between Jewish and general culture. To travel to Poland is to experience the height of Jewish creativity—and the depth of human depravity. Traveling to Israel is about seeing, feeling and touching the Jewish past, present and future. Jewish educational travel does encompass well-defined subject matter, and a great deal of cognitive learning takes place, but it happens through seeing, visiting, touching and participating, rather than through lectures or "looking in from without".[17] Travel programs often create a sense of community and also are usually regarded as great fun. Like the "bunk", the "bus" connotes not only a vehicle of physical transportation but a newly formed bonded group of peers deriving support, reinforcement and pleasure from being together.

For many decades a prominent form of informal Jewish education was Jewish youth movements and organizations. These terms refer to frameworks in which young Jews participate in cultural, educational, ideological and social activities within a peer group context. (Youth *movements* encompass both ideological and associational dimensions, whereas youth *organizations* focus more on the latter.) The power of the peer group and culture is a striking dimension of youth movements and organizations. Many young people enjoy being together and "hanging out" with friends in their youth groups. Youth movements and organizations are often led by charismatic and engaging "counselors" that are close in age to the participants. These leaders have the ability to excite and inspire their younger charges, and there is often a great

---

[14] Jonas Soltis, *An Introduction to the Analysis of Educational Concepts* (Reading, MA: Addison-Wesley, 1978), pp. 29–30.

[15] Amy Sales and Leonard Saxe. *How Goodly Are Thy Tents: Summer Camps as Jewish Socializing Experiences.* (Hanover, NH: Brandeis University Press, 2004).

[16] This characteristic is described in Goffman's classic essay "On the Characteristics of Total Institutions" in E. Goffman.*Asylum* .(New York: Anchor Books,1961), pp. 1–125.

[17] Two volumes that attempt to describe the Israel educational experience are Shaul Kellner. *Tours That Bind: Diaspora, Pilgrimage, and Israeli Birthright Tourism* (New York: New York University Press, 2010) and Leonard Saxe and Barry Chazan, *Ten Days of Birthright Israel: A Journey in Young Adult Identity* (Waltham, MA: Brandeis University Press, 2008).

sense of identification with them. Youth movements frequently address topics that are immediate and of interest to young people. The participants are excited about attending weekly meetings, going away for weekends and spending summers together with friends and colleagues from the "movement" or the "club." The whole experience of taking part in these youth activities carries an aura of enthusiasm and fun.

In some circles, Jewish Community Centers have been referred to as examples of informal Jewish education.[18] JCCs are multipurpose institutions established to provide a diversity of recreational, cultural, social, athletic and Jewish and general educational activities for a broad cross-section of Jews. In recent decades, in communities in Latin America and North America, they have proven to be a new kind of "Jewish neighborhood". Jews of all ages pass through the JCC's halls, and it is one of the few places where Jews of all kinds meet together. It is a center of diverse kinds of Jewish and general activities: pre-school teachers sing Hebrew songs, staff members study Jewish history; _hallot_ are baked on Friday morning, parents and children swim together, fathers and mothers work out and play basketball ("Jewish oxygen flows in this place and it is breathed by millions of Jews who enter its doors."[19]). JCCs lack a "curriculum" in the sense of a fixed set of subjects or books, but they do have a broad menu of Jewish programs, activities, learning and observances. Jewish activities happen at JCCs in a way and in a constellation that differs from traditional school models. JCC staff includes highly skilled professionals with "people skills" who are also knowledgeable and committed Jews. Many JCCs have full-time Jewish educators who, in addition to teaching, also "hang out" in the health club and the gym as well as in the study room or library. As is true of all the other forms of informal Jewish education, it's engaging and fun to go to the JCC.

In general education (and in Jewish life, too) adult learning is often denoted as "informal education".[20] This framework refers to programs established to enable adult Jews to enrich their Jewish knowledge and acquire Jewish skills in warm and non-threatening settings. These settings are voluntarily chosen, revolve around text study and form fellowships of discussion, reflection and bonding.[21] Adult learning involves interactive and learner-centered educators, presenting the texts in ways that relate to the lives and life settings of the participants. Beyond being knowledgeable, the teachers are skilled at making adults—and young people—feel comfortable about Jewish learning. The learning has nothing to do with grades or advancement on a hierarchical ladder. Those who gather to learn become more than a class, and very often in the case of adult learning they are transformed into a "family-like" group.[22] This field has developed a strong network of ardent believers and noteworthy spokespeople.[23]

Other areas that are sometimes denoted as informal Jewish education are Jewish family education, the internet, preschools and museums. Moreover, some analysts of the modern Jewish day school imply that these "schools" might be better seen as total Jewish "cultures"—formal and informal—rather than as "schools" in the narrow sense.[24] Day schools "educate" as much by the environs, community and culture they create as by the facts they transmit. These additional examples underscore qualities that were prominent in the kinds of education we saw above: the importance of the learner, the role of the group, involvement, the total setting and the fun and excitement of the experience.

---

[18] Barry Chazan. _What Is Jewish Education in JCCs?_ (Jerusalem: Jewish Community Centers Association, 1996); Barry Chazan and Steven Cohen. _Assessing the Jewish Educational Effectiveness of JCCs: The 1994 Study_ (New York: Jewish Community Centers Association, 1994); Barry Chazan and Mark Charendoff, eds., _Jewish Education and the Jewish Community Center_ (Jerusalem: Jewish Community Centers Association, 1994); Patricia Cipora Harte, Richard Juran and Alvin Mars, "Jewish Education in the JCCs" in Goodman, Flexner and Bloomberg, _What We Now Know about Jewish Education_, op.cit., 417–422.

[19] Chazan (1996), _Ibid,, p. xx.

[20] Paulston, _op.cit._ Steven Brookfield. _Understanding and Facilitating Adult Learning._ (SanFrancisco: Jossey Bass, 1988).

[21] Janice Alper, ed., _Learning Together: A Source Book on Jewish Family Education_ (Denver: Alternatives in Religious Education, 1987). Diane Schuster; Betsy Katz.

[22] Betsy Katz and Jonathan Mirvis (1997). _Israel and Adult Jewish Education._ Jerusalem: Keren Karev, Jewish Agency Department of Education, Mifgashim Centre.

[23] Betsy Dolgin Katz. _Reinventing Adult Jewish Learning_ (Jersey City, N.J.: Ktav, 2012); Lisa Grant and Diane Tickton Shuster. "Adult Jewish Learning: The Landscape" in _International Handbook of Jewish Education: Part II_, pp., 669–689.

[24] Steven M. Cohen and Judith Veinstein, "Who You Know Affects How You Jew—The Impact of Jewish Networks in Childhood Upon Adult Jewish Identity" in _International Handbook of Jewish Education: Part 1 op.cit._, pp. 203–,218, Tali Hyman (2008) _The Liberal Jewish Day School as Laboratory for Dissonance in American Jewish Identity-Formation._ Unpublished doctoral dissertation. New York University. New York, NY.

THE DEFINING CHARACTERISTICS OF INFORMAL JEWISH EDUCATION

These examples reflect the phenomenon I have been attempting to explain for over three decades. After looking, thinking and deeply engaging in these and other examples, I believe that it is possible to identify eight (generic) characteristics that are common to these and other examples of "informal Jewish education". These characteristics constitute what I regard as the phenomenological attributes of informal Jewish education. The uniqueness of informal Jewish education lies in the configuration and synergy of these characteristics.

1. **Person-centered Jewish Education.** The central focus of informal Jewish education is the individual and his/her growth. Underlying this focus is the belief that human beings are not simply empty vessels waiting to be filled,[25] but rather the individual is an active dynamic organism who grows and is shaped through his/her own active engagement in learning. Hence, this kind of education places primacy on the person's own involvement and progress. He/she is considered an active partner in the educational dynamic. Educationally, this implies what is often called a "person-centered pedagogy," which means that people learn best when there is a focus on personal interests, listening as much as telling, starting with questions, identifying interests and collaborating rather than coercing. [26] In terms of informal Jewish education, the person-centered principle means helping each individual to grow and find meaning as a Jew. The emphasis is on personal Jewish development rather than the transmission of Jewish facts, and the individual is actively engaged in his/her own journey of Jewish growth.

   The preoccupation with the person in informal Jewish education also implies concern with affecting the learner's *total* being. While selected activities may focus on a specific Jewish skill or Jewish topic (such as learning to speak Hebrew or build a *sukkah*), the ultimate aim of informal Jewish education is building the person's overall Jewish character. Thus, informal Jewish education does not see "Jewish growth" as exclusively intellectual but rather as a synthesis of aesthetic, affective, moral, behavioral and cognitive dimensions.

2. **The Centrality of Experience.** Informal Jewish education is rooted in a belief that the experience is central to the individual's Jewish development. The notion of experience in education derives from the idea that participating in an event or a moment through the senses, the body and the mind enables one to understand a concept, fact or belief in a direct and unmediated way. Experience in education refers to learning that happens through participation in events or by direct observation or hearing. John Dewey expanded upon this idea by suggesting that people are active centers of impulse rather than passive vessels and they learn best when they are actively rather than passively engaged in experiencing an idea or an event. Such experiencing is rooted in the interaction of the idea or event with the person's life and with a continuum of ideas that enables the experience to contribute to ongoing personal growth.[27] The focus on experience results in a pedagogy that attempts to create settings which enable values to be experienced personally and events to be experienced in real time and in genuine venues, rather than their being described to the learner. Over the years this notion of experiencing has become closely identified with "experiential learning", often seen as the "calling card" of informal education. [28]

   In terms of informal Jewish education, learning occurs through enabling people to undergo key Jewish experiences and values. For example, an experiential approach to Shabbat focuses on enabling people to participate in Shabbat in real time—buying flowers Friday afternoon, lighting candles at sunset, hearing *Kiddush* before the meal and eating *challah*. This approach does not deny the value of learning *about* Shabbat in classes and from texts, but it does suggest that exclusively verbal learning about an experience cannot replace the real thing.

---

[25] Charles Dickens. *Hard Times* (1981), Chapters 1–3.

[26] Alfie Kohn, *The Schools Our Children Deserve* (Boston: Houghton-Mifflin, 1997).

[27] J. Dewey, *Experience and Education* (New York: Macmillan, 1937).

[28] In my reading over the years of the writings of John Dewey, I have not found any precise citation where he uses the phrase "experiential" education as it is popularly used in Jewish education.

Jewish education lends itself particularly well to the experiential approach because so many of the concepts that we wish to teach (such as Shabbat, holidays and daily blessings) are rooted in actual experiences. The moral system of Judaism—honoring parents, helping the needy, social justice—is rooted in deeds. The cultural life of Judaism—songs, food, holidays—is rooted in meals, singing, ritual objects and specific celebrations. Israel in Jewish life is not an abstract concept but a real place that can be visited, touched, walked and inhaled. Jewish education is extremely well suited to giving primacy to experience, and informal Jewish education is the branch of Jewish education that highlights that primacy.

3. **A "Curriculum" of Jewish Experiences and Values.** The word "curriculum" has been generally associated with formal rather than informal education. "Curriculum" is commonly understood as courses of studies, with lists of subjects to be covered, books to read, ideas to be learned and tests to be given. In the last decades of the twentieth century, this notion of "curriculum" was subject to much discussion, and a more generic and broader concept has emerged in contemporary curriculum theory which understands the term to refer to an overall blueprint or plan of action which guides the broad range of teaching or educational activities of an educational institution.[29] In this new sense, "curriculum" is very much part of informal Jewish education. "Curriculum" in informal education is rooted in a well-defined body of Jewish experiences and values which is presented in a pedagogic style that is dynamic and flexible and which closely relates to the lives of the learners.

In contemporary Jewish life there is a diversity of views regarding what are the core experiences and values of Jewish tradition or culture. Religious approaches are likely to emphasize prayer, study, holidays and rituals. Ethnic approaches are likely to emphasize Hebrew, holidays, music and customs. National approaches are likely to emphasize the Land of Israel, travel to Israel, Hebrew and Jewish history. Because of this diversity, it is difficult to arrive at one agreed-upon core curriculum for teaching experiences and values. However, there are some Jewish experiences that seem to be shared by the majority of informal Jewish educational systems: (1) Jewish holiday and calendar experiences; (2) Jewish lifecycle experiences; (3) studying Jewish texts; (4) Jewish cultural and peoplehood experiences; and (5) acting upon Jewish values. Most forms of Jewish informal education throughout the world—whether in the Deportivo in Mexico City, a NFTY retreat in Oconomowoc, or a Counterpoint Seminar in Melbourne—present programs around such themes as the Passover seder, Shabbat candles, *tikkun olam*, *tzedaka* and rallies for Israel or Jews in need.

A central dimension of informal Jewish education's curriculum is its flexibility and dynamism. The methods of teaching "core contents" and the sequence in which they are taught are open to change and adjustment. These core experiences and values may be "taught" in a variety of ways, depending upon time, place and the individual pace of each learner.

4. **A Pedagogy of Inter-Activity.** Informal Jewish education is rooted in the belief that the active interchange between students and students and between students and educators is a critical dimension of Jewish learning. Interaction refers to a reciprocal effect or influence between two or more people. The behavior of one, it is assumed, acts as a stimulus for the behavior of the other. People learn and grow through active social interaction, which stimulates ideas, causes us to think and rethink views and helps us to re-conceptualize our beliefs and ideologies. The active dialogue back and forth with others is not simply pedagogically useful; it is, in a more basic sense, a pivotal factor in shaping our ideas, beliefs and behaviors.[30] The principle of interactivity implies a pedagogy of asking questions, stimulating discussions and engaging the learner. To stimulate interactivity, educators must create an environment which invites learners to listen to each other and to react with dignity and decency.[31] The pedagogy of informal Jewish education is rooted in techniques that enfranchise openness, encourage engagement, instigate creative dialectic and insure comfort of diversity and disagreement.

---

[29]William Piner, William Reynolds, Patrick Slattery, Peter M. Taubman. *Understanding Curriculum* (New York: Peter Lang, 1995).

[30]Martin Buber, "Teaching and the Deed," in *Israel and the World* (New York: Schocken, 1948); Lawrence Kohlberg, *The Philosophy of Moral Development* (San Francisco: Harper and Row, 1981); David Brooks. *The Social Animal* (New York: Random House, 2011).

[31]S. Haroutinian-Gordon, *Turning the Soul: Teaching Through Conversation in the High School* (Chicago: University of Chicago Press, 1991); N. Burbules, *Dialogue in Teaching: Theory and Practice* (New York: Teachers College Press, 1993).

For example, students may be asked what they think; how great rabbis of the past might have reacted; what the Jewish content means for their lives; and what they agree or disagree with.

Informal Jewish educators cannot really complete their work unless there is a dynamic interactive process between student and educator, student and student, student and text, and student and Tradition. Neither ingenuous nor instrumental, this interaction is an inherent element of informal Jewish education's theory of learning. It is important to add that this characteristic—like others in our analysis—is not unique or idiosyncratic only to informal education. Interactivity is central to several approaches in formal education, therapy and group work.

5. **The Group as Educator.** In informal education, the group is an integral component of the learning experience. Groups are important factors in shaping of identity; the groups of which we are part shape our minds, language and selves in very central ways. Educating a group is not simply about transmitting knowledge to an aggregate of individuals gathered in one room, but rather is very much about the dynamic role of the collective in expressing and reinforcing values that are part of the culture of the society that created the group. Indeed, groups are not simply aggregates of people learning individually in parallel fashion; they are social networks that teach ideas and values through the essence of the group process.[32] The group often serves as a mirror of selves or identities—a reflection of others who are like "me" in many ways and who at the same time exemplify ideas, values and behaviors to which I might aspire. In the best of cases the group could be a kind of creative hall of mirrors to help me see and shape my identity. Thus, the group experience is an additional educational resource to create culture, to present values, to expedite experiences and to help touch the individual. The group is especially relevant in informal Jewish education because of the centrality of the concept of "group" to Jewish civilization: *klal yisrael* (the totality of Israel), *am yisrael* (Jewish people), *kehillat kodesh* (holy community) and *tikkun olam* (correcting the world) are experienced through the collective group experience of Jewish peoplehood.

As some critics note, a group emphasis can sometimes lead to tribal triumphalism.[33] This is an important reservation, and co-opting the group phenomenon to education need not be exclusively for group loyalty or supremacy. In informal Jewish education the group is another contributing component in the journey to personal growth and identity.

6. **An Immersive Culture.** Informal Jewish education is concerned with creating a culture or a setting that in its totality immerses participants in the ideas, values and behaviors being presented. This approach utilizes the total environment to create a context in which the walls, the design, the architecture, the colors, the food—as many components of the venue as possible—"breathe" and "teach" the desired contents. This approach aspires to create an environment that exudes the educative moment and, as it were, fills the room with the oxygen from within rather than transmitting knowledge from without. This educational perspective (called the culturalist perspective[34]) ultimately is focused on enabling education to, as much as possible, imitate real life.

This means that logistical and organizational considerations are neither incidental nor secondary to the educational program; they are themselves inherently educational issues. On the Israel trip, for example, it is the educator and not the bus driver or innkeeper who should determine routes and room allocation. The dinner menu on the first night of a Jewish summer camp is as much an issue for the camp educator as it is for the business manager or dietician. The latter are rightly focused on finance or nutrition, while the former, zeroing in on the transition of the campers (and possible "newness panic"), seeks to create a warm Jewish home atmosphere.

The notion of an "educational culture" also implies that education is not limited to specific locales such as classrooms or school buildings; it can occur anywhere. The notion of a culture of education also suggests that no one agency has a monopoly on Jewish education. Such a culture can be created wherever Jews are found: in community centers, Jewish family service offices, sports clubs; at

---

[32] Charles Kadushin. *Understanding Social Networks* (New York: Oxford University Press, 2012).

[33] Steven M. Cohen and Arnold Eisen. *The Jew Within* (Bloomington, IN: Indiana University Press, 2000).

[34] Michael Cole. *Cultural Psychology* (Cambridge: MA: Harvard University Press, 1996). Jerome Bruner. *The Culture of Education* (Cambridge, MA: Harvard University Press, 1996).

retreats and conferences; during meals and bus rides. Some of these places may well be ideal venues for Jewish education because they are real settings where Jewish experiences can be lived out. The task of the educator is to shape all settings so that they may serve the larger educational vision.

7. **The "Playfulness" of Informal Education.**[35] Informal Jewish education intensely engages and co-opts participants and makes them feel positive about being involved.[36] Because of its focus on the individual and on issues that are real to him/her, informal Jewish education is often described as "fun," "joyful" or "enjoyable." This should not be taken as a sign of frivolity or lack of seriousness. The Dutch historian Johan Huizinga suggested that, at the core, humans and societies are *homo ludens*—playing people and societies.[37] Erik Erikson and others have taught us that identity is in part a sense of positive and "glad" feelings about a group or a world view or one's self.[38]

Positive feelings play a very important role in the development of identity. The literature of identity development, happiness and well-being emphasizes the significant role of "flourishing", enjoying and feeling positive as important linchpins of positive identity.[39] In that context, it may well be suggested that Jewish life has over-emphasized the lachrymose—crisis, suffering, the struggle for survival—and instead would do well to emphasize the joyful, the playful and the fun motifs which are part of our culture and history (perhaps it is time to replace the traditional Yiddish epitaph that "It is difficult to be a Jew" with the joyful proclamation of the twentieth-century poet Muriel Rukeyser that "To be a Jew is a gift"[40]).

8. **The Holistic Educator.** The informal Jewish educator is a total educational personality who educates by words, deeds and by shaping a culture of Jewish values and experiences. He/she is a person-centered educator whose focus is on learners and whose goal is their personal growth. The informal Jewish educator is a shaper of Jewish experiences. His/her role in this context is to create opportunities for those experiences and to facilitate the learner's entry into the moments. The informal Jewish educator promotes interaction and interchange. One of his/her major tasks is to create an environment that enables this interactivity to flourish. This requires proficiency in the skills of asking questions, listening and activating the engagement of others.

The informal Jewish educator is a creator of community and *kehillah:* he/she shapes the aggregate into a group and utilizes the group setting to teach such core Jewish values as *klal Yisrael* (Jewish peoplehood), *kvod ha-adam* (the dignity of all people), *shutfut goral* (shared destiny, and *shivyon* (equality). Informal Jewish educators are creators of culture; they are sensitive to all the elements specific to the educational setting so that these will reflect values and experiences they wish to convey. The task in this instance is to make every decision—big or little—an educational decision. Informal Jewish educators must be able to engage those with whom they work and make their learning experience enjoyable. The stimulation of positive associations is part of the informal Jewish educator's work. The informal Jewish educator needs to be an educated and committed Jew. This educator must be knowledgeable, since one of the values he/she comes to teach is *talmud torah*—Jewish knowledge. He/she must be committed to these values, since teaching commitment to the Jewish people, to Jewish life and Jewish values is at the heart of the enterprise. Commitment can only be learned if one sees examples of it up close. Finally, informal educators must, in the words of Parker Palmer, "teach from within"[41]. They must harness their innermost self and allow it to give voice to its commitments, beliefs and feelings as a model of the engaged person.

Informal Jewish Education Defined. Having identified these characteristics, we can spell out a definition of informal Jewish education:

---

[35] Over the years I have wrestled with various terms to describe this phenomenon, including "fun", "play", "engagement" and "playfulness".

[36] Van Clive Morris, *Existentialism in Education* (New York: Harper and Row, 1966).

[37] Johan Huizinga, *Homo Ludens* (London: Paladin, 1949).

[38] Erik Erikson. *Identity and the Life Cycle* (New York: Norton, 1980) Erik Erikson. *Toys and Reasons* (New York: Norton, 1977).

[39] Martin E.P. Seligsman. *Flourish: A Visionary New Understanding of Happiness and Well-being* (New York: Free Press, 2011); M. Csikszentmihalyi, *Creativity, Flow, and the Psychology of Discovery and Invention* (NY: Harper Perennials, 1997).

[40] Muriel Rukeyser. *Collected Poems of Muriel Rukeyser.* (Pittsburgh: University of Pittsburgh Press, 2006).

[41] Parker Palmer. *Teaching From Within* (San Francisco: Jossey-Bass, 1998).

Informal Jewish education is aimed at the personal growth of Jews of all ages. It happens through the individual's actively experiencing a diversity of Jewish moments and values that are regarded as worthwhile. It works by creating venues, by developing a total educational culture and by co-opting the social context. It is based on a curriculum of Jewish values and experiences that is presented in a dynamic and flexible manner. As an activity, it does not call for any one venue but may happen in a variety of settings. It evokes fun in the present, pleasurable feeling, and warm memories. It requires Jewishly literate educators with a "teaching" style that is highly interactive and participatory, who are willing to make maximal use of self and personal lifestyle in their educational work.

WHAT IS UNIQUE ABOUT INFORMAL JEWISH EDUCATION?

The synergy of the eight characteristics. Informal Jewish education is not defined by any one of its characteristics. As noted, each of these characteristics is also a component of other kinds of education and other professions that involve working with people. The coming together of the various characteristics in the new construct called "informal Jewish education" is the key to understanding the concept. By way of analogy: Chicken soup on Friday night requires not only the combination of water, vegetables and chicken, but also the presence of candles, <u>h</u>allah, dusk and a loving family to become part of the Shabbat experience. Likewise, a person-centered approach, an emphasis on Jewish experience, a curriculum of experiences and values, interactivity, group process, a culture of education, an engaged mood and a holistic Jewish educator are all required to add up to informal Jewish education.

Informal education and informal Jewish education. Jewish and general informal education share some of the defining characteristics: both are person-centered, experience-oriented and interactive, and both promote a learning and experiencing community, a culture of education and content that engages. At the same time, informal Jewish education is a unique sub-category of informal education that is related to other faith-based forms of education. It differs from general informal education in two major respects: its curriculum of experiences and values and its holistic educator.

The first difference has to do with the goal of curriculum in Jewish as opposed to general informal education. Informal Jewish education is inherently about affecting the lifestyle and identity of Jews. All forms of informal Jewish education are ultimately education for Jewish character or lifestyle. It is true that there are specific examples of informal Jewish education that seem to be about well-defined topics, rather than about identity. The adult learning class on "The Rhythm of Jewish Life" helps participants acquires knowledge about the Jewish calendar. The trip to Poland enables a better understanding of the role of the Holocaust in Jewish life. But in both cases the larger, overall goal is Jewish character or identity education.

In general informal education, on the other hand, a class or workshop may be about learning a skill or improving one's skills. It might also be about recreation and use of free time. But it is not always necessarily about ultimate identity or about character education. In informal Jewish education the specific Jewish experiences (holidays, visits to Jewish sites, the Israel trip) that make up the "curriculum" are really about a curriculum of Jewishness *in toto*, whereas in general informal education the specific experiences and skills (sports, ceramics, music, learning about other cultures) that make up the curriculum are the ends in themselves.

The second difference has to do with divergent conceptions of the role of the informal educator. Educators in informal Jewish education are inherently shapers of Jewish experience and role models of Jewish lifestyle. They need to be skilled in the facts of the Jewish calendar or the history of Polish Jewry, but ultimately their unique mission is to create Jewish experiences and affect Jewish identity. If an educator's sole role is giving a good lecture about the Polish *kehilla* in the nineteenth century, he/she is called a "visiting lecturer". A person whose sole task is to take a group through the streets of Prague or Krakow is a tour guide. Only if the mission is to affect the total Jewish being of the traveler is the guide an "informal Jewish educator".

WHERE INFORMAL JEWISH EDUCATION DIFFERS FROM OTHER FORMS OF EDUCATION OR WORK WITH PEOPLE

Our analysis of informal Jewish education helps us to clearly see that it is not confined to a place, even though it does seem more likely to happen in certain venues such as camps, educational travel, youth movements or retreats. Many of its methods are shared by other forms of "the helping professions," such as social work, therapy and good school classes. At the same time, it is true that certain methodologies such as group process, dialogue and experiencing are very central to the practice of informal Jewish education. Let us take a closer look at informal Jewish education and (1) schools; (2) Jewish communal service; (3) therapy; and (4) life itself.

Informal Jewish education and Jewish schools. As we have seen, the most common comparison is between informal Jewish education and that which takes place in Jewish schools. In fact, we have been suggesting that there are important similarities: Both are rooted in some overall Jewish vision or ideology. Both have a program or a "curriculum" that guides their work. Both are populated by people whose role is to "shape," "teach" or "guide" and others who are in the setting to learn and grow. Both happen in specific social and cultural contexts and are conducted by some public or private agency. Both are concerned for the Jewish future.

At the same time, there are also sociological differences that seem to suggest some differences between Jewish schooling and informal education in the reality of twenty-first-century life. Generally, contemporary schooling—Jewish and general—has become associated with the task of transmitting knowledge.[42] Schooling does have important socialization and acculturation objectives, but the transmission of knowledge remains a central focus. This knowledge is usually categorized in terms of a curriculum or course of study which becomes the definitive "map" of what should be taught. These contents have usually been seen in cognitive terms, and they are often linked to the idea of a core intellectual "canon", a culture or a society's body of basic texts. The central personalities in schools are generally called "teachers", whose roles are multiple but certainly linked to transmitting knowledge. Much of general schooling is aimed at progressing along a hierarchical ladder of educational achievement, which means advancing to the next rung of schooling and ultimately to a profession. Jewish day schools must be effective in advancing their charges on this ladder. Schooling over the years has very much become linked to a system of sanctions rooted in grades and outside evaluative measurements.[43] Given the realities of contemporary life, some of our day schools have sometimes seemed to emphasize the primacy of grading and academic achievement and the sharp distinction between Jewish and general studies.

Informal Jewish education, as we have seen, emphasizes experiences, the role of the learner, and the educator as shaper of environment, group process and interaction. It is undoubtedly true that many contemporary Jewish schools also value these attributes, and in that sense Jewish schools and informal Jewish education are often close relatives rather than opposing forces. Jewish schools have played and will continue to play a central role in the education of the individual and the advancement of societies; informal Jewish education proposes acting as a viable and vibrant partner in that process.

Informal Jewish Education and Jewish Communal Service. Informal education is sometimes equated with Jewish communal service. In training programs, journals and professional development, these two spheres often are aligned, and it is worthwhile to examine their relationship.

Informal Jewish education shares the concerns of Jewish communal service and social work for the needs of the Jewish people and Jewish communal life. In addition, informal Jewish education and Jewish communal service also share the grounding in group dynamics and group process, and focus on the person. Both of these approaches are rooted in the helping professions and in the rich social science tradition of individual psychology, social psychology, organizational theory, the clinical process and group relations.

---

[42] E.D. Hirsch, Jr. *The Schools We Need and Why We Don't Have Them* (New York: Doubleday, 1996).
[43] Alfie Kohn, *Schools We Deserve, op.cit.*

However, informal Jewish education and Jewish communal service are not exactly the same. The former is an overt form of Jewish education in its concern with presenting individuals at various stages of their lives with a Jewish vision that will be meaningful for them. With its main task the Jewish growth of the learner, informal Jewish education is centrally concerned with Jewish experiences, Jewish lifestyle and Jewish worldview. Jewish communal service responds to the various needs of Jews and the Jewish community—social, cultural, recreational, welfare. It comes to help Jews wherever they are, and it aims to advance Jewish communal improvement. It is not contradictory to the goals of informal Jewish education, but it is not exactly its equivalent.

Informal Jewish education and therapy. Informal Jewish education is influenced by presuppositions that underlie certain major approaches to therapy in the past century. These approaches share with informal Jewish education the concern with the individual and the individual's needs as the "client". Both therapy and informal Jewish education require the engagement of the individual in order to do their work. Both are committed to words and to dialectic as a central technique for engaging clients and for enabling them to grow.

There are, however, major differences. Therapy is ultimately very much about helping and healing people: "Psychotherapy aims, in general, to reduce or eliminate distress and disability that are a consequence of the neurotic person's reaction against himself. In short it aims simply to repair."[44] While it can also be said to help people grow, therapy's tasks are adaptive and rehabilitative. It does not replace education, but very often it is an adjustment to and even antidote for education. Informal Jewish education is overtly about educating, building and helping to give shape to a Jewish way. It is not about healing or repairing (although it sometimes does that), but about creating and unfolding.

The major difference is ultimately related to worldview. Therapy comes to help individuals confronting personal dilemmas to find their way, and it generally does not propose or promulgate any one worldview. It is ultimately a technique to help a person function better and make choices. Informal Jewish education shares therapy's commitment to individual choice, but it also speaks in the name of Jewish values and lifestyles that it regards as desirable. It is not just a technique; it is also content-based, ultimately rooted in a worldview that is Jewish. It may be diverse, and it certainly does not come to impose the worldview, but it does represent a belief that there are values and behaviors that are integral to the Jewish perspective and are good and valuable.

Informal Jewish education and life. It is appealing to say, "All of Jewish life is informal Jewish education." Informal Jewish education, like life itself, encompasses diverse Jewish experiences in a variety of settings. However, while we do learn many things from Jewish life, there is a critical distinction. Jewish life is a complex pattern of personalities, events and processes over which no one person or force has definitive control. General events, the economy, world forces and other religions and cultures all shape Jewish life, as do the dynamics of Jewish organizations, Jewish leaders and Jewish communities. Jewish life as a whole is not something that can "set" goals and outcomes or build a curriculum of experiences. It does "educate" in the sense that it has an impact upon us, but it doesn't have the ability to "choose" this. The events of Jewish life—like all of life—are the outcome of a multitude of historical, political and sociological forces over which we do not have total control.

In contra-distinction, informal Jewish education *deliberately* selects Jewish experiences with the conscious intent of affecting the learner. Jewish life is a haphazard flow of events, the outcome of a multitude of historical, political and sociological forces. Informal Jewish education is a conscious effort to shape what Jewish life is. Jewish education chooses to be.

THE SOURCES OF INFORMAL JEWISH EDUCATION

Informal Jewish education is an eclectic theory that is informed by several diverse sources. The development of the literature of this field is still at an early stage and will require time and a willingness to roam

---

[44]David Shapiro, *The Psychotherapy of Neurotic Character* (New York: Basic Books, 1989).

wide and far in Jewish texts and in history, world literature, philosophy and the social sciences. We are at the very beginning of the journey.

One important source for understanding informal Jewish education is the history and texts of Jewish tradition. The great texts of our civilization, along with the social history of Jewish life throughout the ages and across continents, reveal much about basic educational approaches and practices in Jewish communal and religious life. There is no one definitive classical Jewish text on "education". Thus, we need to learn and be taught by the rich comprehensive canon of Jewish texts to learn about education. Important resources include: biblical and Talmudic texts, the history of Jewish education and community in *Eretz* Israel and in Babylonia, the academies of the great rabbis, the classical yeshiva, the *kehilla* of nineteenth-century Poland, Jewish camping and youth movements in the twentieth century and the thinking of such diverse personalities as Rabbi Akiva, the Salanter Rebbe, Martin Buber, the Lubavitcher Rebbe and Janus Korczak.

In recent years there is increasing wisdom to learn from emerging work in the field of Jewish educational research and thinking and from case studies of prominent forms of contemporary informal education in the Jewish world and the world at large.[45] This arena has been in its early stages, but there are signs that it has a small but growing group of interested parties. The practice of informal education is blossoming and is worthy of serious and diverse modes of research and analysis.

General intellectual and educational thought is a critical resource for understanding informal Jewish education and includes the ideas of such figures as: Socrates, St. Augustine, Maria Montessori and Sigmund Freud; John Dewey, Carl Rogers, Bruno Bettelheim, Paolo Freire, Michel Foucault, Claude Levi-Strauss and Oliver Sacks. While most of them did not write about "informal education" per se, their thinking about education, knowing, learning and context are critical for the shaping of the theory of informal education.

I believe that there are extremely significant new directions in the neurosciences and cognitive sciences which will have significant implications for the very essence of how we look at education—and concomitantly for thinking about informal education. Daniel Kahneman's path-breaking work on "Thinking Fast and Slow" describes not just two diverse ways of "thinking" that characterize humans, but may have significant implications for the settings and educational techniques used to develop these two types.[46]

The research summarized by David Brooks in *The Social Animal* suggests new frontiers about the sources of being human and the process of "educating".[47] Together with Csikszentmihalyi's notion of "flow",[48] Ariely's notion of "rationally irrational"[49] and Seligman's emphasis on a positive psychology which is aimed at the concept "happiness"[50] suggest significant new directions being studied by serious scholars and researchers which may break down and rebuild the phenomenon called "education". We may be on the cusp of dramatic reworkings of the entire domains of formal and informal education.

IN DEFENSE OF INFORMAL JEWISH EDUCATION

Over the years a host of reservations about informal Jewish education have been raised. In this section I shall attempt to address some of these and provide answers to my interlocutors.

"Informal Jewish education has no Jewish content or curriculum." Informal Jewish education does have Jewish content. Its content is a body of Jewish experiences, values and behaviors that its proponents wish to present and help learners internalize. Informal Jewish education comes to enable a person to confront and internalize basic dimensions of being Jewish by experiencing them. It is true that this content is not the same as a body of facts and ideas about Judaism organized according to academic categories

---

[45] Joseph Reimer has devoted much effort to documenting such case studies.

[46] In an email to a student of mine, Kahneman indicated that he had not thought a great deal about educational implications, but it was an important question (Spring, 2012).

[47] David Brooks. The Social Animal (New York: Random House, 2011).

[48] Cskizentmihayli, *op.cit.*

[49] Dan Ariely. Predictably Irrational: The Hidden Forces that Shape Our Decisions (New York: Harper Collins, 2008).

[50] Seligman, *op.cit.*

or presented in books. Its contents are not limited to bodies of knowledge or texts but rather encompass the internalization of Jewish knowledge, facts and values into a personal life style. There is an informal Jewish educational curriculum, and it is well defined and explicit, but the dynamics of its teaching are not carved in stone. The curriculum of informal Jewish education doesn't look like *school* curricula with lists of themes, dates, facts, generalizations and specific lesson plans for the day. It is more likely to be organized around key value concepts, kinds of experiences and moments in time, and it is much more flexible and adaptive in nature.

"Informal Jewish education neglects the Jewish canon." The "canon" is a popular contemporary term referring to a compendium of basic texts regarded as the core of Jewish culture and civilization. This canon is typically held to include: Bible, Talmud, commentaries, Midrash, rabbinic literature, *siddur* and other texts that are assumed to comprise the core of Jewish learning. Teaching the canon is central not only to Jewish education but to Jewish life and continuity and must be incorporated into any comprehensive Jewish program of learning. Teaching the canon requires knowledgeable and talented teachers and structured settings. Informal Jewish education is informed and shaped by the canon and reflects its best principles; however, its ultimate task is not the transmission of the canon per se but rather the canon's underlying values and ideas. While informal Jewish education may not specifically teach the texts of the canon, it is inherently shaped by them. The traditional texts are certainly a part of informal Jewish education's own eclectic "canon".

Studying texts surely is serious and one of the cornerstones of Jewish education. But other Jewish experiences also can be serious, in the sense of life shaping life. The study of great Jewish books should be treated very seriously, but so should the experiencing of Shabbat, visiting the Jewish cemetery in Warsaw or strolling through the hills of the Galilee on a spring day. Informal Jewish education is not a replacement for the canon but rather makes its ideas and teachings come alive.

"Informal Jewish education is 'touchy-feely.'" It is true that informal Jewish education is concerned with attitudes, feelings and choices, but that does not mean that it is unconcerned with substantive teaching of Judaism. Adult learning programs, camp programs and Israel trips help students become more knowledgeable about Judaism although their ultimate goal is knowledge that leads to action and lifestyle. Affect is clearly an important part of identity and of Jewish life, and neglect of this fact in Jewish education is often lamented by the unattached. The emphasis on affect and behavior is not a rejection of intellect and understanding. Indeed, informal education may be about correcting the bifurcation between affect and intellect and restoring the organic harmony between deeds, intellect and emotion.

"Informal Jewish education is simply having fun." Informal Jewish education isn't "simply" fun, but fortunately for Jewish life it certainly does seem to be enjoyable! Calling informal Jewish education "fun" is significant because this says that there are kinds of Jewish experience and education which can engage and ignite people. But it is also education, and when done properly it can advance Jewish understanding and living. We should not be afraid or skeptical of things that are fun—we should jump at the educational opportunity they present.

Informal Jewish education is play in the sense of deep involvement in a comprehensive activity that completely engages the learner. Many studies tell us how central play can be in child therapy,[51] in the cultural life of a society and in personal relationships. Erikson looked to toys as a key to understanding young people,[52] and Giamatti compared the end of the baseball season and the advent of Rosh Hashanah as important transitional moments in the year's lifecycle.[53] Informal Jewish education is not playing in the sense of being irrelevant and casual—it is play in the sense of engaging and energizing.

"Informal Jewish educators are not serious professionals." Informal Jewish education in fact calls for extremely serious educators and training! To be a truly professional informal Jewish educator one needs Judaic knowledge; a Jewish lifestyle; a knack for group dynamics; the ability to be interactive and

---

[51] Saralea Chazan. *Profiles of Play* (London and Philadelphia: Jessica Kingsley Publishers, 2002).

[52] Erikson, *Toys and Reasons, op.cit.*

[53] A. Bartlett Giamatti. *Take Time for Paradise: Americans and Their Games* (NY: Summit, 1989).

to listen; the ability to engage others; and the ability to impart ideas and values twenty-four hours day, seven days a week. One has to be accomplished in many areas—encompassing both content and method, Jewish and general—often demonstrating proficiency over and above that required of teachers. Thus, the training and work of informal Jewish educators is very challenging, to the extent that some of my critics have regarded it as a "mission impossible".

It is indeed a difficult and challenging profession, but the work can be done. The theory is based on real life, real experiences and real people. There are masters of this work out there accomplishing this kind of education, and many readers of this treatise have been affected by them. Some readers are these educators. The fact that something is complicated does not mean it is impossible.

"Informal Jewish education is simply another way to say 'good education.'" "Informal education" is not simply a synonym for "good education." "Informal Jewish education" is a term that exists in common language and a phenomenon that exists in contemporary educational practice in countries throughout the world. I have attempted to show that there are formal dimensions which define this phenomenon and distinguish it from other kinds of education. Moreover, all informal education is not *mutandis mutandi* "good education"; there can be good informal education or mediocre informal education or bad informal education. In contemporary educational parlance and practice, the term "informal education" is a formal category that describes an idea and a form of education.

"Informal education does not exist." This argument encompasses two contentions. The first position is that these two fields *shouldn't* be separated.[54] This position seems to me to be an ideological stance of what should or shouldn't be and not an analytic point of how we do talk and think about concepts. The second contention is that "informal education" has become a way of collecting all the "goodies" about education and wrapping them neatly with the emotively positive term "experiential" or "informal". As already indicated, I am not at the moment interested in what is "good" or "bad", but rather with what "is". I believe there is a thing called x (Informal or Experiential), and I want to understand it.

"Where does the thinking of Chazan and Reimer and Bryfman agree and/or disagree?" My colleagues Joe Reimer and David Bryfman have made important contributions to the advance of experiential/informal education. I believe the three of us agree about more things than we disagree. We agree that there is an important educational phenomenon that has been denoted as either "informal" or "experiential" Jewish education. We agree that this phenomenon is important for Jewish life and worthy of serious study and implementation. We agree that it is a potentially seminal force in affecting identity and life. I have identified eight characteristics of informal Jewish education. They speak of three distinct initiatives which are involved in experiential learning: recreation, socialization and challenge. Their notion of recreation is parallel to my fifth and sixth characteristics—an immersive culture and the playfulness of informal education. Their notion of challenge as the stretching and growing of an individual parallels my notions of learned centered and a pedagogy of interactivity. Their notion of socialization has informed my thinking and caused me to expand my comments on the group dimensions of informal Jewish education and the rich potential of informal Jewish education.

Where we differ is: 1) I posit some additional characteristics that they do not emphasize, i.e., a curriculum of values and behavior; pedagogy of interactivity; and a holistic educator. 2) I agree that socialization to be an active member of the Jewish community is a goal of informal education, although for me it is not the primary nor exclusive goal. 3) I believe that any discussion of informal Jewish education involves certain type of skills that need to be fostered in educators to make it happen. 4) I agree that the criteria I propose are "lofty", but I do not believe that they are unrealistic. Over the years I have observed these qualities in many people and institutions. They are real, accessible and happen in practice. Moreover, I think that informal Jewish education will not be serious or taken seriously until it is willing to establish lofty goals, no less rigorous than those for being a rabbi, educator or professor. Overall, my thinking has

---

[54]Cytryn and Doff, *Op.cit.*

grown because of the writings of David, Joe and others, and I believe that these articles are best read as a shared, ever-evolving creative compendium.

THE PROMISE AND LIMITATIONS OF INFORMAL JEWISH EDUCATION

What is the promise of informal Jewish education? This kind of education is uniquely equipped to introduce people of all ages to some of the great experiences and moments of Jewish life. Its focus on the person and its emphasis on actually participating in significant moments offer great promise for affecting individuals and the Jewish community very powerfully. It offers great promise for affecting Jewish feeling and behavior. It can deepen some Jewish skills very well—for example, speaking Hebrew or reading Torah or building a *sukkah*—because in informal Jewish education one learns by doing. It is very effective in helping individuals advance on their personal journeys and growth, as a plethora of voices from summer camps, Israeli trips and other kind of informal education attest.

Informal Jewish education may be less effective for systematic Jewish text learning, for a systematic expansion of Jewish literacy and for the meta-analysis of Jewish ideas. In that sense it is less effective in the overall goal of imparting Jewish culture, an important objective for the Jewish people as a whole. Informal Jewish education's strength is not in guaranteeing transmission of the Jewish canon and cultural legacy, which is so important for Jewish survival. Informal Jewish education is not anti-intellectual, but it does not make the cognitive and the intellectual its sole or even main preoccupation. It does seem fair to say that schooling has several potential advantages in enabling systematic Jewish learning.

Finally, because informal Jewish education is so focused on the individual and his/her personal journey and choice, it cannot guarantee collective cultural outcomes. The hope of informal education is that the learners will choose a Jewish path, but they may or they may not. Ultimately, the bottom line is that the learning that occurs in informal Jewish education and that which occurs in formal Jewish education are both critical, and they should work in tandem. We cannot afford a Jewish education that is only formal, just as we cannot afford a Jewish education that is only informal. We should look forward to the day when these two kinds of education work side by side, hand in hand and interchangeably, to touch the young and old learner alike, and from all sides.

CONCLUSION: INFORMAL EDUCATION AND JEWISH LIFE IN THE POSTMODERN ERA

The bifurcation of education into formal and informal is in many ways artificial and inefficient. While we begin the twenty-first century with formal and informal Jewish education, this state of affairs is not irreversible. In the decades, years and century ahead we may yet succeed at restoring the organic unity that once was. We should work hard to correct the notion that informal and formal Jewish educations are separate entities. In fact, they should be seen as partners in the overall goal of developing knowledgeable and committed Jews. Each has much to learn from the other: Formal Jewish education can learn to be more person-centered and participatory, and informal Jewish education can learn to be more literate and rigorous. We should be talking about "the deformalization of the formal" and "re-formalization of the informal" rather than opposing philosophies. The time has come to unite these two critical worlds.

Informal Jewish education, as an approach that maintains that people learn by being actively involved, is a good fit with the diversity, mobility and longevity that characterize the twenty-first-century Jewish world. With its emphasis on experience and values, informal Jewish education seems uniquely equipped to help people on that most important of human endeavors—the search for personal meaning. The twenty-first century warmly welcomes an education that reaches out to each of us as unique human beings and helps us grapple with the search for answers to life's big questions. The days of informal education being "supplementary" or "extra-curricular" are over. Informal Jewish education is ready to assume a major new educational role in twenty-first-century Jewish life.

BIBLIOGRAPHY

Alper, Janice, ed. (1987). *Learning Together: A Source Book on Jewish Family Education.* Denver: Alternatives in Religious Education.

Bellah, Robert, et al. (1996). *Habits of the Heart: Individualism and Commitment in American Life.* Berkeley: University of California Press.

Bereiter, Carl (1973). *Must We Educate?* Englewood Cliffs, N.J.: Prentice-Hall.

Bettelheim, Bruno (1950). *Love is Not Enough.* New York: Collier Books.

Blyth, A., ed. (1988). *Informal Primary Education Today.* Lewes: Falmer Press.

Boal, A. (1992). *Games for Actors and Non-Actors.* London: Routledge.

Boud, D., and N. Miller, eds. (1997). *Working with Experience: Animated Learning.* London: Routledge.

Brew, J. M. (1946). *Informal Education: Adventures and Reflections.* London: Faber.

Brookfield, Steven (1988). *Understanding and Facilitating Adult Learning.* San Francisco: Jossey-Bass.

Bruner, Jerome (1996). *The Culture of Education.* Cambridge: Harvard University Press.

Buber, Martin (1947). "Education" and "The Education of Character." In *Between Man and Man,* London: The Fontana Library.

    (1948). "On National Education" and "Teaching and the Deed." In *Israel and the World.* New York: Schocken.

Burbules, N. (1993). *Dialogue in Teaching: Theory and Practice.* New York: Teachers College Press.

Chazan, Barry, ed. (2002). *The Israel Experience: Studies in Jewish Identity and Youth Culture.* Jerusalem: Andrea and Charles Bronfman Philanthropies.

    (1996). *What is Jewish Education in JCCs?* Jerusalem: Jewish Community Centers Association.

    (1994). "The Israel Trip: A New Form of American Jewish Education." In *Youth Trips to Israel: Rationale and Realization.* New York: JESNA (Jewish Educational Services of North America).

    (1991). "What is Informal Jewish Education?" *Journal of Jewish Communal Service* 67, no. 4 (Summer 1991).

    (1981). "What is Informal Education?" *Philosophy of Education, 1981.* Carbondale, IL: Philosophy of Education Society.

    (1979). *Jewish Identity and Education in Melbourne.* Jerusalem: Institute of Contemporary Jewry, Hebrew University.

    and Steven Cohen (2001). "What We Know about Young Jews." *Journal of Jewish Communal Service.*

    and Steven Cohen (1994). *Assessing the Jewish Educational Effectiveness of JCCs: The 1994 Study.* New York: Jewish Community Centers Association.

    and Mark Charendoff, eds. (1994). *Jewish Education and the Jewish Community Center.* Jerusalem: Jewish Community Centers Association.

    and Perry London (1990). *Jewish Identity and Psychology.* New York: American Jewish Committee.

Chazan, Saralea (2002). *Profiles of Play.* London and Philadelphia: Jessica Kingsley Publishers.

Cohen, Erik H., and Eynatt Cohen (2000). *The Israel Experience* Jerusalem: Jerusalem Institute for Israel Studies.

Cohen, Steven M., and Arnold Eisen (2000). *The Jew Within.* Bloomington: Indiana University Press.

Cohen, Steven M., and Susan Wall (1994). "Excellence in Israel Trips." In *Youth Trips to Israel: Rationale and Realization.* New York: JESNA (Jewish Educational Services of North America).

Cole, Michael (1996). *Cultural Psychology.* Cambridge, MA: Harvard University Press.

Coombs, M. (1968). "Non-Formal Education: To Catch Up, Keep Ahead, and Get Ahead." In *The World Educational Crisis: A Systems Analysis.* New York: Oxford University Press.

Cremin, Lawrence (1961). *The Transformation of the School.* New York: Vintage Books.

Csikszentmihalyi, M. (1997). *Creativity, Flow, and the Psychology of Discovery and Invention.* New York: Harper Perennials.

Dewey, J. (1937). *Experience and Education.* New York: Macmillan.

Dickens, Charles (1981 ed.). *Hard Times.* New York: Bantam.

Doyle, M. E., and M. K. Smith (1999). *Born and Bred: Leadership, Heart and Informal Education.* London: YMCA George Williams College/Rank Foundation.

Dreeben, Robert (1966). *On What Is Learned in Schools.* Reading, MA: Addison-Wesley.

Durkheim, Emile (1957). *Education and Sociology.* Glencoe, IL: Free Press.

Dushkin, Alexander (1985). *Living Bridges.* Jerusalem: Keter.

Edwards, C. (1998). *The Hundred Languages of Children.* London: Ablex.

Erikson, E. (2000). "Toys and Reasons." In *The Erik Erikson Reader*. New York: W. W. Norton.

Fantini, M. D., and R. L. Sinclair, eds. (1985). *Education in School and Non-School Settings*. Eighty-fourth yearbook of the National Society for the Study of Education, part 1. Chicago: University of Chicago Press.

Finklestein, Louis. *Akiva: Student, Scholar, Saint*. New York: Jewish Publication Society.

Giamatti, A. Bartlett (1989). *Take Time for Paradise: Americans and Their Games*. New York: Summit.

    (1998). *A Great and Glorious Game*. Chapel Hill: Algonquin.

Gladwell, Malcolm (1997). "Listening to Khakis: What America's Most Popular Pants Tell Us About the Way Guys Think." *New Yorker* (July 28, 1997).

Goldman, Israel (1975). *Life-Long Learning Among Jews*. New York: Ktav.

Goffman, I. (1961). *Asylums*. New York: Anchor Books.

Gordis, David (1976). "Towards a Rabbinic Philosophy of Education" In *Exploring the Talmud*, ed. Haim Dimitrovsky. New York: Ktav.

Grenz, S. (1996). *A Primer on Postmodernism*. Grand Rapids, MI: Wm. B. Eerdmans.

Gur-Ze'ev, Ilan, ed. (1996). *Education in the Era of the Post Modern Discourse*. Jerusalem: Magnes Press.

Haroutinian-Gordon, S. (1991). *Turning the Soul: Teaching Through Conversation in the High School*. Chicago: University of Chicago Press.

Henze, R.C. (1992). *Informal Teaching and Learning: A Study of Everyday Cognition in a Greek Community*. Hillsdale, NJ: Lawrence Erlbaum Associates.

Hirsch, E. D., Jr. (1996). *The Schools We Need and Why We Don't Have Them*. New York: Doubleday.

Hyman, Tali E. (2008) *The Liberal Jewish Day School as Laboratory for Dissonance in American Jewish Identity-Formation*. Unpublished doctoral dissertation. New York University. New York, NY.

Illich, I. (1973). *Deschooling Society*, Hammondsworth: Penguin.

Jeffs, T., and M. Smith, eds. (1990). *Using Informal Education*. Buckingham: Open University Press.

    (1999). *Informal Education: Conversation, Democracy, and Learning*. Ticknall: Education Now.

    (1999). *Informal Education*. Leicester: NIACE; London: Zed Books.

Jewish Community Centers Association (2002). *Annual Report*. New York: JCCA.

Joselit, Jena (1994). *A Worthy Use of Summer: Jewish Summer Camps 1900–1950*. www.nmajh.org/exhibitions/summercamp.

Kahane, Reuven (1997). *The Origins of Postmodern Youth: Informal Youth Movements in a Comparative Perspective*. Berlin: Walter de Gruyter.

Katz, Betsy (2012). *Re-Imagining Adult Jewish Education*. New Jersey: Ktav.

Katz, Betsy, and Jonathan Mirvis (1997). *Israel and Adult Jewish Education*. Jerusalem: Keren Karev, Jewish Agency Department of Education, Mifgashim Centre.

Kellner, Shaul. *Tours That Bind: Diaspora, Pilgrimage and Israeli Birthright Tourism*. (2010) New York: New York University Press.

Krasner, Jonathan (2011). *The Benderly Boys and American Jewish Education*. Waltham, MA: Brandeis University Press.

Kaufman, David (1999). *Shul with a Pool: The "Synagogue Center" in Jewish History*. Hanover, NH: Brandeis University Press.

Kirschenbaum, H., and V. L. Henderson (1989). *The Carl Rogers Reader*. Boston: Houghton Mifflin.

Knowles, M.S. (1973). *The Adult Learner: A Neglected Species*. Houston: Gulf Publishing.

Kohlberg, Lawrence (1981). *The Philosophy of Moral Development*. San Francisco: Harper and Row.

Kohn, Alfie (1997). *The Schools Our Children Deserve*. Boston: Houghton-Mifflin.

Lavi, Zvi (2000). *Is Education Possible in Times of Postmodernism?* Tel Aviv: Sifriat Poalim.

Lindeman, E. C. (1989). *The Meaning of Adult Education*. Norman: University of Oklahoma Press.

Maller, Julius (1949). "The Role of Education in Jewish History." In *The Jews: Their History, Culture, and Religion*, ed. Louis Finklestein. New York: Harper and Row.

Matzner-Bekerman, Shoshanna (1984). *The Jewish Child: Halakhic Perspectives*. New York: Ktav.

Miller, Helena, Alex Pomson, Lisa Grant (editors) (2011). *The International Handbook of Jewish Education*. Heidelberg: Springer.

Mead, G. H. (1934). *Mind, Self, and Society*. Chicago: University of Chicago Press.

Morris, Van Clive (1966). *Existentialism in Education*. New York: Harper and Row.

Paulston, Rolland (1972). *Non-Formal Education: An Annotated International Bibliography*. New York: Praeger.

Pinar, William F., William M. Reynolds, Patrick Slattery, Peter Taubman (1995). *Understanding Curriculum*. New York: Peter Lang.

Pratte, Richard (1973). *The Public School Movement*. New York: David McKay.

Putnam, Robert (2000). *Bowling Alone: The Collapse and Revival of American Community*. New York: Simon and Schuster.

Redl, Fritz, and David Wineman (1957). *The Aggressive Child*. Glencoe: Free Press.

Reimer, E. (1971). *School is Dead*. Hammondsworth: Penguin.

——— (2007). "Beyond More Jews Doing Jewish: Clarifying the Goals of Informal Education." *The Journal of Jewish Education*, Vol. 73, pp. 5–23.

——— (2007). "Response." *The Journal of Jewish Education*, Vol.[xx, pp.—.]

——— (2011). "Informal Education: the Decisive Decade: How Informal Education Was Transformed in Its Relationship with Jewish Philanthropy." *The International Handbook of Jewish Education*. Hamburg: Springer.

——— and David Bryfman (2008). "Jewish Experiential Education" in *What We Now Know About Jewish Education*. (Los Angeles: Torah Aura).

Reisman, Bernard (1979). *The Jewish Experiential Book*. New York: Ktav.

——— (1991). *Informal Jewish Education in the United States*. A Report for the Mandel Commission. New York: Mandel Foundation.

Roberts, L. C. (1997). *From Knowledge to Narrative: Educators and the Changing Museum*. Washington: Smithsonian Institute Press.

Rogers, C., and H. J. Freiberg (1993). *Freedom to Learn*. New York: Charles Merrill.

Rolnick, Eran (2012). *Freud in Zion: Psychoanalysis and the Making of Modern Jewish Identity*. London: Karnac.

Rukeyser, Muriel (2006). *Collected Poems of Muriel Rukeyser*. Pittsbugh: University of Pittsburgh Press.

Saxe, Len, Charles Kadushin, Shaul Kelner, Mark Rosen and Erez Yereslove (2002). *A Mega-Experiment in Jewish Education: The Impact of Birthright Israel*. Waltham, MA: The Cohen Center for Modern Jewish Studies, Brandeis University.

Saxe and Sales (2004). *How Goodly Are Thy Tents: Summer Camps as Jewish Socializing*. Hanover, NH: Brandeis University Press.

Saxe, Leonard, and Barry Chazan (2008). *Ten Days of Birthright Israel: A Journey in Young Adult Jewish Identity*. Waltham, MA: Brandeis University Press.

Scheffler, Israel (1958). "Philosophical Models of Teaching" in *Philosophy and Education*. Edited by Israel Scheffler. Boston: Allyn and Bacon, Inc.

Scult, Mel (1993). *Judaism Faces the Twentieth Century: A Biography of Mordecai Kaplan*. Detroit: Wayne State University Press.

——— (2001). *Communities of the Spirit: The Journals of Mordecai Kaplan*, vol. II *1913–1934*. Detroit: Wayne State University Press.

Seligman, Martin (2011). *Flourish*. New York: Free Press.

——— (2002). *Authentic Happiness: Using the New Positive Psychology to Realize Your Potential for Lasting Fulfillment*.

Shapiro, David (1965). *Neurotic Styles*. New York: Basic Books.

——— (1981). *Autonomy and Rigid Character*. New York: Basic Books.

——— (1989). *The Psychotherapy of Neurotic Character*. New York: Basic Books.

Simkins, T. (1977). *Non-formal Education and Development*. Manchester: Manchester University Press.

Spring, Joel (1975). *A Primer on Libertarian Education*. Montreal: Black Rose Books.

Twain, Mark (1981 ed.). *The Adventures of Huckleberry Finn*. New York: Bantam.

Weber, Lillian (1971). *The English Infant School and Informal Education*. Englewood Cliffs, NJ: The Center for Urban Education.

World Leisure and Recreation Association (1993). *International Charter for Leisure Education*. Jaipur: WLRA.

Wright, Robert (1994). *The Moral Animal*. New York: Vintage Books.

Yalum, Irvin (1992). *When Nietzsche Wept*. New York: Harper Perennial.

——— (2001). *The Gift of Therapy*. London: Piatkus Press,

THE POWER OF OPTIMAL JEWISH EXPERIENCES: EXPERIENTIAL JEWISH EDUCATION A DECADE AFTER CHAZAN

Joseph Reimer

INTRODUCTION

During the past decade the organized Jewish community in North American has placed ever-greater emphasis on the importance of informal educational settings for engaging young Jews in their Judaism. With the growth of programs like Birthright Israel and Jewish summer camps there has been a greater need to understand how these informal settings work to engage their participants and set them on a journey to pursue intensive Jewish meaning in their lives (Sales and Saxe, 2004; Saxe and Chazan, 2008).

Fortunate for Jewish education has been the pioneering work of Barry Chazan (1991, 2003), who has long been thinking about the educational potential of these informal settings. In this essay I will review Chazan's work and then build upon it by asking how educators working within these informal settings can raise the stakes by challenging participants to go beyond the minimal expectations of their program to find deeper meaning in their experiences. I will offer two illustrative examples of programs that maximize the challenge in ways that inspire participants to take greater risks to discover how rich the personal and communal rewards can be when you give this effort your all.

From these examples I will generate steps that educators in any informal program can follow to maximize the Jewish educational value of working experientially with participants.

STARTING WITH CHAZAN

From my first reading of Barry Chazan's paper (2003) I knew that here we had a clear, defensible philosophy of informal Jewish education upon which we in this field could build a more coherent educational enterprise. I have applauded his bringing a singular clarity to what educators can aim to accomplish and his calling this field to a higher purpose than simply increasing the numbers of Jews "doing Jewish" in an explosion of programmatic options.

Rereading Chazan's (2003) essay, I find that these key points still stand out:

1. While informal Jewish education takes place in multiple settings and is often identified with the best-known of those settings (camps, Israel trips, etc.), Chazan contends it is best thought of as an *approach* to Jewish education rather than being identified with any particular settings or methods.

2. Informal Jewish education is poorly named because "informal" suggests both a high degree of informality and an opposition to formal education. Yet Chazan cautions against seeing those as defining the field. "Informal" is not a style of working with people, but an approach to how that work should be carried out in many different settings, including Jewish schools.

3. Informal education is often identified with feeling rather than cognition and with fun rather than serious learning. While Chazan embraces the role that fun and feelings play in informal education, he also believes that serious cognitive learning has its place and would reject easy dichotomies between feeling and thinking, fun and learning. This approach includes all these elements in interactive configurations.

5. Informal education is often thought of as taking place spontaneously as educators seize on teachable moments. While informal educators do need to seize upon such moments, Chazan emphasizes that much of the work of informal educators involves serious preparation to structure the environment so that the teachable moment can work effectively. What people call "magic moments" actually result from good educational planning by well-trained, thoughtful professionals.

6. Informal education begins with a concern and a respect for the learner's experience and proceeds by helping learners connect their experiences in building meaningful worldviews. In a Jewish context this involves creating cultural contexts that inspire learners to identify with positive role models, connect with networks of peers and create for themselves experiential models of what a compelling Jewish life might look like.

While all these points remain central, I have focused my research primarily on the fifth: the nature of experiential Jewish learning. I have tried to remain faithful to Dewey's (1938) fundamental insight that while many experiences might delight us, only a handful prove to be educative. Educative, or optimal, experiences build a chain of learning that in their cumulative effect change the ways we both understand and act in the world. I have been drawn to exploring the ways that informal Jewish settings—such as residential summer camps—can provide these types of optimal experiences for their participants (Reimer, in press).

DISTINGUISHING INFORMAL FROM EXPERIENTIAL JEWISH EDUCATION

While Chazan has made a significant contribution, when Bryfman and I (2008) looked at how the term "informal education" is used in the general education literature, we found that it does not map well to Chazan's usage. Even Chazan has acknowledged that the term "informal" throws people off in understanding this approach to education. We therefore prefer to use "informal Jewish education" as a broad umbrella term to refer to the familiar settings of Jewish education outside of schools. We use "experiential Jewish education" to describe the transactive process between educators and learners in a learning environment that promotes experientially based Jewish learning (Bryfman, 2011). Yet we join Chazan in advocating that experiential Jewish educators learn and practice the approach to education he has put forward.

Fundamental to this approach is the claim that experiential educators should aim higher and not settle for what is commonly viewed as success. What would it mean to aim higher? Imagine an experiential educator planning a *shabbaton* for high school students. Much of the planning needs to focus on establishing a workable Shabbat routine that the teens can joyfully inhabit. An educator might argue, "If I can get these teens to turn off their electronic gadgets and enter into the spirit of Shabbat, I will have succeeded." I would agree: She has succeeded in setting up a socializing environment that teaches this group to experience a meaningful Shabbat together.

That is a wonderful first step. But what if this group is part of a program that will have them attending annual Shabbatonim over the course of three years? How will this educator deepen their Shabbat experience from year to year? Will it be enough to repeat the same routine each time so they get more accustomed to its rhythms, or does the educator also have a responsibility to introduce new learning elements that initiate them into more complex patterns of Shabbat celebration? Following Chazan's advocating for "a curriculum of Jewish experiences and values" (Chazan, 2003, p. 6), I believe that to be true to the goals of experiential Jewish education, she needs to aim to deepen the participants' Jewish learning by introducing more complex elements of Jewish living each year.

What are examples of deepening a Shabbat experience? This will depend on the group and its background, but let's imagine a community day school tenth grade class planning for its second annual shabbaton. The educators—perhaps working with a student planning committee—might review what this grade most enjoyed a year earlier and ask: How can we build on those successes and deepen them? Let's imagine they remember a song session that everyone loved. They might then ask: How can we introduce *z'mirot* (traditional Shabbat songs) that are new, but which we think they can learn to sing and enjoy? Can we make people aware of *z'mirot* and why they have become integral to the Shabbat experience? Can we design the learning so what we teach becomes more musically complex as we move from song to song?

The example is simple, but the principle is worth articulating. A *socializing* goal reinforces what people have already learned and makes that part of their ongoing routine. It builds on the pleasure of repeating the familiar in the company of peers to win greater allegiance to this group and its norms. Socializing is essential to maintaining Jewish life by enhancing a sense of "I know how to be part of this community and enjoy belonging to it" (Sales and Saxe, 2004). But *educational* goals aim for one step deeper: to move participants beyond the familiar to explore and learn aspects of Jewish life that are new and challenging. They push the envelope of comfort and dare the learners to ask, "What could I learn to make my Jewish life more complex, but also more satisfying?" (Reimer, 2007).

Building experiential Jewish education around both *socialization* and *educational* goals more effectively insures that we speak to participants' need for being part of something larger as well as their need to pursue their own interests and talents in ways that are more challenging and yet truly enjoyable; to even dare for what Maslow (1968) has called "peak experiences" within their Jewish realm.

LEARNING FROM EXPERIENCE

The field of informal Jewish education primarily focuses on planning programs and events: the field trip, the Purim bash, the Sukkah party, the Israel experience and the camp season. Professionals invest great energy in marketing these events and insuring participants will walk away feeling, "I enjoyed that Jewish event and would welcome more." Professionals justify this investment by saying, "Jews in North America need the experience of being together with their peers in a Jewish environment where they enjoy doing Jewish together. That is what builds Jewish identity." And there is much empirical evidence to support the claim that when Jews voluntarily associate with one another in events that are recognized as being Jewish in nature, they tend to identify more clearly as members of the Jewish community (Cohen and Kotler-Berkowitz, 2004; Horowitz, 2000).

But those who are influenced by the work of John Dewey (1938) will never be satisfied with this formulation of the goals of informal Jewish education. For Dewey does not view human experience as a collection of isolated events, but as forming a potentially connected network of *learning opportunities*. Dewey reminds us that the experience need not and should not end with the original event. No matter how rich a program may be and how wonderful the momentary experiences, the most significant educational questions are: What comes next? How do these experiences build toward the next set of Jewish experiences? What tools are provided for the participants to keep their Jewish learning alive? For the ultimate goal is not to keep people coming back for more programs, but launching them on a learning journey to become more skilled and engaged with Jewish living (Schuster, 2003).

The crucial distinction is between *having* an experience and *learning* from that experience. We *have* many experiences, but we only *learn* from a few where the conditions promote a type of reflection that continues over time. Typically people seek to replicate the pleasurable experiences they have had. If these are associated with being Jewish, people may identify being Jewish with having good times and come to identify as members of a voluntary Jewish community.

But a communal strategy of simply providing good times can set low expectations. Its implicit message is: "As long as the Jewish community provides *you* with pleasurable experiences, you will continue to identify with that community." This places people in a passive and dependent position waiting for their next shot of Jewish excitement. It does not teach that living a dynamic Jewish life is more like a participatory "sport" in which each participant needs to be upgrading his or her skill sets to get the most out of this "game."

If active Jewish living is the ultimate goal, I am suggesting that educators need to build into Jewish experiences an element of challenge. For *challenge* entails designing active experiences that simultaneously capture the participants' interest and yet ask them to stretch themselves in unanticipated ways (Csikszentmihalyi, 1990). Challenge has been a common theme in outdoor adventure education and now needs to become a cornerstone for designing learning-based experiences in the Jewish community. These experiences build upon participants' interests, satisfy their need for belonging and yet challenge them to actively pursue their Jewish learning as part of the experience (Bryfman, 2008).

Few people wake up each morning asking, "What risks can I take today to further my learning?" Educational risk-taking needs a context that teaches that if learners are willing to take certain risks, they will be supported. In most cases educators need to initiate learners into the quest and provide a safe and productive path for risk taking (Peters, 1973). To illustrate how educators can initiate participants, I will present two quite different case studies of how educators have designed challenging Jewish learning experiences that proved to be educative in Dewey's sense of the term. In the first, the learning grew out of an individual quest to understand Judaism at a different level of complexity, and in the second the learning involved a group's quest to master a challenging task within a camp context.

AWAKING TO THE POWER OF IDEAS

My first encounter with challenging Jewish learning experiences dates back to my being invited by a high school teacher to an end-of-the-summer retreat sponsored by Yeshiva University. This Talmud teacher had noticed that I was rebelling against the strictures of Orthodoxy and generously offered me a scholarship to attend this four-day retreat that was designed primarily for college students to meet with exciting thinkers from that world. He expressed a confidence that though I was young I could handle the challenge of this program.

The retreat took place at a Jewish summer camp and began on a Thursday with interesting facilitated discussions on current topics that were never even mentioned in my school's curriculum. As Shabbat approached a palpable excitement arose among the participants: Hartman was coming. I had no idea who Hartman was; but on Shabbat evening after services and the meal, we all entered the hall to hear Hartman speak. David Hartman, it turned out, was a young rabbi from Montreal who had already developed a reputation in these circles as an exciting thinker and brilliant speaker.[1] With everyone else, I listened with rapt attention to his talk. But I did not understand a word; he was speaking—as it were—in a foreign language. Afterward I would remember only two words: "Heschel" and "revelation". Hartman repeated those often, yet I did not know who Heschel was and what revelation meant.[2]

Though I understood little, I sensed that Hartman was speaking about ideas, big ideas, big Jewish ideas, and the room was alive with excitement. It did not matter to me that I could not grasp those ideas; what did matter was that such ideas filled the air, and I could feel the passion with which Hartman spoke and the effect that his passion had on my older peers. I had never before been in a room filled with a passion for ideas.

After the talk I listened to my peers' conversations. What moved me was how deeply they cared about what Hartman had said. I could sense that his ideas were compelling to them, and I wished I could join the conversation. At fifteen I could not, but listening had a deep effect on me. First, I felt welcomed by my older peers who included me in their circle. Second, when they reframed what Hartman had said, I could better grasp what we were talking about. Third, they gave me a feeling that these ideas were not in some abstract realm beyond reach, but were accessible if you worked at trying to understand them. Indeed, after going home I bought my first books of philosophy and tried to read them. I felt that what I had experienced put me on a path toward a destination that I could barely glimpse. Yet I needed to prepare myself for that journey.

---

[1] David Hartman—then a young rabbi—would go on to become a professor at the Hebrew University in Jerusalem, the founding director of the Shalom Hartman Institute in Jerusalem and the author of many books on Jewish thought, the most famous of which is *A Living Covenant: The Innovative Spirit in Traditional Judaism* (1997).

[2] Hartman was talking about the work of Abraham Joshua Heschel, and most probably his book *God in Search of Man* (1959), in which Heschel presents a striking account of how God reveals God's presence.

I wish I had received support from my teachers to follow up on this powerful summer experience, but I did not. Like so many adolescents who come home excited by their summer experience, I was alone in my quest and often in trouble with my teachers. Looking back, I am proud of that fifteen-year-old who did not back down from the challenge of making sense of a complex experience and did not let go of its personal significance. I can now see that this summer encounter provided me with *a mental model of what is possible and a desire to recreate that model in other contexts.*[3] I could not find support in my high school, but I when I got to college I found the contexts to understand the ideas that Hartman was engaging. This singular experience pointed me in a direction and accomplished what experiential Jewish education at its best can do: *open participants to the possibility of living actively in a Jewish world where they will undertake the challenge of trying to understand Judaism in all its marvelous complexity.*

Significant moments like this do not happen in a vacuum, but often are part of a well-designed intentional learning environment. In this instance, the four days seemed like an ideal time frame for this learning experience. The facilitated discussions on the first day got us into a serious mode of conversation without feeling overwhelmed. Preparing for and entering Shabbat together built a sense of a spiritual community. Anticipating Hartman's coming built a shared excitement that was richly realized in his breathtaking talk on *erev* Shabbat. The rest of Shabbat allowed us to reflect on what he had said and what those ideas meant for us. And as Shabbat was ending Hartman returned to lead us in singing *nigunim* (religious melodies), which felt like closing a magical circle of spirit, thought and feeling.

This pivotal encounter with Hartman was nicely balanced by several acts of support. First was the generosity of the teacher who could see I was drowning in a sea of negativity and reached out to make this opportunity possible. Second were my older peers who welcomed me and provided reflective moments to glimpse in more understandable terms what these ideas meant. Third were the educators who planned and implemented this seminar in ways that bound us together as a community of searchers. Challenge and support need to balance one another so that participants can feel that in taking risks they are not alone but are borne on the wings of a caring community.

STAGING *OLIVER!* AT CAMP RAMAH IN WISCONSIN

I encountered a second vivid, but very different, example of educators creating a challenging Jewish learning environment during the summer of 2008 while doing research at Camp Ramah in Wisconsin.[4] I witnessed there a unit of fourteen-year-old campers preparing for and performing their *edah* play, the Broadway musical *Oliver!* Several features of this performance struck me. First, the entire performance was in Hebrew. I had been walking around that camp and not hearing campers speaking Hebrew. Yet here they were—this group of fourteen-year-olds—staging this lovely musical in Hebrew. Second, virtually the whole *edah* was performing on stage. This was not the work of the few kids who knew Hebrew well and could sing and dance. Third, when the performance was over the campers and staff together launched into such a joyous celebration that you might have thought they were a sports team that had just won the national championship.

I wondered: How did the camp educators motivate this group of American teens to take on the challenge of mastering all the Hebrew needed for the dialogue and songs of *Oliver!?* Why were these teens willing to do this, when in most other Jewish camps plays are regularly performed in English? And why did completing the performance occasion such an ecstatic reaction by both campers and staff?

We cannot understand this single performance outside its cultural context. This camp has a long tradition of staging Broadway musicals in Hebrew. In fact, when you enter the main social hall you can glimpse a wall of plaques that memorialize each of the unit productions that have been staged since 1980. These fourteen-year-olds had been witness to the productions of their older peers since they were the youngest campers, and they had anticipated that their turn would come to perform in Hebrew. They

---

3 I am thankful to my colleague Rabbi Bradley Solmsen for this formulation.
4 I am thankful to Rabbi David Soloff, the executive director of Camp Ramah in Wisconsin, for supporting this research and to Jacob Cytyrn for helping to decode the meaning of these camp traditions.

would be very proud when their plaque went up on the wall and they joined the generations of Ramah campers who have staged such plays in Hebrew. They could also anticipate that in the coming two summers they would be performing other plays in Hebrew, and that each summer the challenge would grow incrementally with their maturing talents. For the high point each summer was when the oldest campers performed, and then the celebration I witnessed was exceeded by several decibels.

Yet it is not always the case that campers respond with such enthusiasm to camp traditions. Some traditions grow tired and fade in their allure. The educators at this Ramah certainly rely on the power of camp tradition, but they also wisely have updated and enhanced the procedures by which they prepare campers for performing these plays. It is those enhanced procedures that, I believe, may have made the difference in keeping campers so involved in the preparation and performance of this play.

The educational staff has developed over the years a highly sensitive support system or scaffolding that allows the campers as an *edah* to take on this challenge fully believing that they can succeed (Rathunde, 1988). Some of the finer points of this scaffolding are:

1. *Providing choice*: Campers have to participate but have a choice of how to become involved, which allows them the opportunity to think about their talents and interests and how to match those to many roles available in the production.

2. *Providing focused facilitation*: Campers are not left on their own to master the challenges, but at every turn are met with staff members whose task is to provide feedback, reflection, support and encouragement.

3. *Matching challenge to available talent*: The drama staff is not charged with producing a Broadway–caliber production, but rather, the best performance that these campers can give. The script and score are often revised to make the challenge meaningful for the talent available in this group.

4. *Encouraging full commitment*: The attitude of the *edah* staff is crucial, because the counselors need to feel that this production is crucial to the success of their program and that they are there to support all the campers so everyone feels he or she has an integral role to play in achieving the group's goals (Reimer, in press).

Creating these conditions helps make the staging of these shows a qualitatively different experience than what happens at many summer camps where the drama program touches only those campers with a special interest in drama. Ramah Wisconsin has made the staging of these plays an optimal experience for most of their campers, and perhaps that is why such joy is expressed when the performance is complete. This is an instance in which taking on a big challenge resulted not in resistance and frustration, but joy and celebration.

FLOW, CHALLENGE AND ENJOYMENT

Csikszentmihalyi (1990) provides a psychological framework for understanding how to employ challenge that will result in achievement and enjoyment rather than anxiety and frustration. He is best known for introducing and describing "flow"—that experience of bring so engaged by an absorbing project that one can lose a sense of time and even ego boundaries. Initially he studied artists and then scientists who, in pursuing their creative work, experienced flow. But then Csikszentmihalyi (1990) broadened his research to ask how flow works in the lives of ordinary people, including several studies of high school students in the Chicago area (Csikszentmihalyi et al, 1993). From these studies we can derive important lessons for experiential Jewish education.

Flow theory provides guidelines for how to make any complex cultural activity more engaging for learners primarily by creating interest, building upon existing talents and choices and creating the right balance between existing skill levels and the complexity of the tasks the learners are faced with. The key is the relationship between challenge and enjoyment. We do not enjoy challenges that we experience as overwhelming; they make us anxious, and we avoid them. But when we are attracted to a challenge—perhaps because we see attractive models that thrive on that challenge—we are willing to try that activity as long as we encounter conditions that keep our interest growing and our anxiety in check.

That was the design issue facing the drama staff at Camp Ramah. Had they insisted that only those campers who already knew Hebrew well enough to recite the lines of *Oliver* could be in this production, they would have had a small corps of actors. But they employed the key strategies of diversifying the tasks so that many different talents could be engaged and carefully monitoring the challenge level so that the actors, singers and dancers faced a manageable challenge in their roles. The Ramah staff, I would say, intuited the basic insights of this theory when they set clear goals, monitored campers' progress and offered constructive feedback on how to improve. When young people experience that consistent interest and feedback, they are more likely to feel "We can do this, and although this is challenging, we want to get better at it."[5]

A drama production—in ways similar to a sports team on a championship run—can be an ideal setting for a group experiencing a shared sense of flow. There is a clear common goal to achieve, and each player knows that for the group to succeed he or she has to perform his or her part at the highest possible level. There is openness to constructive feedback and space to reflect on how the group and each of its members can improve their performance. Everyone puts aside personal issues and unites for the common push for success. When that is achieved, everyone feels the elation and that he or she is special for having been part of the winning effort.

But what follows in the wake of that successful performance? What happens when the campers go home and return to the more mundane settings of their home communities? While we do not have definitive answers, flow theory provides useful guidelines for thinking about this dilemma. Csikszentmihalyi (1996) believes that we need to study creative settings such as this summer camp for clues about how to enhance the learning possibilities in the many settings where we know most learners are not experiencing the joy of creative challenges.

A drama production has many unique qualities, but there are aspects of this experience that can be adapted to other settings. We know that teens—and many adults—do better with learning tasks that feel like a challenge and can be undertaken in the company of others working together as a team. Teams work better when they are given goals whose achievements are doable, measurable and have visible real-life outcomes. To the extent that educators can structure their educational programs to provide participants with these conditions and the constructive feedback that learners need to improve their performance, many more learning tasks could take on the flow-like qualities that were evident in staging *Oliver!* at Ramah.[6]

BEYOND THE CIRCLE OF THE HIGHLY COMMITTED

These two case studies—for all their differences—have this in common: They describe settings in which highly committed Jews have gathered to deepen their Jewish engagement. How would this approach to experiential education work in settings with participants who have less firm Jewish commitments and less extensive Jewish knowledge?

I will answer by referencing Shlomo Bardin, the founder of the Brandeis Institute. Bardin arrived in Southern California in the 1940s and set out to serve a population of Jews that "retained only faint memories of Jewish life in the Northeast and Midwest" and barely "knew how to practice any forms of Jewish ritual observance" (Moore, 1999, p. 202). Bardin developed a style of Jewish engagement that meets Chazan's criteria for informal Jewish education and matches the blending of challenge and support that I am advocating. I spent time with Bardin toward the end of his life and also learned much from talking with his disciple Bruce Powell. From their work I can suggest these guidelines for experiential educators working with diverse Jewish populations.

---

[5] Feedback in this theory plays much the same role as reflection does in Kolb's (1984) model of the learning cycle. When a teen is struggling with performing her role, well-placed feedback creates a space in which she can reflect on what she is doing and ask: How can I be approaching this role differently so that I can perform it more effectively?

[6] Ron Berger (2003) provides several detailed examples of this expeditionary approach to educating. Though he works in a public school, his examples have great relevance to Jewish education.

1. *Setting matters greatly.* Bardin was the master of creating an exceptional setting for experiential Jewish education. Most educators can learn to create a setting that takes participants out of their daily routines and announces "We are now in a special space where the rules of daily business are suspended for the opportunity to live in Jewish space and by Jewish time."

2. *Begin by building trust and comfort.* When Bardin invited participants into his space they felt like guests in his home. Most educators can learn to extend that sense of trust and comfort to participants by taking the time to get to know each one and making that person feel that you care that he or she has come.

3. *Use Jewish music and movement to help participants open up.* Bardin invested greatly in his music and dance professionals and understood that for Jews who feel insecure about their Jewish knowledge, you begin with melody and movement. Most educators can find similar ways to begin by touching the heart before reaching for the mind.

4. *Employ intentional Jewish rituals to build community.* Bardin made the most of Shabbat preparation and ritual to build community and understood that even the most reluctant Jews can feel the spirit of those rituals if they are well prepared. Most educators can learn how to create special occasions with intentional rituals that bind people together.

5. *Present great Jewish ideas in ways that make their appeal apparent.* Bardin brought Jewish scholars to his institute, insisting that they teach in ways that spoke to participants in the language of the day. Most Jewish educators can learn to present Jewish teachings that speak directly to the concerns of their participants.

Bardin was a master of creating these conditions for Jewish learning. Most educators are not masters, but they can learn how to adapt these principles to their settings. The crucial point is that following Maslow's (1968) hierarchy of needs, educators need first to build trust and safety, then open up on a level of feeling and only gradually move toward the more challenging level of Jewish ideas. The ideal is to create a magic circle of spirit, feeling and thought—always moving carefully from one phase to the next and then back around the circle to keep participants feeling they are well held as they are being challenged to reach for the great teachings of our tradition.

I follow Bardin in insisting there is no Jewish education without a challenging encounter with great Jewish ideas. This encounter can come in many different forms and through the multiple intelligences that Gardner (1999) describes. But to settle for less may meet the criteria of Jewish socialization, yet fall short of what experiential Jewish *education* aims to accomplish.

CONCLUSION: A CALL TO EXPERIENTIAL JEWISH EDUCATORS

Chazan's (2003) work has set the stage for my inquiry into how experiential Jewish education can be designed to be both challenging and rewarding. His call that this field needs to aim higher has inspired my project of spelling out the conditions for supporting participants who are willing to take a risk and go deeper in exploring Jewish living in all its complexity.

What can experiential Jewish educators do to create these conditions for Jewish growth? I suggest that educators begin by exploring their own areas of deep Jewish interest and pursuing those as a basis for educating others. Participants respond to passion and to those whose passionate interests ignite their curiosity and potential explorations.

Yet passion needs to be balanced by both care and professional skill. If passion ignites interest, care protects participants from excess. Care bounds the passion and sets the challenge at levels that participants can safely manage. Care is what the Ramah educators exercised when they made themselves available to help their campers manage their anxiety over how to learn all the Hebrew they would need to perform in *Oliver.*

Professional skill is the capacity to design the overall experience so that it leads the learners along a structured path to an outcome they can be proud of. When I watched the Ramah campers on the last days preparing for their performance, I admired the pacing and relative calm of the staff rehearsing these fourteen-year-olds. They were demanding much but keeping the pressure at a manageable level. Professional skill involves knowing how to motivate, lead and ask a lot without pushing over that delicate line into frenzied anxiety. Risk and challenge need to be introduced at the right level and with the proper supports. It is helpful to have models to show how to move forward with clear goals and markers than indicate progress. It is vital for participants to receive clear feedback so they can be reflective and correct for possible errors and misdirection.

Above all, it is essential that participants believe that they are involved in an effort that has a larger purpose. Participants need to believe that their efforts are contributing to building a better world in ways that can be seen and felt. David Hartman had an unusual ability to make his listeners feel that they were engaged in crucial conversations. What was at stake was nothing less than the essential relationship between God and humanity.

The most precious gift we can give our participants is the invitation to join us in the challenge of Jewish discovery. That is what I experienced in the encounter with Hartman. He invited us to think together about the meaning of revelation as suggested by the work of Heschel, a Jewish thinker we might never have encountered. I was surely in over my head, but the conditions were right to struggle with what was difficult to grasp.

The result was an optimal moment for growth: I went home determined not to allow this experience fall away because it was so challenging. The power of an optimal experience is that it can inspire participants to take on life challenges that otherwise might be out of reach.

REFERENCES

Berger, R. (2003). *An Ethic of Excellence: Building a Culture of Craftsmanship with Students.* Portsmouth, NH: Heinemann.

Bryfman, D. (2008). "The Challenge of Experiential Jewish Education." In J. Reimer (ed). *How Jewish Experiential Learning Works.* Waltham, MA: Institute for Informal Jewish Education.

Bryfman, D. (2011). "Experiential Jewish Education: Reaching the Tipping Point." In Miller, H., L.D. Grant, A. Pomson (eds.) *International Handbook of Jewish Education Part Two.* London: Springer.

Chazan, B. (1991). "What Is Informal Jewish Education?" *Journal of Jewish Communal Service.* 67(4), 300–308.

Chazan, B. (2003) "The Philosophy of Informal Jewish Education." *Encyclopedia of Informal Education. http://www.infed. org/informaljewisheducation/* informal-jewish-education.htm.

Cohen, S. M., and L. Kotler-Berkowitz. (2004). "The Impact of Childhood Jewish Education upon Adults' Jewish Identity: Schooling, Israel Travel, Camping and Youth Groups." United Jewish Communities Report Series. *http://www.ujc.org/ nips.* Report 3.

Csikszentmihalyi, M. (1990). *Flow: The Psychology of Optimal Experience.* New York: Harper Collins.

Csikszentmihalyi, M.(1996). *Creativity: Flow and the Psychology of Discovery and Invention.* New York: Harper Collins.

Csikszentmihalyi, M., K. Rathunde and S. Whalen (1993). *Talented Teenagers: The Roots of Success and Failure.* New York: Cambridge University Press.

Dewey, J. (1938). *Experience and Education.* New York: Macmillan Company.

Gardner, H. (1999). *Intelligence Reframed.* New York: Basic Books.

Hartman, D. (1997). *A Living Covenant: The Innovative Spirit in Traditional Judaism.* New York: The Free Press.

Heschel, A.J. (1959). *God in Search of Man: A Philosophy of Judaism.* Philadelphia: JPS.

Horowitz, B. (2000). *Connections and Journeys: Assessing Critical opportunities for Enhancing Jewish Identity.* New York: UJA-Federation of New York, Commission on Jewish Identity and Renewal.

Kolb, D. A. (1984). *Experiential Learning: Experience as the Source of Learning and Development.* Englewood Cliffs, NJ: Prentice-Hall.

Maslow, A. (1968). *Toward a Psychology of Being* (2nd ed.). New York: Van Nostrand Reinhold.

Moore, D.D. "Inventing Jewish Identity in California: Shlomo Bardin, Zionism and Brandeis Camp Institute." In S.M. Cohen and G. Horenczyk (eds.), *National Variations in Jewish Identity: Implications for Jewish Education*. Albany: State University of New York Press.

Peters, R.S. (1973). *Authority, Responsibility and Education*. London: George Allen and Unwin.

Rathunde, K. (1988). "Optimal Experience and the Family Vontext." In Csikszentmihalyi, M., and I.S. Csikszentmihalyi (eds.), *Optimal Experiences: Psychological Studies of Flow in Consciousness* (pp. 342–263). New York: Cambridge University Press.

Reimer, J. (2007). "Beyond More Jews Doing Jewish: Clarifying the Goals of Informal Jewish Education." *Journal of Jewish Education* 73 (1) 5–23.

Reimer, J. (in press). "Providing Optimal Jewish Experiences: The Case of Camp Ramah in Wisconsin." *Journal of Jewish Education*.

Reimer, J., and D. Bryfman (2008). "Experiential Jewish Education." Goodman,R.L., P.A. Flexner and L.D. Bloomberg (eds.), *What We Now Know about Jewish Education*. Los Angeles: Torah Aura Productions.

Sales, A. L., and L. Saxe (2004). *"How Goodly Are Thy Tents:" Summer Camps as Jewish Socializing Experiences*. Hanover, MA: Brandeis University Press.

Saxe, L., and B. Chazan (2008). *Ten Days of Birthright Israel*. Waltham, MA: Brandeis University Press.

Schuster, D.T. (2003). *Jewish Lives, Jewish Learning: Adult Jewish Learning in Theory and Practice*. New York: URJ Press.

EXPERIENTIAL JEWISH EDUCATION:
IMPACTING THE FORMATION OF JEWISH IDENTITY[1]

Shuki Taylor

INTRODUCTION

This chapter presents my understanding of what is concretely "Jewish" about experiential Jewish education. The term "experiential education" connotes flexibility and adaptability, whereas the word "Jewish" can evoke tradition and rigidity. The combination of these two terms generates rich tension that can ignite meaningful conversation.

Most of the works that discuss the subject of experiential Jewish education focus on the implications of applying the methodologies of experiential education in a Jewish setting. Very few works present a philosophy that seamlessly integrates the "Jewish" and "experiential education" components of experiential Jewish education and suggest how this philosophy might be applied.

In this chapter, I attempt to do this. I argue that because experiential education creates fertile ground for self-exploration, experiential Jewish education has the tremendous potential to impact the formation of Jewish identity. I argue that the best way to actualize this potential is by using the methodologies of experiential education to communicate Jewish content and values.

The first section of this chapter lays out my understanding and definition of experiential Jewish education. I do so by first reviewing some of the main attributes of the general field of experiential education. I then explore how these attributes relate to Jewish education and propose a definition for experiential Jewish education. I conclude this section by analyzing the communal implications of my definition. The second section of this chapter outlines what I refer to as the four foundations of experiential Jewish education: Imparting Values, Creating Experiences, Cultivating Communities and Self-Development. In my outline of these foundations, I focus primarily on how each foundation relates to the ultimate goal of impacting the formation of Jewish identity.

Aside from defining and describing the goals of experiential Jewish education, I offer practical structures and models throughout this article that can help organize the field and assess its impact.

Many prominent academics have already proposed definitions for experiential Jewish education. This chapter is informed by the work of the scholars who pioneered research in this field. Specifically this chapter is informed by the works of Dr. David Bryfman, Dr. Barry Chazan and Dr. Joseph Reimer. I hope to contribute to the conversation surrounding the definition, role and goal of experiential Jewish education by presenting my understanding of the field—an understanding born out of a deliberate collaboration between practitioners and theorists, experienced and emerging educators, and formal and experiential Jewish pedagogues. My aim is both to strengthen the field of research and knowledge surrounding experiential Jewish education and to provide practical tools to help educators enrich their learners' Jewish identities.

---

[1] Much of this article is based on the curriculum of Yeshiva University's Certificate Program in experiential Jewish education, which was launched in 2010 with support from the Jim Joseph Foundation. The curriculum—developed in consultation with experts from a variety of areas, both within and beyond the field of Jewish education—expresses my current, evolving understanding of the field.

• • I am grateful to my Marc Fein and Mijal Bitton for their advice in structuring this article. I am deeply indebted to Anosh Zaghi, who spent countless hours giving words to my thoughts. I am also thankful to Rabbi Dr. JJ Schacter for his thoughtful feedback.

[A] DEFINING EXPERIENTIAL JEWISH EDUCATION

1. EXPERIENTIAL EDUCATION

The field of experiential education advocates learning through action and reflection. It operates on the premise that the more immersed a student is in the process of his or her learning, the more impactful that learning process will be.

Several thinkers have constructed paradigms to help both educators and learners understand the process of experiential education. In practice, these paradigms allow learners to draw individually conceptualized skills, tools, feelings, knowledge, traits and ideas from their educational experiences that they can then apply in new settings.

One of the most prominent of these paradigms was developed by David A. Kolb. Kolb's model of experiential education[2] suggests four distinct stages. The first two stages include the experience itself and the reflective observation that follows. In the third stage—abstract conceptualization—the learner turns what he or she has learned into concrete tools and skills. In the fourth stage of Kolb's model the learner applies these tools and skills in active experimentation. This fourth stage sparks a novel experience and starts the cycle anew.

Drawing from my observations, I believe that there are three important factors that contribute to the success and/or failure of experiential education:

1. **The learner must own his or her learning process.** Experiential education affords the learner the autonomy to experiment, explore and take ownership of his or her learning process. The more the learner controls his or her own learning process, the more successful this process will be.

2. **The educator must facilitate the learning process.** The more the educator directs and dictates to the learner, the less ownership the learner will have over the experience and the less impactful this learning process will be. Thus the educator plays the role of facilitator rather than lecturer.

3. **Prescribed outcomes negatively affect the learning process.** The learner will truly master the subject matter only if given permission to be openly reflective about his or her learning and to draw and then apply his or her own conclusions about the subject matter. Any attempt by the educator to tamper with the learning process—either by interjecting or by leading the learner toward prescribed outcomes—will negatively affect the learner's ability to have an authentic learning experience.

2. EXPERIENTIAL EDUCATION AND EXPERIENTIAL JEWISH EDUCATION

One of the primary challenges in applying the methodologies of experiential education in a Jewish context relates to the third factor mentioned above.

Jewish education aims to achieve a wide variety of prescribed goals and outcomes. I believe that the main, broadly defined goal of most Jewish educators is to help learners reach heightened commitment to, or relationship with, Jewish values, heritage and tradition. Jewish education works to help learners forge and foster deep, rich and meaningful Jewish identities.[3] (I cannot justify such an assertion with reference to a single, authoritative source, because of the plurality of understandings vis-à-vis what Judaism is and what being a successful, educated Jew means. Nonetheless, I choose this definition, as it is broad enough to serve a pluralistic community.)

---

[2] Kolb, D. A. (1984). *Experiential Learning: Experience as the Source of Learning and Development.* Englewood Cliffs, NJ: Prentice-Hall.

[3] My underlying assumption in this chapter is that Jewish education has the ability to significantly impact the formation of Jewish identity. For more on this topic see:

   1. Fox, Seymour, Israel Scheffler and Daniel Marom, eds. *Visions of Jewish Education.* New York: Cambridge University Press, 2003.

     Specifically: *"The Jewish component in the education of the Jewish child, in Israel as in the Diaspora, plays a decisive role in the formation of his identity. The shape of this component will determine the shape of the child's Jewishness—the awareness that he is heir to a tradition rich in values, one that invites him to fulfill himself through it" (Greenberg 122).*

   2. Cohen, Steven M., and Laurence A. Kotler-Berkowitz. *The Impact of Childhood Jewish Education on Adults' Jewish Identity: Schooling, Israel Travel, Camping and Youth Groups.* United Jewish Communities, July 2004.

     Specifically: *"Many, but not all, forms of Jewish education exert measurable, positive impacts upon almost every form of Jewish identity examined here. Israel travel leads in the informal education, with camping and youth groups also demonstrating across-the-board effects" (Cohen 17).*

   3. Horowitz, Bethamie. *Connections and Journeys: Assessing Critical Opportunities for Enhancing Jewish Identity—Full Report.* UJA-Federation of New York, June 2000.

     Horowitz suggests nine hypotheses regarding factors that affect adult Jewishness. Two of them deal with education, one looking at early Jewish training, the other at voluntary experiences.

Given this understanding, I find there to be an inherent conflict between the goals of Jewish education and the methodologies of experiential education. In attempting to accomplish both, the experiential Jewish educator needs to grapple—almost constantly– with how to serve as the facilitator of authentic learner-centered experience, while simultaneously directing toward goals and outcomes.

To illustrate this challenge, consider the following scenario. An experiential Jewish educator decides to run a Shabbat program. The educator does a tremendous job as facilitator. She puts together a magnificent Shabbat experience and allows her learners the time and space to reflect. Given this space, the learners might conclude that they love Shabbat and would like it to remain an integral part of their lives. They might determine to henceforth set aside time for family, community, prayer, rest and reflection. However, if the educator does not also direct her learners to some degree, she might achieve unwanted outcomes. Her learners might decide that the best time for them to practice this Shabbat–style experience is not on Saturdays but on Sundays.

Has this educator succeeded in her goals? For many, if not most, the answer is no. Clearly, Jewish educators have prescribed outcomes—however broad—for what "Jewish identity" looks like. Yet the moment the educator directs learners toward these outcomes, he or she tampers with the self-exploratory, learner-centered experiential learning process. In other words, the experiential learning process is no longer wholly authentic.

3. DEFINING EXPERIENTIAL JEWISH EDUCATION

As described above, one of the ultimate goals of Jewish education is to enable learners to form relationships with their Jewish past, present and future—and to take ownership of this relationship. It makes sense to apply the methods of experiential education to this goal, as experiential education affords the learner the opportunity to own his or her learning process. Ultimately, the successful integration of content that promotes ownership of the Jewish story into experiential education methodologies that allow for an individualized learning process to occur is what impacts the formation of Jewish identity.

> Hence, the role of the experiential Jewish educator is, as I see it, to facilitate active learning experiences that utilize Jewish content in order to achieve the outcomes of identify formation. Throughout this learning experience, the educator must perform the difficult task of facilitating self-exploration while guiding towards desired goals and outcomes.[4]

In my example of facilitating a Shabbat program, the experiential Jewish educator might create an experience that portrays the importance of Shabbat as a sacred day. The educator might discuss how the idea of Shabbat relates to the creation of the world, thereby generating opportunity for reflection, *tefillah* and family time. The educator will allow ample space for reflection, conceptualization and experimentation, but she will guide her learners toward valuing Shabbat in a particularistic way. Her challenge will be to carefully balance content (Shabbat and the values it promotes), possible outcomes (such as practice of Shabbat–related values and rituals as core components of Jewish identity, however they may practically be defined) and methodology (an active learning process that allows for authentic self-exploration).

In light of the above discussion, the process of experiential Jewish education should encompass the following components:

1. It must be content- and value-driven, guiding learners toward possible **outcomes** (however broad they may be).

2. It must contain experiences that allow for learners to authentically experience, reflect, conceptualize and experiment. That is to say, it must allow for **self-exploration.**

3. It must mix the elements of predetermination and self-exploration in order to achieve the goal of **Jewish identity formation**.

---

4 In current practice, the term "outcome" is often used to define very specific and measured results. Below I argue that this practice poses a significant challenge to experiential Jewish education. Since this chapter refers to "outcome" in context of identity formation, I use the term more loosely, in that it signifies change rather than a result. More specifically put, "outcome" in this article refers to *one or more changes that may occur as a response to an educational intervention.*

Thus I propose the following definition for the field of experiential Jewish education:

Experiential Jewish education is the deliberate infusion of Jewish values and content into engaging and memorable experiences that impact the formation of Jewish identity.

Said differently, the broad outcome of experiential Jewish education is impacting the formation of Jewish identity; the input is relevant Jewish content and values; and the activity is an experience that is infused with the input and guides toward the outcome.

This article will explore how a variety of different models, theories and structures can help experiential Jewish educators impact the formation of Jewish identity. The article will also highlight the implications of this practice.

4. COMMUNAL IMPLICATIONS FOR THE PROPOSED DEFINITION OF EXPERIENTIAL JEWISH EDUCATION

My proposed definition of experiential Jewish education suggests that when applied to a Jewish context, experiential education is far more than a methodology that imparts content in an interactive fashion. Rather, experiential Jewish education is a philosophy that is concerned with the symbiotic relationship between matter and method and considers the intimate connection between the values that are imparted, the methods used to impart these values and the joint outcomes of this connection.

It is important to note that while my definition of experiential Jewish education describes the elements that make this mode of education successful in impacting Jewish identity, it does not stipulate or require predetermined or prescribed definitions for what Jewish identity should look like. Therefore, educators from across the Jewish spectrum can adopt this definition of experiential Jewish education while adapting it to their specific target populations, based on their own religious practices.

The two common denominators that, based on my definition, experiential Jewish educators should agree upon are:

1. Experiences should be infused with Jewish content (without necessarily having to agree on what that content is).
2. The goal of these experiences should be impacting the formation of Jewish identity (without necessarily needing to agree on what Jewish identity should look like).

To exemplify how different educators might infuse experiences with different types of Jewish content, consider the following. Two experiential Jewish educators facilitate a service learning experience. While one educator infuses this experience with the values of *Tikkun Olam* to help learners achieve a heightened sense of commitment to world poverty, the other educator infuses the experience with the values of Jewish observance and commitment to help learners attain a heightened sense of commitment to Jewish ritual and practice. Both of these educators infuse the experience with Jewish values and impact the formation of their learners' Jewish identities. The experiences' values and outcomes, however, are vastly different.

In short, my suggested definition of experiential Jewish education can have a broad impact in that it is:

1. A unique and independent philosophy rather than an applied methodology.
2. Positioned to empower learners to play an active role in the development and continuity of Jewish identity.
3. Applicable to all walks of Jewish life, as it accomplishes uniform goals without determining uniform outcomes.

[B] THE FOUR FOUNDATIONS OF EXPERIENTIAL JEWISH EDUCATION

In order to successfully navigate the process of experiential Jewish education, I propose that there are four foundations the experiential Jewish educator should master. Each of these foundations requires specific training that addresses the knowledge experiential Jewish educators must champion, the skills they must possess, the tools they must utilize and the traits they must embody. Together these foundations create the holistic field of experiential Jewish education. When implemented correctly, these foundations can interact to form and strengthen Jewish identity.[5]

FOUNDATION ONE: IMPARTING VALUES

The core of experiential Jewish education is to impart values and content rooted in the rich tradition of Judaism. The foundation of imparting values stresses that Jewish substance should serve as the catalyst for identity development. Without this substance, experiences will be void of meaning and significance.

SELECTING VALUES AND CONTENT

The specific type of content and values that experiential Jewish educators should seek to impart are those that develop and inform Jewish identity. Consequently, experiential Jewish education is not the art of delivering Jewish content in an experiential manner (i.e., it is not applying the methodologies of experiential education to Jewish content). Rather, it is the art of selecting *unique identity-impacting* Jewish content and values and infusing this content into engaging experience.

In a camp setting, for example, various methods can be employed to create an immersive Hebrew environment. Food labels in the cafeteria can be written in Hebrew, counselors can speak to campers in Hebrew and Hebrew signs can be posted around campus. However, in the absence of an overarching Jewish value aimed at impacting identity, teaching Hebrew fits into the category of teaching a skill. Though the aforementioned experiences may be valuable and memorable, they do not necessarily impact Jewish identity.

Because Hebrew is a core component of Jewish liturgy and history, there are many values that may be appropriate to focus on. One value around which to design experiences may be the Jewish relationship to heritage; another might be the significance of language to Jewish peoplehood. The methods described above of posting Hebrew labels and signs and having counselors speak Hebrew can all remain a part of the core experience, so long as educators infuse the experience with intentionality and the value they wish to impart.

To that effect, in measuring this experience's success, the experiential Jewish educator will be interested in evaluating not how fluently his learners speak Hebrew, but how connected these learners feel to the Hebrew language or whether they speak Hebrew with pride and passion.

In summary, the subject matter that experiential Jewish educators decide to impart must be subject matter that has the ability to directly impact identity.

DEVELOPING CONTENT

It is the role of the experiential Jewish educator to expose her or his learners to ideas and values that will stimulate self-exploration and lead to newfound resolutions.

In day-to-day life, events that stimulate self-exploration occur naturally. Often these events are so powerful that they can even impact identity. By way of example, consider the following: Two people meet, fall in love and entertain the possibility of living their lives together. While entertaining this possibility they might consider whether or not they share the same values and belief systems. Both individuals will be launched into a state of self-search and exploration. They might evaluate which personal values or rituals they do not feel comfortable compromising on and which ones they feel are less integral. They are likely to ask themselves questions that have never surfaced before: "What type of education do I want to give my children?" or "Which communities or social circles do I feel most comfortable being part of?" etc.

---

[5] While there is much to write about each of these four foundations, in this article I will focus on the foundations only as they relate to the process of impacting the formation of Jewish identity.

The relationship that these individuals have developed with each other imposes upon them a series of conflicts that they must explore and resolve before moving forward. As a result of this journey of exploration they will further define and refine their own identities.

In order to significantly intervene in learners' lives—to engage learners in experiences that compel them to seriously reconsider their identities—experiential Jewish educators must simulate natural events (like the one described above) and then guide learners through the processes of self-exploration that ensues. Experiential Jewish educators must create experiences in which learners are compelled to ask themselves identity-impacting questions—either questions that they have never before asked or questions that they have thought about but have not yet fully explored.

In order to simulate events that invite a process of self-exploration and result in identity formation, educators must very carefully develop the content that they wish to impart and ensure that it is extremely relevant. In addition, educators should be sure to give learners enough room to engage in authentic self-exploration while keeping the desired outcomes in mind.

THE CONTENT DEVELOPMENT MODEL

The paradigm that best simulates a natural identity-impacting event is a model employed in the field of script writing. This model can be used as a guide for developing content for experiential Jewish education. *The Content Development Model*, as I have labeled it, contains four components that stories must include to be both inviting and involving.

In context of scriptwriting,[6] the stages are:
1. **Exposition.** In the exposition the audience receives background information that humanizes the characters and the settings in a way that makes them relatable.
2. **Conflict.** The conflict is where the characters confront an obstacle that drives the remainder of the story. This is one of the most crucial points in a script, and it is usually accompanied by rising action and suspense.
3. **Journey.** During the journey the audience sees where the characters' actions lead them and observes as the characters negotiate a process of investigation and discovery that builds to a dramatic climax.
4. **Resolution.** The resolution occurs when the climax's outcome becomes apparent as the story reaches dénouement. During this stage the audience learns the final fate of the characters in the story.

The reason that I have chosen to build upon this model is that it simulates a natural life cycle that engages and involves an audience. Successful implementation of this model results in relatability, relevancy and empathy—all of which are crucial to experiential Jewish education.

In context of experiential Jewish education, the model translates as follows:

Exposition is where the educator introduces the content in a relatable manner that evokes feelings of comfort. The exposition displays the content's relevancy to learners' lives and encourages learners to want to learn more about the content.

Conflict is the heart of the educator's intervention. At this stage the educator poses a conflict significant enough to make the learner sincerely consider or reconsider his or her relationship with the subject matter. If the question is not presented in a relevant, interesting or pragmatic fashion, the learners will have no desire to remain involved. The conflict must be a force strong enough to engage learners in an authentic process of self-exploration that has the potential to impact their identities.

Journey is the process of self-exploration. It is where learners discover aspects of the subject matter of which they were previously unaware and/or had not considered. The learners' relationships with the subject matter evolve as they open themselves up to new ideas, thoughts and feelings related to the subject matter.

---

[6] I would like to acknowledge and thank professional actor and playwright John Adam Ross for outlining this model for us. The language I use to present this model is his.

Resolution is where the learners obtain a newfound understanding of the subject matter and/or discover their relationship with it as a result of having confronted the conflict and navigating their journeys. It is at this point that learners recognize the subject matter's impact on their identities.

In summary, in order to impart a value that will have an impact on the learner's identity, the experiential Jewish educator must ensure that the value is imparted through an exposition, which provides relevancy; a conflict, which provides motivation to explore; a journey, which allows for authentic self-exploration; and a resolution—a lasting personal connection to the value presented.

I will now demonstrate how to apply the *Content Development Model* to one of experiential Jewish education's most complex undertakings: addressing the challenge of intermarriage—in effect, the attempt to influence whom learners marry.

In the exposition the educator will raise the topic of choosing a life partner. Since the exposition demands relevancy and relatabilty, it automatically dictates the age group and life stage for which this topic is most appropriate.

A deep and relevant conflict will emerge from questioning whether—or to what extent—one should allow feelings and emotions to flourish when these feelings and emotions directly conflict with core values. The conflict can thus be, "What values are most important to me, and can I maintain those values in this relationship?" or "What is more important to me—my feelings or my values?"

The above exposition and conflict apply to most, if not all, human love stories. The difference here is that the values in my example relate to leading one's life as a Jew. The conflict can therefore go deeper: "Do I have a responsibility toward Jewish continuity? What social circles would I like to identify with?"

The journey is the learner's exploration of the values that contradict or compliment her or his personal relationship. During the journey the educator creates space for learners to engage in conversation and develop their own connection to the topic. Learners can be encouraged to look into their pasts: Where did they come from? What type of sacrifices did or didn't their parents and grandparents make for the sake of Jewish continuity? Learners can be encouraged to contemplate the future: What types of relationships do they want to have with Judaism? How would they want to raise their children? They can also be encouraged to consider what is changeable and what is not changeable in their lives. How involved an educator decides to be in the process of the journey will depend on how focused that educator is on achieving a particular outcome. If the educator wants to ensure that learners will not conclude that intermarriage is acceptable, she or he will need to be actively involved in guiding the learners' journeys.

In reaching a resolution, learners will have greater clarity as to which values are most important to them. At this point learners will be well equipped to make informed and meaningful choices regarding the role these values play in their lives.

Although the Content Development Model was derived from script writing, it mimics a human learning cycle. Very often we are exposed to certain occurrences that cause us to question, search and reach resolution. The goal of experiential Jewish education is to simulate this process.

The Content Development Model can be applied to any experience, from a ten-minute *d'var Torah* to a yearlong learning curriculum. Nuances and details may vary, but the overall learning cycle follows the same principles.

In summation, the foundation of imparting values stresses the importance of experiential Jewish education as a value-driven field.

1. The values and content selected must have the potential to impact identity formation. (Utilizing experiential education for the purpose of Jewish knowledge or skill acquisition does not amount to experiential Jewish education.)

2. In order to impact the formation of Jewish identity, experiential Jewish education must simulate real-life learning cycles. In order to achieve this goal, I suggest utilizing the **Content Development Model**.

FOUNDATION TWO: CREATING EXPERIENCES

BALANCING EXPERIENCE AND CONTENT

In recognizing that the ultimate success of experiential Jewish education lies in how it imparts values so that they impact the formation of Jewish identity, I must consider the role that experiences play in this process. In referring to experiences, I mean the methodologies utilized to impart content. These methodologies should use a diverse range of space, environment, sense and intelligence in order to convey information in an experiential manner. Furthermore, these methodologies include the means by which they themselves are processed—through reflection, conceptualization and experimentation.

Thus the foundation of "Creating Experiences" refers to three areas:

1. The methodologies utilized to deliver experiences.
2. The structures utilized to process these experiences.
3. The relationship between content and experience.

My goal in this chapter is to discuss the implications of experiential Jewish education as an identity-impacting enterprise. In this section I will focus primarily on the relationship between content and experience.

Ideally, only once experiential Jewish educators have selected the values they wish to impart and have developed a content structure with the appropriate level of intentionality are they ready to apply methodologies to present content.

In working closely with practicing experiential Jewish educators, I have found that more often than not they approach their work in a reverse fashion: first they design and plan activity, and only afterward do they consider the values and/or content that they wish to impart.

The fact that content comes "first" does not mean that it is more important than experience, which is the means of delivering content. Just as language (a means of delivery) is no less important than thought (the content one wishes to impart), experience is no less important than content.

In working closely with experiential educators I have found that there are three approaches to the relationship between content and experience:

1. **The experience is deemed secondary to the content.** The primary inclination of the educator is to consider the subject matter and the outcome.
2. **The content is deemed secondary to the experience.** The inclination of the educator is to first consider the activities, the schedule or the event.

    In both of these instances, educators will often find themselves attempting to artificially insert experience into content or vice versa.
3. **The experience and content are seamlessly integrated** so that the experience serves as language for the content.

I believe that the last approach is the most desirable one. Implementing it is not without difficulty. Just as children must learn how language expresses intention and thoughts, we as experiential Jewish educators must learn how the language of experiences can express the content we wish to impart.

JUDAISM'S EXPERIENTIAL NATURE

The simplest way to demonstrate the seamless integration of content and experience is by observing Judaism's rich tradition of imparting content and values by means of experience.

The manner in which Jewish values have been imparted from generation to generation is fully experiential—a fact that greatly contributes to the preservation of Judaism. The following examples demonstrate this point.

1. In the Torah's description of the Ten Commandments[7] many verses are devoted to describing the Jewish people's experience during this event. Moreover, the event's significance is also delivered through experiences that imply specific values. By being told not to touch Mount Sinai,[8] the Jewish people understand the value of creating a separation between holy and unholy. By being commanded to refrain from sexual conduct,[9] the Jewish people understand the need to elevate themselves from human desire in preparation for hearing the word of G-d. The Jewish people are provided with experiences that represent values and content. It is the experiential nature of this event that makes it so long-lasting.

2. The seder night's content can be presented formally in one sentence: The Jewish people were slaves, they cried out to G-d, G-d redeemed them, and it is the Jewish people's responsibility to pass this message from generation to generation. However, in order to ensure that this content passes from generation to generation, the author of the haggadah imparts it in an experiential manner. Methodologies incorporated throughout the seder night utilize space and environment, stimulate all senses and speak to people with varying types of intelligences: those who are musically inclined, intellectually inclined, artistically inclined and emotionally inclined.

3. The period of atonement that culminates with Yom Kippur is also experiential. Days before Yom Kippur, crowds of people gather to chant *Seliḥot* and listen to the shofar's blasts, utilizing their senses and creating spaces and environments. On Yom Kippur we are commanded to suppress our senses in order to elicit a higher sense of spirituality. The day is filled with moments of silence and moments of singing. We pray to G-d, come together as a community and mend relationships with those whom we've wronged.

None of these examples places primary emphasis on content over experience or on experience over content. Rather, they seamlessly integrate one into the other so that the experience is the language through which content is conveyed—explicitly and implicitly. Without the values, the experiences would be meaningless, and without the experiences the values would never be internalized.

I derive from this analysis two important points:

1. In order to impact the formation of identity, content and experience are of equal importance and need to be seamlessly integrated into each other.

2. The practice of experiential Jewish education is inherent in Judaism, as almost all lasting events of significance in Jewish tradition have followed this model.

FOUNDATION THREE: CULTIVATING COMMUNITIES

THE MAGNITUDE OF IMPACTING THE FORMATION OF JEWISH IDENTITY

Whereas the foundations of Imparting Values and Creating Experiences speak to the content the experiential Jewish educator imparts and the structures and methodologies used to impart this content, the third foundation—Cultivating Communities—focuses on the recipients of the educational intervention.

In order to impart values and orchestrate experiences, experiential Jewish educators need to excite, enlist and empower the communities they service. Mastering the art of listening to and identifying with an audience's passions, struggles and challenges is fundamental in enabling experiential Jewish educators to ensure that their content is constantly relevant and that the experiences they share are captivating.

---

[7] Exodus, Chapters 19-20
[8] Exodus, Chapter 19: Verses 12–13
[9] Exodus, Chapter 19: Verse 15

While the primary recipients of this intervention are the direct learners, the communities I refer to also include the larger circles that are impacted by experiential Jewish education's process of intervention. These larger circles may include:

1. The **learners'** broader circles, such as parents, family, friends and spouses.
2. The **educators'** broader circles, such as the institutions and ideologies that the educator represents and additional stakeholders such as donors, board members and colleagues.

To understand the breadth and depth of these relationships, the educator must have great clarity about what outcomes he or she would like to achieve and whom these outcomes will affect. The following example helps illustrate the broadness of the experiential Jewish educator's impact.

An educator creates an experience with the goal of bolstering learners' commitment to the State of Israel by means of an immersive Israel experience. The Israel immersion program is captivating and powerful, and it significantly impacts the learners' identities. One learner declares, as a result, that he would like to make *aliyah*. Aside from the dramatic shift in perspective this experience caused the learner to undergo, several other impacts are likely to follow. The learner's family might be shocked or dismayed, the learner's friends might feel neglected and the learner's girlfriend might feel betrayed. The experiential Jewish educator cannot ignore these outcomes. If the goal of experiential Jewish education is to impact identity, the outcomes will be far-reaching. The educator must at least be aware of these outcomes and preferably anticipate and address them.

The following four segments address the responsibilities of the experiential Jewish educator when cultivating communities. Each of these responsibilities is a corollary of the experiential Jewish educator's goal to impact the formation of Jewish identity.

SENSITIVITY

In this article, I speak of the experiential Jewish educator's goal as one that impacts the formation of Jewish identity. My choice of words is deliberate: the educator should provide experiences that *impact the process* of identity formation. She or he should not, however, *actively form* Jewish identity. This distinction is of the utmost importance as the active forming of identity, in many instances, amounts to what might be defined as brainwashing.

Moreover, experiential Jewish educators should constantly be aware of how this very personal learning process unfolds in learners' lives. By providing safe spaces where learners feel nurtured and cared for—not imposed upon—experiential Jewish educators can ensure that learners do not lose control of their learning process and do not walk away feeling brainwashed. Educators should encourage learners to reconsider their values and consider new ones, but should constantly be mindful of the learners' state of mind and environment.

In many if not most cases, the learner will feel vulnerable during his or her process of identity formation .This feeling of vulnerability is what allows the learner to be receptive to growth and change. While attempting to be truly receptive—to act as open vessels, if you will—learners are likely to feel that they are losing control over their own learning processes, especially if learners become too receptive. Thus, it is the educator's responsibility to ensure that her or his learners have full ownership over their learning experiences and their processes of exploration.

AUTHENTICITY AND TRANSPARENCY

As with any process of intervention, the intervener must have a series of potential outcomes in mind—he or she must know what success looks like. In the field of experiential Jewish education as an identity-impacting process, this intervention is accomplished by carefully balancing outcomes with a process of self-exploration. In order to carry out an identity-impacting intervention, the experiential Jewish educator must carefully work towards outcomes while simultaneously allowing for self-exploration.

Educating towards pre-determined outcomes often contradicts educating towards self-exploration. Balancing the two requires a high measure of intentionality, authenticity and transparency.

Often, experiential Jewish education initiatives claim to encourage complete, non-determined processes of self-exploration, when in fact these initiatives are geared towards producing specific outcomes (or are at least uncomfortable with certain outcomes).

By way of example, consider the following two scenarios:

1. An outreach initiative claims to guides participants towards discovering and practicing Judaism. This initiative, however, invites learners to go on journeys of "self-discovery" to discover their "inner selves". Clearly, the initiative is specifically outcome driven, but operates under the pretense of self-exploration.

2. A pluralistically inclined initiative encourages a multiplicity of journeys, voices and outcomes. All the while, this initiative does indeed have a red line. For example, it would not want learners to turn against the organization's core values (or, in line with the example at the beginning of this article, it would not want learners inspired by Shabbat to celebrate Shabbat on Sunday). Though this initiative does foster self-exploration, it falsely claims to have no pre-determined outcomes.

Experiential Jewish education allows room for both types of initiatives, but these initiatives must be both internally and externally authentic and transparent. Learners should never think that they are engaging in a process of self-exploration when in fact a journey has been scripted for them. Similarly, learners should not be told that any and every outcome is acceptable when, indeed, educators discourage certain outcomes, even if implicitly.

FACILITATION

In order to foster self-exploration while guiding learners towards predetermined outcomes, the educator must develop two distinct types of facilitation skills:

1. **Reflection**: Reflection allows for the process of self-exploration to emerge and flourish. By asking questions that allow learners to respond to and reflect upon the experiences and the content to which they have been exposed, educators can allow learners to access the space they need and can help learners achieve an authentic process of self-exploration. Educators should ask open-ended questions that focus on thoughts about and feelings towards the experience.

   In order to ensure authentic self-exploration, the educator should validate whatever feelings and thoughts learners express and should permit any type of reaction. This type of reflection will allow a multiplicity of voices, opinions and approaches to emerge.

2. **Framing and contextualizing**: This type of facilitation is geared towards pre-determined outcomes rather than self-exploration. The educator will frame and contextualize the experience in a specific fashion, so that it builds a narrative that can result in the outcome. When using these skills, the educator does not want to gauge what learners might be feeling, but wants to guide learners towards outcomes. This facilitation technique utilizes guided—rather than open ended—questions.

   When engaged in this type of the facilitation, if the educator is not satisfied with an answer, she or he should ask if anyone has another opinion. In this way, the educator will be able to build a narrative by asking directed questions and respecting whatever answers are given.

Both types of facilitation skills are necessary. If educators merely fosters reflection, learners might get lost in the process of exploration and lose sight of the overall narrative. In such a case, learners might not recognize the deliberate connections that the educator tries to make between activities and experiences. On the other hand, if educators spend too much time framing and contextualizing experiences, they will not enable any form of self-exploration. As a result learners are likely to lose their unique voices.

Once again, intentionality is crucial: the educator must recognize when it is necessary to use each type of facilitation skill in order to ensure a seamless process of intervention that balances pre-determined outcomes with self-exploration.

EVALUATING AND MEASURING SUCCESS

Because impacting the formation of Jewish identity is such a complex task, measuring the success of experiential Jewish education is often difficult.

One challenge that might arise relates to the process of self-exploration inherent to experiential Jewish education. When educators, institutions, ideologies and communities are geared towards producing specific outcomes, success is relatively easy to measure—have learners achieved these specific outcomes? However, when educators allow for self-exploration, many more outcomes are likely to ensue. The more possible outcomes there are, the harder it becomes to quantify success. Experiential Jewish educators must realize this reality and resist the urge to narrowly define success.

The second challenge that might arise relates to my definition of experiential Jewish education. The current practice of evaluation requires that outcomes be measured based on how specific, measurable, attainable, realistic and timely (S.M.A.R.T[10]) the outcomes are. Naturally, most behavioral outcomes satisfy these criteria. However, impacting the formation of Jewish identity does not always result in behavioral outcomes.

Some of the most powerful outcomes of identity impacting experiences are change in temperament, value system and belief and increased sense of pride. Learners often describe experiential Jewish education as "life changing." This description and the aforementioned outcomes do not neatly fit into the S.M.A.R.T rubric. In order to appropriately measure the success of a field that is geared towards identity formation, educators should focus less on S.M.A.R.T outcomes and find alternative ways to measure temperament, feelings, traits, and beliefs, as well as overall cultural changes. Though these outcomes are more difficult to measure, they speak to the essence of successful experiential Jewish education.

FOUNDATION FOUR: SELF-DEVELOPMENT

This foundation deals with the experiential Jewish educator's self-development. Aside from possessing organizational and leadership skills, the experiential Jewish educator must master the skills, traits and knowledge that are unique to the field of experiential Jewish education. These may include authentic use of self, role modeling, sensitivity towards use and abuse of power, the creation of healthy relationships, and balance of personal and professional life.

Below, I will highlight the skills, traits and behaviors that are most relevant to the experiential Jewish educators' role of impacting the formation of Jewish identity.

EMPATHY

In order to guide learners through a reflective process of self-exploration, experiential Jewish educators must possess skills that allow for such a process to take place. These skills are acquired primarily through constant self-reflection on the educator's part. Just as craftsmen need to constantly sharpen their tools in order to perform their craft, experiential Jewish educators must constantly revisit their own journeys of self-exploration and reflect upon them. By doing so, the experiential Jewish educator will gain empathy towards, and a deep understanding of, the journeys that they prompt learners to embark on.

ROLE MODELING

Because experiential Jewish educators promote the adoption of Jewish values, and often use themselves as authentic examples of such adoption, they assume positions as role models, willingly or unwillingly.

---

[10] Doran, G. T. (1981). There's a S.M.A.R.T. way to write management's goals and objectives. Management Review, Volume 70, Issue 11 (AMA FORUM), pp. 35-36

Serving as a role model is an unbelievable opportunity for a community of learners to experience the embodiment of passionate Jewish living and a value driven lifestyle.

However, serving as a role model can also be very burdensome. Though educators might guide their learners towards certain ideals, they themselves might be struggling to attain these very ideals. It is not easy to require an experiential Jewish educator to serve as a *dugma ishit*, a constant personal example of the values he or she preaches. Serving as a role model, though a powerful opportunity is also a substantial responsibility that requires guidance and mentorship from experienced and well-seasoned educators.

JEWISH LITERACY—A JEWISH EDUCATOR MUST FIRST BE AN EDUCATED JEW

More often than not, sought-after experiential Jewish educators in today's world are those who are creative, dynamic and excellent at fostering relationships. Though these traits are important, they are not sufficient. In order to infuse experience with identity-impacting content, experiential Jewish educators must be well versed in such content. An experiential Jewish educator must possess the literacy, knowledge and resources of a formal Jewish educator, with the creativity and vibrancy of an experiential educator.

USE AND ABUSE OF POWER AND THE FORMATION OF HEALTHY RELATIONSHIPS

In impacting the formation of Jewish identity, experiential Jewish educators play a very significant role. As a result, learners often feel dependent on their educators and view them as "saviors" who have changed their lives. Unfortunately, experiential Jewish educators sometimes, even if subconsciously, welcome this feeling of dependency and become dependent on it themselves. Alternatively, educators may abuse the positions of tremendous power they occupy.

In light of these situations, it is imperative that educators form and maintain healthy and well-balanced relationships with their learners. A formal code of conduct should be put in place from the outset to ensure that lines are not blurred and that educators understand what interactions are and are not objectively appropriate.

CONCLUSION: BUILDING A FIELD

In this article I have attempted to define experiential Jewish education as a field that has the potential to impact the formation of Jewish identity and ensure Jewish continuity.

I have suggested that in order to successfully achieve this goal, it is necessary to:

1. Deliberately infuse experiences with Jewish content and values in order to impact the formation of Jewish identity.
2. Select values and content that can in fact impact the formation of Jewish identity.
3. Impart content by utilizing and simulating natural learning cycles.
4. Constantly balance outcomes with authentic journeys of self-exploration.
5. Recognize that experience is a language that expresses content but cannot replace it.

By way of defining, illustrating and describing the goals of experiential Jewish education I have also offered structures and models that organize the field and its process of impact.

In addition, I have addressed several points that follow from and supplement my definition of experiential Jewish education as a field that impacts the formation of Jewish identity.

1. The importance of recognizing that the impact of identity is far-reaching and does not end with the learner.
2. Understanding the difference between impacting the formation of Jewish identity and actively forming Jewish identity. The latter can amount to brainwashing.
3. The need for authenticity and transparency about the methods used to achieve the outcome of identity formation.

4. The realization that different facilitation skills will result in different outcomes.

5. The need for new instruments with which to measure success.

6. The unique skills, knowledge and traits that are necessary for accomplishing the task of impacting Jewish identity formation.

7. The need for a code of conduct.

The common thread that permeates this article is the need for intentionality. Following a strong theory of experiential Jewish education, and utilizing successful and proven models to apply this theory, allows—and requires– experiential Jewish educators to be intentional in all aspects of their work.

A NOTE ABOUT LANGUAGE AND THEORY

Impacting the formation of Jewish identity is not a small goal; it comes with tremendous responsibility. Experiential Jewish educators essentially intervene in the lives of their learners in order to impact their very essences. Experiential Jewish educators must realize that it is their duty to carefully develop a responsible and successful practice based upon principled theory. They must appreciate that every aspect of the work they do can have tremendous implications. Additionally, the fact that their ultimate goal is of such large import demands that the community at large give the field of experiential Jewish education the respect and credibility it deserves.

In this article I used language and theory that are broad enough to be shared among practitioners across the spectrum of Jewish education. There are a number of significant benefits to adopting shared language and theory—all of which can contribute to building a strong field framework.

1. By using shared language, models and theories, experiential Jewish educators can easily form communities of practices and support networks through which they can inform and develop one another.

2. Shared language can strengthen the experiential Jewish educator's career trajectory. Currently, because theory, language and terminology are not shared, the career span of an experiential Jewish educator is short. If shared language is created, the experiential Jewish educator can move freely from camp to school to synagogue. The setting might be different, but the language and the process of impact that educators in each setting must be familiar with are similar.

3. If experiential Jewish educators conceptualize their ideas into standardized language, they will be able to experiment with these ideas in a variety of different realms. Shared language and theory will allow for fluidity within the field, as educators will be able to apply concepts to different experiences and to different communities with varying interests.

It is my hope that by using common language and by encouraging true deliberation and intentionality, we can build a strong field that will attract the respect and investment it deserves and enable the growth of a strong and passionate Jewish community.

CITED REFERENCES

Bryfman, D. (2008). "The Challenge of Experiential Jewish Education." *How Jewish Experiential Learning Works, An Anthology.* Edited by Joseph Reimer with Susanne A. Shavelson.

Chazan, B. (2003). "The Philosophy of Informal Jewish Education." *The Encyclopedia of Informal Education.* Retrieved September 1, 2006, from *www.infed.org/informaleducation/informal_jewish_education.htm.*

Reimer, J., & D. Bryfman, (2011). "What I Know About Experiential Jewish Education." In Goodman, R., P. Flexner & L. Bloomberg (eds.), *What I Now Know About Jewish Education.* Los Angeles: Torah Aura.

Reimer, J. (2003). "A response to Barry Chazan: The philosophy of informal Jewish education," *The Encyclopedia of Informal Education,* www.infed.org/informaleducation/informal_jewish_education_reply.htm.

Reimer, J. (2007). "Beyond More Jews Doing Jewish: Clarifying the Goals of Informal Jewish Education," 73: 1, 5–23.

NEUROSCIENCE AND EXPERIENTIAL JEWISH EDUCATION

Scott Sokol

"One whose deeds exceed his wisdom, his wisdom endures. But one whose wisdom exceeds his deeds, his wisdom does not endure" (*Pirkei Avot*, 3:10).

"First-hand experience is the most important foundation stone in discovering who you really are and what you might become" (Smit, cited in McNeil, 2009).

"…the bi-partite character of the brain implies that understanding is itself an emergent process, the result of an essential interplay between experience and reflection" (Dalke et al., 2007).

As a cantor-educator who also happens to be a cognitive neuropsychologist, I have lived much of my professional life at the intersections of the worlds of education, religion, music and neuroscience. The link between the cantorate and Jewish education is, to my mind at least, a given. Cantors spend the majority of their time involved in Jewish education, whether training b'nei mitzvah students, leading services in the religious school or conducting a synagogue choir. I think it also fair to say that the majority of a cantor's spiritual and educational directive is experiential in nature, although cantors certainly are engaged in more formal educational modes as well.

As for the link between Jewish education and neuroscience, this is not as obvious, although I believe fruitful connections do exist. More than a decade after the official "Decade of the Brain" ended, educators across the content spectrum continue to be fascinated by neuroscience and what its insights might offer to pedagogical understanding and practice. Indeed, a whole new scientific field known as educational neuroscience has recently emerged. At the same time, the realms of theology and neuroscience, which since Descartes have largely kept each other at a polite distance, have started up a serious conversation (e.g., the excellent recent work of Rabbi Ralph Mecklenburger, *Our Religious Brains*). It is within the framework of these ongoing courtships that I hope to place the present discussion.

My thesis—if you can call it that—is that matters of concern to cognitive neuroscience are similarly concerns to experiential Jewish education, and therefore that knowledge of educational neuroscience will enhance our work as Jewish educators. Furthermore, as educators (whether or not we are labeled special educators), each of us is concerned with understanding our student's neurocognitive status, and with linking that assessment to sound pedagogical practice. Greater familiarity with learning disabilities, social impairments and other neurocognitive conditions such as attention-deficit disorders is critical if we are to reach all our students effectively. Although we may think of these difficulties as impacting more directly in the traditional classroom (e.g., teaching children with dyslexia how to read Hebrew), a student's learning style and challenges obviously have significant impact within more informal settings as well.

With these general ideas in mind, I have organized this chapter so as to highlight several areas in which I believe neuroscientific findings should prove interesting to experiential Jewish educators, and then discuss what some of the relevant connections to this work might be.

THE CHANGING BRAIN

Perhaps the most important fact about the brain is that it changes throughout our lives, a process known as neural plasticity. When discussing the limits to plasticity, the received wisdom has been that we are born with all the neurons that we will have as adults. Although recent research suggests that this assertion is probably true (Larson et al., 2006), such a finding may not be that determinative. In the first place, more important than the total number of brain cells are the number and quality of the connections among those cells. Infants are born with as many as a trillion connections already "hard-wired" in their brains. Throughout life, many of these connections will be "pruned" as they become unneeded. Many new connections are laid down at the same time, however, more than balancing out the number pruned. It is through these connections that learning ultimately takes places.

Another known fact about neural development and plasticity is that the brain increases in volume between birth and early adulthood; indeed, there is a four-fold increase in volume (Johnson, 2001). Increased volume is associated with increased learning; put a bit simplistically, as we learn, our brains get bigger. There has been an enormous amount of research focused on identifying what actually happens in the brain during learning, and what effect environmental factors (broadly construed) have on changes in brain structure. Much of this research has direct application to education.

Implications for experiential Jewish education. As experiential Jewish educators, especially those working with children and adolescents, the most important implication of this work on neural plasticity is that all of our experience truly has an effect on the development of our brains' unique structural pathways. The literature in cognitive neuroscience abounds with clear evidence that changes to the brain occur on neurochemical, neurophysiological and neuroanatomical levels depending on the nature and quality of our experiences, and although there may be more potential for gross reorganization of brain structures in early childhood, these changes continue throughout our lives. In other words, lifelong learning yields lifelong brain development.

GETTING THE SIGNAL IN: THE ROLE OF ATTENTION IN EDUCATION

William James, early psychologist and philosopher, was among the first to research the role of attention in learning. Attention is a function of the mind, but it results in significant changes in the brain. Focusing our attention on an object creates neural networks that show enhanced excitation when in the presence of that object later on, gaining collective strength by their repeated firing. As Donald Hebb, another early psychologist, put it, "Neurons that fire together wire together" (Hebb, 1949).[1]

One of the factors most important to our attentional system is novelty. When something is novel, it tends to catch our attention more readily than something we are already accustomed to. In some cases attention goes awry, moving its resources to every new experience it comes in contact with, sort of like a strobe light. In fact, this is a fairly apt description of what occurs in some individuals with attention deficit disorders (especially of the inattentive subtype). A properly functioning attentional system, in contrast, filters out what is unimportant and focuses on what is salient in the moment.

To assist children and adults with attention deficits, I first try to explain activation and how this concept relates to performance. Put simply, a cognitive system has to be activated in order to learn, but peak activation levels vary from person to person. For many individuals with attention disorders, their resting neurocognitive systems (especially in the frontal lobes) are under-aroused, requiring a higher degree of arousal/activation than is typical.

There are several ways that arousal can be enhanced. The first is through reinforcement or reward. Parents know this tack well: "If you work consistently for the next thirty minutes on your *Haftarah*, then you can play video games until dinner." (By the way, one of the reasons that people with AD/HD so enjoy and can focus on video games for hours at a time is the high degree of constant stimulation that these games

---

[1] This famous line of Hebb's might serve as a good metaphor for Jewish community as well.

supply to their attentional systems.) Another method to increase activation is to engage only with material one is already interested in; such material is intrinsically rewarding and thus more likely to maintain arousal. It is unclear whether many *Haftarot* would be learned, however, if this method were the only one chosen (let alone many required academic subjects).

These are, of course, more extrinsic means of increasing attentional activation as well. A common method is by means of a stimulant medication such as Ritalin. The stimulant acts to enhance activation on a neurological level, elevating neurochemical activity in synapses, which aids in initiating and focusing attention. Stimulants have been used in the treatment of AD/HD for more than seventy-five years and have helped many people, although they are not appropriate for everyone. Recently computer-based programs have been developed that have been empirically proven to increase attention and working memory (e.g., Cogmed). Neurofeedback has also proven effective in many cases.

Implications for experiential Jewish education. As just described, attention is driven by novelty and reinforcement, as well as by evolutionary hard-wiring that makes certain sorts of information immediately accessible to the brain (e.g., information that correlates with biological necessities, such as fear, hunger, reproduction, etc.). To make learning more attentionally compelling, then, we need to increase novelty and reward and/or link the material to be learned through chains of association to biological imperatives.

I would argue that experiential education tends to do these things more naturally than formal education. Sitting in classrooms day in and day out, having information coming to the learner in highly predictable and consistent ways, is frankly a recipe for lowering arousal to levels that are not conducive to typical learners, let alone those with attention deficits. Experiential education such as camps, youth groups, or activity-centered learning has greater inherent novelty. Many such activities are also tied more directly to intrinsic, rather than extrinsic, reward. Finally, these activities typically have higher degrees of connectedness to biological drives (e.g., a camp ropes course is frightening and exciting; Jewish youth activities have potential for attracting mates; Sephardic cooking classes appeal to our appetites). Experiential Jewish education, therefore, seems consonant with what we know about activating and maintaining attention.

Another aspect of attention that is relevant to Jewish education is belief. This is a more complex point that might fall outside of present consideration, but I will nonetheless try to make it succinctly because I think it is relevant to identity formation. Attention has long been linked to consciousness—when we pay attention to something, we literally become "conscious" of it. Many view consciousness as the summation of those aspects of the world that we pay attention to. Put differently, consciousness arises out of the interaction of the physical world and our attentional system.

In his book on religion and the brain, Rabbi Ralph Mecklenburger goes a step further, not merely arguing that attention is the basis of consciousness, but that it is related as well to the need for a belief system and ultimately a theology. The basic idea here is that given the dizzying amount of information in our daily lives, we need a go-to system that permits us to ignore certain information that has been processed previously—a filter, if you will, that considers some information to be "given" and other information as needing to be explored. This filter is (for Rabbi Mecklenburger, at any rate) belief. I will return to this notion later in the section on social learning. But for now, suffice it to say that our religious beliefs (if we have them) actually influence what we pay attention to and what we don't. We know this to be true on a micro level; for example, someone who keeps kosher may attend to a chemical on an ingredient list called sodium caseinate, knowing that it is a milk product, whereas someone who doesn't care about mixing meat and dairy products may simply think it a preservative and ignore it. But Mecklenburger's observations here have a broader focus as well, positing belief as a building block of our cognitive systems more generally.

LEARNING

Once attention has been engaged, learning can follow. Learning is the result of the collaborative efforts of many regions of the brain. Although quite complex in its details, the basic mechanisms of learning are fairly well understood at this point. That said, the nature of the explanation will be quite different at different levels of analysis (e.g., cognitive, biochemical, neurophysiological and neuroanatomical). For the purpose of this discussion I will paint a very broad "neurobehavioral" account.

Information comes to us through our senses or, if internally generated, by our thinking or our memory. The information is initially sent to the thalamus—a deep brain structure—for preliminary processing. It then gets routed simultaneously to the amygdala—a subcortical area largely responsible for emotional processing—and to different parts of the cerebral cortex, depending on the type of information. For example, visual information from the retina is decoded by regions in the occipital lobe of the brain, whereas auditory information such as spoken language gets decoded in the temporal lobe. If the information is surprising or alarming, the amygdala will recruit other brain areas to respond, largely the sympathetic nervous system. If not, information is processed and held by the frontal lobes of the cortex for a few seconds to determine if it is important to us. Most information is not deemed important and quickly fades; indeed, it may never even reach our conscious awareness. If the information is important or interesting, however, it draws our attention and gets sent for further processing both by the hippocampus and cortical structures. The role of the hippocampus is to organize and consolidate the information, which it then links (associates) to appropriate areas of the cerebral cortex for long-term storage.

Implications for experiential Jewish education. It is apparent that learning is reliant on access to sensory information, and also on a properly functioning attentional system. Initial learning, as well as the consolidated learning that takes place over the course of our lives, is something of an iterative process in which information gets fed from processor to processor and back again, and moreover where different information gets tagged or associated with other information, thus deepening the connections into an associative network. This collaborative process seems well suited to multi-modal learning, a point that will be made again in a moment in our discussion of memory. Educators therefore need to engage students through a variety of sensory inputs, a recommendation that is supported as well by thirty years of research and practice integrating the theory of multiple intelligences (e.g,. Gardner, 1983). The methods and modalities of experiential Jewish education seem highly consonant with this methodology.

MEMORY

One might say that the result of the process of learning is memory (although some aspects of memory interact with attention earlier in the cognitive flow). On the neurological level, memory—like much else in cognition—is represented in a diffuse manner across our brains. Different regions of the brain are responsible for coding different types of memory, whether by duration or content. Understanding the neural substrates of memory has in fact been one of the most highly studied areas in all of cognitive neuroscience.

There are, of course, many competing cognitive theories of memory, but despite these varied accounts there is broad agreement on a number of aspects about memory. First is that there are different memory systems for different durations of time (i.e., sensory memory, also known as "very-short-term memory," which is less than a second; short-term memory that lasts about twenty seconds without rehearsal; long-term memory, which may last hours or days, and remote memory, which we store for years or perhaps our entire lives). Next, it is known that there are qualitatively different types of memory. For example, there is working memory (extremely important to attention and learning), which is the type of memory we rely on when we need to hold information while computing something (e.g., reversing the order of a list of numbers). There is also a distinction between episodic memory (memory for events that have happened to us), semantic or declarative memory (memory for facts or other "known" information, such as names) and procedural memory (memory for skills such as driving or cooking). Finally, there are distinct memory systems for different input modalities (e.g., visual versus auditory memory).

Implications for experiential Jewish education. One critical fact about memory is that it is associative: The more information we can link together about something, the more likely we are to remember it and recall it later (and yes, there is definitely a difference between remembering and recalling). Indeed, one of the most often quoted "facts" about memory is that it is more "reconstructive than reproductive," a quote usually attributed to the British psychologist FC Bartlett (Bartlett, 1932). The point that Bartlett was making is that our memories are not like video or audio recordings but are psychological representations of bits of information that we actively piece together (whether consciously or subconsciously) in trying to reconstruct our memories.

With respect to experiential education, the reconstructive and associative nature of memory implies that the more varied and interwoven our associations are, the more likely information will be recalled. This is again, in part, why educators stress the importance of multi-modal learning. The more sensory modalities that come into play when learning information, the richer will be the cognitive and neurological associations of that information. These associations can support one another when we try to reconstruct that information from memory, "triggering" the neural connections and producing a neurophysiological cascade that can reconstruct the relevant representations. An obvious example of this is learning the words of a prayer through music. The melody becomes connected to the lyrics, thus aiding in recall of the text.

With respect to values education, Jewish observance and religious behavior, memory is also an important aspect of our decision-making. As neuroscientist Steven Rose puts it, "Memory defines who we are and shapes the way we act more closely than any other single aspect of our personhood." If we want children to learn to give tzedakah, we need to provide them with examples of others giving (modeling) and plenty of opportunities to do so themselves, thus establishing behavioral memory for the mitzvah. Then, to really seal the deal, we should support this behavioral memory through other modalities of reinforcement (e.g., text study and songs about tzedakah), thus creating multi-modal memory.

EMOTIONS

We tend to think of memory (and even learning) as a purely "cognitive" act, and by that I mean one that can be explained through mechanisms of thought alone. But more and more, cognitive scientists and neuroscientists are coming to acknowledge the vital importance of emotions to memory. One layer of association that is quite important to memory is emotion. As Eric Jensen puts it:

> Mind and emotions are not separate; emotions, thinking and learning are all linked. What we feel *is* what's real—even if only to us and no one else. Emotions organize and create our reality (Jensen, 2005, p. 68).

Indeed, burgeoning research in neuroscience has confirmed the importance of emotions to learning and memory. Emotions determine what we attend to, help to establish meaning, regulate behavior and help us to organize our worlds. Furthermore, we know that emotions are implicitly involved with establishing and maintaining long-term memories (Damasio, 1994, Lane and Nadel, 2000, LeDoux, 1994).

Implications for experiential Jewish education. For experiential Jewish educators, the significance of emotions to learning and memory is among the most important confirmations of the work we are engaged in. One of the things that makes teaching effective is engaging students on emotional levels. This is because when information has emotional salience, it is far more likely to be remembered than when it doesn't. This fact is now understood to arise from a complex interplay of affective and cognitive representation in the brain. Moreover, when students come to value learning—when the act itself has emotional importance to them—then learning becomes self-propagating. As Covington puts it:

Ultimately it is the value and meaning of what is learned—more particularly, the sense of satisfaction arising from enhanced understanding—rather than accumulating knowledge for the sake of power or prestige that will ultimately determine whether the will to learning is maintained.

This, to my mind, is also the essence of *Torah l'Shma*, and I believe it is at the heart of what makes experiential Jewish education so valuable. Finally, when learning is linked organically to emotionally charged experiences (e.g., a *Yom ha-Shoa* commemoration with a survivor's account) that learning will have much more effect and greater staying power.

SOCIAL LEARNING

Human beings are, of course, social beings. Once again, new insights in the field of neuroscience have shown that the development of social relationships (or the lack thereof) has significant effects on the brain. Indeed, these insights have resulted in a whole new field known as social neuroscience. Neuroscientists Stephen Quartz and Terry Sejnowski (the latter of whom was coincidentally the chair of my doctoral defense committee many years ago) co-authored an intriguing work (*Liars, Lovers and Heroes: What New Brain Research Reveals about How We Become Who We Are*), which attempts to identify the neurological underpinnings of human social (and antisocial) behavior. They favor a "cultural biology" and describe the resulting relationship succinctly: "Culture helps to shape your brain, which in turn creates culture, which acts again on the brain."

The issues that Quartz and Sejnowski raise are broad-based, but the basic abilities that human beings have in the social domain are, of course, intrinsic to the individual. Social intelligence, emotional IQ and social skills development are terms that speak to the clear observation that human beings differ in their ability to understand the motivations, expressions, affect, etc. of other people. In extreme cases, impairments of social cognition are the hallmarks of neurocognitive disorders such as autism and influence those affected at many levels of functioning.

Research over the last couple of decades has concluded that social contact affects human biology in highly significant ways, ranging from the very expression of genes to physiological effects on blood pressure and the immune system (Suomi, 1999, Uchino et al., 1996, Padgett et al, 1998). In terms of learning and cognition, social interaction is a key factor as well. Peer pressure and reinforcement, cooperative goal-setting and group accountability are all significant motivators in learning (Jensen, 2005, Johnson and Johnson, 1999). It is important to note that social cognitive skill development proceeds over a long stretch of time and that it, like many other cognitive skills, needs to be nurtured and sometimes taught explicitly. We know, in fact, that the part of the brain responsible for social cognition (i.e., the prefrontal cortex) doesn't fully develop until the late teens or early twenties (Durston et al., 2001).

<u>Implications for experiential Jewish education</u>. To my mind, the most important finding from research on social cognition is the extent to which people benefit from learning in social groups. Indeed, cooperative learning has been shown to be more effective than competitive learning (Walberg, 1999), a finding that anyone who has worked in <u>hevrutot</u> will not find surprising. Jensen (2005) suggests that much of the social time students need to optimize learning can occur in informal groupings. He also suggests that attempts to work on social skills should not be limited to elementary school–aged children but should be continued through adolescence at least. "When blended into the curriculum, teaching social skills takes little extra time. And you may get a significant payoff, [including]… better overall feelings about the learning."

The relationship between social learning in general and values education should also not be underestimated. As the famous Israeli psychologist Reuven Feuerstein has remarked, "Our parents and relatives, acting as the agents of culture, impose meaning on the stimuli that constantly bombard us, and in this way ensure the transmission of values from one generation to another." This is perhaps the most significant role of social learning within experiential Jewish settings.

COGNITIVE DOMAINS: ACQUIRING KNOWLEDGE

For many individuals engaged in the field of educational neuroscience, their interest lies in understanding the algorithmic and neurological substrates of various domains of cognition. The most important and most often studied content areas, not surprisingly, comprise the classic "three R's": reading, writing and arithmetic. I myself was engaged in this work for the majority of my career as a scientist, studying language and mathematical cognition through the window of impairment—first by working with adults with acquired brain injury, and later with children with learning disabilities.

The approach I took in my research, and (not coincidentally) the one that I believe has yielded the most direct application to education, is known as cognitive neuropsychology. The methodology of cognitive neuropsychology uses data from individuals with cognitive impairments to model normal cognition, in much the same way that one might learn how a car works by examining a broken engine. The assumptions of this work are important to unpack. First we need to assume *universality*—in essence, that all cognitive systems share the same basic hardware (i.e., human brains), despite individual differences in behavior. Second, we have to assume *transparency,* which states that cognitive systems (or engines, for that matter) do not reorganize themselves so drastically after brain damage that they no longer reflect the same original system. Both of these assumptions have been supported by decades of neuropsychological research and form the basis for using patterns of impaired performance to model normal cognition (see Caramazza, 1986).

This work may not seem at first blush to be of direct interest or relevance to Jewish education, but I would argue that it is, especially in the domain of reading. It turns out that the insights offered from the study of children and adults with reading impairments have direct application to the teaching of Hebrew reading to beginning readers, whether those with or without reading difficulties.

In addition to this very specific set of insights, an important general insight has been consistently supported in this line of research having to do with the highly modular nature of the brain's cognitive functioning. What cognitive neuropsychological research has demonstrated across domains is that virtually every cognitive system (e.g., reading, math, memory) is made up of several smaller, functionally (and neurologically) separable processing units. Importantly, these processing units develop at different times and in response to content-specific learning.

To take a concrete example, mathematical ability comprises several modular competencies, including knowledge of algorithmic procedures (e.g., in solving the problem 26 x 8, first find the product of 8 and 6, carry the tens digit, etc.), fact retrieval (knowing that 8 x 6 = 48) and conceptual knowledge (understanding that multiplication involves successive addition; cf. McCloskey et al., 1991). Children are not equally good at acquiring each of these knowledge sets, nor will they acquire them naturally at the same time. More importantly, acquiring one will not necessarily predict success in another (e.g., students can be good at procedures but bad at remembering facts; understanding math conceptually will not guarantee efficiency in problem solving, etc.). The modularity of these cognitive sub-processes is supported by corresponding neurological modularity as well.

Implications for experiential Jewish education. In a domain perhaps closer to the work of many reading this chapter, growing up in a kosher home does not imply explicit knowledge of the laws of kashrut, but neither does understanding the *halachah* necessarily result in a desire to live by its strictures. Singing the *Shema* each night with your child may insure the she is able to recite it by heart (not an insignificant achievement), but an understanding of the theology of *Shema* will obviously require a different sort of instruction. Moreover, the order in which these different "*Shema*-related" knowledge bases will likely be acquired (and thus will most successfully be taught) is not arbitrary but arises from specific facts about brain maturation. Experiential Jewish educators understand that frontal learning is insufficient to acquire the sort of knowledge that will inculcate values of Jewish living. They need also to understand, however, that experience without explicit supporting knowledge will likewise be unlikely to bring about this goal.

COGNITIVE MEDIATORS AND OTHER TOPICS

Exercise and learning. Child psychiatrist John Ratey has reviewed a significant body of scientific evidence that proves the connection between physical exercise and learning. He argues that in order to enable our brains to operate at peak performance our bodies need to exercise. Aerobic exercise pumps more blood to the brain: "More blood means more oxygen and thus better nourished brain cells." Functionally, exercise influences the way we think and feel and cues the building blocks of learning in the brain. It has also been shown to affect our mood-state and our attention (Ratey, 2008).

There are a number of learning programs that have been designed with exercise in mind. Most of these have attempted to modify traditional educational settings to allow for a time and place for exercise as well as provide a structure in which exercise supports learning objectives. Of course, many of the environments in which experiential Jewish education takes place (most especially Jewish camping) can easily promote physical activity along with learning. Considered from this perspective, there is great truth in the statement *"Nefesh briah b'guf bari."*

Stress and learning. There has been a great deal of research into the effects of stress on learning. The neurochemical and neurophysiological reactions that stress causes in our body are fairly well understood. Acute stress causes the release of cortisol, a steroid that initially has a useful effect on the body, giving it a little burst of energy, dulling pain and maximizing those body systems that we need to respond to the stressor. However, over time excessive stress brings about detrimental effects to the body. In addition, and more relevant to the present discussion, chronic stress has been shown to impede learning and memory.

One of the leading clinical experts on stress and its relation to learning is neuropsychologist Jerome Schultz (whose wife happens to be a noted Jewish educator and my colleague at Hebrew College). Schultz has written a new book on the effects of stress on students with attention-deficit disorders and learning disabilities. He has also offered a useful model for stress reduction in school and other educational settings (Schultz, 2011). Many of the suggestions that he makes are consistent with experiential educational strategies, including creating learning and social environments that neutralize risk, building in opportunities for movement and exercise and providing multiple opportunities to acquire mastery and maximize experiences of success.

Schultz's model provides hope to individuals and families who want to reduce the stressors in their educational lives. He also reminds us of the importance of positivity in our attitudes and behaviors, quoting the words of Eric Kandel, Nobel laureate and perhaps the leading neuroscientist of our age:

> Behaviors and thoughts that relate to hope, love and happiness can change the brain—just as fear, stress and anxiety can change it. It's completely symmetrical (Kandel, 2008; quoted by Schultz, 2011).

MUSIC

Since I'm a musician, it may come as no surprise that I am greatly interested both in the neurological basis for human musical competence and the use of music in learning. I am not alone, though. The cognitive neuroscientific *zeitgeist* of the twenty-first century has placed increasing importance on elucidating the cognitive and neurological substrates of musical processing and has shown significant promise to offer insights into broader areas of scientific inquiry. Popular works such as *This Is Your Brain on Music* by cognitive neuroscientist Daniel Levitin have done much to support this growth of interest. Musical ability is also one of the eight domains that comprise Gardner's theory of multiple intelligences, thus assuring it an important seat at the cognitive table.

Of course, in the Jewish world music has always had a unique place among the arts, serving as a carrier of tradition and a conduit of our liturgical and cultural heritage. Music is used in all facets of Jewish living and learning, including *lernen shteigers* (melodies used for studying and reciting of Jewish text such as the Mishnah), holiday celebrations, prayer and connecting to Israeli society (to name just a few). When music is coupled with text it is a powerful carrier of culture and emotion (e.g., *Kol nidrei*, whose pleading tones seem to embody the sense of Yom Kippur perfectly). Finally, music has always served an important mnemonic function in the oral traditions of Judaism. It is in this role that it may have the greatest relevance to our previous discussions of memory and learning.

RELIGION AND LEARNING

I began this chapter by referencing some recent work by rabbi/theologian Ralph Mecklenburger on religion and neuroscience. Mecklenburger's is not the first treatment of this subject; there is also the 2010 book by philosopher of religion John Hick entitled *The New Frontier of Religion and Science: Religious Experience, Neuroscience and the Transcendent*. Mecklenburger's perspective as a rabbi, however, results in insights particularly relevant to Judaism. His primary thesis is that religion provides a structure of meaning through which we view the world. He argues that the brain itself seeks out such structure, and that without some rubric to serve as an organizing force we would be hard pressed to process all the information we encounter in the world. According to Mecklenburger,

> We must believe in something (or several somethings) not to drown in all the possibilities… we construct our world and we assign its meaning, and the potential actions and interpretations are dizzyingly manifold. Not choosing is not an option. The brain craves patterns and connections, creates meaning. That is who we are, what our brains, at all levels including this highest level, do. The issue is not *whether* we will select, privileging some ways of interpreting over others. The issue is only *what* ways of thinking we shall give our allegiance to.

But lest we think that religion's only function is this broad organizational one, there are data suggesting that the effects of living a religious life have far more specific effect as well. For example, a 2003 research paper by Jeynes finds that individuals who report living a religious life perform better on tests of academic achievement than their non-religious counterparts.

FINAL REMARKS

In this chapter I have tried to provide a brief primer of the cognitive and affective processes of the brain that give rise to the human ability to learn and retain information. Along the way I have considered some basic features of these processes that I believe are supported by the methodologies of experiential Jewish education. Synthesizing different types of material to create a unified explanatory fabric is always difficult; indeed, in Judaism it is sometimes explicitly prohibited (e.g., wool and linen). In this case, however, my hope is that the resulting tapestry is not only permissible but has served a useful purpose.

Allow me to end with one final summative thought taken from a position paper on neuroscience and education:

> Biology provides no simple limit to our learning, not least because our learning can influence our biology.…Considerable caution needs to be applied when attempting to transfer concepts between neuroscience and education. Such attempts need to be well-informed by expertise from within both fields. On the other hand, to ignore the relevance of present neuroscientific understanding to education flies in the face of a common-sense connection. There is a belief, shared by an increasing number of researchers in both fields, that neuroscience has a fundamental and increasing relevance to education that, together with related psychological perspectives, needs to be cautiously explored.

Howard-Jones, 2007

REFERENCES

Arns, M., S. de Ridder,, U. Streht, M. Breteler and A. Coenen (2009). "Efficacy of Neurofeedback Treatment in ADHD: The Effects on Inattention, Impulsivity and Hyperactivity: a Meta-Analysis." *Clinical EEG and Neuroscience 40:3*, 180–189.

Bartlett, F. C. (1932). *Remembering.* Cambridge: Cambridge University Press.

Caramazza, A. (1986). "On Drawing Inferences about the Structure of Normal Cognitive Systems from the Analysis of Patterns of Impaired Performance: The Case for Single-Patient Studies." *Brain & Cognition,* 5, 41-66.

Covington, M. (1999). "Caring about Learning." *Educational Psychologist, 3(2),* 127–136.

Dalke, A., K. Cassidy, P. Grobstein and D. Blank (2007). "Emergent Pedagogy: Learning to Enjoy the Uncontrollable and Make it Productive." *Journal of Educational Change 8:7, 111–130.*

Damasio, A. (1994). *Descartes' Error: Emotion, Reason and the Human Brain.* New York: Vintage.

Feuerstein, R., R.S. Feuerstein and L.H. Falik (2010). *Beyond Smarter: Mediated Learning and the Brain's Capacity to Change.* New York: Teacher's College Press.

Gardner, Howard (1983). *Frames of Mind: The Theory of Multiple Intelligences.* New York: Basic Books.

Hebb, D. (1949). *The Organization of Behavior.* New York: Wiley.

Hick, J. (2010). *The New Frontier of Religion and Science: Religious Experience, Neuroscience and the Transcendent.* London: Palgrave Macmillan.

Howard-Jones, P. (2007) *Neuroscience and Education, Issues and Opportunities: A Commentary by the Teaching and Learning Research Programme.* London: University of London.

Jensen, E. (2005). *Teaching with the brain in mind: Second edition.* Alexandria, Virginia: ASCD.

Jeynes, W. (2003). "The Effects of Black and Hispanic Twelfth Graders Living in Intact Families and Being Religious on Their Academic Achievement." *Urban Education,* 38: 35–57.

Johnson, M. (2001). "Functional Brain Development in Humans." *Nature Reviews Neuroscience, 2:7,* 475–483.

Johnson, T. and R. Johnson (1999). *Learning Together and Alone: Cooperative, Competitive and Individualistic Learning.* Boston: Allyn and Bacon.

Lane, R. and L. Nadel (eds.) (2000). *The Cognitive Neuroscience of Emotions.* New York: Oxford University Press.

Larsen, C.C., Bonde Larsen, K., Bogdanovic, N., Laursen, H., Graem, N., Samuelsen, G.B., and B. Pakkenberg, B. (2006). "Total Number of Cells in the Human Newborn Telencephalic Wall." *Neuroscience* 139:3, 999–100.

LeDoux, J. (1994). "Emotion, Memory, and the Brain." *Scientific American, 270(6),* 50–57.

Levitin, D.J. (2006). *This Is Your Brain on Music: The Science of a Human Obsession.* New York: Dutton.

McCloskey, M., Aliminosa D., and S.M. Sokol (1991). "Facts, Rules and Procedures in Calculation: Evidence from Dyscalculia." *Brain and Cognition 17,* 154–203.

McNeil, F. (2009). *Learning with the Brain in Mind.* London: Sage Publications.

Mecklenburger, R. (2012). *Our Religious Brains: What Cognitive Science Reveals about Belief, Morality, Community and Our Relationship with God.* Woodstock, VT: Jewish Lights Publishing.

Padgett, D.A., R.C. MacCallum and J.E. Sheridan (1998). "Stress Exacerbates Age-related Decrements in the Immune Response to an Experimental Influenza Viral Infection." *Journals of Gerontology Series A: Biological Science and Medical Science 54(4),* B347–353.

Quartz, S.R., and T.J. Sejnowski (2002). *Liars, Lovers, and Heroes: What the New Brain Science Reveals about How We Become Who We Are.* New York: William Morrow.

Ratey, J. (2001). *A User's Guide to the Brain.* New York: Little, Brown.

Ratey, J. (2008). *Spark: The Revolutionary New Science of Exercise and the Brain.* New York: Little, Brown and Company

Rose, S. (1992). *The Making of Memory.* New York: Bantam.

Schultz, J.J. (2011). *Nowhere to Hide: Why Kids with ADHD and LD Hate School and What We Can Do about It.* San Francisco: Jossey-Bass.

Suomi, S. (1999). Attachment in Rhesus Monkeys. In J. Cassidy and P. Shaver (eds.), *Handbook of Attachment* (pp. 181–197). New York: Guilford Press.

Uchino, B., J. Cacioppo, J. and J. Kiecolt-Glaser, J. (1996). "The Relationship between Social Support and Physiological Process: A Review with Emphasis on Underlying Mechanisms and Implications for Health." *Psychological Bulletin* 119, 488–531.

Walberg, H. (1999). "Productive Teaching." In H.C. Waxman and H. Walberg (eds.), *New Directions for Teaching Practice and Research* (pp. 75–104). Berkeley, CA: McCutchen Publishing Corp.

"GET GLUE": HOW GOOD JEWISH EDUCATORS USE CURRICULUM AND PEDAGOGY TO HOLD IT ALL TOGETHER

Robyn Faintich

PERCEPTION OF INFORMAL EDUCATION METHODS

In their book *Informal Education: Conversation, Democracy and Learning* (rev. edition), Tony Jeffs and Mark K. Smith have contended that curriculum is an element of distinction between formal and informal education. They write, "Informal education is…not curriculum-based" (Jeffs & Smith, 2005, p. 78). They argue that curriculum theory was formulated within the context of formal schooling with the goal of specifying in advance the structure, and therefore there are complications when educators try to apply it to informal forms of pedagogy.

Clearly, I don't agree, and therefore I lay out the way that curriculum and pedagogy enhance experience-based and experiential education encounters.

THE EXPERIENCE-BASED EDUCATION CURRICULUM

> What does the curriculum for your learning community look like? How does the curriculum you have in place get determined and implemented? Do you move from one program/event to another without a thread tying it all together? Try to articulate that thread.

Peter Jarvis is an expert in the field of adult learning, and in his book *Human Learning* he writes, "…One way of viewing curriculum is that it is a selection from culture. Culture is all the knowledge, skills, attitudes, beliefs, values and emotions that we, as human beings, have added to our biological base" (Jarvis, 2006, p. 55). This description mirrors how many people describe the ways in which Jewish identity is expressed—in knowledge, skills, attitudes, beliefs, values and emotions. So how do we, as educators using experiential techniques, develop the curriculum for building Jewish identity? What are the components to consider?

In an ideal world, when developing any curriculum, some key meta-components include: educational philosophy; process and plan; goals; pedagogy; implicit and explicit content; context/environment; and methodologies. The micro-components include (but are not limited to) opening community-building activities; transitions and set inductions; assessment and reflection; and responsibilities and roles. This next section will walk you through these components using a preferred lens of experience-based education.

EDUCATIONAL PHILOSOPHY

> Have you ever written your educational philosophy? If you have, when is the last time you reviewed it? Does it reflect your commitment to experiential education techniques?

An education philosophy is a position statement about how you view the learning transaction that takes place between you (or educators in your environment) and the learners. Your education philosophy is a reflection of your experiences and training and ultimately your belief in how your training and experiences come together in the execution of teaching.

Understanding the reflexive nature of education, regardless of the methods we utilize, is a critical piece of being a self-aware educator. The process of developing an educational philosophy is one method for guiding our deliberation. Gert Biesta, a professor of education at the University *of* Stirling in Scotland, reflects that as quality educators we need to question thinking that leads us to teach just for utilitarian purposes; rather, we need to "identify ways in which philosophy of education might contribute to what are deemed to be desirable educational outcomes…. It requires that we reflect on what it means to be a teacher, what it means to be a student, what it means to educate, what it means to listen, what it means to know, what it means to think and reflect, what it means to be critical and what all this does to selves: the selves of teachers and the selves of students" (Biesta, 2010, p. xi). Continually assessing how we view these aspects directly impacts the curriculum we develop in order to deliver the education we hope to impart.

When educators choose to utilize experience-based education techniques or choose to align themselves with an informal education environment, there is something in their own experiences and knowledge of education that drives them toward these conditions. Sometimes we just have a gut feeling or a hypothesis that these are better circumstances for students to learn in, but framing that intuition in a written education philosophy helps concretize its origins and execution. In their journal article "Assessing the Consistency Between Teachers' Philosophies and Educational Goals" Martha J. Livingston, Benjamin R. McClain and B.C. DeSpain write that "Teachers develop viewpoints, values and goals about the purposes of education and about how students are to be educated. Within the practice of every classroom teacher are beliefs that shape educational opportunities for students. Operationally, philosophy influences how we educate students. A systematic view of philosophical thought and goals can provide a framework for the professional to gain insight into the nature of instruction" (Livingston, McClain and DeSpain 1995, p. 124).

One reason for writing an education philosophy is to hold ourselves accountable to the consistency between our educational vision and our execution. Jon W. Wiles and Joseph C. Bondi, in their book *Curriculum Development: A Guide to Practice*, shape the continuum on which all education philosophy sits. They situate the philosophy between "two variables—structure and flexibility—[that] are used to facilitate the analysis of fifteen major dimensions of schooling" (Bondi and Wiles 1993, p. 49). Some of these dimensions include community involvement; learning spaces; the use of learning materials; the teaching strategies; teacher roles; and student roles. They claim, "Examining the school by such criteria, in a systematic manner, will help you see a school in its totality. The underlying beliefs about educating will become more obvious, and the program congruence or inconsistencies will be more visible."

In considering writing your education philosophy, or in revisiting one you have previously drafted, taking into consideration all that these education philosophers and master educators articulate will help you clearly develop the blueprint that shapes every other piece of your curriculum and its execution.

PROCESS AND PLAN

> When you begin to conceptualize a learning program, what are the first three steps you take in order to shape the ideas and pieces into something you can implement? Is there room in your plan to seize an unexpected educational moment?

H. Lynn Erickson is a consultant recognized as a national expert in the areas of concept-based curriculum design and teaching for deep understanding. She wrote the foreword in the book *Getting Results with Curriculum Mapping,* in which she asserts, "Leaders pay attention to *process* when introducing and implementing an initiative" (in Hayes Jacobs, 2004, p. vii). One of my biggest critiques of education leaders in informal settings is that they often do not pay attention to the process (a key reason for my writing this chapter). Curriculum is the roadmap for the process. Erickson writes, "A strong curriculum is the foundation for strong teaching and learning" (in Hayes Jacobs, 2004, p. ix).

In the chapter on the language of experiential Jewish education Jeffs and Smith make a distinction between informal education and non-formal education, and while they believe curriculum isn't a hallmark of informal education (by their definition), they do actually offer us a clear understanding of what a curriculum does in its role in non-formal education. "A curriculum is just one way of organizing the work of educators. It is a proposal for action—something we build before the educational encounter" (Jeffs and Smith 2005, p. 74).

If we consider that curriculum is a proposal for action, we inherently understand that our plan needs to be flexible and that we need to leave space for the unexpected to occur. A trademark of informal Jewish education is the Jewish Educational Moment (JEM) or Jewish Teachable Moments—"Teachable moments are serendipitous moments…[in which] every interaction with a child has a potential Jewish-educational impact" (Sales and Saxe 2002, p.10). One definition of Teachable Moment is that "a teachable moment is not something that you can plan for; rather, it is a fleeting opportunity that must be sensed and seized by the teacher. Often it will require a brief digression that temporarily sidetracks the original lesson plan so that the teacher can explain a concept that has inadvertently captured the students' collective interest" (Lewis, n.d., paragraph 2).While the idea of "Teachable Moments" in informal settings seems simplistic, the implementation involves significant pedagogical theory, serious staff training and significantly more planning and collaboration than traditional frontal education (Cohen and Bar Shalom 2010).

GOALS

What do you want to accomplish by utilizing experiential education methods? What content goals do you want to achieve?

Within the conversation about goals in experience-based curriculum there are actually two dimensions to explore. One is the goal of the education method you are choosing—experiential education—and one is the goal you have for the learner vis-à-vis the content. This may be a diversion from traditional methods of approaching curriculum, in which the method is applied to the content once the content is chosen; here I am recommending that we have chosen the experience-based education method because of its value and that we are looking for ways to apply it to all content.

In order to understand of our goal for using specific experience-based methods we can explore what experts have articulated. The goals of experiential education are widely defined among the philosophers. Several authors emphasize the importance of inspiring learners to be continuously curious and want to learn while increasing their capacity to learn (Rousseau 1762/1972; Pestalozzi 1894; EDTA, 1999); however, Dewey says it best: "The most important attitude that can be formed is that of a desire to go on learning" (Dewey 1938, p. 48). Shifting the goal from the content of learning to the yearning to learn is a different approach to education than many educators employ.

Beard and Wilson take this shift and tie it to the long-term impact of education. "A much more effective and long-lasting form of learning is to involve the learner by creating a meaningful learning experience" (Beard and Wilson 2006, p. 1). The authors go on to explain, "The greater the involvement of the participant in the learning activity, the deeper will be the participant's learning and therefore the effect on future thought and behavior" (Beard and Wilson 2006, p. 6).

The idea of life-long learning is often a central theme in Jewish education. One reason for this is that in contrast to secular educational institutions, Jewish institutions feel the responsibility to engage learners at all ages and to make the learning meaningful and applicable to Jewish action. Reimer and Shavelson say, "Why care about experiential Jewish learning? Because involved Jews of all ages hunger for the experience of being Jewishly engaged, not just simply more knowledgeable about Judaism" (Reimer and Shavelson 2008, p. 8).

In addition to the emphasis on life-long learning and developing a desire to learn, education philosophers also focus on the amount and high impact of knowledge the learner in an experiential environment can take in versus a learner in a frontal environment. Rousseau asserts about a learner that "… You may expect him to learn more in one hour's work than he would retain after a whole day's explanation" (Rousseau 1762/1972, p. 160). One can assume that Rousseau's belief about this is based on a foundation of Pestalozzi's similar declaration, "To arrive at knowledge slowly, by one's own experience, is better than to learn by rote facts that other people know" (Rousseau 1762/1972, p. 35).

One can surmise from these statements that the goals of experiential education are to inspire an aspiration and inquisitiveness to learn; to provoke a learner to life-long learning; and to transmit knowledge with a higher impact and deeper modality. If this is the case, it is important for us to write a curriculum in which this goal is reflected. If our curriculum only focuses on content goals, then we might be missing an over-arching goal of our entire education initiatives—and therefore undercutting our specific and immediate content goals. In their book *Experiential Learning: A Best Practice Handbook for Educators and Training*, authors Colin Beard and John P. Wilson say, "The challenge for educators…is to find the right type of experience that is immediately appealing to the learner and also has a longer-term impact" (Beard and Wilson 2006, p. 30).

PEDAGOGY—DEVELOPMENT

> Reflect: Do you deliver your education content in a planned, systematic way?

What is pedagogy? Pedagogy is "the art or method of teaching—a way of doing something, especially a systematic way; implies an orderly, logical arrangement (usually in steps)" (http://thefreedictionary.com/pedagogy). It is:

- The study of the process of teaching.
- The examination of the correct use of education methods.
- The building blocks of education/understanding required to teach the next thing.

So many youth educators I have encountered consider pedagogy an element of concern only to formal education. But then I ask: Is teaching someone how to swim done in a formal education setting? Is it done with formal education methods? And, of course, I am told that swim lessons are done through experience-based techniques in informal settings. So then I ask: What do you need to know how to do before you can swim laps doing the breaststroke? People are quick to respond: breathe out without taking on water, float, kick, etc. Swim instructors understand that there is a clear pedagogy to teaching someone how to swim safely and with confidence. But what is the pedagogy for teaching Jews how to participate in communal worship? What is the pedagogy for teaching Jews how to host a Shabbes dinner? Experience-based education programs need to have a well-thought-out pedagogy that should be reflected in a well-thought-out curriculum.

CONTEXT/ENVIRONMENT

> Use five adjectives to describe the physical space your learning encounters take place in.

Wiles and Bondi make a well-defined claim to the role that environment plays in any education experience. "It is clear that environments, both real and perceived, set a tone for learning. What people feel about the spaces that they occupy or in which they interact causes them to behave in certain ways" (Wiles and Bond 1993, p. 49). This is evident in the utilization of informal environments for Jewish education. On numerous occasions I have facilitated the same activity and discussion in a school building and also in a retreat center, and without fail two things happen: 1) Learners express themselves in the informal environment in a much more open tone with a level of vulnerability they rarely reach in a classroom, and 2) The learners themselves will evaluate the experience in the camp setting as a better education encounter than those learners who experienced it in a formal environment.

In the early 1980s my mom served as the curriculum supervisor for a large Reform congregation in St. Louis. I have a clear memory of her constructing a huge plastic bubble in our basement using duct tape and clear plastic sheeting. When she attached a box fan to the contraption it inflated into a giant enclosed room. The next thing I knew, my third grade religious school class was all seated inside this giant bubble to simulate our airplane ride to Israel. I don't remember much about third grade religious school, but I remember the feeling of sitting in this giant plastic space and hearing the rotation of the fan blades. In recent years, as I have become entrenched in the field of experience-based education, I have acquired the terminology to frame the educational goals she wanted to accomplish with the erection of this learning environment in the center of the synagogue hallways.

Beard and Wilson dedicate an entire chapter in their book examining the role of the learning environment. They express their belief that the consideration of the setting and how it impacts the education encounter constitutes "a pedagogy of space and place for consideration" (Beard and Wilson 2006, p. 10). Wilson and Beard call to task educators who focus primarily on the learning program and less on the environment in which it will take place, saying, "This can reduce learning effectiveness." Quality educators, in their opinion, spend a great deal of time attempting to understand "the role, value and function of places and spaces that enhance learning" (Beard and Wilson 2006, p. 79). In this recognition of the role they also call attention to the function that the labels used to describe the spaces has on the learning and learners. They make the cogent point that experiential education can successfully take place in both formal and informal settings, but that referring to those formal settings as "learning spaces" and not as "classrooms" has its own impact on the education encounter. (I believe this use of language can be extended to consider the terms "school" versus "learning community," and the difference the term "teacher" makes as compared to "educator" or "facilitator". We will explore other areas in which the language impacts the concept.)

Even if you are an educator whose primary environment is a formal setting, such as a school, the way you speak about the space and utilize the space will drastically impact the learning that occurs. Experience-based educators should consider how to transform spaces, create breakout areas, change the expected environment, link indoor and outdoor locations, convert walls and floors to education resources and develop flexible constructs. The steps you will take in accomplishing this are outlined in detail as a part of your curriculum.

METHODOLOGIES

> What are three experiential learning methodologies you are familiar with?

When Jay W. Roberts makes the distinction between experiential learning and experiential education, he does so on the back of Christin M. Itin's article "Reasserting the Philosophy of Experiential Education as a Vehicle for Change in the Twenty-first Ccentury," in which the author writes, "If experiential education is correctly identified as a philosophy, it allows for the various expressions of this philosophy (service learning, cooperative learning, adventure-based, problem-based, action learning, etc.) to be linked together under this single philosophy" (Itin 1999, p. 97).

The curriculum you develop will specify which of these methodologies (or other experiential learning methods) you will employ. In some cases you might create a hybrid method that should be described in detail as part of your curriculum.

COMMUNITY BUILDERS

> Do you view "icebreakers" as an element of the education encounter? How do you transition your learners from whatever they were doing prior to entering your environment into the learning?

In their book Beard and Wilson outline a seventeen-point experiential learning program typology and say that one of the important considerations of the typology is the sequencing of the activities. In many ways this goes back to the conversation about pedagogy. As a layer to the typology the authors set forth a "four-stage sequence or activity wave" of which the first step is "Awaken participant enthusiasm with icebreakers and energizers" (Beard and Wilson 2006, p. 119).

In the world of informal youth education we often refer to these as mixers or team builders, in addition to using the icebreaker lexicon. For some reason, activities termed in these ways seem separate and sometimes a throwaway in the overall experience. But when Beard and Wilson frame them as "primer activities" we can see the important role they play in setting the stage for the overall success of the learning encounter. On one hand these activities are designed to "to reduce inhibitions or to create trust, empathy and teamwork" (Beard and Wilson 2006, p. 119), but they are also designed to spark the initial thinking of the learners and to help them transition from whatever they were doing when they walked through your door.

If we look at these primer activities as a critical part of the education experience, we begin to consider how they feed the content learning and how their success or failure impacts the positioning of the rest of the learning. Every quality experiential education curriculum will include well-thought-out and intentional primer activities.

SET INDUCTIONS AND TRANSITIONS

> Who gives the instructions and directions to the learners? How much preparation time do they spend planning for that introduction?

Just as the primer activities are essential pieces of a quality experiential education curriculum, so are the introductions to and the transitions between learning activities. I have seen entire programs fail or succeed based on the way they were introduced to the learners, how directions were given and how much thought and attention was given in advance to the critical role set inductions play in the overall learning encounter.

Researcher and educator Robert F. Schuck, in his article "The Impact of Set Induction on Student Achievement and Retention," defines set induction as "the initial instructional act on the part of the teacher for the purpose of establishing a frame of reference deliberately designed to facilitate the creation of a communicative link between the experiential field of the pupil and the desired behavioral objectives of the learning experience. The purpose of the set induction process is to focus pupil attention on some commonly known experiential referent (orientation), which becomes a mechanism by which the teacher makes the passage from the known to the new material (transition), thereby building continuity from lesson to lesson" (Shuck 1981, p. 228). And while Schuck's milieu is formal education settings, if we, as educators in informal environments, changed the language slightly from "pupil" to "learner" and from "lesson" to "activity," we can see the way he makes the connection between the set induction, the content and the learner's life experiences.

But how important are the set induction and the planned transitions to the learner's success? Schuck's article asserts that these make a substantial difference. He writes, "The fact that teachers can be trained in the teaching skill employed (set induction) and that teachers so trained are judged to be more effective by their students is documented in previous studies....Pupils taught by teachers who incorporated set induction into their instructional strategies scored significant gains in achievement," (Schuck 1981, p. 227).

If we have evidence that the planning and use of set inductions makes an impact on learner achievement, how can we not incorporate them into our experience-based learning curricula? In developing each experiential learning activity, consider how you are going to bring the learners' prior experiences and knowledge into the discussion from the beginning. Concretizing that plan is an important element in your curriculum and the success of your planned education encounter.

ASSESSMENT AND REFLECTION

> At the end of an education encounter, how do you know if your learners understood new material? What measurements do you have in place to assess mastery?

In formal learning environments assessment and progress measurement take the form of formal methods such as tests and grades. In many cases the reasons for learner evaluation is to either place a student in a leveled-learning class or to determine if s/he is familiar enough with a concept to move on. With the current environment of standardized testing, the methods for assessment are often in place to examine a learner's knowledge of factual information, concepts and specific skills. When we utilize experience-based techniques or are functioning in an informal setting, the purpose of assessment tends to be significantly different—it focuses on meaning-making, internalization and personal growth. Curriculum development theorists and consultants Jay McTighe and Grant Wiggins are the leading experts in the Understanding by Design (UbD) curriculum development method. They refer to the measurement of learning as "Evidence of Understanding" and outline how to transform "Understandings into Performance" (McTighe and Wiggins 1999, p. 133).

The writer who penned the foreword in one of McTighe and Wiggins' books wrote, "From years of experience developing, testing and critiquing assessment tasks, the authors [McTighe and Wiggins] have concluded that performance is the key to assessing understanding" (Brandt in McTighe and Wiggins 1998, p. vi).

So how can we use performance assessments to ascertain if our learners have understood the content we have introduced to them? How can informal check-ins help learners achieve true understanding? How can we assess their meaning-making, internalization, and personal growth?

McTighe and Wiggins teach us that we need to write into our curriculum a mix of informal checks, observation/dialogue, academic prompts and performance projects. They write, "Because understanding develops as a result of ongoing inquiry and rethinking, the assessment of understanding should be thought of as a collection of evidence over time instead of an event" (McTighe and Wiggins 1999, p. 126).

When developing your curriculum, specify the places in the learning process where the facilitators should inject the informal checks, which McTighe and Wiggins explain are "oral questions, observations, dialogues, student logs [reflections], self-assessments and peer assessments." While educators in informal settings might use a different label, the academic prompts that McTighe and Wiggins suggest are completely appropriate for use in experience-based education methods. They explain, "Academic prompts are open-ended questions or problems that require students to think critically, not just recall knowledge…[there is] no single best answer or solution strategy" (McTighe and Wiggins 1999, p. 127).

This description is in perfect alignment with the goals of experience-based education methods. If we fail to implement them as a part of our planned curriculum, then a large piece of quality education is missing.

While the informal check-ins and the academic prompts are important elements of a quality experiential education curriculum, the higher level of assessment is the utilization of performance tasks and projects. McTighe and Wiggins describe these as "complex challenges ... authentic ... ranging in length from short-term to long-term, multi-staged projects...[that] require a tangible product or performance" (McTighe and Wiggins 1999, p. 128). If we are staying true to the DEEP definition of experiential education (and to Kolb's), we know that these kinds of performance tasks will, in themselves, provide the space and prompt for reflection, growth and the transfer of knowledge. A quality curriculum will provide the guidelines for learners to complete these performance tasks. McTighe and Wiggins offer a list of over sixty "performance verbs" that educators can use to help plan these projects. The performance verbs fall into one of six categories: explanation, interpretation, application, perspective, empathy and self-knowledge (McTighe and Wiggins 1999, p. 136). We can see how these categories flow easily into our concept of experiential education. We can also begin to see that if we spend time concretizing the use of performance tasks—via our curricula—in the education encounters we offer, we strengthen the education itself.

ROLE OF PRACTITIONER

> If you were going to write a job description of the lead educator in your learning community, what would be the five primary responsibilities?

In formal education the teacher is often found delivering content in a frontal mode, whereby students can only take in information in audio and sometimes basic visual methods. This approach to education provides the teacher with considerable power over the learning itself. All of the literature on experiential education outlines a very different role for the educator.

Within experiential learning the function of the educator shifts from formal teacher to facilitator and guide. This assertion is consistent among all of the literature—historic and contemporary, secular and Jewish. Dewey offers the foundation of this claim and uses quite strong language when he says, "When education is based upon experience and educative experience is seen to be a social process, the situation changes radically. The teacher loses the position of external boss or dictator but takes on that of a leader of group activities" (Dewey 1938, p. 59). Even the juxtaposition this statement frames between a dictator and a leader is quite powerful.

The consistent message of the literature is that the educator must still have an active role: controlling the environment, arranging the educative experience, offering critical questions and suggestions, helping a learner with intelligent interpretation and contributing to the learning process (Dewey 1938; Roberts 2012; Wiles and Bondi 1993) Both the DEEP document (EDTA 1999) and Beard and Wilson (2006) specifically call the educator "facilitator". In her chapter in *Contemporary Theories of Learning: Learning Theorists ... in Their Own Words*, Robin Usher writes, "Educators are forced to assume the role of commentators and interpreters rather than legislators and 'enlightened' pedagogues. Educational practitioners, rather than being the source/producers of knowledge/taste, become facilitators helping to interpret everybody's knowledge and helping to open up the possibilities for further experience" (in *Illeris*, 2009, p. 171–172).

In addition to all that is described above, Reimer and Shavelson offer additional roles for the experiential education leader. "We advise educators to think of themselves as having three primary roles[:] ...create a group space in which every participant feels safe ... create a sense of purpose ... challenge individuals" (Reimer and Shavelson 2008, p. 5). It is important that these authors include safety as a part of the experience. With some interpretation, readers can extract that these authors mean emotional as well as physical safety. This emotional safety allows the learner to explore and take risks without fear of judgment.

David Bryfman, in his contribution to the Reimer and Shavelson anthology, writes, "As experiential educators, Jewish educators aim to encourage participants to undertake the challenge of stretching themselves and growing toward a more complex participation in Jewish life" (Reimer and Shavelson 2008, p. 34). That safe emotional space offers the buffer that enables the learner to stretch and grow. This is one of the key components of experiential education.

The understood function of the lead educator plays a major role in the development and execution of the curriculum. And because there is a clear shift in the traditional role of this educational leader, this leaves room for others to have leadership roles within the learning community and education encounter.

RESPONSIBILITIES/ROLES

> Besides the lead educator, who in your learning community has responsibility for implementing the content? How do the various people come to know and understand their roles in this education encounter?

The Jewish concept of *tzimtzum*, contraction, is based on the idea that in order for anything else to exist in the world, God has to contract. If, in experience-based education and informal settings, the practitioner shifts from a full frontal teaching role to that of a facilitator, this leaves room for others to step into the teaching process. This could be co-leaders, parents, learners, community members or guests.

Roland S. Barth is the founding director of the Harvard Principals' Center and a consultant to schools, school systems, state departments of education, universities and foundations. He is quoted in Thomas Sergiovanni's book *Building Community in Schools:* "Schools are seen as places where children learn and adults teach." His vision is of school as a place where everyone is involved in learning and everyone is involved in teaching. He says, "An anthropologist friend tells me that dramatic, profound learning takes place in societies in which people of all ages, generations and positions—grandmother, father, child, adolescent…—live, work and learn together simultaneously. … Everyone is a teacher and everyone is a learner" (in Sergiovanni 1994, p. 143). Informal learning environments lend themselves naturally to creating this multi-generational teaching and learning community. When considering your learning community and the curriculum you are developing, it's important to consider what teaching and facilitating roles each member of the community has.

THE IMPLICIT PEDAGOGY AND CURRICULUM OF JEWISH LEARNING COMMUNITIES MADE EXPLICIT

> Take a moment and think about the education encounters you facilitate. When people "graduate" from your program, what would you want them to know? How would you want them to learn it?

The work of Etienne Wenger and Jean Lave has focused on situated learning, and they use apprenticeship and communities of practice as examples. In considering the role that education plays in these environments, they begin to frame the difference between a teaching curriculum and a learning curriculum and the role that curriculum plays in building community meaning and developing relationships. They write, "A learning curriculum consists of situated opportunities….The learning curriculum…evolves out of participation in a specific community of practice engendered by pedagogical relations and by a prescriptive view of …subject matter, as well as out of the many and various relations that tie participants to their own…institution. A learning curriculum is essentially situated…and thus characteristic of a community....participation in an activity system about which participants share understandings concerning what they are doing and what that means in their lives and for their communities" (Wenger and Lave 1991, p. 97-98).

Their words resonate with what we have discussed before—that there is a curriculum and pedagogy within informal environments. What we focus on here is attention to the role of community building, community participation, developing meaning and the relationships built within this community of learning. So this leads us to explore how we build the transmission of *ruach* (the spirit/energy in our communities); the intentionality of creating community and social connectedness; the enculturation into organization traditions and language; and the cultivation of community ethics into the learning curriculum within experience-based education.

COMMUNITY BUILDING AND SOCIAL CONNECTEDNESS

In what ways do you include community-building techniques in your education environment? How do learners in your environment know that building a safe community is a core value?

In the book *Learning, Teaching and Community: Contributions of Situated and Participatory Approaches to Educational Innovation*, educator Margaret Gibson writes that "Learning is a social process and... it occurs through active participation within social communities...it follows that the nature of one's membership within a...community plays a critical role in shaping one's manner of participation" (in Pease-Alvarez 2005, p. 47). She goes on to say, "A sense of belonging and acceptance enhances participation [and]...ultimately learning." Later in the chapter Gibson refers to work by Carol Goodenow and Kathleen E. Grady in their 1993 article in the *Journal of Experimental Education*, in which they write, "Unless students identify with the school to at least a minimal extent; feel that they belong as part of the school; and believe themselves to be welcomed, respected and valued by others there, they may begin the gradual disengagement process" (in Pease-Alvarez 2005, p. 48). These sentiments about the role of belonging in a learning environment are essential regardless of the learning being in a formal setting or an informal setting. The goal of creating a learning experience where people don't disengage—and in fact are inspired to life-long learning—is a critical element of Jewish education experiences.

Wenger and Lave also put emphasis on the role social connectedness has on learning. They write, "Learning [is] a process by which a learner internalized knowledge, whether 'discovered,' 'transmitted' from others or 'experienced in interaction' with others....The social character of learning mostly consists in a small 'aura' of socialness that provides input for the process of internalization viewed as individualistic acquisition of the cultural given....Concentrate on processes of social transformation.... Insist on starting with social practice, on taking participation to be the crucial process .... Participation in a social practice... suggests a very explicit focus on the person, but as a person-in-the-world, as a member of sociocultural community" (Wenger and Lave 1991, pp. 47–52). As Wenger and Lave highlight "participation" several times in this excerpt, we have to link back to a key element of experience-based education methods: the active participation the learner has his/her own education.

As stated earlier in the "Role of Practitioner" section of this paper, Reimer, Shavelson and Bryfman emphasize the need for a safe space in which learners can challenge and stretch themselves. This safe space and development of community dynamics does not happen by accident. It needs to be a critical piece of the explicit curriculum. Oftentimes, when I am exploring this issue with educators, they lament the lack of time they have to deliver content, much less implement community-building programs. One way to accomplish both is to develop ways to deliver the content via community-building methods. A quality experience-based curriculum will foster relationships and build connections.

Even the grandfather of educative experiences, John Dewey, gives a nod to the role of the social community in learning. He writes that one role of the educator is "moving the spirit of the whole group. The control is social, but individuals are parts of the community, not outside of it " (Dewey 1938, p. 54).

RUAH

> What collective emotional experience do you want your learners to have? What elements of your learning program are designed as a catalyst for building emotional group experiences?

Gustave LeBon was an early twentieth-century social psychologist who specialized in crowd psychology and the collective mind. He proposed that "groups provide contexts for intense contagious emotional experiences" (in Niedenthal, Krauth-Gruber and Ric 2006, p. 235).

It is exactly this intense, contagious emotional group experience that educators utilizing experiential education methods within Jewish learning environments hope to create. In some cases this will manifest itself in a song session and in other cases via a spiritual healing service. Often summer camps and youth groups utilize cheers, logo regalia and friendly competition to create those emotional experiences.

An entire field of study is dedicated to understanding the psychology of emotion. In their book *Psychology of Emotion: Interpersonal, Experiential, and Cognitive Approaches,* authors Paula Niedenthal, Silvia Krauth-Gruber and Francois Ric write about the power of a shared experience. "An entire group can share or experience the same emotion for the same reason. These are called 'group-based' emotions…. Groups or crowds are considered capable of extreme emotional movements" (Niedenthal, Krauth-Bruber and Ric 2006, pp. 234–235). In our work these extreme emotional moments may take the form of overpowering joy and excitement and they may take the form of significant emotional attachment. I have heard experiential educators say that they know they did a good job if someone cries. It's the process of reflecting and meaning-making within the experience and group setting that often brings someone to tears.

Niedenthal, Krauth-Gruber and Ric know that this group emotional experience doesn't happen all by circumstance, and that in fact it needs to be planned. They write, "Changes in a group affective state can be the consequence of deliberate attempts to modify the others' affective state—due to controlled processes (in the sense of processes that are engaged consciously, effortfully and with intention)" (Niedenthal, Krauth-Gruber and Ric 2006, p. 245). It's the intentional, conscious planning that we call curriculum.

TRADITION AND LANGUAGE

> What traditions have been developed in your learning community that you need to explain to outsiders? What language (including acronyms and organization names) is a natural part of your program, but may not be natural to newcomers?

Each time I walk into a Jewish youth community I enter a place steeped deep in tradition and language. Some of the traditions of these youth programs or camps take on a life of their own, with their own history, their own meaning and their own level of holiness. But how do outsiders or newcomers learn the execution of these traditions and also somehow make meaning of them for themselves?

Peter Jarvis says, "Crucial to this process is learning the language of the people, since it is through language that meaning, knowledge and so on are conveyed….Language, as such, is arbitrary and symbolic; no word, thing or event has intrinsic meaning, and it only assumes meaning when meaning is given to it, which occurs through narrative" (Jarvis 2006, p. 57).

The narrative is given structure through curriculum. There is a pedagogy to learning the traditions and culture of an organization, and we have to consider how that pedagogy is built into our informal settings and experiential-learning methods.

COMMUNITY ETHICS

> What Jewish ethics frame the culture of your organization? How is this communicated with all members of your organization's community (i.e., learners, teachers, parents, board members)?

One of the primary goals of any Jewish education experience is to cultivate the ethics of the greater Jewish community—in essence, to produce *mensches*. This is in addition to developing a nuclear set of ethics that might guide and be a piece of the cultural fabric of any particular organization.

Jewish educator Steve Bailey also supports this core goal. "An area of Jewish education that comes closest to consensus is the goal of producing an ethical, socially mature student, sensitive to Jewish values….The goal of Jewish education must include an effective pedagogic model of ethical education—educating toward *menschlichkeit*. It is critically important that [Jewish education institutions] graduate students who integrate Jewish ethical values into their social lives, career goals and community responsibility" (Bailey 2010, p. 4). Bailey challenges each of us as Jewish educators to consider what pedagogic model we are going to utilize to instill these values—basically outlining that it doesn't happen by accident for our learners.

No matter the environment—formal or informal—we as Jewish educators must take seriously our role in the cultivation of these values. In considering how many educators using experience-based methods to tackle the task of teaching ethics and values, many see it as an implicit part of the environment, with some occasional learning about a specific ethic—most of the time *Tikkun Olam*. However, in understanding the importance that Bailey places on the critical role of teaching ethics in education, we need to examine how to put them into an ongoing curriculum and how that curriculum functions in an informal education setting or embedded in every experiential education encounter.

Seymour Fox and Israel Scheffler assert that a curriculum would "help the student develop love of learning and commitment to tradition" (Fox and Scheffler 2007, p. 9). They suggest the best Jewish education settings for this to occur are those where it can "be lived and require a community—it is doubtful that such an education can be undertaken only in schools or in formal settings. It most likely needs to be undertaken in enclaves that offer a subculture where the students can experience and learn what it means to act on ideas and where their search for meaning can be responded to." This description certainly brings the image of many of our informal environments.

RECOMMENDATION AND CONCLUSION

The most assertive recommendation I can make is for all educators, regardless if they work in informal or formal settings, and no matter which education methods the educators implement—formal or experience-based—to spend considerable time learning about and experimenting with the components of a quality curriculum. It might mean that we need to enroll in formal courses ourselves in order to learn the basics, or it could be that we should sit with colleagues and collaborate on curriculum development, exploring our own formal vs. experience-based learning encounters.

Experiential Jewish education and education in informal environments have proven to have a significant impact on Jewish identity development. We cannot afford to approach our utilization of these methods in a haphazard manner.

REFERENCES

Bailey, S. (2010). "Educating for an Ethical Jewish Community." *Jewish Educational Leadership* 8(3).

Beard, C., and J.P. Wilson (2006). *Experiential Learning: A Best Practice Handbook for Educators and Trainers.* London and Philadelphia: Kogan Page.

Biesta, G. (2010). "What's the Use of Philosophy of Education?" *Philosophy of Education* xi-xiii. Retrieved from *http://ojs. ed.uiuc.edu/index.php/pes/article/view/2989/1069.*

Cohen, E. H., and Y. Bar Shalom (2010). "Teachable Moments in Jewish Education: An Informal Approach in a Reform Summer Camp." *Religious Education* 105(1), 26–44.

Dewey, J. (1938). *Experience and Education* (1997 ed.). New York: Simon & Schuster.

Experiential Training and Development Alliance (1999, March). *The DEEP Document: The Definition, Ethics and Exemplary Practices of Experiential Training and Development.* Deerfield, IL: Bronson, et al. Retrieved from *http://www.etdalliance. com/Resources/Documents/DEEP.pdf.*

Fox, S., and I. Scheffler, (2007). "Jewish Education and Jewish Continuity: Prospects and Limitations." *Monographs from the Mandel Foundation,* 1–13.

Gibson, M. A. (2005). "It's All about Relationships: Growing a Community of College-oriented Migrant Youth." In L. Pease-Alvarez and S. R. Schecter (eds.), *Learning, Teaching and Community: Contributions of Situated and Participatory Approaches to Educational Innovation* (pp. 47–68). London: Routledge.

Hayes Jacobs, H. (ed.) (2004). *Getting Results with Curriculum Mapping.* Alexandria, VA: Association for Supervision and Curriculum Development.

Horowitz, B. (June2000; rev. 2003). "Connections and Journeys: Assessing Critical Opportunities for Enhancing Jewish Identity" Retrieved from http://www.ujafedny.org/assets/documents/PDF/who-we-are/Connections-And-Journeys-Opportunities-for-Enhancing-Jewish-Identity.pdf.

http://www.infed.org/i-intro.htm

http://www.thefreedictionary.com/pedagogy

Illeris, K. (ed.) (2009). *Contemporary Theories of Learning: Learning Theorists ... in Their Own Words.* London: Routledge.

Itin, C.M. (1999). "Reasserting the Philosophy of Experiential Education as a Vehicle for Change in the Twenty-first Century." *Journal of Experiential Education* 22(2), 91–98.

Jarvis, P. (2006). *Human Learning: Towards a Comprehensive Theory: Vol. 1, Lifelong Learning and the Learning Society.* New York: Routledge.

Jeffs, T., and M.K. Smith (2005). *Informal Education: Conversation, Democracy and Learning* (rev. ed.). Ruddington, Nottingham: Educational Heretics Press (original work published 1996).

Jeffs, T., and M.K. Smith (eds.) (2010). *BASW Practical Social Work: Youth Work Practice.* United Kingdom: Palgrave Macmillan.

Kolb, D.A. (1984). *Experiential Learning: Experience as the Source of Learning and Development.* Englewood Cliffs, NJ: Prentice-Hall, Inc.

Lewis, B. (n.d.) About.com Elementary Education: *Teachable Moments.* Retrieved from: *http://k6educators.about.com/od/ educationglossary/g/gteachmoment.htm.*

Livingston, M. J., B.R.McClain and B.C. DeSpain (1995, Fall). "Assessing the Consistency between Teachers' Philosophies and Educational Goals." *Education* 116(1), 124–129. Retrieved from *http://web.ebscohost.com/ehost/detail?sid=0b7c0f5e-ad13-4176-8e47-7b150743404b%40sessionmgr111&vid=1&hid=119&bdata=JnNpdGU9ZWhvc3QtbGl2ZSZzcZ29wZT 1zaXRl#db=f5h&AN=9511290972.*

McTighe, J., and G. Wiggins (1998). *Merrill Education/ASCD College Textbook Series: Understanding by Design.* Upper Saddle River, NJ: Merrill Prentice Hall.

McTighe, J., and G. Wiggins (1999). *The Understanding by Design Handbook.* Alexandria, VA: Association for Supervision and Curriculum Development.

Niedenthal, P. M., S. Krauth-Gruber and F. Ric (2006). *Psychology of Emotion: Interpersonal, Experiential, and Cognitive Approaches.* New York: Psychology Press.

Palmer, P.J. (1997). *The Courage to Teach: Exploring the Inner Landscape of a Teacher's Life.* San Francisco: Jossey-Bass Publishers.

Pestalozzi, J.H. (1894). *The Education of Man: Aphorisms.* New York: Philosophical Library.

Reimer, J., and S. Shavelson (eds.) (2008). *How Jewish Experiential Learning Works: An Anthology.* Boston, MA: Brandeis University Press.

Rousseau, J.J., and B. Foxley (trans.) (1762/1972). *Emile.* London: Everyman.

Roberts, J. W. (2012). *Beyond Learning by Doing*. New York: Routledge.

Sales, A. L., and L. Saxe (2002). *Limmud by the Lake: Fulfilling the Educational Potential of Jewish Summer Camps*. Center for Modern Jewish Studies, Brandeis University.

Schuck, R. F. (1981, March/April). "The Impact of Set Induction on Student Achievement and Retention." *The Journal of Educational Research* 74(4), 227–232. Retrieved from http://www.jstor.org/stable/27539820.

Sergiovanni, Thomas J. (1994). *Building Community in Schools*. San Francisco: Jossey-Bass.

Wenger, E., and J. Lave (1991). *Situated Learning: Legitimate Peripheral Participation*. New York: Cambridge University Press.

Wiles, J., and J. Bondi (1993). *Curriculum Development: A Guide to Practice* (4th ed.). New York: Merrill.

MEASURING SUCCESS: BETTER UNDERSTANDING EXPERIENTIAL JEWISH LEARNING

Bradley Solmsen

When it is successful, experiential Jewish education can help people develop an appetite for a lifetime of Jewish learning and exploration and at the same time create an environment within which powerful relationships are formed—relationships to other people, to our texts and to the Jewish calendar. The question this chapter will explore is: What strategies can we employ to know when experiential Jewish education is successful?

By definition experiential Jewish education is about the experience. The content or the cognitive is often secondary. This is not to say that the content is not important; it absolutely is. But if our education is experiential, then we have to pay attention first and foremost to the culture we are creating, the culture of learning.

Deborah Meier, in her book *The Power of Their Ideas*, paints a picture of a public school that helps its students develop habits of mind. The five habits of mind that Meier shares include the following:

1. Concern for evidence: How do you know that?
2. Viewpoint: Who said it and why?
3. Cause and effect: What led to it, and what else happened?
4. Hypothesizing: What if, supposing that?
5. Who cares? (41)

Meier's list does three things simultaneously. First, it presents a vision for a culture of learning. Second, it provides the educators and the learners with a framework—a map of sorts—with which to guide their learning. Third, it provides a clear mechanism to measure learning. I share this with you as one extremely powerful tool we might consider as we think about experiential Jewish education. What habits of mind might we want to articulate? What are the key questions we want to put in front of our educators and learners to be able to help them understand how to move forward on their journey of learning and how to know what they are getting out of this same journey?

Asking questions about measuring the success of experiential Jewish learning forces us to examine the foundations of our work. Our work must pass a challenging threefold litmus test:

1. How is the work experiential? Can we point to intentional experiences the learners are having?
2. What is the Jewish context or setting? Have we defined context or a milieu[1] with clear Jewish connections?
3. What are the participants learning?

Once we have answers to these three questions we can move forward with greater confidence in developing measurement strategies. If we have a difficult time answering one or more of these questions, it might indicate that we are not clear about what we are doing or that what we are doing is not necessarily experiential Jewish education. This is helpful information to have and respond to. The secret of measuring success is that it helps us at the very beginning of our work to make it clearer and stronger while

---

[1] Schwab, J. (1983). The Practical 4: Something for Curriculum Professors to Do." *Curriculum Inquiry*, vol. 13, no. 3, 240–265.

also helping us understand the outcomes of our work. This chapter will strive to help experiential Jewish educators get clarity on different approaches to measuring the outcomes of our work.

WHY MEASURE

It may seem fairly obvious why we would include a chapter on measuring success in a book about experiential Jewish education. Put simply, it's an opportunity to determine if we as educators are successful. But measurement and success, especially in relation to experiential Jewish education, are not necessarily easily defined or straightforward concepts. Many educators find themselves undertaking efforts to measure their work as a response to external forces: a supervisor, board or funder. While it is completely legitimate for various stakeholders to want to know the results of a given educational endeavor, my position is that measurement must start with the practitioner, and the most effective strategies for measurement are developed early on in the process of envisioning experiential Jewish education.

I want to suggest an approach to the measurement of experiential Jewish education that is practitioner-inspired and -designed. I first encountered the concept of measuring my work as something imposed upon me from the outside.

Measurement is most effective, and I would argue that education is most effective, when the educator is thinking about his or her strategy from the beginning of the planning and conception phases. In my practice, the measurement lenses I have employed help me to focus my goals at the earliest stages of planning and ask, "How do we tell if we are meeting our goals? What would success look/sound/feel like?" Experiential Jewish educators, who are frequently working with results that are not easily quantifiable, are even more dependent on having clearly articulated goals that can be measured in some way. The measurement process is crucial to help achieve this target.

If the practitioner is to weave the measurement agenda into his or her practice from the very outset, the experiential educator must be comfortable with the theory and practice of a variety of different forms of measurement. She needs to be trained in theory and methods (especially those most applicable to experiential Jewish education). The experiential Jewish educator needs to see measurement not as an intrusion and interruption at the end of her work but as a self-conceived, beneficial initial (and then ongoing) component of her work.

DEFINITIONS

What do we mean by measurement?

The easiest way to answer this question is to say that this chapter will focus on the question: How do we determine the extent to which we are meeting our goals? I am defining a goal as an outcome that can be measured in some way. For example, a goal might be: At the end of the program participants will have had meaningful conversations with peers they did not know before the program started. There are several different ways to determine if this goal has been met. Staff can create opportunities for these conversations to take place. Subsequently staff can observe the conversations and note who is speaking with whom. Participants can be asked to reflect on the conversations they have, and they can be given opportunities to take the initiative to seek out people with whom they want to speak. At the end of the program participants can be asked about this goal of the program in terms of the number of conversations they had, the nature of those conversations and what they learned (or took away) from the conversations.

An example of a goal that would be challenging to measure would be: By the end of the summer each participant's Jewish identity will be strengthened. Many Jewish educators (and our stakeholders) desperately want this to happen, and this type of goal is commonly found in early drafts of our planning work; however, it cannot be adequately measured, and therefore it does not fit our definition of a "kosher" goal.

Being serious about measurement means being serious about initial planning and goal setting. Clear goals allow for stronger programming. Staff better understand their work, learners better understand their roles and outcomes are easier to identify.

Up to this point I have tried to avoid using the terms "assessment" and "evaluation". Educators often use these terms interchangeably. On one hand, there is confusion about these concepts, which I will try to address here; on the other hand, I do not want to get distracted by too much theory, and instead I will focus on how we can learn about the outcomes of our practice, whether that be through evaluation or assessment approaches.

Assessment focuses on learning, educating and outcomes. It provides information for improving learning and educating. Assessment is an interactive process between participant and educator that informs the educator how well her participants are learning. The information is used by educators to make changes in the learning environment and is shared with participants to assist them in improving their learning habits.

Evaluation focuses on outcomes and may reflect components other than content and mastery level. These could include discussion, cooperation, attendance and verbal ability.[2]

Dimension	Assessment	Evaluation
Timing and Primary Purpose	Ongoing, to improve learning	Final, to gauge quality
Focus of measurement	Process-oriented: how learning is going	Product-oriented: what's been learned
Findings	Diagnostic: identify areas for improvement	Judgmental: arrive at an overall grade/score

To a practitioner, assessment feels as if it is the more appropriate methodology to measure experiential Jewish education. Experiential Jewish education tends to be more process-oriented, collaborative between learner and participant and iterative in terms of its development. However, it is vital that experiential Jewish education and its practitioners enthusiastically embrace evaluation alongside assessment as we think about measurement strategies. Why? For too long, experiential Jewish education has been viewed by some as lacking integrity and rigor. Veteran experiential Jewish educators know that their practice is substantial and impactful—what we need to do is demonstrate this clearly and irrefutably. This means we need to think about evaluation; we need to develop creative evaluation and assessment tools that complement our pedagogical methods. Only when we embrace both of these approaches to measurement will we be able to be clear about the efficacy of experiential Jewish education and make the strongest case for its role in a broad array of opportunities for learning.

WHAT ARE WE MEASURING?

The remainder of this chapter will focus on measuring the non-cognitive elements of experiential Jewish education. We need to do a better job of demonstrating how we help participants develop attitudes, change behaviors, grow spiritually and build relationships and how all of these things contribute to learning and to building a stronger Jewish community. Retention rates, rates of participation, participant satisfaction surveys, parent satisfaction surveys, influencer surveys, focus groups—these are all helpful pieces of data, but they do not necessarily contribute to learning the most about experiential Jewish education. We certainly will employ all of these techniques, but we also want to consider other elements that, combined with these tools, will allow us to become even clearer about what we are achieving and how we are achieving it.

What makes education Jewish?

---

[2] Angelo, T., and K.P. Cross 1993. *Classroom Assessment Techniques: A Handbook for College Teachers*, p. 42.

This question is challenging and vital to address in this chapter. I do not believe there is one answer, but I do believe that we as educators need to be able to articulate the Jewish substance within our work. I would suggest that our work have some connection to the established fields of the formation of identity, commitment, behavior, belief and relationship. We might not be doing all of these things at the same time, but certainly we need to be clear about what we are doing and how we are doing it.

Finally, it is helpful to distinguish between the concepts of education and learning. Education is the broader system of thinking about what is being taught, what is being learned and how (the pedagogy) this takes place. Learning is the process of understanding and meaning making a person goes through. I often find it helpful and more focused to concentrate on the learning process instead of on the larger, more complex question of education.

THE CHALLENGES

Measuring the success of *any* educational endeavor is challenging for experienced professionals, even under ideal circumstances. To arrive at measurements that are helpful, clear goals must be articulated from the outset. Additionally, a strategy for collecting data needs to be defined at the outset to accurately measure the extent to which goals are being met. Even when these two critical conditions are met there is debate among Jewish educators regarding how to best demonstrate success. For example, there are vigorous debates taking place today, in the wake of the No Child Left Behind Act and its successors, regarding how to determine if children are learning and how schools, teachers and administrators are performing. There is a growing movement of educators who want to place the emphasis not on test scores or even mastery of subject matter, but rather on helping learners build clearly defined habits of learning.[3]

If measuring the success of education overall is a challenge, measuring the outcomes of experiential Jewish education is even more challenging. Educators, organizations and stakeholders often look to (and sometimes make claims about) experiential Jewish education's ability to strengthen a person's identity, improve her Jewish commitments and help her build strong life-long relationships to practice, text and other people. Even once more specific goals are articulated, experiential Jewish educators face the challenge of demonstrating the value of engaging, powerful experiences. Indeed, if beliefs are challenged, new relationships formed and thinking deepened—all major ambitions of experiential education—these achievements will most likely have more long-term consequences and outcomes than short-term ones.

My goal here is not to intimidate. The more we understand the formidable challenges before us, the better equipped we will be to address them. Experiential Jewish educators need to be well prepared to face these challenges and to embrace the role of measuring our performance not as something painful and frightening, but rather as the way to demonstrate the power of our approaches, to better understand how to improve our practice and to reveal to our colleagues from different educational perspectives and practices the import of what we do and how we do it.

IMPLICATIONS FOR PRACTICE: SETTING GOALS

Setting goals seems obvious and is often taken for granted. We usually believe we have clear goals in our head and do not feel a need to write them down or share them with colleagues or stakeholders. We cannot measure our effectiveness or achievements without a clear set of written, shared goals.

The process of writing the goals down on paper accomplishes several things. First, it forces us to make sure we have thoroughly thought out what we want to do and to accomplish. Once written down, we can begin to ask the question, "How would we tell if we have met this goal?" If we cannot answer this question (that is often the case in the first iteration of goal setting) then we must go back and reexamine the goal, revise it or remove it. This can be a difficult and painful process of realizing that what we hoped to accomplish might be a challenge, need to change or impossible. But it is vital to explore this at the beginning of the process and not toward the end, only after the educational programming has taken place.

---

[3] Meier, D. (1995). *The Power of Their Ideas: Lessons for America from a Small School in Harlem.*

Second, we are able to bring key stakeholders into the educational process in a more meaningful way when our goals are transparent and clear. When considering a new educational endeavor, the organization and its leadership must define its goals. But the educators who will be facilitating the programming also must have an opportunity to both fully understand the goals and further define their own. Ideally the learners need to go through a similar process at the earliest possible stages of their involvement. We might not call it goal setting, but it is vital for all participants (the organization, its leadership, educators and learners and possibly other stakeholders as well) to have the opportunity to ask and answer the question, "Why are we doing this?" Once they have begun to answer this question they will need to explore the question, "How will we know if we are successful?"

From this perspective, thinking about goals is actually the first part of developing the actual educational program. It is the opportunity to engage all of the participants, and it is the set of tools we have to sharpen our ideas and make sure that there are tight connections between what we are thinking, saying and doing. In experiential Jewish education it is essential to have this solid framework in place to allow us to be as creative, improvisational and spontaneous as possible.

INTERVIEWS /ONE-ON-ONES

A structured or semi-structured interview may be the single best way to gather data in experiential Jewish learning settings. A structured interview is one that takes place with a standard set of questions (also known as a protocol) that have been determined in advance. The set of questions might be based on questions used in similar research, assessment or evaluation because they have proven to be effective in gathering a specific type of data. A semi-structured interview is one that begins with a standard set of questions but allows for (usually a specified set of) follow-up questions, also known as probes, that may vary based on the types of responses received. Interviews such as these are ideal for learning more about the process (assessment) of a given educational program, but when carried out according to appropriate standards, they are also more than acceptable for evaluation purposes. It is also possible for these interviews to be one-on-one or small groups (focus groups).

At this point I want to highlight several different ways in which I have used these techniques in my practice. After my first few summers at Brandeis University running experiential Jewish educational summer programs for high school students, it became clear to us that the educators we hired, as well as the participants who attended our programs, did not come with a strong sense of the main purposes of the program (the goals). We realized that the classic job interview (for staff)and the application process (for participants) were the first opportunities for us to begin the process of clarifying our intentions, measuring our impact and beginning to determine the goals of our staff and high school participants. For me, this initially defied logic; I did not realize how early in the process the measurement strategy needed to be employed. The leadership of the program had to gather data about who would be carrying out the program and what their background, perspectives and skills were. The facilitators and participants needed ample time to begin to consider what they would be doing within the framework of the program and how they would be doing it. The more advance notice we gave, the earlier we provided and collected information, the better we were at meeting our goals. Our job interview became a semi-structured interview. We had a standard set of questions and follow-up questions we asked all applicants. On the participant side, we were not able to actually interview the each individual, but each participant did have to answer two short essay questions as part of the application process. We saw these essay questions as opportunities to learn about the participants and, equally important, for them to learn about the program and our expectations.

At the very beginning of an educational program it is extremely helpful to learn about the attitudes and expectations of the learner. Many programs utilize pre-program questionnaires to collect quantitative and qualitative data, but it is also helpful to conduct pre-program or early program interviews. Again, the measurement strategy involves both gathering data and helping the learner or educator to clarify her own goals and anticipated outcomes. The program's strategy for measurement should include helping the educator and learner develop their own related strategies for measurement as well.

Interviews are often helpful midway through an educational program to help both the educator and learner reflect on progress and any changes that should be considered.

Finally, toward the conclusion of an educational program an interview can provide essential data as well as a critical opportunity for the learner and educator to reflect on what they have learned. This is where the semi-structured interview is crucial. The interviewer has the opportunity (some might say the obligation) to help the learner and/or the educator articulate what he or she has learned. A skilled interviewer will listen carefully for indications of evidence of learning—especially learning that might not be anticipated. Again, the final interview serves a two purposes by both providing data and solidifying the learning process. Measurement and data collection are not external to the learning process but fundamental parts of the learning process.

An example of semi-structured (or open-ended), established interview questions might be helpful to illustrate how the data collection process works. William Perry developed a model to assess intellectual development that has been successfully employed to assess experiential education in higher education and other settings. Initial questions used with college students to assess outcomes from experiential learning included:

1. What is your view of an ideal college education?
2. In a situation where information is not clear-cut, how do you go about making a decision?

A few questions such as these stretched into an intense hour of student talking as the interviewer probed with further questions, such as:

- How did you arrive at that view? Have you always felt that way?
- You said _____. What did you mean by that?
- If someone else decides differently, are they wrong? How would you view that person?
- What do you see as the relationship between knowledge and truth?[4]

Interviews are especially suitable for experiential Jewish learning settings. However, as with any strategy for data collection and measurement, the educator and others responsible for data collection need to be sensitive to the extent to which data is collected. We do not want to over-measure the subjects or the educators and risk measurement fatigue. When you develop the strategy for data collection and measurement it is vital to think about the number of points of data collection connected to a given program and the nature of those measures. Experiential Jewish educators and the people who collect data about experiential Jewish education must continue to challenge themselves to get more creative about how they collect their data in response to the concern that they might be over-collecting data.

EVALUATION AND REFLECTIVE PRACTICE/PD

Lee Shulman, a professor emeritus from Stanford University and past president of the Carnegie Foundation, believes that one way to gauge the efficacy of a school or other educational endeavor is the extent to which the organization creates a learning environment for its educators.[5] It is true that data can be collected and measured by external specialists or consultants (and I will discuss this in the following section), but I maintain that the nature of experiential Jewish education practically demands that the educator be the one to collect the data and conduct the measurement, or at least be an instrumental member of the measurement team. Experiential Jewish education, by definition, is extremely process-centered. In order for the educator and the learner to take full advantage of educational experiences, the educator and learner must be part of the measurement process. The measurement process should

---

[4] Pavelich, M.J., and W.S. Moore,"Measuring the Effect of Experiential Education Using the Perry Model," *Journal of Engineering Education*, October 1996, 287–292, p. 289.

[5] Shulman, L. S. (1988). "Teaching Alone, Learning Together: Needed Agendas for the New Reforms." Moore, J.H., and T. J. Sergiovanni (eds.), *Schooling for Tomorrow: Directing Reforms to Issues That Count.* p. 166.

ideally be co-generated on some level between leadership, educators and learners. This goes a long way toward ensuring that goals are clear and clearly measured.

Educators and learners in experiential (Jewish) settings need the opportunity to apply what they are learning to their work. This means having the time and structure to reflect on new information and incorporate it into learning experiences. Similarly, it is extremely beneficial for educators and learners in experiential settings to have opportunities for iterative processes. Simply put, the chance to repeat an experiential learning program and apply what they learned from previous programs is essential. One step further involves establishing an environment in which educators and learners can collaborate with one another, provide feedback and ask critical questions about their practice and learning. At this stage the process of measurement can become a full-blown opportunity for in-service professional development for educators. Educators can stretch this process even further by defining questions for investigations of their work while they are educating. This results in several layers of measurement: Educators measure the work they are doing as educators with their learners, and they measure themselves against larger meta-questions regarding their practice. Experiential Jewish learning must be built upon a foundation that includes learning opportunities for our educators that are also carefully measured. In fact, I believe it is easier to measure the success and effectiveness of our staff learning than our students' learning, and that if our educators are learning while they are teaching, it virtually guarantees that our students will be meaningfully engaged as well.

"By engaging teachers, small schools stand a chance to engage their students, too. As we become capable of being strong, powerful, lifelong learners and citizens of our schools, so too will our students stand a better chance of being lifelong learners and citizens of a free society."[6]

The larger educational organization will have its own defined goals and strategy for measuring them, the educators will define their own goals as well as meta-questions about their practice and the onion will get peeled when the culture of measurement is introduced to the learner who considers why she has taken part in a given experience and what she has learned from it. Only then will it become abundantly clear to all involved that we are always learning and that our experiences can provide us with some of the most valuable lessons in life if we employ the tools needed to pay careful attention to them.

WHO IS COLLECTING THE DATA

The question "Who is collecting the data and doing the measuring?" is a vital component of the overall measurement strategy. As I have written earlier, I have found it to be ideal when the educators serve as the data collectors and facilitators of measurement. There are many legitimate reasons to consider alternative approaches to the question of who is collecting the data and facilitating the measurement strategy. First, practitioner-based data collection and measurement is demanding. The educators must be trained, experienced and supervised in these areas. Even when educators are well prepared, the organizational leadership must consider the demands on the educators' time and their priorities. While I believe that this more holistic approach leads to more effective practice and outcomes, it might not always be feasible.

When the educators are not involved in data collection and measurement there are at least two additional models worth considering. First, it is common and sometimes required to work with an outside specialist to collect and interpret data. Often funders or grants require the participation of an evaluator or assessment professional who is an independent consultant not part of your educational team. I have encountered many misconceptions about working with outside measurement consultants. While they are meant to be more objective and removed from the direct educational team, it is still vital to engage this professional early in the design process of your work—as early as possible. The earlier this external member of your team is involved, the better she will understand the foundations of your work. This understanding and early involvement will allow the consultant to develop the most appropriate strategies for both data collection and review. All too often educators begin the process of searching for

---

[6] Meier, D. (1995). *The Power of Their Ideas: Lessons for America from a Small School in Harlem.*

an outside consultant only after the program has been fully designed and is about to be implemented. This is a disservice to the consultant, the program and the measurement process.

A third approach is a hybrid of these first two directions. It is possible to work with an outside consultant to help train the educational staff about data collection and interpretation as a part of their educational work. This approach might be employed when a funder demands an external consultant and you still want to involve your staff in the process. This approach is also helpful when you are working with a staff that might be less familiar with data collection and interpretation methods.

CONCLUSION

We know in our guts, anecdotally and—now more clearly than ever—through emerging data analysis and research that experiential Jewish learning is a powerful, essential force. We have more work to do to help experiential Jewish educators become more comfortable measuring the impact of their own work. I hope this chapter has helped move this conversation forward and has made the point clearly that measurement is not separate from experiential Jewish learning but a core component of quality experiential Jewish learning.

Jewish educators need to continue to strive to articulate their goals as precisely as possible in ways that make sense first to themselves, then to all of their stakeholders. This is the starting point for impactful experiential Jewish learning. Jewish educators today must insist on a chair at the table when the measurement conversations are taking place. We should no longer fear measurement but see it as a crucial tool for improving our work and the larger field. Our organizations must understand that the educator is an essential member of the measurement team, even when outside consultants are being utilized.

Experiential Jewish learning often places an emphasis on asking the best questions as opposed to finding the right answers. Measurement, evaluation and assessment all revolve around this focus on the key questions. Our educational institutions, our educators and our learners will all benefit from this rededication to asking hard questions about our practice in an effort to do the best work possible.

REFERENCES

Angelo, T., and K.P. Cross (1993). *Classroom Assessment Techniques: A Handbook for College Teachers*. San Francisco: Jossey-Bass.

Apple, D., S. Beyerlein, S. Carroll and M. Ford. "The Learning Assessment Journal As a Tool for Structured Reflection in Process Education." Unknown.

Cohen, R., and S. Rosenblatt, S. "Evaluation 101: Evaluating Jewish Youth Programs." Retrieved from http://www.jesna.org/home/156-articles/649-evaluation-101-evaluating-jewish- youth-programs.

Ghere, G, J.A. King, J. Minnema and L. Stevahn (2001). "Toward a Taxonomy of Essential Evaluator Competencies." *American Journal of Evaluation*, Vol. 22, No. 2, 229–247.

Goldenberg, M., and K. Soule (2011). "How Group Experience Affects Outcomes from NOLS Programs: A Means-End Investigation." *The Journal of Experiential Education*, Volume 33, Issue 4, 393–397.

Gosen, J., and J. Washbush (2004). "A Review of Scholarship on Assessing Experiential Learning Effectiveness." *Simulation and Gaming*, Vol. 35, No. 2, 270–293.

Henry, M. E., E.R. McKinney-Prupis, L.M. Molee and V.I. Sess (2010). "Assessing Learning in Service-Learning Courses Through Critical Reflection." *Journal of Experiential Education*, Volume 33, No. 3, 239–257.

Isaacs, L. W., and W.J. Rosov (2008). "Program Evaluation in Jewish Education." In L. D. Bloomberg, P. A. Flexner & R.L. Goodman (eds.), *What We Know about Jewish Education* (517–526). Los Angeles: Torah Aura Productions.

Luo, H. (2010). "The Role for an Evaluator: A Fundamental Issue for Evaluation of Education and Social Programs." *International Education Studies* Vol. 3, No. 2, 42–50.

Meier, D. (1995). *The Power of Their Ideas: Lessons for America from a Small School in Harlem*. Boston: Beacon Press.

Moore, W. S. and M.J. Pavelich (1996). "Measuring the Effect of Experiential Education Using the Perry Model." *Journal of Engineering Education* Volume 85, Issue 4, 287–292.

Schwab, J. (1983). "The Practical 4: Something for Curriculum Professors to Do," *Curriculum Inquiry* vol. 13, no. 3, 240–265.

Shulman, L. S. (1988). "Teaching Alone, Learning Together: Needed Agendas for the New Reforms." In J. H. Moore and T. J. Sergiovanni (eds.), *Schooling for Tomorrow: Directing Reforms to Issues That Count* (166–187). Boston: Allyn and Bacon.

SECTION 2:
WHO ARE EXPERIENTIAL JEWISH EDUCATORS?

SKILLS AND CHARACTERISTICS
OF EXPERIENTIAL JEWISH EDUCATORS

Daniel Held

I carry clear memories of my camp counselors. Elliott had a magical way of setting original stories to classical music. Each night at lights out he would read a chapter, weaving his words with the movement of the music playing in the background. The cliffhanger at the end of the reading left us hounding him with questions throughout the next day. Jonah imbued Jewish curiosity. When he returned from a day off with a new poncho he wondered aloud if he needed to put *tzitzit* on the four-cornered garment. The next night, after lights out, we went to the library and learned the *halakha* with one of the camp educators. Ofer, a *shaliach*, only spoke to us in Hebrew. It still isn't clear to me if this was clever pedagogy or a demonstration of his poor English. At the start of the summer we couldn't understand him, but with enough repetition and charades, by the end of the summer his mealtime requests in Hebrew for the milk or napkins to be passed down the dining hall table were clear, even to those with no prior Hebrew.

Two decades after my experience as a camper, I look back and wonder what was special about these counselors. What personal characteristics enabled them to engage young learners, and what skills and knowledge helped enliven the learning of camp? While the examples I cite above are of camp counselors, the same questions can be asked of experiential educators in other settings—youth movements and Hillels, travel experiences and service learning.

This chapter has two goals. First, through a close read of the literature I seek an understanding of the educators who enliven experiential education—to understand them, their work and the skills and characteristics that catalyze success. While the literature focused specifically on experiential Jewish educators is sparse, the chapter will draw upon what literature does exists to build upon Chazan's (2003) characteristics of informal Jewish educators. Second, the chapter will consider the contemporary scene. What new roles do experiential educators play, and how does a description of the skills and characteristics of the contemporary educator layer upon Chazan's description from a decade ago?

WHAT DO WE KNOW ABOUT EXPERIENTIAL EDUCATORS?

The last quarter century has borne unprecedented growth of participation, investment and research in experiential Jewish education. The overwhelming majority of this research, however, has focused on the experience of the learner, as researchers investigate the impact of these programs on Jewish identity and the efficacy of such investments for strengthening Jewish continuity. Most of what has been written about the educators who animate experiential learning takes the form of peripheral anecdotes and narrative comments in articles focused on other issues.

Among the early works describing experiential educators is Bernie Reisman's (1990) report to the Commission on Jewish Education. The report offers a snapshot of the field at a critical moment in history—shortly before the release of the 1990 National Jewish Population Survey, and before it underwent significant growth and investment. There Reisman draws a distinction between part-time and full-time professionals.

Part-time experiential educators work a few hours each week throughout the year. They may be youth movement advisors or youth directors or hold jobs in synagogues or day schools. Like part-time staff, seasonal educators work full-time for short periods, usually in immersive programs during school vacations. These may be summer camp counselors, *Taglit*-Birthright Israel *madrikhim* or educators in various service learning or travel programs. Part-time and seasonal staff make up the vast majority of front-line experiential educators. While in most cases they play the central role in running experiential activities, they usually have little formal training and are often planning, or already working in, careers in unrelated fields.

Full-time educators, as Reisman describes, enter the field from a variety of educational and professional backgrounds—rabbis and educators, lawyers and business people, social workers and others. The unifying theme among these educators "lies in the area of methodology, a way of working with people sometimes referred to as 'process'" (p. 7). In most cases there is an inverse relationship between the hours worked and the level of front-line engagement—the more full-time one becomes, the less direct contact one has with students. In addition to educative work, full-time experiential educators have a wide range of administrative responsibilities, from budgeting to development, recruitment to physical plant.

Tracking how many experiential educators work full-time and how many are part-time or seasonal staff is difficult. In the 1998 Youth Professional Study commissioned for the North American Alliance for Jewish Youth (Sales, 1998) 79% of respondents were full-time employees and 21% part-time, defined as employed for 35 hour per week or fewer. According to a 2011 study of New York Jewish teen engagement (Sales, et al., 2011), 51% of teen engagement practitioners are full-time employees and 49% are part-time. These figures, however, are only demonstrative of those who completed the respective surveys—a task more likely to be completed by full-time than part-time employees.

While a deeper exploration of the work of full-time experiential educators would facilitate a fuller conception of experiential education as a field and as a profession, for the purposes of this chapter the focus will remain on the skills and characteristics needed for the interactive process of teaching and learning in experiential education—a task taken up primarily by part-time and seasonal staff.

STARTING WITH CHAZAN

While Chazan's (2003) Philosophy of Informal Jewish Education is not the first work defining experiential education, it does offer a good starting point for this chapter. Chazan's first seven characteristics of informal education describe an approach to pedagogy: person-centered education, the centrality of experience, a curriculum of Jewish experiences and values, an interactive process, the group experience, the "culture" of Jewish education and an education that engages. It is the final characteristic, "informal Jewish education's holistic education," that shifts the focus of his work away from philosophies and pedagogies and onto the educator. The section reads:

INFORMAL JEWISH EDUCATION'S HOLISTIC EDUCATOR

The informal Jewish educator is a total educational personality who educates by words, deeds and by shaping a culture of Jewish values and experiences. He/she is a person-centered educator whose focus is on learners and whose goal is their personal growth. The informal Jewish educator is a shaper of Jewish experiences. His/her role in this context is to create opportunities for those experiences and to facilitate the learner's entry into the moments. The informal Jewish educator promotes interaction and interchange. One of his/her major tasks is to create an environment that enables this interactivity to flourish. This requires proficiency in the skills of asking questions, listening and activating the engagement of others.

The informal Jewish educator is a creator of community and *kehillah:* he/she shapes the aggregate into a group and utilizes the group setting to teach such core Jewish values as *klal Yisrael* (Jewish peoplehood), *kvod haadam* (the dignity of all people), *shutfut goral* (shared destiny) and *shivyon* (equality). Informal Jewish educators are creators of culture; they are sensitive to all the elements specific to the educational setting so that these will reflect values and experiences they wish to convey. The task in this instance is to make every decision—big or little—an educational decision. Informal Jewish educators must be able to engage those with whom they work and make their learning experience enjoyable. The stimulation of positive associations is part of the informal Jewish educator's work. Finally, the informal Jewish educator needs to be an educated and committed Jew. This educator must be knowledgeable, since one of the values he/she comes to teach is *talmud torah*—Jewish knowledge. He/she must be committed to these values, since teaching commitment to the Jewish people, to Jewish life and Jewish values is at the heart of the enterprise. Commitment can only be learned if one sees examples of it up close (Chazan, 2003).

In two paragraphs it is impossible to fully explicate the multifaceted work of these educators, as well as the skills and characteristics needed to be effective. As a result, "informal Jewish education's holistic educator" reads like a long laundry list of the idealized educator. In one breath Chazan argues that the educator must be a creator of community and a shaper of individualized experiences, a person-centered educator and a facilitator of group interaction and exchange, an educated Jew and one committed to Jewish values. While Chazan's listing is helpful, each statement can offer only the *dibur ha-Matkhil*, the opening words, on topics that need greater interpretation. To begin this work this chapter now offers a brief overview of the literature related to experiential educators and will use these writings as fodder to produce a commentary on Chazan.

REFINING CHAZAN THROUGH OTHER WRITINGS

Reimer (2003), in responding to Chazan's work, zooms in on one of the eight characteristics: the centrality of experience. Reimer returns to Dewey and emphasizes the role of the educator in shaping experience, challenging learners, offering interpretation and narrative to these experiences and encouraging reflection and meaningful conversation. Reimer writes, "If experience is not simply what happened, but what we make of what happened, then whoever helps construct the narrative interpretation is educating. This activity is not teaching or even modeling. It is the more basic educational work of helping to provide an interpretive lens through which one views the social world."

This role is echoed by Bryfman (2011), who demonstrates that experiential Jewish education is "purposeful learning that occurs when an educator and learner interact, and that causes learners to experience something for themselves" (773). The purposefulness of this interaction speaks to the planning and intentionality of the learning. Moreover, the centrality of the learner's personal experience as the source of interpretation and meaning making differentiates experiential learning from other forms of education in which one learns from the experience of another—a textbook, teacher, etc.

The skills drawn out by Reimer (2003) and Bryfman (2011) are twofold. At once the educator must plan and execute activities that will actively involve the learner in the experience, while at the same time framing reflections, pushing the learner to draw on his own bank of experiences and emotions in interpreting the activity. The educator must be both a theatre director staging an educational experience and a facilitator of reflection, driving participants to make meaning of the crafted experience by considering their own feelings and history in relation to those of others.

Bekerman (2006) describes this facilitative role as the core work of the experiential educator. In contrast to classroom settings, where the teacher develops a bilateral discussion pattern, the experiential educator's primary skill lies in building a multi-directional group process. The facilitator is required to develop a sense of trust among the group, ask probing questions, actively listen, and help participants learn from one another. In describing the work of Israeli Zionist educators, Bekerman highlights their focus on process over content, developing trust and relationship as a prerequisite for delving into deeper issues and ideas.

Zeldin (1989), too, sees the work of the experiential educator as broader than content alone. Comparing the work of NFTY youth group advisors and religious schools teachers, Zeldin tests a framework to differentiate between formal and experiential education. While in a school the teacher is the central authority, in experiential learning the educator works to share power among the teachers and learners. Similarly, while the formal educator's focus is the teaching of content—the overt curriculum—the experiential educator has an eye toward the hidden curriculum, including social interaction, aesthetics and social and emotional learning. Moreover, Zeldin demonstrates that the experiential educator pays close attention to the minutiae of culture, language and aesthetics to create an environment ripe for experiential learning. From the arrangement of chairs to the menu, the experiential educator recognizes the influence of seemingly mundane factors on learning.

In their study of residential summer camps, Sales and Saxe (2004) describe camp counselors as "the essential key to Jewish life and learning at camp" (97). They demonstrate that both the buy-in and ability of staff to craft a Jewish environment are prerequisites for the rich experiences in Jewish education and socialization to which these settings aspire. When counselors are committed to the Jewish mission and have the knowledge and skills to enliven the Jewish nature of the environment, magic can happen. When they adopt a lackadaisical attitude or lack the knowledge and skills to turn ordinary moments into teachable moments, the camp's educational role can flounder.

Sales and Saxe debate whether the human resource cup of camp is half full or half empty. On one hand, they found that the great majority of staff has been active in youth movements, previously attended or worked at summer camps and have traveled to Israel. More that 75% of those surveyed believe that they know enough to serve as Jewish role models for their campers, and 50% have taken a Jewish studies course in the last two years. At the same time, however, Sales and Saxe note that one quarter of Jewish staff at camp lack these backgrounds and commitment, and an equal number do not know enough to be "real Jewish role models".

To contrast the Jewish knowledge of camp counselors with those year-round teen engagement practitioners who responded to the New York Teen Engagement Study (Sales, 2011), the year-round educators hold higher levels of education; 37% attended Jewish day school or yeshiva for an average of ten years; 70% attended part-time Jewish school for nine years, and only 7% report no formal Jewish education.

As demonstrated by Chazan and others, a measure of knowledge, however, is not enough. While Sales and Saxe (2004) and Sales et al. (2011) measure prior experiences as learners in Jewish settings, educators must have solid Judaic content knowledge and must be able to translate their own learning into activities, lessons and teachable moments that both engage and challenge their campers. In this regard experiential educators must be Jewishly knowledgeable, strong pedagogues and motivated to apply their knowledge and skills to work with learners.

In many respects, this last piece is the most challenging. Since experiential educators hold the dual role, as Sales and Saxe describe, of teacher and friend, without strong motivation and educational vision it is often easier for the educator to emphasize the recreational elements of camp and other settings of experiential learning and deemphasize the educational program. To this end, in addition to strong Judaic knowledge and skills as a creator of experience and facilitator of reflection, motivation and self-assuredness as an educator are key characteristics of the successful educator.

A COMMENTARY ON CHAZAN

With a review of some of the literature relating to experiential Jewish educators, we can circle back to Chazan's two paragraphs on informal Jewish education's holistic educator and attempt to write the *Rashi* for his *Diburai ha-Matikhil,* the commentaries for his opening words:

(Text from image above copied below)

Total educational personality: When hiring an experiential educator we are not merely hiring a pedagogue but also a *Dugma Ishit*, a personal example. In addition to teaching through planned lessons and activities, the experiential educator models action and thought. Especially in immersive environments such as camps and travel programs, the modeling of actions such as caring and religious practice, are paramount. When hiring, we look for alignment between the mission and vision of the program and the educator himself. The complex role of this near-peer *dugma ishit* is drawn out in Sales and Saxe's (2004) description of the camp counselor. Educates by words and deeds: The experiential educator sees learning not as a series of didactic lessons, but as a holistic experience including the creation of cultural and interpersonal norms (Zeldin). As such the ways the educator communicates – through words, writing and body – are key elements of his pedagogy in creating normative culture and teaching values. Person-centered educator: The experiential educator sees each individual as an ends rather than a means. Education is created to support the individual in his growth and to shape his personal journey. The experiential educator not only customizes learning by offering choice in the content and modalities of learning, but personalizes it by placing the learner and his experiences, emotions and personal growth at the center. See Gilmore and Dine (2000) for more on personalization.

Shaper of Jewish experiences: The focus of Reimer (2003) and Bryfman's (2011) understanding of experiential learning, the experiential educator both crafts educative experiences and facilitates the learner's use of prior experiences as fodder for learning. To shape experience, the educator must be able to put himself in the shoes of the learner, to consider what he will see, hear, feel and learn while imagining what prior experiences he may use to contextualize the learning. Key to the use of experience is opportunity for the learner to reflect on and make meaning of the experience for himself both individually and within the group context. Promotes interaction and interchange: The experiential educator is an expert facilitator of productive and provocative dialogue using discussion as a tool for personal reflection and meaning making and as a means to learn from the experiences of others. Beckerman (2006) builds on this concept in his description of the Israeli Zionist educators and their facilitation of group discussions. Create an environment: A set designer, stage manager, prop master, time keeper, chef, and marriage counselor, Zeldin demonstrates that the experiential educator thinks intentionally about details such as the physical environment, nutrition, variety and timing of meals, pacing, and inter-personal relationships in order to shape an environment most conducive to

Informal Jewish education's holistic educator.

The informal Jewish educator is a total educational personality who educates by words, deeds, and by shaping a culture of Jewish values and experiences. He/she is a person-centered educator whose focus is on learners and whose goal is their personal growth. The informal Jewish educator is a shaper of Jewish experiences. His/her role in this context is to create opportunities for those experiences and to facilitate the learner's entry into the moments. The informal Jewish educator promotes interaction and interchange. One of his/her major tasks is to create an environment that enables this interactivity to flourish. This requires proficiency in the skills of asking questions, listening, and activating the engagement of others.

The informal Jewish educator is a creator of community and *kehilla*: he/she shapes the aggregate into a group and utilizes the group setting to teach such core Jewish values as *klal Yisrael* (Jewish peoplehood), *kvod haadam* (the dignity of all people), *shutfut goral* (shared destiny), and *shivyon* (equality). Informal Jewish educators are creators of culture; they are sensitive to all the elements specific to the educational setting so that these will reflect values and experiences they wish to convey. The task in this instance is to make every decision—big or little—an educational decision. Informal Jewish educators must be able to engage those with whom they work and make their learning experience enjoyable. The stimulation of positive associations is part of the informal Jewish educator's work. Finally, the informal Jewish educator needs to be an educated and committed Jew. This educator must be knowledgeable since one of the values he/she comes to teach is *talmud torah*—Jewish knowledge. He/she must be committed to these values since teaching commitment to the Jewish people, to Jewish life, and Jewish values is at the heart of the enterprise. Commitment can only be learned if one sees examples of it up close.

sees recreation as an element of education. Reimer and Bryfman (2008) place recreation as the foundation of their taxonomy of experiential learning. The educator himself engages in the recreational activities, building relationships and culture through games of Frisbee, late night chats, and integrates humor and enjoyment through educational activities. Educator must be knowledgeable: Because of the dynamic nature of experiential learning, the educator must be ready to shape and reshape the infusion of Jewish content to meet the particulars of the experience. Jewish knowledge used in experiential education is not limited to particular fields – Tanach, Hebrew, History, Zionism, Prayer – but is integrated. To this end, the educator must have both a breadth and a depth of Judaic knowledge. Committed to these values: The experiential educator is an authentic model of Jewish values. Linking back to the first of Chazan's *Diburei Hamatchil* the educator must be committed to the particular vision and philosophy of the program and institution

learning. Asking questions, listening, and activating the engagement of others: Facilitation is not merely ensuring the flow of conversation, but driving it to challenge participants to explore new thoughts and engage in the process of learning. The educator guides both planned and impromptu conversations, punctuating them with probing questions, synthesis, and idea-tracking. Moreover, as noted by Beckerman (2006), these important tasks require the creation of trust as a prerequisite. Creator of community: Placing an emphasis on the socialization of participants into a cohesive, unified unit, the educator builds community around values, rituals and culture conducive to the vision and philosophy of the program. Reimer and Bryfman (2008) expand on this through their description of recreation, socialization and challenge. Teach core Jewish values: While the curricula of Jewish experiential education are diverse, ever-present is the curriculum of Jewish values, taught both overtly and through modeling. Sensitive to all the elements specific to the educational setting: From the placement of chairs to the timing of meals, from the design of source sheets to the make up of groups, the experiential educator makes educational decisions based on a complex and dynamic set variables. To the greatest extent possible, the experiential educator seeks to anticipate, pre-plan and control these variables in order to shape the strongest educational experiences possible. (Zeldin) Make every decision—big or little—an educational decision: While pre-planning is essential to the creation of an educational setting, the educator is flexible to make calm thought-through on-the-spot decisions with educational goals in mind as variables change. When possible, the educators takes time to 'STAR' – Stop, Think, Act, and Reflect. Engage those with whom they work: Experiential learning is active and interactive. Educators must make the learning engaging in order to encourage high levels of participation. As Reimer (2007) would say in the name of Mihaly Csikszentmihalyi, experiential learning must push the learner into a state of flow, a state in which the learner is immersed in a feeling of energized focus, full involvement, and a sense of success in the process of the activity. Make their learning experience enjoyable: The experiential educator knows that experiential learning is often voluntary (Chazan, 2003). To this end, realizing the importance of group cohesion, comfort and participant buy-in, the educator

The informal Jewish educator is a **total educational personality** who **educates by words and deeds** and by shaping a culture of Jewish values and experiences. He/she is a **person-centered educator** whose focus is on learners and whose goal is their personal growth. The informal Jewish educator is **a shaper of Jewish experiences**. His/her role in this context is to create opportunities for those experiences and to facilitate the learner's entry into the moments. The informal Jewish educator **promotes interaction and interchange**. One of his/her major tasks is to **create an environment** that enables this interactivity to flourish. This requires proficiency in the **skills of asking questions, listening and activating the engagement of others**.

The informal Jewish educator is a **creator of community** and *kehillah:* he/she shapes the aggregate into a group and utilizes the group setting **to teach such core Jewish values** as *klal Yisrael* (Jewish peoplehood), *kvod ha-adam* (the dignity of all people), *shutfut goral* (shared destiny) and *shivyon* (equality). Informal Jewish educators are creators of culture; they are **sensitive to all the elements specific to the educational setting** so that these will reflect values and experiences they wish to convey. The task in this instance is to **make every decision—big or little—an educational decision**. Informal Jewish educators must be able to engage those with **whom they work** and **make their learning experience enjoyable**. The stimulation of positive associations is part of the informal Jewish educator's work. Finally, the informal Jewish educator needs to be an educated and committed Jew. This **educator must be knowledgeable,** since one of the values he/she comes to teach is *talmud torah*— Jewish knowledge. He/she must be **committed to these values,** since teaching commitment to the Jewish people, Jewish life and Jewish values is at the heart of the enterprise. Commitment can only be learned if one sees examples of it up close.

Total educational personality: When hiring an experiential educator we are not merely hiring a pedagogue but also a *dugma ishit*, a personal example. In addition to teaching through planned lessons and activities, the educator models action and thought. Especially in immersive environments, the modeling of caring and religious practice are paramount. We look for alignment between the mission and vision of the program and the educator himself. The complex role of this near-peer *dugma ishit* is drawn out in Sales and Saxe's (2004) description of the camp counselor. **Educates by words and deeds:** The experiential educator sees learning not as a series of didactic lessons, but as a holistic experience including the creation of cultural and interpersonal norms (Zeldin, 1989). As such, the ways the educator communicates—through words, writing and body—are key elements of his pedagogy. **Person-centered educator:** The experiential educator not only customizes learning by offering choice but personalizes it by placing the learner and his experiences, emotions and personal growth at the center (Gilmore and Pine, 2000). **Shaper of Jewish experiences:** The experiential educator both crafts educative experiences and facilitates the learner's use of prior experiences as fodder for learning (Reimer, 2003) To shape experience, the educator must be able to put himself in the shoes of the learner, to consider what he will see, hear, feel and learn, while imagining what prior experiences he may use to contextualize the learning. **Promotes interaction and interchange:** The experiential educator is an expert facilitator of productive and provocative dialogue, using discussion as a tool for personal reflection and meaning making and as a means to learn from the experiences of others (Bekerman, 2006). **Asking questions, listening and activating the engagement of others:** Facilitation is not merely ensuring the flow of conversation, but driving it to challenge participants to explore new thoughts and engage in the process of learning. The educator guides both planned and impromptu conversations, punctuating them with probing questions, synthesis and idea-tracking. These important tasks require the creation of trust as a prerequisite (Bekerman, 2006). **Creator of community:** Placing an emphasis on the socialization of participants into a cohesive, unified unit, the educator builds community around shared values, rituals and culture conducive to the vision and philosophy of the program. Reimer and Bryfman (2008) expand on this through their description of recreation, socialization and challenge. **Sensitive to all the elements specific to the educational setting:** Zeldin demonstrates that the experiential educator is a set designer, stage manager, prop master, timekeeper, chef and interior designer. The experiential educator thinks intentionally and plans for details such as the physical environment, nutrition and timing of meals, pacing and interpersonal relationships in order to shape an environment most conducive to learning (Zeldin, 1989). **Make every decision—big or little—an educational decision:** While meticulous planning is essential to the creation of an educational setting, the educator is flexible to make calm, thought-through-on-the-spot decisions with educational goals in mind. When possible, the educators takes time to 'STAR'—Stop, Think, Act, and Reflect. **Engage those with whom they work:** Experiential learning is active and interactive. Educators make the learning engaging in order to encourage high levels of participation. Citing Csikszentmihalyl, Reimer (2007) states that experiential learning pushes the learner into a state of flow in which the learner is immersed in a feeling of energized focus, full involvement and a sense of success in the process of the activity. **Make their learning experience enjoyable:** Experiential learning is often voluntary (Chazan, 2003). Realizing the importance of group cohesion, trust, comfort and participant buy-in, the educator sees recreation as a cornerstone of education (Reimer and Bryfman 2008). The educator himself engages in recreational activities, building relationships, trust and culture during games of Frisbee and late-night chats. **Educator must be knowledgeable:** Because of the dynamic nature of experiential learning, the educator must be ready to shape and reshape the infusion of Jewish content to meet the particulars of the experience. Jewish knowledge used in experiential education is not limited to particular domains—*Tanakh*, Hebrew, History, Zionism, Prayer–but is integrative. To this end, the educator must have both a breadth and a depth of Judaic knowledge. **Committed to these values:** The experiential educator is an authentic model of Jewish values. Linking back to the first of Chazan's *Diburei Ha-Matkhil,* the educator must model the particular vision and philosophy of the program and institution.

WHAT'S MISSING?

Absent from the both literature and Chazan's description is discussion of the hard skills used by experiential educators. From budgeting to the use of Facebook, time management to graphic design, human resources to physical plant management, computer savvy to basic first aid, the list of hard skills required is diverse. While further research is required to determine exactly what hard skills are needed by which educators, these are specific skills that can be catalogued and taught.

More difficult to define and even more challenging to teach, certain personal characteristics and qualities empower successful experiential educators to build connections with participants, bring cohesion to a group and facilitate a learning process built around experience, reflection and meaning making.

In selecting corps members, Teach For America tests for eight criteria believed to be linked to success in the classroom: prior personal achievement, organizational ability, motivational ability, respect for others, leadership experience, perseverance, critical thinking ability and fit with the Teach for America mission *(http://www.teachforamerica.org/why-teach-for-america/who-we-look-for)*. In studying the correlation between these characteristics and student learning, Dobbie (2011) found that "a teacher's prior achievement, leadership experience and perseverance are associated with student gains in math. Leadership experience and commitment to the TFA mission are associated with gains in English. The TFA admissions measures are also associated with improved classroom behavior" (11). In a vein similar to TFA's work in identifying the characteristics that make for successful teachers, studying the personal characteristics and traits of experiential educators will buttress our efforts to recruit, train and retain high-quality educators.

THE NEW JEWISH EDUCATORS: SKILLS AND CHARACTERISTICS OF THE TWENTY-FIRST CENTURY

In creating his characteristics of informal Jewish education, Chazan used a process called generic-type analysis to parse out characteristics common to settings colloquially called "informal education". As a result, the skills and characteristics he outlines offer descriptions of experiential educators in roles that have existed for decades—youth movement advisors and camp counselors, JCC educators and Israel trip staff. While increased thought and reflection have infused these settings with a more critical eye on the skills and characteristics required of their staff, in many cases the roles have not changed significantly from those that were envisioned decades ago.

The twenty-first century has borne new roles and responsibilities for many experiential educators, new thinking about the skills and characteristics required for their work and new nomenclature to describe the work. Adene Sacks (2007) of the Jim Joseph Foundation notes that as the foundation surveyed the field, she found that a number of professionals used terms such as "translators" and "connectors" instead of describing themselves as educators. Sacks offers definitions for each of these skills.

> **Connectors:** Connectors, by virtue of knowing many people in a diversity of subcultures, bring people together to disseminate new ideas and connections. Jewish connectors link non-engaged constituents into a network of (presumably Jewish) people and Jewish–oriented activities/conversations. The network can be institutionally driven or not. Key to the connector and to the network is the focus on a platform and delivery, often bringing non-engaged constituents of the community into Jewish engagement through non-traditional, non-institutional access points (Malcolm Gladwell, *The Tipping Point)*.

> **Translators:** Translators broaden the definition of what it is to "be" Jewish or to "do" Jewish. Using Gladwell's construct, the translator is a "maven" or someone who brings esoteric expertise and authority to the table. Key to the translators in a Jewish context is an emphasis on integration of the particular (Judaism) and the universal (everything else). Most commonly the translator acts as a link between the engaged individual's primary identity (activist, environmentalist, atheist, etc.) and Judaism—and typically translators themselves have strong roots and skills in both worlds (Sacks, 2007).

Two new positions, both funded by the Jim Joseph Foundation and both in their nascent forms, embody these characteristics: Hillel's Senior Jewish Educators (SJEs) and BBYO's Directors of Jewish Enrichment (DJEs). By examining the job descriptions of these educators, a deeper understanding of the skills and characteristics of the new educators can be derived.

Hillel's Senior Jewish Educators seek to build relationship with college students who are otherwise unconnected to Jewish life on campus. By doing so the SJEs help students explore, through a Jewish lens, the "big questions" associated with the stage of life called emerging adulthood (Parks, 2000). In looking to fill such a position Hillel seeks an individual who is:

1. **An Authentic Jewish personality**—the Senior Jewish Educator will be a living model of how to live an integrated Jewish life and will be able to inspire students, through his or her own story, to make Judaism integral to their own life choices and expressed Jewish values.

2. **A Relationship Builder**—The Senior Jewish Educator will be capable of building rapport and developing meaningful relationships with a wide variety of students.

3. **An Informal Educator**—The Senior Jewish Educator will be experienced with the theory and practice of informal education and will use that knowledge to model and teach others, particularly the Hillel professionals on his or her campus, how to create the most effective opportunities for meaningful Jewish experiences.

4. **Knowledgeable**—The Senior Jewish Educator will be highly educated in areas of Jewish content and excel at bringing that knowledge into the realm of popular culture and experience. This could range from traditional Jewish texts to Zionism, contemporary Jewish culture and Jewish social and political activism, thus providing the educator with a reservoir of knowledge to share with students. Ordination is not a requirement for the position; the Senior Jewish Educator might be a rabbi but also might not.

5. **A Strategic Community Organizer**—The Senior Jewish Educator will think strategically about how to reach and impact students not involved in the traditional networks and will utilize methodologies of community organizing in order to manage and strategize for success.

6. **A Pastoral Counselor**—The Senior Jewish Educator is familiar with the psycho-spiritual dramas common to the college experience (Who am I? Why am I?) and is capable of speaking one on one with students about the challenges in their lives and giving them ways to understand those challenges in a Jewish framework.

On a note similar to Hillel's SJEs, BBYO, one of North America's largest high school-aged youth movements, recently created the position of Director of Jewish Enrichment (DJE). Placed in hubs around the country, the DJEs will work with teen leaders, volunteer advisors and BBYO professionals to raise the bar of the Jewish character of BBYO programming. In written job descriptions BBYO states that they are looking for professionals with a creative program mind; good facilitators and trainers; people who like working with teens, staff and advisors; people who thrive as part of a team (*http://old.b-linked.org/intranet/article.php?id=2272&p=*). Taken alone, this description resembles many of the characteristics defined by Chazan. In tandem with the written description, however, BBYO also produced a YouTube video (http://www.youtube.com/watch?v=8_F9HoPbYuo) of teens making the pitch for the DJEs. This script stated:

> BBYO is looking for a few good Jewish educators…This isn't your average teaching gig. We're looking for someone who is going to make this week's Parasha sound like the latest must-see TV show. Come on, you gotta entertain me. We're looking for someone who is a people person and a deal closer. Someone that is going to connect BBYO to exciting new partners. We want someone who is going to know how to find us on Facebook, Twitter and YouTube without us having to teach them first. We want someone who is passionate about sharing a love of Judaism with people from all walks of life… .We want someone who is comfortable charting their own course, creating their own strategies and measures of success… .We want someone who is good at meeting teens where they are at and ready to do some serious staff, teen and advisor training. Teach us to be great teachers.

Reading the SJE and DJE job descriptions with the lens of Sacks' connectors and translators, we uncover important skills and characteristics of the contemporary experiential educator not fully elucidated in Chazan's characteristics. The contemporary educator is an authentic personality, someone who uses his personal narrative and Jewish journey as an educational tool; an engager who uses social networks—both human and digital—to reach the under-engaged; a translator who is both Jewishly knowledgeable and can make the weekly parasha as appealing as the hottest TV show; and a community organizer who catalyzes campus engagement interns and teen leaders to act as educators themselves. Most importantly, however, the contemporary experiential educator is an entrepreneur willing to blaze his own path, take initiative and think creatively in how he goes about the work of translating and connecting.

HUMAN RESOURCE CHALLENGES FACING EXPERIENTIAL LEARNING

Elliot, Jonah and Ofer were excellent counselors. Each, in his own way, shaped powerful camp experiences for me and for my fellow campers. Measured against the rubric of skills and characteristics of an experiential educator outlined above, however, likely none would pass the test of the broad and diverse skills described. To this point, the limited discussion of the skills and characteristics of experiential educators is prescriptive rather than descriptive—it details the skills and characteristics of an ideal experiential educator but does little to describe the attributes and work of those active in the field. Recognizing that the majority of those working in the field are part-time or seasonal employees with little training, no certification and limited intention to make a career in experiential learning, the chasm between the espoused theory and the reality on the ground remains stark.

Reimer and Bryfman (2006) state that the field of experiential education would be buttressed by research exploring questions like "What skills, knowledge and dispositions should characterize these educators?" Alongside the prescriptive research they propose, descriptive research profiling the current state of human resources in experiential education is required. These two studies taken together will offer the information needed to recruit, train and retain top educators.

FINDING A NAME FOR OURSELVES

Notwithstanding their impact on my education and personal growth, Elliot, Jonah and Ofer likely wouldn't call themselves educators. Across Hillels and youth movements, camps and travel programs, many who do educative work—connect youth to Jewish activities, enact experiences and model Jewish values—do not take on the label of educator, often reserving that title for those who teach formal classes. Instead, amorphous terms like engagement professional, youth worker or youth professional are bandied about.

The recent study "Engaging Teens: A Study of New York Teens, Parents and Practitioners," commissioned by UJA Federation of New York, defined this challenge:

> There are several challenges to defining "teen engagement" as a field of practice. At the simplest level is the question of what to call the adults responsible for this work. "Youth professional" seems inadequate, as 14% of our respondents are volunteers, not paid professionals. "Teen worker" or "youth worker" are misleading titles. They suggest a relatively low-level position, but 32% of our sample are at the top of their organizations (rabbis, principals or executive, associate or assistant directors). These titles also suggest that the person's job is primarily dedicated to teens, when the reality is that 34% spend less than half of their time with teens. To avoid misnomer we decided to refer to the adults whose job it is to engage teens in Jewish life during the school year as "Teen Engagement Practitioners" (TEPs) (Sales et al., 47).

Sacks, who offered the terms translators and connectors, is similarly ambivalent on the applicability of these descriptors to the contemporary educator. She states, "Given that interactions between the translators/connectors and their constituency are open-ended and that outcomes, by definition, are undefined, it is too soon to make any strong claims that translators and connectors are the new Jewish educators" (6). Echoing the hesitancy of these leaders to take on the label educator, Sacks quotes Eli Raber of BayTribe as saying, "It doesn't mean we are not educators, it just means we …do not want to appear different and/ or separate from the communities we lead. It is imperative for a leader in this generation to be from and to be within the population [the leader serves])." While this hesitancy to view one's work through the lens of an educator may not diminish the impact on Jewish youth, it does make it more difficult to define experiential education as a professional field.

The gap between the prescriptive skills and characteristics and the reality on the ground, as well as the hesitancy of these youth workers to take on the label "educator", is further compounded by high turnover. The New York Teen study notes that "almost half of the professional TEPs in New York (48%) and a quarter of the volunteer TEPs (24%) are somewhat or very likely to leave their current position in the next two years. Together these figures represent 47% of the TEPs in our sample" (51). Therefore, even if we were able to offer training to bridge the gap between the actual and the idealized and foster a self-perception as an educator among those in the field, the high rates of turnover would thwart the ongoing impact of these efforts, leaving us recreating the wheel with each new cohort of short-lived employees.

CONCLUSION

An attempt to break down the core skills and characteristics of experiential Jewish educators could be perceived as an academic exercise, more helpful to framing experiential learning as a field or profession than to improving practice. If, however, the process of parsing out these skills and characteristics buttresses our ability to recruit and hire the right people, train them in the skills that will benefit their work and retain them for longer careers in the field, the exercise will successfully bridge an academic pursuit with benefit for the field.

This chapter has begun that work. By enumerating the characteristics described by Chazan, adding the commentary of other literature and layering on top of these conceptions the work of experiential educators in newly formed positions, we have begun to tease out the ingredients necessary to reach the goal of successful recruitment, training and retention. But, to paraphrase Rabbi Tarfon in *Pirke Avot*, "The day is short, the labor vast, the workers [don't] idle, the reward is great and the Master of the house is insistent" (Avot 2:20).

REFERENCES

BBYO's Hiring: Looking for a Few Good Jewish Educators. 2011. Film.

Bekerman, Zvi, Nicholas C Burbules and Diana Silberman-Keller. *Learning in Places: the Informal Education Reader.* New York: P. Lang, 2006. Print.

Bryfman, D. "Experiential Jewish Education: Reaching the Tipping Point." *International Handbook of Jewish Education* (2011): 767–784. Print.

Chazan, Barry. "The Philosophy of Informal Jewish Education." *Encyclopedia of Informal Education* 2003.

Dobie, W. "Teacher Characteristics and Student Achievement: Evidence from Teach for America." Harvard University, July (2011): n. pag. Web. 6 Nov. 2012.

Ethics of Our Fathers. Vol. 2:20. Print.

Gladwell, Malcolm. *The Tipping Point: How Little Things Can Make a Big Difference.* Hachette Digital, Inc., 2000. Print.

II, B. Joseph Pine, and James H. Gilmore. *The Experience Economy: Work Is Theater and Every Business a Stage.* Harvard Business Press, 1999. Print.

Kessel, David M. "Director of Jewish Enrichment Position."

Parks, Sharon Daloz. *Big Questions, Worthy Dreams: Mentoring Emerging Adults in Their Search for Meaning, Purpose, and Faith.* John Wiley & Sons, 2011. Print.

Reimer, Joseph. "A Response to Barry Chazan: The Philosophy of Informal Jewish Education." *The Encyclopedia of Informal Education* 2003.

—-. "Beyond More Jews Doing Jewish: Clarifying the Goals of Informal Jewish Education." *Journal of Jewish Education* 73.1 (2007): 5–23. Web. 26 June 2012.

Reimer, Joseph, David Bryfman and Linda Dale. "What We Now Know About Experiential Education." *What We Now Know About Jewish Education : Perspectives on Research for Practice.* Los Angeles: Torah Aura Productions, 2008. Print.

Reisman, Bernard. *Informal Jewish Education in North America : a Report Submitted to the Commission on Jewish Education in North America.* Commission on Jewish Education in North America, 1990. Print.

Sacks, Adene. "The New Jewish Educators?" 15 Nov. 2007.

Sales, Amy L. *1998 Youth Professional Study.* North American Alliance for Jewish Youth, 1998. Print.

Sales, Amy L, Nicole Samuel and Alexander Zablotsky. *Engaging Jewish Teens: A Study of New York Teens, Parents and Practitioners.* 2011. Print.

Saxe, Leonard, and Amy L Sales. *"How Goodly Are Thy Tents": Summer Camps as Jewish Socializing Experiences.* UPNE, 2004. Print.

"Who We Look For." Teach For America. Web. 30 Dec. 2012.

Zeldin, Michael. "Understanding Informal Jewish Education." *Journal of Reform Judaism* (1989): 26–34. Print.

PREPARING EXPERIENTIAL JEWISH EDUCATORS

Jeffrey S. Kress, Abigail Uhrman, Mark S. Young

In this chapter we address enhancing the work of experiential educators through staff training and supervision. Our goal is to discuss theory and make suggestions, drawn from our experiences and research, relevant to organizational leaders working with their staff members. We frame our discussion broadly rather than for one particular type of setting, while acknowledging that the application of these ideas and suggestions will differ significantly from setting to setting.

Given the nature of this volume, it makes sense to take Barry Chazan's (2003) seminal article as a jumping-off point. This article is cited as a watershed event that serves as a rallying flag lending coherence to what had been at best a loosely organized set of initiatives and theories. Chazan's article also set the course for the ideas and practices he described to be framed within the discourse of, or under the heading of, *education*. As the years have passed there has been much discussion (e.g., Reimer and Bryfman 2008) about the first word—*informal*—while the word it modifies—*education*—seems to have been taken for granted. The *educational* framing of this work has created both momentum and challenges for the field and for preparing those who work within it.

The words and terms we use for ideas or objects can activate strong associations that color our perceptions. One the one hand, *education* connotes a certain seriousness of purpose and rigor of method. Looking at a bunk, a tour bus or a *Shabbaton* as an educational experience implies higher expectations than for participants simply to have fun. Rather, they should walk away changed in some way, having grown as Jews. And if the people working in these settings are doing *education*, then they are *educators*, and they stand with other recognized and respected members of this category—schoolteachers, professors, etc. Certainly they should be prepared for their roles! As such, the terminology and associated framework of *education* provides the rationale for thinking about enhancing the work of people in these roles. There is more to being a camp counselor, for example, than being "good with kids."

On the other hand, however, the term *education* is associated with *school*, and this can be quite foreign to the way that those who work in informal[1] settings conceptualize their work. Informal settings are generally seen as a break from the rules, exams and stresses of school. Further, the term *education* may be associated with primarily cognitive approaches to learning—gaining knowledge *about*—which is but one component of our goals for Jewish outcomes (as is discussed elsewhere in this volume). Experiential educators working in the field may themselves be students (in universities or, in some settings, high school) and find it difficult to group themselves with other *educators* in their lives. To them, education might imply passivity or disempowerment. More than thirty years after its release, the Pink Floyd lyric "We don't need no education, we don't need no thought control" is familiar to many of today's youth. Thus the term *education* might also complicate efforts to enhance the work of what we might consider avocational experiential educators who may not embrace this framing of their work.

An organizational leader must be aware of the possibility of such associations with the term *education* and be sensitive to their implications. It would be misguided to simply use the term *education* with an assumption that the word holds the same resonance with staff as it does with leadership. Of course, one

---

[1] While correct nomenclature is an ongoing discussion, here we follow Reimer and Bryfman's (2008) suggestion to use "experiential" to denote an approach to education and "formal" or "informal" to refer to venues.

option would be to try to modify the association staff members have with the word *education* and try to broaden their understanding of what might be meant by this term. Another option would be to work with language that might have less "loaded" connotations, such as talking about *growth* and *development* rather than *learning*. In this way staff might come to understand the connection of their work to the range of cognitive, affective and behavioral outcomes that Jewish educational settings strive to achieve. Regardless, a key initial goal of enhancing the work of avocational experiential Jewish educators is to develop an understanding of the educational/developmental aspects of their work; that is, that someone in their role (counselor, advisor, etc.) can be a major influence on the Jewish growth trajectories of the youth they serve.

To achieve this, it is helpful to build on the staff members' own experiences, prompting them to reflect on the Jewish experiences—in whatever context they occurred—that led them to be who they are today. These experiences can then be "unpacked" with regard to active ingredients: What was it about experience X that made it impactful? Following this individual reflection, staff can compare notes in groups to find commonalities among their experiences. One outcome of this activity is that staff come to realize the diversity of experiences that can be impactful and the range of individuals who have been important in their own development, who have been their *educators*.

Further, this activity can serve as a springboard for discussion of the "active ingredients" of impactful experiences and how educators in informal settings can create experiences that include such characteristics. We have found the active ingredients of impactful Jewish experiences to be fairly consistent among the many Jewish educators (of varying experience and in a wide range of settings) who have participated in this activity. Further, the elements identified are highly consistent with the research literature on impactful developmental experiences (as reviewed in Kress, in press; Kress and Reimer 2009). These include:

1. A safe and respectful learning environment.
2. Caring relationships between and among educators and learners; a sense of community.
3. Opportunities for participants to have significant input into the learning environment and to connect what is learned with their own experiences.
4. Multiple pathways of connection to Judaic content in ways that span cognition and emotion.
5. Opportunities to reflect on one's experiences.

One very basic implication of this is that organizational leaders can work with their staff to enhance their abilities in creating environments marked by these five elements. That is, staff training can focus on how to create safe and respectful environments, build community, understand and work with the passions of their participants, meaningfully integrate Jewish content into their work and facilitate reflection. In our experience, this happens frequently and manifests in training sessions on communication skills, conflict resolution, developmental issues, etc. Training in this regard can take place for educators in so-called "formal" settings as well as informal ones (Epstein & Kress 2011). We heartily endorse a focus on these elements as the subject matter of training.

We think, however, that there is a more challenging implication of these elements of impactful experiences. If we take these principles to be fundamental to any learning or growth experience, it makes sense to apply these to the *process* of staff training as well. Just as with our program participants, our goal with staff training is to provide lasting and meaningful educational experiences—experiences that will encourage staff to learn and grow and inspire them to create similarly powerful teaching moments. Such an approach to staff training—an approach that genuinely values the learning experiences and trajectory of the staff—requires the leadership to embrace a particular stance toward education. Education, in this context, occurs at all levels of the organization. From the senior administration to the program participants, everyone involved is actively engaged in the learning process. Staff training, then, must reflect this understanding of the staff's dual roles as learners and educators. Sessions should have personal and professional resonance and model the educational principles and practices we hope to see in staff's work and interactions. These principles should not only be the subject matter of training, but should inform and guide the *process* of training.

APPLYING ELEMENTS OF IMPACTFUL EXPERIENCES

1) A SAFE AND RESPECTFUL LEARNING ENVIRONMENT

For several reasons, this is more difficult to achieve than one might imagine. Staff training, by definition, involves staff trying out new ideas or actions. While some may readily embrace what they are learning, others will find it more challenging to integrate what they are learning into their practice. Staff might doubt their ability to implement these changes. Some might worry whether they will lose legitimacy or control with program participants. Others may wonder how their efforts may impact their performance evaluation: Will I look foolish for trying something new, something with which I am not yet comfortable? Can I express my concerns to my supervisor, or will that detract from his/her impression of me?

Understanding staff as learners *and* educators means that the above concerns should be taken seriously. Staff needs to feel that, like program participants, they are engaged in a learning and growth process. They are provided opportunities to try new things and push the boundaries of what is natural for them. A safe and respectful learning environment encourages these kinds of healthy explorations. It allows staff time and space to experiment with new ideas and consider the implications of their learning for their work. Furthermore, staff should be encouraged to ask questions. Discussion and reflection should be embedded in training sessions, allowing staff a forum in which to assimilate new ideas and consider their practical applications.

Such learning environments, however, are not formed instantaneously; they require getting to know and trust staff and build relationships with them. They necessitate significant investment from the organizational leadership in terms of time—the amount of time devoted to staff training as well as the regularity of training sessions—and planning. Careful forethought on such issues, logistical as well as theoretical, is critical when developing successful staff training programs. Also, expanding beyond one-shot training opportunities (to be discussed further) gives the message that skill development is an ongoing process, not something one achieves overnight.

2) CARING RELATIONSHIPS BETWEEN AND AMONG EDUCATORS AND LEARNERS; A SENSE OF COMMUNITY

The language of *community of learners* has become very popular in staff training and in professional growth in general (e.g., Novick, Kress and Elias 2002; Wald and Castleberry 2000). When staff members come together to share ideas and support one another's work, everyone gains. This idea carries particular resonance for training experiential educators, many of whom are at developmental stages (adolescence, late adolescence) at which peer relationships take center stage. For many, particularly at immersive settings such as camps, *hanging out with my friends* is the not-so-secret motivation behind the decision to work at a particular setting. The group can serve as a powerful vehicle for growth.

To that end, considering the group dynamic is an important focus of staff development. Not only will this meet the developmental needs of many experiential educational staffs, but it also provides a remarkable opportunity to build group cohesion, foster trust and engagement and build meaningful relationships. Ultimately these types of connections are among the most meaningful and lasting to staff, both in terms of their personal lives and their professional associations. In order to build a *community of learners*, group bonding and teamwork need to be expressed goals of staff training. While such relationships can form organically, they are often the product of careful planning. Making time for staff to get to know and feel comfortable with one another is critical to creating positive and successful staff learning.

Providing opportunities for ongoing collaboration, group work and discussion is also important. This means creating partnerships among staff who are already close as well as working to forge new bonds among staff members who may not know one another well or work together on a regular basis. Not only are such strategies good educational practices in general, but they also allow opportunities for staff to continue to build strong connections with their co-workers. Finally, as a practical consideration, it is important to honor the staff's desire to *hang out with my friends* by respecting their time both during and outside of training sessions. Pay attention to their needs and interests, and work to incorporate their needs and interests into planning. Also, be prompt—start and end on time—and allow staff the opportunity to attend to personal matters, work on something else or simply spend time with one another in another context.

3) OPPORTUNITIES FOR PARTICIPANTS/LEARNERS TO HAVE SIGNIFICANT INPUT INTO THE LEARNING ENVIRONMENT AND TO CONNECT WHAT IS LEARNED WITH THEIR OWN EXPERIENCES

Why are we doing this again? The answer should go beyond *Because it is our new way* or *Because it is important.* For staff members to learn a new skill or adopt any new set of procedures the change has to mean something; it has to connect to something they feel is important about their work, who they are and what they are passionate about.

One implication of this is that any new staff initiative should be flexible enough for staff members to find multiple points of entry and connection. This is true both in terms of how the content is framed and how it is presented. *What* is being taught needs to be carefully conceived so that staff feels invested in the learning and the outcome. They need to understand what they are doing and its relevance in the larger organization picture, their personal growth and/or the experiences of the program participants. The key here is to be explicit and upfront about goals and objectives and expressly state the purpose of the training. Making the linkages clear and straightforward directs the focus toward the learning. While meaning-making will occur simultaneously, taking the bulk of the guesswork out of the equation allows staff to be directed and intentional from the start of the session.

How the material is presented is equally critical in providing staff multiple points of entry and connection. Just as with program participants, it is necessary to think about the diverse learners and learning styles in the group. This means finding creative ways for staff to engage with the material being presented, utilizing a range of different modalities and providing opportunities for individual, small group and whole group work. This also means building in time for thoughts and feedback. Particularly when presenting a new initiative or idea, it is important to allow staff time to make sense of what they are learning. Although providing such a space can elicit a unique set of challenges (e.g., staff might disagree), figuring out a way to work through the challenges is, in the long term, well worth the initial investment upfront. To that end, planning is crucial. Thinking through what reactions staff might have and coming prepared to help staff manage their questions and concerns can help make this a smoother process for all involved. Finally, as with all training, follow up with staff. In addition to providing time for reflection in the moment, check in with staff both formally and informally about their thoughts and progress. This is not only a helpful assessment tool, but it also reminds staff that their needs are heard and valued.

4) MULTIPLE PATHWAYS OF CONNECTION TO JUDAIC CONTENT IN WAYS THAT SPAN COGNITION AND EMOTION

As noted above, staff members will likely have a range of associations—not all of them positive—with the notion of Jewish education. The range of Jewish expressions to which they have been exposed might be limited, and they may not have focused on the intersection of Judaism and their primary areas of interest (e.g., music or technology). Staff training benefits from a broadening of this horizon, an expansion of the ways one can be engaged Jewishly; and keeping both objectives in mind—training Jewish educators and providing rich learning opportunities that facilitate the staff's personal and, in this case, Jewish growth—means taking this responsibility seriously and doing this well.

Practically, this translates into several key principles. First, it requires making time for Jewish learning, in whatever form the Jewish learning may take. Jewish learning can be integrated throughout training or it can be a separate piece of the staff development, but either way there must be time and space for Jewish learning to occur. Second, Jewish learning should be engaging and exciting. It needs to capture the attention and imagination of the staff in order for it to feel powerful, interesting and relevant. Using a range of modalities is one way for Jewish learning to come to life. The same strategies that are used with program participants apply to staff—be creative, use different techniques and media, and design sessions that appeal to diverse learners. Third, choose topics that speak to the staff and the questions with which they are struggling and/or are interested in pursuing. It is critical to remember the audience if the learning is to be meaningful and lasting.

Finally, remember that the staff, as educators *and* learners, are on their own Jewish journeys. For some this may mean dedication and passion, and for others this may mean doubts and challenges. For the latter group, their role as "Jewish educators" may prove a bit more challenging, and it is important to acknowledge and honor where each person is in his or her Jewish explorations. Also, it provides a space to discuss how to manage these issues when working with program participants and either provide some general suggestions or set more clear expectations while affirming their engagement with the tradition and the honesty and legitimacy of their Jewish paths.

One last note: Particularly when working with a young staff, sensitivity to tone is crucial. Exploration and consideration may be embraced, while preachiness will likely result in an emotional shutdown. This is true with all audiences, but especially so with emerging adults who are considering a host of related questions and unknowns about themselves and their futures.

5) OPPORTUNITIES TO REFLECT ON ONE'S EXPERIENCES

A key component distinguishing an "experience" from a "learning experience" is the reflective process (Reimer 2003). In order for learning to have meaning, it needs to have a reflective element. All learning experiences, therefore, need to include this critical component. Time and thought needs to be given to reflection, and for staff training this means planning for these moments in and between every training session. A *coaching* framework—such as that used in sports or other activities—can provide a useful set of guidelines in this context. In coaching the acquisition of new skills is enhanced by opportunities to try them out in increasingly complex situations (progressively harder drills, then scrimmages, then the big game) with feedback provided throughout. Certainly staff training should not be seen as a one-shot deal. In planning multiple sessions, resist the urge to see each meeting as an opportunity to add new information or expectations. Instead, include time for reflection about how their efforts are going, what challenges they encountered and how they handled these situations.

Be sure to include time for reflection during every training session as well. Allow time for the staff to ask questions, make sense of what they're learning and concretize new ideas and concepts. This can be anything from a group share to journaling. The methods can and should vary, as long as there is ample time allotted for reflection to occur.

IDEAS IN ACTION

So how might this application or framework of training look on the ground—i.e., in the *hadar o'khel* (dining hall), in the JCC/recreation center or even in the temple atrium? We now turn to three examples of these principles in action.

A–Z TO NOAH'S ARK—EXPERIENTIAL PROFESSIONAL DEVELOPMENT AT JEWISH CAMP

Picture a camp director who must inform and train his or her young staff about the rules and regulations of camp during staff training. Many include foreigners whose English is a second language, Israeli *shlihim* experiencing culture shock and those young counselors barely out of high school. It seemed like just yesterday that these were the campers sneaking out of their bunks and acting out when the hand would go up (and the mouth is supposed to go shut). The policies are an endless list: where campers can go and can't go on their own around camp, when they must be supervised, when is curfew, what is the vision of camp, what can or can't occur during rest period...and the list goes on.

The director might choose the A–Z approach to staff training: sitting the entire staff of, say, 100–150 teens and twenty-somethings in the _hadar o-hel_ for hours on end to go over all the specifics. The director and senior staff take turns in lecture style reciting every rule. Yes, there is an opportunity to ask questions, but there is no rationale or context; rules are what they are, and we must follow them. The training asks for little or no creativity or input from those who are supposed to enforce the rules when the campers arrive. "Oh," the director adds, "campers are supposed have fun, too."

Alternatively, the director can ask the staff to build a boat, Noah's ark style. Imagine the director dividing the staff into several different teams, mixing up the groups so teammates are not with their friends but with new acquaintances—those they might not have much in common with (other than getting paid modestly to work 24/7 for the next eight weeks). Each team has a task, a shared challenge. They must gather the supplies need to build Noah's ark, the ark they need to survive when the flood (of campers?) arrives and threatens to take them away. There are constraints (rules), there is a limited amount of time (a regulation), only certain supplies they can use, and they must demonstrate _ruah_ (spirit), to receive additional "points" from the judges, senior staff who will score their ability to complete the task, their teamwork and their excitement about the challenge.

It may appear that the director who goes with Option B is not doing his or her job. Where in building Noah's ark does it say that staff must be in their bunks by midnight? At what point do staff learn how to design an evening program? These rote procedures are not explicitly being articulated while the boats are being built and the teams are devising their cheers; what is happening is real and in-depth training, preparation for the staff, these experiential educators, to do their job when the kids come.

In their common task they must work together and learn about one another (building relationships and establishing community). They must learn to trust one another and become unafraid to share and ask questions to accomplish the task (creating a safe space and requiring the need for participant input and connections). They are challenged to think beyond auditory rote learning by having to physically build a boat while creating cheers and communicating with one another under the auspices of a biblical story/ framework (multiple pathways and multiple Jewish pathways to learning). And chances are the staff are engaged, achieving a sense of _flow_ (Csikszentmihalyi 1990) in the activity and having a great time bonding with their colleagues and friends for the summer. They are learning to create and maintain a safe, fun and amazing camp experience by creating a safe, fun and amazing camp experience for themselves.

So when do the rules and regulations come in? In this example, through two final steps: One, through the director asking reflective questions of the staff: What did you learn from this task? Why was it important? How does this relate to your role as staff? How does this relate to a broader, Jewishly based vision of community at camp that integrates values such as _kavod_ and _derekh eretz_ (respectful and appropriate behavior)? In their own words, the staff (through facilitated guidance) articulates perhaps not the rules themselves, but the meaning and reasoning behind these rules (for example, "Ah, one staff must be in the cabin the entire night the first week so the campers are safe and we can better identify and work with homesick campers. I get it!"). Two, through a challenge, the staff go through the rules, a staff handbook, in small groups and on their own, now with a real understanding of adhering to and enforcing rules in ways that still make camp "camp". They may also see themselves as educators, not merely the "oldest folks" at camp still coming _only_ to see their friends and be at camp.

Of course, there are rules and regulations that need to be said out loud because they are that important (sex, drugs, rock 'n' roll?). This important note aside, empowering a diverse, young and energetic staff to "build a boat like Noah and his team" is an experiential way to train experiential educators that follows a modeling approach and that may accomplish more with one's staff training then going A to Z, and is in the spirit of what Jewish camp wishes to accomplish. It can serve as a way of framing the "rules" conversation so that staff can come, on their own, to see the importance of having shared understandings of whatever is being taught. This example illustrates a change in stance on the part of the leader from "What do I need to tell them?" to "What do they, the staff, need to walk away with, and how can that best be achieved?"

LINKING CUSTOMER SERVICE TO STAFF SERVICE IN A JEWISH COMMUNITY CENTER

A Jewish Community Center director aims to train his or her staff to provide exemplary customer service to its patrons. The walls and floors should be clean, the smiles extended and friendly from the security desk to the lifeguard stand, and the communication to patrons in programs from promotion to follow-up consistent, warm and helpful. Sounds like a place any patron would want to be. The JCC director, to launch the customer service campaign, brings the staff together and says, "This is our new mission, our new direction, to treat every member of our community who walks through that door with ideal customer service, friendly, warm, helpful and sincere." Then she or he asks, "How are you being treated? More importantly, how would you like to be treated as a member of the staff community?"

This is not simply lip service. This is a director's embracing the idea that professional development in order to achieve the objectives of the educational institution can be participatory and reflective, not simply dictated. The staff, hesitant at first, responds with ideas and sincere thoughts. The director listens and reflects and poses a challenge to their staff: How can "we" develop the principle of our customer service and staff service (service to each other) together?

Again, the staff—diverse as many Jewish educational institutions, of various ages, backgrounds, educational degrees—all become educators, engaging in a challenge they must facilitate together and reflect on in order to achieve a common goal, one from which they will either benefit if successful or feel the burden of if they are not successful. The leader, recognizing that changes in practice do not come easily, plans follow-up meetings for staff in small groups to discuss situations during which it is hard for them to maintain a professional demeanor and to problem-solve around how such situations can be handled. Throughout the process the director weaves Jewish values such as *hakhnasat orkhim* (welcoming visitors) into the discussion.

Consider this mode of professional development in contrast to the director emailing a set of "customer service principles" that the staff must follow when working with patrons, with no mention of how staff should be treated (or how they treat each other), with none of their input or participation, with no establishment of safe grounds for the staff to challenge, with no acknowledgment of the different ideas, backgrounds and strengths of the collective body, and certainly with no time for personal reflection other then maybe confusion or resentment about the emailed document in front of them.

A JCC is an example of a place where all employees—whether in maintenance, marketing, music or management—have opportunities and instances when they can be in the role of experiential Jewish educator, or at least play a significant role in creating a program and environment whose aim is to foster exemplary Jewish experiential learning. Approaching a professional development opportunity that changes the framing of professional development from "here you go" to "let's hear from each other, work on this together and acknowledge the strengths and opinions of those around us," the staff is modeling what they are being asked to carry out. The JCC, in becoming a model of customer service, becomes of model of staff service. The organizational leader is an educator, too, who needs to live by what he or she is preaching or teaching. The leader would need to have a happy, satisfied staff in order for that to translate to the consumer/customer. Through an experiential learning approach to professional development, the staff collectively learn to create an environment that will foster exemplary Jewish experiential education for their patrons.

INVITING, NOT IMPOSING, A NEW INITIATIVE IN A SUPPLEMENTAL SCHOOL

Just as experiential Jewish education can take place in settings lacking lakes or rustic dining halls, our approach to staff training is equally relevant to so-called "formal" settings. Our five key components of impactful experiences apply to promoting growth in general, even though the specific content or goals of training may vary from setting to setting. Our next example involves a supplemental school director who aims to introduce a new initiative (whether this involves a curriculum, a set of procedures or what have you[2]). Typically the director would introduce the initiative in a staff meeting or training session (or, as we have seen, even in a memo) and then expect the initiative to become standard operating procedure in the setting. We believe that approaches such as this help explain the multitude of unused curricula, unheeded instructions and ignored memos that can be found in many schools (cf. Kress and Elias 2006).

Contrast this with a director who asks educators to attend a staff meeting and to bring with them an artifact representing their favorite Jewish memory, perhaps a menorah from when they first celebrated Ḥanukkah with their kids, the tallit from their bar or bat mitzvah ceremony or the ḥallah cover they made while teaching their class. The director asks, "What does this mean to you as a person, and what does this mean to you as an educator?" Through this discussion the director begins to establish a space where it is safe for educators to share, and the educators identify areas of their own passion related to Jewish education, connect with their peers and think about how their work can best reflect their passions. A director who wishes to bring in a new initiative creates a safe and trusting space that encourages participant input in a learning and supportive community. The director is better able to help staff members connect elements of the initiative to their areas of passion. Staff members are encouraged to identify their own connections that may enable them to tap into their strengths and think creatively and passionately when preparing for their classes, though the initiative might be new. Of course, this director also understands that introducing the initiative, even in this positive emotional context, is just the first step toward successful implementation. Educators will face challenges and doubts during the process and will need a venue in which to exchange ideas with their peers, problem-solve together and, importantly, share their successes and innovations. In this way a new initiative may feel more like an *invitation* than an *imposition*.

CONCLUSIONS

These examples illustrate efforts to make staff training sessions more impactful by helping participants go beyond *learning about* new procedures, rules, or skills. The goal of staff training in these examples is to create experiences that help staff grow and develop vis-à-vis new procedures, rules or skills. The leaders in these examples recognize that successful change in educational settings is rooted in individuals joining in a new vision and successfully implementing changes to their practice (Evans 1996). The participating staff members are not passive recipients of information or directives but are rather empowered to connect with information or procedure on their own.

This paradigm parallels the goals of experiential Jewish education in creating impactful holistic growth experiences. Wherever staff training takes place, and whatever its content may be, the process must take into account feelings of safety, the power of relationships and community, connections to staff members' interests and perspectives, multiple ways to engage emotionally with Jewish content and ongoing opportunities to reflect on progress and challenges. These examples also show that while out-of-the-box activities can be helpful in staff training, experiential education does not require a pyrotechnic sound and lights extravaganza that has participants running and climbing around the setting. The five elements can be enhanced in quiet, reflective discussion as well as by raucous, energetic activity.

It is important to note the interdependence of these five elements, even though we have discussed each individually. Failure to attend to any of one of these will complicate achievement of the others and will attenuate the impact of the overall learning experience. Further, while we isolate the implications of

---

[2] Although we are discussing a generic case for which the actual content of the innovation is less relevant, it should be noted that the principles of effective developmental educational programming can themselves be important subject matter for staff in "formal" settings to learn and to incorporate into their practice. The principles can be *what* the educators learn as well as guidelines for *how* the training is structured.

these elements for staff training, these training efforts are situated within the broader context of the setting. This means that in addition to applying these elements to staff training, leaders must make sure that they are modeled and promoted in ways that help them permeate the setting as a whole.

Of course, implementing experientially based staff training is not a simple matter. It is far easier to think about planning a "one and done," frontal-lecture format training session than to map out a series of experiences in which staff members grapple with new ideas, plan for their implementation and reflect on their progress. However, it is our assertion that staff members who participate in training in ways that are meaningful for them as learners, as opposed to simply being informed about new procedures, are more likely to adhere to these new procedures in the long run, leading to greater training success. As Chazan (2003, italics in the original) noted, experientially based education *"works by creating venues, by developing a total educational culture and by co-opting the social context."* The work of experientially based staff training is ongoing, individualized and communal. However, as with experiential Jewish education in general, if we take our goals for growth seriously, then the effort is worthwhile.

REFERENCES

Chazan, B. (2003). The philosophy of informal Jewish education. Retrieved March 30, 2009, from *http://www.infed.org/informaljewisheducation/informal_jewish_education.htm*.

Csikszentmihalyi, M. (1990). *Flow: The Psychology of Optimal Experience*. New York: Harper and Row.

Epstein, S., and J.S. Kress (2011). "Not Just Fun and Games: Preparing Day School Teachers for Meaningful, Constructivist, Experiential Education." *HaYidion*, 50–51, 62.

Evans, R. (1996). *The Human Side of School Change: Reform, Resistance and the Real-life Problems of Innovation*. San Francisco: Jossey-Bass.

Kress, J. S. (in press). *Development, Learning, and Community: Educating for Identity in Pluralistic Jewish High Schools*. Brighton, MA: Academic Studies Press.

Kress, J. S., and M.J. Elias (2006). "Building Learning Communities through Social and Emotional Learning: Navigating the Rough Seas of Implementation." *Professional School Counseling Journal, 10*, 102–107.

Kress, J. S., and J. Reimer (2009). "Shabbatonim as Experiential Education in North American Community Day High Schools. In A. Pomson and H. Deitcher (eds.), *Jewish Day Schools, Jewish Communities* (pp. 341–360). Oxford: Littman Library of Jewish Studies.

Novick, B., J.S. Kress and M.J. Elias (2002). *Building Learning Communities with Character: How to Integrate Academic, Social and Emotional Learning*. Alexandria, VA: Association for Supervision and Curriculum Development.

Reimer, J. (2003). A Response to Barry Chazan: The Philosophy of Informal Jewish Education. Retrieved March 30, 2009, from *http://www.infed.org/informaljewisheducation/informal_jewish_education_reply.htm*.

Reimer, J., and D. Bryfman (2008). "Experiential Jewish Education." In R. L. Goodman, P. A. Flexner and L. D. Bloomberg (eds.), *What We Now Know about Jewish Education: Perspectives on Research for Practice* (pp. 343–352). Los Angeles: Torah Aura Productions.

Wald, P. J., and Castelberry, M.S. (2000). *Educators as Learners: Creating a Professional Learning Community in Your School*. Alexandria, VA: Association for Supervision and Curriculum Development.

MEETING THEM WHERE THEY ARE: ON THE EDUCATIONAL POTENTIAL OF ENGAGING ADOLESCENTS AS EDUCATORS

Jacob Cytryn

The recent work undertaken in the field of Jewish education to develop graduate programs in Informal Jewish Education (IJE)[1] and to develop our conception of the knowledge, skills and dispositions that should characterize a professional in this sub-field is crucial and important. These advances, however, especially combined with the significant financial resources that major philanthropic foundations and others have mobilized to enable and support them, cannot by themselves raise the level of IJE in general. Other articles in this volume that may imagine a future in which the position of "informal educator" in Jewish institutions evokes clear images of job descriptions, talents, skills and more are necessary but not sufficient.

Indeed, as the legions of Jewish professionals for whom IJE is already an important component of their job description—at JCCs, day schools, synagogues, Hillels, Israel programs, community organizations, summer camps and more—know all too well, their administrative, logistical, development and recruiting responsibilities leave little room for the type of educational interaction that, in all likelihood, attracted them to their positions in the first place. Additionally, for every student working toward a master's degree in Informal Jewish Education or a more advanced degree (Rabbi, Ph.D.) with the hope of doing similar work, there are dozens (hundreds?) of in-the-trenches informal educators employed on part-time or seasonal bases to staff our summer camps (day and overnight), Israel trips, youth group events and conventions, service-learning trips and the litany of other non-school–based Jewish programming with educational potential and profound impact on the socialization of Jewish children and adolescents.[2] These informal educators are the footsoldiers in the American Jewish community's ongoing war against assimilation and apathy. They are our best chance to continue the renaissance underway in vibrant Jewish living in North America, to grow the community benefiting from it and to realize what ought to be everyone's goal: a thriving, evolving, pluralistic and exciting Jewish community that relegates anxiety over "Jewish continuity" to the periphery where it has always belonged.

This article will focus on the unrealized possibilities of helping these footsoldiers be more effective in their jobs, a potential that would both enhance the programs they staff and, in a phenomenally beneficial side effect, catalyze their own thinking about and engagement with Judaism and their Jewish communities. These hordes of counselors, advisers and trip leaders will already, in all likelihood, make up the core of the next generation's committed Jewry. To bring their level of discourse about and knowledge of Jewish education to the next level will, in turn, have far-reaching positive implications for the future Judaism they will create and support. Additionally, though few, if any, institutions currently work with such populations in the manner suggested here, we need not recreate the wheel in determining how best to approach the problem. The best practices of teacher education programs and the research on those programs provides a counter-intuitive and inspirational approach to redefine Jewish education in the twenty-first century.

The core of this article will describe and explore the implications of an effort to achieve these goals undertaken at Camp Ramah in Wisconsin in 2002 with a group of fifteen high school students in their final summer as campers. The campers participated in a course called Programmatic Informal Education (PIE), designed and taught by the author, which was repeated in a less intensive fashion with similar groups in 2005 and 2006. At the conclusion of the article I will present a vision for a "laboratory campus" built on the principles on which PIE is based, the best practices of teacher education and the needs of the IJE field. Such a campus could serve as a national incubator for emerging lay and professional leadership in Jewish education and a research and development site for the theory, practice and program of Jewish education that would ground an intensive academic environment in the day-to-day realities of a living educational institution.

SCOPE AND CONTEXT

Before delving into PIE, two brief introductory notes are in order about this article's implications for the entire field and a crucial, underdeveloped distinction that speaks to the core assumptions of my work. Both are undertaken in the spirit of full disclosure and in the hope of allowing for clarity of expression and maximal impact.

Though I have experienced IJE as a participant and/or staff member in many contexts—day schools, supplementary schools, synagogues, Hillels, Israel programs, service-learning trips and JCCs—my thinking on the topic and the vast majority of my experience is in residential summer camping. My natural idioms and the vast majority of my examples will emerge from the world of Jewish summer camp as I have experienced it at Camp Ramah in Wisconsin over the last twenty summers. While I may remain limited by the form of my educational experience and thinking, the *content* of that thinking and experience is applicable in every setting. Each setting in which IJE may take place has its own essential characteristics, and there are settings that have more and less in common with each other, but all of them share a general shared approach. The building blocks of IJE, then, the creation of educational experiences built by developing social interactions with Jewish content and Jewish peers with goals for impacting those peers' minds, allow for the possibility of extrapolating, however imperfectly, from one setting to the next. The discussion below has implications for all settings and all stakeholders in IJE—participants, their parents, staff members, aspiring professionals, experienced professionals, funders, communal leaders and more—and it has consequences for every setting, every professional trajectory and every child's Jewish learning and growth.

As I have already explored elsewhere in greater depth (Cytryn, 2011), I reject the simple dichotomy between so-called "formal" and "informal" education. Rather, I suggest that we recast the discussion around Jewish education in terms of our commitment—or lack thereof—to intensive, content-driven experiences that allow for the greatest learning and growth. I wish well to the sections of the Jewish world that commit themselves to the types of Jewish socialization described by Saxe and Sales (2003) and others while preferring to throw my lot in with Reimer (2007) and others who compel us to strive for more. Though the building blocks may be the same from one IJE setting to the next, the core premises on which the approach outlined below is based may not resonate with every reader, and the consequences of the approaches laid out may not, in fact, apply to every eligible institution (though that would not result from a specific institution's setting but from the choices underlying its educational approach and vision).

ANIMATING IDEAS: IMPETUS FOR PIE

THE MISSING PARADIGM IN STAFF TRAINING: EDUCATION AT THE CENTER

The creation of the Programmatic Informal Education (PIE) curriculum attempted to fill a gap in the transitioning of campers to counselors at Camp Ramah in Wisconsin. The vast majority of campers spend more than three summers at camp, and more than eighty percent of campers in the final summer (rising juniors in high school) apply to return as junior counselors two years later. Even so, there are few formalized professional development opportunities to help the campers transition to become staff members; and to the extent that such opportunities do exist, they are focused heavily—as is the professional development that takes place for staff members each summer during a pre-season staff week and summer-long professional development seminars—on issues of interpersonal communication, the psycho-social profiles of children, health and safety concerns and the management of group dynamics. While each of these topics is essential to a counselor succeeding in her role, in an institution like Ramah Wisconsin (and many others) there appears to be a missing paradigm: utilizing the aforementioned components (and others) to maximize the educational impact on one's campers.

In a camp that prides itself on providing surpassing educational programming, the lack of a formalized approach for introducing educational ideas to young staff, discussing issues of their jobs that relate specifically to education and nurturing their development as Jewish educators seems odd, to say the least. This is surely not a problem that plagues only Ramah Wisconsin, the Ramah camping movement or educationally intensive residential summer camps, but one that is pervasive in most, if not all, Jewish summer camps and, in all likelihood, Jewish IJE settings in general. I leave the surely interesting and possibly valuable explorations of why, exactly, this is the status quo and its implications to a different forum. The devised solution, however, follows from these facts: an attempt to fill the void by engaging with soon-to-be staff members in an extended series of discussions about the educational potential of Ramah; developing with them some theory about how the educational process may occur and how we might imagine it could occur; and bolstering these campers' educational potential as staff members in the future.

FOCUSING ON THE WRONG THING: EDUCATION AS A GOAL, NOT LEADERSHIP

Before outlining the fundamental principles that shaped PIE—and contributed to its possible success—and drawing conclusions from the experience of crafting and teaching the course, two contextual, related, and as-yet-absent topics deserve attention: "leadership training" and approaches to staff training.

Wading into the minefield that is questions of leaders versus followers and the future of the Jewish community outside of Israel (and perhaps within it) is far outside my focus here. What is wholly relevant, however, is the educational community's obsession with programs, institutes, initiatives and more dedicated to the alleged enhancement of "leadership skills." Even leaving aside questions of anyone's ability to teach and the resulting importance of charisma, integrity, eloquence and similar qualities we may seek in our leaders, and the various theories of leadership espoused by different institutions dedicated to the task within the Jewish community, I remain befuddled by our goals in such endeavors. For even in those situations where a clear, cogent and compelling theory of leadership frames the discourse and where meaningful and achievable goals are laid out for the program, I cannot distinguish "leadership" from a mishmash of workshops aimed at building character, communication skills and a sense of responsibility or, at worst, entitlement in creating something that other members of the community are supposed to want or need. The skills we are attempting to teach are skills practically all of our community members will require to survive as economic contributors and engaged citizens in the twenty-first century. And while I embrace the role of (and have benefited enormously from) programs to build leadership that consciously collect some elite cohort of Jews with similar rationale and purposes, I remain skeptical of the leadership development potential, per se, of any such program and am wary of the development of such programs as what seems like a primary objective of the Jewish community in North America.

It need not surprise the reader to learn that PIE and future, improved versions of a curriculum based on similar premises that attempt to create cohorts of educators tasked with bolstering the teaching and learning of Jewish children, adolescents and adults, are not "leadership development" programs. Rather, they are unabashed attempts to create educational visionaries, thinkers and practitioners. The issue here is not just semantic; educators are interested in the teaching and learning of content to a group of living human beings in a specific context. Though they may represent a subset of "leaders" or share significant qualities with them, their task is laden with fundamentally different connotations. The more individuals we can bring into a rigorous, stimulating, in-depth conversation about the grounded potentials and pitfalls of Jewish education, the better off the community will be. For the act of learning, teaching and innovating *is* the fundamental, sustained activity of Jewish communities throughout history. Let leadership take care of itself; the sea change the Jewish community is in desperate need of is more people, in every age bracket and level of commitment, engaged with the fundamental questions of education.

These fundamental questions of education, in my experience, are not at the core of training in our residential summer camps and elsewhere. Active throughout high school, college and the ensuing years in a Jewish youth group at local, regional and international levels; the product of programming geared toward my professional growth in an educationally minded residential Jewish summer camp as a camper, junior staff member and member of the administration; and deeply engaged in multiple capacities with the Hillel on a college campus, the hundreds of hours of programming attempting to prepare me to plan and execute programs, to shape the institutions themselves and, ultimately, the broader Jewish community, I found that this preparation always seemed to be about something other than educational impact. As I moved up through the ranks at Ramah in my early years on staff, such frustrations boiled over in an early session of the PIE curriculum. There, in a pique of late-adolescent idealistic simplification, I suggested that what the camp requested of its staff was achievable by anyone with basic human empathy and around eighteen years of life experience. The intellectually complicated parts of the job that could have further inspired my colleagues seemed to be wholly ignored by our supervisors and mentors in professional development seminars, the elephant in the room ignored so we could settle for providing a lowest-common-denominator experience.

Today, in spite of a more nuanced (and, I hope, reasonable) approach to the contributions that my colleagues who have developed and implemented the staff training program at Ramah Wisconsin and elsewhere have to offer our staff members—and that those working in other settings offer to trip leaders, Hillel professionals, day camp counselors, and others—I remain wholly convinced that though an appreciation for psycho-social profiles of our campers; development, teamwork and communication skills, health and safety rationales and regulations, an appreciation for the nuances of risk management and more are *necessary* for success, they are neither sufficient nor do they belong at the center of our work. We owe it to ourselves and to the motivating mission of our institutions to aim higher, to engage fully in a conversation about how best to effect learning, to design and capitalize on transformational experiences and to nurture our campers/students/participants/program attendees toward acquiring the building blocks of Jewish literacy and then interpreting those puzzle pieces into something meaningful to them in their circumstances. This re-centering of education at the core of our joint work is the central animating idea of PIE, and it is an approach that is applicable in all settings.

THE PIE CURRICULUM: AN OVERVIEW

A full analysis of PIE as curriculum and experience would require an analysis of a curricular binder that reached five hundred pages, in-depth interviews with the fifteen campers who participated in the fully realized version in the summer of 2002 and an attempted reconstruction of the educational experience in the class and its lasting impact, all activities better undertaken by a different author. Depending on the approach taken by this more objective observer, such a study could focus on PIE as curriculum or as learning experience, or on the complicated dynamics the cohort ended up experiencing internal to the class (on the whole, overwhelmingly positive) and the unintended consequences for the social landscape of their age group at Ramah that summer (decidedly less rosy).

The experience itself was built on twenty-four sessions. Even the first cohort, which experienced by far the most robust of the three incarnations, met fewer than twenty times, combining some of the lessons and skipping others. The vision for the class was laid out in a series of documents—a syllabus and abstract, chiefly—handed out along with red three-ring binders at the beginning of our first meeting. In addition to short framing pieces, the syllabus listed all twenty-four classes by cryptic titles and the "task" (i.e., brief homework assignment) to be completed prior to each one. An "agenda"- almost always in the form of a rather opaque outline of the topics and points we would cover—was prepared for each class, and one of the participants volunteered to take notes on a laptop computer. Agendas, notes and supplementary materials were intended, from the outset, to be enhanced, hole-punched and placed in the binders, a project I was unfortunately able to complete (including writing agendas and notes for the classes we had not had time to conduct at camp) only well after the summer and that only a small fraction of the class ever received.

A major challenge of designing the class was that I lacked training in curricular design and had never taken a course in education, let alone one from which I could directly borrow for a class attempting to introduce rising high school juniors to the philosophies and practicalities of education at Camp Ramah in Wisconsin. The class suffered, I am quite sure, from the limits of my own perspective as a twenty-year-old counselor, my own curricular and intellectual predilections that shaped the choices I made (relying, for example, on the curricular technique of "set induction" and its possible "wow" moments to a nauseating degree) and the haphazard way the curriculum was assembled before the summer (and, even more so, the last-second preparations I would try and complete before each and every class). Perhaps not surprisingly, I was more interested in the class looking interesting and academically serious (more on this in a moment) than I was in the participants; learning.

The curriculum consists of twenty-four class sessions, each of which falls into one of three broad areas (see Table 1). Framed by an opening and closing session, the class spans (I) a philosophical introduction to informal education, with a focus on the "Nine Pillars" that represent my philosophy of building educational experiences at Ramah; (II) the application and in-depth discussion of the pillars themselves; and (III) a series of workshops that cover crucial skill sets for executors of the type of informal educational programming on which PIE focuses.

	Topic Heading	Class #s	Sample Titles
I	Philosophical Introduction to Informal Education	#2–6	**Camp's Big Secret: What You're Really Learning To Do; Anti-Semitism in Every City in the Country: Why Education Should Be More Jewish**
II	Practical Applications	#7,9–12;14–20	**How Smart Are The Patients on ER? And Why Do We See the Previews We Do at the Movies?; A Lesson from the Civil Rights Movement: Educational Integration**
III	Skill-building Workshops	#8, 13, 21–23	**A Four-Letter Word We Shouldn't Fear; De Oratione**

PIE attempted to accomplish the best of both worlds, to speak to the intellectual curiosities and significant academic abilities of the participants while resisting the adoption of the stultifying environment many associate with so-called formal settings. Of course, this attempt is not innovative; I hope that many have experienced, as I have, the divine flavoring of the best classrooms where the teacher builds an atmosphere where feelings of community and playfulness are understood to enhance the rigor of the learning. Unfortunately, we find these classrooms all too often in the world of schools where the exceptional educator—blessed, often, with charisma and charm—infuses characteristics most associated with informal settings (abiding sense of community and caring about individual personalities; an air of informality in dress, seating arrangements, language or conversational style; a sense that everything should be fun) into formal ones. I longed, during my many years at camp, in youth group and in Hillel, for someone to make the parallel move into those informal settings, and I kept longing. PIE was an attempt to crystallize a notion of the serious intellectual work I had always intuited was happening at camp, but that few wanted to admit to and, seemingly, no one wanted to call by name.

With PIE I was testing out a core principle of my own emerging theory of the power of so-called "informal" settings: quality attracts; adolescents will gravitate toward even the most rigorous intellectual environment as long as it is presented in an interesting (even entertaining) way. I wanted, then, to build into the design of the class a number of obvious nods to the informal characteristics I mentioned above, even while trusting myself to recreate a feeling in the classroom I had already experienced on multiple occasions in high school and college classes. Thus was born the need for the individual session titles, each of which could be a working title for a popular work in the social sciences. Assigning "homework" in camp seemed as if it could be interpreted as onerous, so with the vast majority of the tasks I attempted to craft clever, simple questions that were quickly doable, would likely provide diverse, meaningful fodder on which we could base the beginning of our discussions and from which I planned to reach my pre-determined conclusions. On the first day, sitting in a classroom in the camp library that was our official home base, we collected suggestions from the participants as to places around camp where they wanted to have class—and then did. Most memorable was the discussion we had about paradigms of institutional change sitting on the soccer field, one participant dutifully typing away on the laptop. And each class would begin with "This is Your Life," an opportunity for two of the participants to briefly check in with the group on how they were doing and what was going on in their camp lives on that day.

Though I doubt that any of these nods to informality would have mattered had I not embraced the implicit assumptions about the informality of the class in each and every moment of interaction, each of these structural approaches helped convey the message at the outset that however different this experience would be, it would resonate with the participants' understandings of the cultural norms of camp. The class became a beloved part of the campers' summers as a majority of them embraced opportunities to meet during free time (usually in the late afternoons and late at night), when it became clear that we would not have enough time to complete the entire curriculum relying solely on our scheduled sessions. PIE may have been successful in many ways, though I lack concrete evidence to demonstrate either success or failure in most regards. I am, however, quite confident that the participants greatly enjoyed themselves and that, as a result, they began conversations about educational philosophy and how the camp might function educationally well before they otherwise would have. That surely is a form of learning, though we lack measured documentation of the learning and its true impact.

CORE PRINCIPLES

Though I have touched on each of them in passing, there are three core principles that motivated the design and implementation of PIE that deserve explicit attention. After discussing them I will briefly note three minor points that, rather than being specific to PIE itself, are essential considerations for anyone attempting to design an educational entrée to prospective informal educators.

Formalizing the education of informal educators. Even with recent attempts to address the challenge in certain ways among specific populations, far too often we assume that wholly informal and implicit training is enough to prepare informal educators. As dangerous is the reigning assumption in the field: that serving as a participant in a program and expressing an interest in returning to help execute future iterations of that program or a similar one somehow qualify an individual to do so. These assumptions build on and conflate a number of others: informal education "just happens;" "leadership training" trains educators; learning the rules of how an institution runs and how it aims to keep those under its care safe and healthy is enough to set up staff members for success.

Valid arguments about the constant nature of human learning notwithstanding, excellent educational institutions, whether they take place in formal or informal settings, do not just happen. They are the result of careful, articulated thought processes and a series of explicit choices. The important role of vision in education (Reimer 2011; Pekarsky 1997; Fox 1997) is well documented, and though visionaries ought not also be micro-managers, compelling visions help classroom teachers, camp counselors and specialists, trip leaders and others make decisions in the moment that are consonant with the values and goals of the institutions they serve.

As mentioned at the outset, the recent investment in training a mid-level cohort of informal educators undertaken by foundations and academic institutions in the recent past is important, but it is not enough. PIE attempted, briefly, to fill a still-extant gaping void in the staff development process of one of the leading examples of educational Jewish summer camping; it set out to provide a modicum of introduction to how Ramah may function educationally. If the vaunted Ramah camping movement has failed to invest in formalizing significant educational training for the line staff vested with the immense responsibility of direct service to campers, the whole field is suffering mightily. (I am not ignorant of the practical and possibly insurmountable challenge that a scarcity of resources—time and money, at the least—poses for fixing this problem. That being said, I am wholly convinced that we can do much more than we currently do.)

With a lack of obvious empirical evidence, embrace what you can. When imagining what a formalized program for aspiring informal educators might look like, we are faced with a challenge that plagues the world of teacher education as well: It is difficult to document education in action. Though innovations in video documentation, collecting student work and teacher diaries have begun to assuage this challenge in the world of teacher education, informal settings may pose even more difficulties. Ethnographic studies, even where they exist (Saxe and Chazan 2008; Reimer 1997; Bekerman 1986; Farago 1971) have their limitations, especially in that they almost never speak directly to a specific setting and context.

A fundamental principle of PIE is to take advantage of what we may, borrowing from Lortie (1977), call the informal educator's "apprenticeship of observation." Especially when dealing with a cohort that has a set of joint experiences, the shared memories of the group, their perspectives on how the setting functions, what specific overt or covert educational attempts have been more and less successful and their own ideas for improving their experience can serve as imperfect but acceptable replacements for hard, dispassionate evidence. This is not to disagree with Lortie's conclusions about the negative consequences of apprenticeships of observation; far from it. There remains, as ever, important work to be done helping aspiring educators change their own preconceptions and impressions of the educator's role from that of student/consumer to professional. Yet the shared memory of the group provides a rich set of aural "texts" that can be studied, challenged and interpreted. The power of this information is further augmented when instructors or mentors of the group who have witnessed some or all of their memories and who also have experience with a given institution can help the group wade through their own fickle memories. This was a particular advantage I had in all three incarnations of PIE.

The applications for this work outside of populations drawn exclusively from the same summer camps, schools or perhaps Hillels will undoubtedly be different than within them. Even so, reflections on participants' recollections from their own lives ought to be scaffolded and framed so that the group can "study" shared material.

In addition to memory, one's resourcefulness in identifying and utilizing other primary documents of participants' experience is crucial. The PIE curriculum devoted two full class periods to reading the write-ups of educational programs that had been developed for Ramah in Wisconsin over previous summers. One full session consisted of analyzing programs these particular campers had experienced over their last two summers at camp. Introducing the participants to the content, process and evaluation (especially when that evaluation can be compared with their own) of concrete programs can help them begin to appreciate the type of conscious decision-making, development of expertise and ability to reflect on, critique and then improve upon one's own work that defines the practice of excellent educators. To the extent that other documents may exist espousing policy rationale or an institution's philosophy, or that a trusted staff member may be open to an interview and discussion about his or her own work, such methods should absolutely be used to help surface and study what is often hidden, silent work.

Theory is not a bad word. In much of the world of education, and especially in conversations *about* education by non-educators, suspicions abound about the value and import of theory. In the world of IJE, theory plays an even smaller role. Yet theory is what helps us make sense of the complicated questions we face and guides us in exploring, in practice, what works and what does not. We all have working theories based on experience, personal values and predilections, and our conceptions of the field and our work within it. In the absence of theory we create our own, either internally or, more often, by interpreting a variety of things we hear and see around us impressionistically. Perhaps as important, the inherent curiosity and skepticism of adolescents creates an intense thirst for explanations of why things happen the way they do. This is not to say that, when exposed to answers to those questions, the adolescents are necessarily likely to agree. But the conversations about why things work the way they do is one of the competing theories that are crucial for us to initiate with aspiring educators.

There is a wide variety of areas of theory that may be relevant to programs designed to prepare educators for IJE settings. Developing such a program from scratch would require making decisions about including a wide variety of theoretical approaches to setting (Zeldin 2006; Reimer 2003; 2007; Chazan 2003) and the learning process within it, from the acclaimed masters (Dewey 1900; 1902; 1916; Vygotsky 1978) to contemporary scholars playing with their own theories of sociocultural learning (Rogoff 1990; Cole 1996; Lave and Wenger 1991). Theories of development psychology (Piaget 1952; Kohlberg & Mayer 1972), of the role of vision (Pekarsky 1997; 2007; Reimer 2011), and many more areas ought at least to be considered.

PIE unabashedly attempted to open up theoretical conversations about how certain components of the participants' experience at Ramah in Wisconsin could be explained. Relying on my own shoddy methods and the answers peers and I had developed over summers together at camp, we presented for discussion theories about the breadth of content, skills and ideas that Ramah hopes to teach its campers; what one of the most emphasized (and hidden) goals is; and how one may be able to explain why camp functions as it does. Some of the theories offered were more compelling to the participants than others. More productively, the introduction of theories from those with more experience at camp may have helped catalyze a process of "legitimate peripheral participation" (Lave and Wenger, 1991), opening up a conversation that the sixteen-year-old participants could already participate in and one to which they could already contribute.

The most significant theory offered in PIE is one I had developed to guide my own approach to educational programming, the planning of which is one of the key components of the role of non-specialist junior staff members. Over the course of three class sessions we discussed the nine pillars of programming and then used the vocabulary of that theory and its content to guide us through nearly the entire rest of the course. Throughout the process I attempted to emphasize that the extent to which my specific theory was compelling and helpful was its only relevance; far more important than one specific theory is that one works to develop frameworks of thought, regularly revisited and, if necessary, tweaked, to guide one's work.

One of the positive consequences of the introduction of theory is that, by necessity, theories provide a technical vocabulary to help describe, in shared terms, that which may not be named by many practitioners. They can also provide a professional shorthand (negatively termed as jargon) that can simplify internal communication and help to build even more substantial theories within a specific cohort.

Additional minor points. In developing PIE I embraced intellectual honesty; demanded excellence from myself, the material and the participants; and consciously attempted to model in my own "classroom" the values and norms I hoped my participants would enact in theirs. When working with adolescents, who possess an inherent skepticism about the status quo and a deep yearning for what they understand as authentic, relevant and important experiences, intellectual dishonesty will get us nowhere. We must be honest with ourselves as educators and, even more important, must be honest with those we are attempting to nudge toward becoming our professional partners. Our own ability to question systems that exist, to freely acknowledge institutional shortcomings and our own personal failures and to unabashedly refer to things as they are need not serve to dishearten our charges or scare them away. Rather, when done appropriately, intellectual honesty will help reveal how deeply committed we are to the visions we attempt to enact, how much we believe in the educational mission to which we have dedicated ourselves and how human we are in our attempts to succeed.

In a marketplace flooded with ideas and products, excellence matters. As we know from our experiences with the up-and-coming institutions that will shape Jewish life for the next decades, they are defined by excellence. We must demand it of ourselves as well. To the extent that it succeeded, PIE worked because of its quality and the quality it demanded from the participants. The binders, the syllabus, the homework assignments and the organization and expectations that they represented sent a powerful message from day one that what happened in PIE would meet the participants at their level: rising high school juniors with elaborate extracurricular involvements on their way to elite universities and promising professional training and careers. Few groups of American Jewish high school or college students will deviate significantly from this characterization. Excellence is also defined by challenging them with intellectual theories, conducting the class as a college seminar and being intellectually honest with myself and them.

The playfulness and seriousness of PIE, the engagement with the participants as people through "This is Your Life," and the creation of a safe space in which any topic was worthy of serious discussion made our time together a model for the cabin environments, programming and general demeanor I hoped the participants would create when they returned as staff members, at home in their youth groups and on their now-quickly-emerging professional lives. These values are consonant with the philosophical vision of Ramah as I understand it, and they are core aspects of my own personal, professional and academic life. The experience of PIE represents a type of holistic approach to Judaism, to educational thinking and to an approach to living that has implications far beyond the circle the sixteen of us created wherever we chose to have class.

A FUTURE OUTGROWTH OF PIE: A LABORATORY CAMP

The takeaways from PIE, its challenges and drawbacks notwithstanding, are significant. First, we need more programs like PIE that welcome prospective future educators into a high-level, nuanced conversation that treats the subject matter, the participants and their future roles with the reverence they deserve. Second, we need more documentation of the learning that happens in IJE settings in the form of the creation and preservation of primary documents, the recording via audio or video of specific experiences, the publication of firsthand researcher accounts (with analysis) and the development of a theory and philosophy that can lead to a professional shared vocabulary that pushes the field forward. Third, the field of IJE—and the Jewish communal world that has turned its eyes to us to ensure its future—needs to fully embrace the significant parallels the discussion above shares with the best practices of teacher education. We need to start treating the educators we rely on to provide maximal impact for their students as well as any educators can be treated.

As the organized Jewish community continues its decades-old war against assimilation (regardless of to what extent we may disagree with its methods, rationale and ultimate goals), those in the trenches of that war—front-line educators in summer camps, Hillels, Israel trips, day schools, service-learning trips and more—need to be acknowledged as key figures. Even better would be an appropriate re-shaping of the communal agenda to note that it is the front-line educators who are young and passionate who very well may receive the *greatest benefits* from these programs, not the participants themselves. To welcome the thousands of camp counselors, thousands of college students helping to plan and execute programming on their campuses and hundreds of Israel trip leaders into a conversation about the philosophy, best practices and idealized impacts of Jewish education on the highest levels is, perhaps, to do more for the future of the Jewish people than anything else. Many of these young adults (nearly all of whom are college students or recent graduates) will become Jewish professionals in their own right, now blessed with a head start in terms of their own thinking about education. Those who end up working for non-obvious educational institutions—major philanthropic foundations, communal agencies and federations, the development wings of all organizations—will have access to and, in all likelihood, be invested in

Jewish education in a way they currently are not. Finally, and perhaps more profoundly, those who do not enter Jewish professional life will consist of the core of the next generation's Jewish community. They will be parents of children with choices to make about educational institutions and spending. They will belong to synagogues (or prayer communities), donate to federations (or their equivalent) and much more. Eventually they will sit on boards, contribute significant monies, serve in major philanthropic and leadership roles in the Jewish community. Why are we not taking advantage of the opportunity to expose this massive underpaid and under-appreciated cohort to a rigorous conversation about Jewish education that, if nothing else, might make the jobs of their children's educators easier in the coming decades?

While this author, at the age of twenty, was limited to attempting to enact PIE as best he could, over ten years later my ambition is greater. Utilizing the outline and goals that PIE introduced, the Jewish community needs to create a laboratory for research into IJE and the professional development of educators. Using a site like Camp Ramah in Wisconsin or similar camps in the Bnai Akiva, URJ and Young Judea movements, or the best educational independent camps, or partnering with a series of organizations encompassing a variety of settings, we need to begin doing this work. In addition to developing curricula and preparing individuals to teach PIE–like classes in their own diverse settings, the laboratory campus would be a place to welcome cohorts of aspiring and seasoned professionals to embark on intensive training programs. It would be a site where researchers would document learning and teaching, reaching toward greater degrees of excellence. It would be a site that would serve as an incubator for cutting-edge programs that may end up proliferating to many sites or finding their permanent footing at one after honing the project.

This laboratory campus would partner with an existing academic institution or develop its own think tank to oversee the dissemination of information, ongoing curriculum development, mentoring, alumni networks, theory development and more. It would embrace the truism that its worth as a laboratory is fully dependent on its ability to provide excellent, cutting-edge programming to its own clientele, and it would hold itself to the highest standards of administration, facilities, fundraising and caring for its participants in order to maximize the import and impact of the crucial work being done at its site.

A laboratory campus need not be a far-fetched dream. It requires only a single, visionary funder or existing institution to plant the seed and begin programming, however modestly. Its creation would represent a true tipping point in the world of IJE and would fundamentally alter the landscape of all Jewish education. In a not-so-distant future the laboratory campus could host a core group of fellows and faculty for an extended period of time while welcoming cohorts of day school teachers, pulpit rabbis, agency professionals and Jewish artists from a variety of disciplines for shorter-term residencies. It would serve as a clearinghouse for new ideas and best practices, committed simultaneously to being relevant and to serving as a powerful stimulus for future growth.

PIE was a dream I had ten years ago, in the spring of 2002. Its implementation was marked by my own inexperience and naïveté. Yet it filled a gap that continues to exist in the landscape of Jewish education—a gap that, if not filled, will continue to plague and stymie educators in the settings for Jewish education that provide the most impact. The lessons of PIE are many, and we ought to scale up this work in order to simply and fundamentally alter the educational potential of institutions engaged in IJE. While the recent development of graduate-level programs in IJE are noble, the creators of those programs cannot be as successful as the community needs them to be without dreaming more broadly and ambitiously about the state of the field.

WORKS CITED

Bekerman, Z. (1986). *The Social Construction of Jewishness: An Anthropological Interactional Study of a Camp System*. Doctoral dissertation. Jewish Theological Seminary of America.

Chazan, B. (2003). "The Philosophy of Informal Jewish Education." *The Encyclopedia of Informal Education*.

Cole, M. (1996). *Cultural Psychology: A Once and Future Discipline*. Cambridge, MA: Belknap Press.

Cytryn, J. (2011). Beyond "Formal vs. Informal": Good Education Is Good Education. *HaYidion: The RAVSAK Journal*. Winter 2011, 18–19.

Dewey, J. (1900). *School and Society*. Chicago. University of Chicago Press.

Dewey, J. (1902). *The Child and the Curriculum*. Chicago. University of Chicago Press.

Dewey, J. (1916). *Democracy and Education*. New York. Macmillan.

Farago, U. (1971). *The Influence of a Jewish Summer Camp's Social Climate on the Camper's Identity*. Doctoral dissertation. Brandeis University.

Fox, S., and W. Novak (1997). *Vision at the Heart: Lessons from Camp Ramah on the Power of Ideas in Shaping Educational Institutions*. Jerusalem: Mandel Institute.

Kohlberg, L. and R. Mayer (1972). "Development as the Aim of Education." *Harvard Educational Review* 42, 449–496.

Lave, J. and E. Wenger (1991). *Situated Learning: Legitimate Peripheral Perception*. New York: Cambridge University Press.

Lortie, D. (1977). *Schoolteacher: A Sociological Study*. Chicago: University of Chicago Press.

Pekarsky, D. (1997). "The Place of Vision in Jewish Educational Reform." *Journal of Jewish Education* 63 (1): 31–40.

Pekarsky, D. (2007). "Vision and Education: Arguments, Counterarguments, Rejoinders." *American Journal of Education* 113 (3), 423–450.

Piaget, J. (1952). *The Origins of Intelligence in Children* (2nd Ed) (M. Cook, Trans.). New York: International Universities Press, Inc.

Reimer, J. (1997). *Succeeding at a Jewish Education: How One Synagogue Made It Work*. Philadelphia: Jewish Publication Society.

Reimer, J. (2003). A Response to Barry Chazan: The Philosophy of Informal Jewish Education. *The Encyclopedia of Informal Education*. Retrieved from: www.infed.org/informaleducation/informal_jewish_education_reply.htm.

Reimer, J. (2007). Beyond "More Jews Doing Jewish": Clarifying the Goals of Informal Jewish Education. *Journal of Jewish Education* 73(1), 5–23.

Reimer, J. (2011). Vision, "Leadership, and Change: The Case of Ramah Summer Camps." *Journal of Jewish Education* 76 (3), 246–271.

Rogoff, B. (1990). *Apprenticeship in Thinking: Cognitive Development in Social Context*. New York: Oxford University Press.

Sales, A. L. and L. Saxe (2003). *How Goodly Are Thy Tents: Summer Camps as Jewish Socializing Experience*. Lebanon, NH: Brandeis University Press.

Saxe, L. and B. Chazan (2008). *Ten Days of Birthright Israel: A Journey in Young Adult Identity*. Lebanon, NH: Brandeis University Press.

Vygotsky, L.S. (1978). *Mind in Society: The Development of Higher Psychological Processes*. M. Cole, V. John-Steiner, S. Scribner and E. Souberman (eds.). Cambridge, MA: Harvard University Press.

Zeldin, M. (2006). "Making the Magic in Reform Jewish Summer Camps." In M.M. Lorge and G.P. Zola (eds.), *A Place of Our Own: The Rise of Reform Jewish Camping*. Tuscaloosa, AL: University of Alabama Press.

THE EMERGENCE OF THE REFLECTIVE PRACTITIONER

Joshua Yarden

INTRODUCTION

Reflection is at the heart of experiential learning. Our fleeting experiences only become memorable through recognition and consideration. Reflective practice is the method through which a facilitator can learn to balance proficiency in subject matter with developing ethical character and cultivating meaningful relationships. The integrity of this equilibrium provides for sustainable life-long learning that supports individual growth within vibrant communities. Part one of this essay offers definitions that characterize the nature and the significance of three key elements of experiential learning. Part two relates a story about emerging reflective practitioners. The concepts discussed in part three explore several key principles of reflective practice that can be applied to any learning process.

EXPERIENTIAL LEARNING

Experiential learning is the process of acquiring knowledge through meaningful encounters. It is bound up in self-exploration, in our relationships with others and with the ideas that connect us. We shed our anonymity by sharing formative experiences, and we become integrated into each other's personal stories. Participants sense a curiously powerful energy during interactions that lead to spontaneous joy, probing investigation or conflict resolution. These instances stand out against mundane routines. Relationships come alive, creating powerful memories and lifelong friendships. As our identities evolve through genuine engagement, we discover the depths of our own character.

REFLECTIVE PRACTICE

Reflective practice is a method of converting common misconceptions into common sense. We often interpret new information to support the premature conclusions that were unsound in the first place. Sticking to one's beliefs is usually seen as a sign of integrity in our society, but some beliefs are unsustainable. We enhance our potential to act as agents of positive change by uprooting self-defeating assumptions. Reflective practitioners learn to investigate and address the discrepancies between what we choose to believe about our thoughts and actions, on the one hand, and what we are actually doing and achieving, on the other.

REFLECTION-IN-ACTION

Reflective practice is a method for promoting one's natural abilities to identify areas of personal growth and professional accomplishment. Just as physical mirrors and lenses enable us to adjust the focus and the depth of field in a telescope in order to look deep into outer space, conceptual reflective lenses enable us to access our insight, to look more deeply into our own minds in order to capture clearer images of what we notice, why we are inclined toward certain beliefs and how we can interpret the significance of our observations. You can expand your ability to achieve your goals by heightening your awareness, sharpening your focus and cultivating your innate capacities for intuitive and perceptive thinking. The objective is to put thoughtful decision making into action during meaningful encounters.

A CASE STUDY

Audrey, Daniel and Joanna worked closely together to plan, implement and assess their work. They also took part in a reflective practice research group. Working with a facilitator, they met weekly for one-on-one sessions and came together for team meetings, and each member conducted an individual investigation of some aspect of their work environment.[1]

Daniel investigated the way the voices of individuals were received within the dynamic of the group. He recognized certain relationships that characterized the subtle and not-so-subtle ways power was harnessed and exercised by members of the staff. He took particular notice of the way that everyone in the group endorsed the idea that the environment should be welcoming and inclusive of all of the participants, yet the more charismatic members tended to dominate planning and decision making, often marginalizing quieter members of the team.

Audrey's investigation focused on how people receive and employ feedback. It turned out that while people often *say* they value input from others, they are not usually very responsive to it and only employ it quite selectively. She observed in her own behavior and in others' that supervisors in particular use positive feedback to motivate their teams; subordinates aim to please their supervisors; and peer colleagues steer clear of negative criticism in order to protect their friendships. People regularly discussed the faults they noticed in others, but never directly, only with their friends and allies on the staff. She identified what she called "the veil of kindness".

Audrey's observations illustrated how feedback, while assumed to be a tool for fixing problems, was actually a method of creating a façade. The team members said they used feedback to improve their work, but their behavior was actually governed by a desire to avoid conflict. She challenged the unspoken assumption that excellence leads to discord, while congeniality leads to mediocrity, and questioned whether colleagues really have to choose between pursuing excellence and maintaining friendly relationships.

Joanna had been investigating the effect of formal and informal hierarchies on working relationships. She observed and explained how the structure of a group of colleagues creates spaces for people to fill, analogous to the way that the structure of a building creates rooms for people to occupy. After listening to Audrey's observations, Joanna realized that all of the information revealed through their investigations had been hidden in plain sight. Just as the walls of solid structures conceal the contents of rooms in a building, so virtual barriers that alienate people from one another in a social structure obstruct their ability to see and understand one another. Joanna observed how her colleagues found what they expected to see, often regardless of evidence to the contrary.

There were five additional team members conducting investigations, and each one provided everyone with a deeper understanding of their shared experiences. The insights reflected one another, as though each was a different facet of the same prism offering an additional perspective on the same subject. How is it that the educators were not initially able to observe some of the challenges they faced? Habit made it difficult, if not impossible, to recognize how their own operating procedures were working against their common interests. They believed they were cooperating by keeping their criticism to themselves, but their collaboration through reflective practice enabled them to uncover a deeper truth: Their mutual dissatisfaction could only be addressed mutually, by examining their behavior together in order to learn from each other's concerns.

Participation in the practitioner research group enabled the members to work through their discomfort in a safe, transparent and mutually supportive setting, but it was not a simple matter. The idea of dismantling the façade of their pleasant demeanor initially made some of the educators uneasy. They were apprehensive about what they might discover. After all, if building the buffer zone had enabled them to cooperate without getting in each other's way, removing it could set a conflict in motion. Their facilitator

---

[1] This case study is a composite illustration that draws upon the experience of several educators, gleaned from my experience over a period of many years as a facilitator of reflective investigation. This section, as well as some of the ideas discussed in section three, draws upon and rework material I collected and discussed in much greater detail in Yarden, J. (2008), *Embracing Complexity: A Reflective Investigation of Cultural Transformation through Experiential Learning*. Dissertation available online. ProQuest. Paper AAI3309528.

acted as both a catalyst for change and a control mechanism to keep the level of intensity of the process manageable and productive.

The educators were able to identify, understand and then abandon the unspoken and unreasonable assumption that it was necessary to choose between good work and good working relationships. They found that by balancing honesty with patience and kindness, they were able to discuss issues they previously considered too hot to touch. They discovered that frank discussions did not have to be callous or uncaring. After identifying the stumbling blocks to their success, they were able to offer each other more constructive feedback and to work together toward achieving their common goals.

IS REFLECTIVE PRACTICE FOR EVERYONE?

Audrey was initially a bit skeptical about making time in her already busy schedule to reflect, but after presenting to the team and listening to the others, she was surprised at how much they were able to learn about themselves, about each other and about how they could improve their outcomes as a team. She asked if reflective practice would work for everyone. Daniel asked if it ever becomes easier to use the "lenses", the frames of reference they had learned to use to examine their work, or if it always requires a conscious effort.

Reflective practice could be for anyone, because we can all learn from examining our experience. We are all subject to the same habit-forming ways of missing or misconstruing what we see. Even so, it will not necessarily work for everyone. You have to have a desire to rethink things you thought you already understood, to hunt your own assumptions and to learn from your own shortcomings as much as from your strengths. It requires an inquisitive mind, the stamina to stick with problems until you figure them out and, occasionally, the integrity to admit that you previously got it wrong. It also requires the sustained humility to realize that once you think you have figured something out, you always need to investigate your new assumptions.

As you gain insight with experience, a reflective outlook can become intuitive. At a certain stage you begin to detect assumptions without really trying, and then you begin to anticipate the misunderstandings they create. You begin to forget that you are "wearing the lenses". You just see more clearly. We are always looking at the world through some frame of reference that filters what we detect and what we ignore. These frames and lenses are always changing. We always begin by seeing without knowing what we are missing. Sometimes we recognize our own lack of familiarity with something of which we were unaware. Figuring out what we previously found perplexing leads us to develop confidence in our knowledge.

Beware of overconfidence; the ease of understanding that comes with experience can encourage us to stop paying close attention to getting the details right. This is why even accomplished specialists and star performers can benefit from various forms of collaborative learning such as reflective practice, artistic direction and professional coaching.[2]

ASSUMPTIONS[3]

We justifiably rely on our assumptions in many instances throughout every day, especially when we need to make instantaneous decisions. The pitfall of assumptive thinking is that we tend to rely upon mental shortcuts even when they lead us in the wrong direction. It is not always convenient to invest the necessary time and effort to discover our errors. It is particularly undesirable to do so if the principle governing our thinking is to prove that we are right, rather than to discover that we might be wrong. We

---

[2] "The key to being great at any given profession … is the ability to recognize failure" ("Atul Gawande: Excellence Is Recognizing Details, Failures," *Harvard Magazine* 10.25.12). "What I found over time, trying to follow and emulate people that were focused on achieving something more than competence, is that they weren't smarter than anybody else, they weren't geniuses … Instead they seemed to be people that could come to grips with their inherent fallibility—fallibility in the systems that they work in, and with what it took to overcome that fallibility." http://harvardmagazine.com/2012/10/excellence-is-recognizing-details-failures Accessed 2.18.2013. See also, Gawande, Atul, "Personal Best. Top Athletes and Singers Have Coaches. Should You?" *The New Yorker*, Oct. 3, 2011 < http://www.newyorker.com/reporting/2011/10/03/111003fa_fact_gawande> Accessed 2.18.2013.

[3] My work on assumptions and critical reflection has been informed by the work of Stephen D. Brookfield, in particular: (1995) *Becoming a Critically Reflective Teacher*. San Francisco: Jossey-Bass; (2005) "Learning Democratic Reason: The Adult Education Project of Jürgen Habermas." *Teachers College Record* 107(6) 2005 1127–1168; (2005) *The Power of Critical Theory: Liberating Adult Learning and Teaching*. San Francisco: Jossey-Bass.

tend to overlook our own biases and inclinations, quickly assuming rather than carefully considering the difference between what we *actually* know and what we only *think* we know. Confidence itself is not a measure of accuracy. Critical thinking is a matter of justifying our understanding according to logic, experimentation and evidence rather than personal preference or convenience.

We misconstrue simple things that inform our decision-making when an important understanding is actually a *mis*understanding. Discerning well-grounded understandings from unfounded opinions begins with learning to recognize the difference between valid and invalid assumptions. It is important to displace false impressions before they become influential frames of reference; once a misperception takes root in our consciousness, we become inclined to rely on it as we continue to construct our knowledge of the world. Evidence to the contrary may not be enough to shake our beliefs. In some cases only overwhelming proof can disabuse us of our errors in judgment. By that stage a shift in confidence can require deep personal transformation.

Technically incorrect assumptions can give rise to two kinds of very practical problems. First, we intuitively ascribe meaning to insignificant coincidences, and we act upon unsound foundations. Additionally, we can miss the actual meaning of connections that we are not predisposed to detect, and we miss those opportunities to gain insight from our experiences. The power of reflective thinking is in our potential to open our minds in order to seek out reliable input, learn to disabuse ourselves of our faulty notions and construct more legitimate interpretations of the situations we encounter.

OPEN SOURCE LEARNING

Learning from experience is a basic element of daily life, but we often rely upon chance to stumble upon our solutions. We tend to approve of our own decisions and actions, and we search out positive reinforcement for our existing beliefs.[4] In doing so, we affirm and continually reaffirm our own judgment in a feedback loop that cannot incorporate ideas or information from outside a closed system.[4] The natural process of trial and error tends to spawn new problems at least as quickly as it generates possible solutions. As a result, people reproduce and in some cases further entrench the very problems they aim to remedy.[6]

The following three interrelated strategies can enable you to avoid becoming another link in the chain that reinforces existing problems.

1. See problems as signs within the context of imbalanced systems.
2. Identify the patterns that indicate the root causes of dysfunction, as well as those that produce desired outcomes.
3. Generate solutions to supplant dysfunction with systems designed to achieve your goals.

The circles in the following series of diagrams represent various lenses or frames of reference. The lens on the left side of the first diagram represents a repeated *action*, and the lens on the right represents a repeated *reaction*.

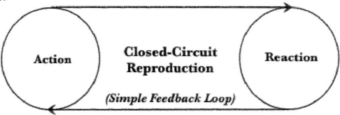

Attempting to overcome a recurring obstacle within a closed loop reproduces the problem.

Diagram 1

---

[4] For an informative review of cognitive biases, see DeLaplante, Kevin. "Cognitive Biases and the Authority of Science," http://www.criticalthinkeracademy.com/014-cognitive-biases-and-the-authority-of-science.html. Accessed 2.18.2013.

[5] Certain elements of this approach are loosely based on the theory of double-loop learning in Argyris, C. S. and D. A. Schön (1974), *Theory in Practice*. San Francisco: Jossey-Bass.

[6] For a thorough discussion of social reproduction, see Bourdieu, P. & J-C Passeron. (1977) *Reproduction in Education Society and Culture*. (2nd ed.) London: Sage. For a very readable review of Bourdieu and an array of subsequent social reproduction theorists, see the introduction to MacLeod, J. (1995), *Ain't No Makin' It*. San Francisco: Westview Press.

This self-perpetuating loop promotes stability, which is fine when a system is functioning well. Dysfunctional systems, however, promote their own eventual demise by resisting challenges rather than reconfiguring to address changing conditions. Perseverance can represent a determination for success, or it can be a mere rationalization for an endless loop of accommodation in the face of recurring failure. A reproduction loop *can* be disrupted either by the systemic collapse of a teetering imbalance or by a system undergoing a correction that establishes equilibrium.

The open-source approach integrates new ideas by seeking out collaborative environments beyond the limits of one's existing network and co-creating learning opportunities. Additional perspectives provide more varied speculation about how to address challenging problems. An active "learning community of practice" aims to view experience through multiple lenses, reflecting a broader and more diverse variety of experiences. Reflective practitioners share ideas, observe one another, learn from relevant literature and access outside sources to expand their comfort zones.

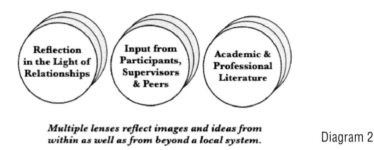

Multiple lenses reflect images and ideas from
within as well as from beyond a local system.

Diagram 2

Open-source learning can expose hidden problems and lead to addressing them in effective ways that would not become apparent in a closed system. It rejects "If it ain't broke, don't fix it" in favor of "I may not know, but I can probably find someone who can help me figure this out." You are unlikely to achieve your best results in a vacuum. Success is often achieved through collaborative effort. Expand the number of sources upon which you draw in order to define and achieve your goals, and you are likely to discover that you have not tapped nearly as much of your own potential as you might have assumed.

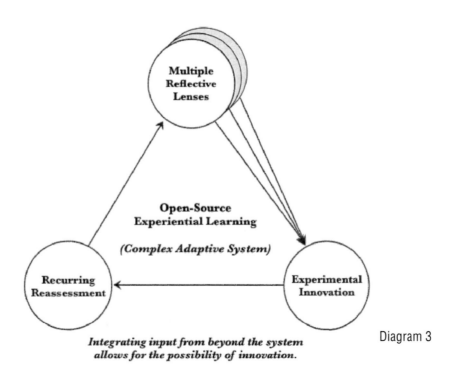

Integrating input from beyond the system
allows for the possibility of innovation.

Diagram 3

USING MULTIPLE REFLECTIVE LENSES

By using several frames of reference you can gather a large pool of useful data in order to generate more reliable interpretations of your observations. It may help to think in terms of capturing images with telephoto, wide-angle and magnifying lenses that help you see more sharply whether you are reading fine print close up, viewing something nearby or looking off into the distance. In a world of inexhaustible repositories of information it is necessary to be selective even as you become open to input from additional perspectives. You are not likely to find significant information every time you attempt to do so, but you are likely to find more indications of venues to pursue by broadening the search in the following directions:

- Examine the field.
  - What academic research relates to the issue at hand?
  - What cultural insights have been expressed through the creative arts?
  - What theories have been generated that may help to explain your observations?
- What and how can I learn by exploring others' perspectives?
  - My colleagues?
  - Those who are learning from me?
  - What can I learn about myself through the eyes of those who encounter me?
- Explore your own experience.
  - What seems to be particularly new or difficult to explain on an intuitive level?
  - How is my own autobiography relevant to my current situation?
  - What insights can I gain as I move through this investigation?

HOW TO: GOALS, CONTENT AND METHOD

The art of experiential learning design is a matter of creating opportunities for essential questions to emerge through open and honest investigation. A strong plan balances inspiring goals, meaningful content and engaging methods. Create a learning space that provides interesting possibilities for participants to become engaged within the learning context by being attentive to their needs and responsive to their contributions. Rather than subordinating learners to teachers, experiential teaching focuses on the learning process. The measure of a program or a course is not in the quantity of the content, but in the qualities of a curriculum that enables learners to internalize meaningful knowledge.

Clearly defined goals enable you to assess the extent to which you are achieving success. They also offer a basis for examining the ways in which you are missing the mark and how to improve your strategy. When your goals are clear, you can determine the appropriate content to communicate your message. If the content you choose is not a good reflection of your goals, then the outcome of your efforts will suffer from a discrepancy between what you set out to do and what you can actually achieve. Finally, employ methods that will communicate your message effectively. Choosing methods is the most important element of all, because your methods are the only part of your plan that the participants actually experience. The following paragraphs focus more specifically on goals, content and methods. The rubric at the end of this section offers a framework for integrating reflection into your practice.

GOALS: IF YOU HAVE NO GOALS, YOU WILL NEVER FAIL… OR SUCCEED

In creating goals for experiential learning encounters, we aim to provide opportunities for emotional, intellectual and behavioral growth. How does your plan for success touch on each one of those areas? How will your work inspire participants, transmit vitality through the learning experience and motivate them to become life-long seekers of knowledge? These qualities are not easily quantified. One way to gauge success is to begin with the expectation that everyone involved will have an opportunity to become both a learner and a teacher.

Ask how the experience itself, rather than some sort of exit exam or evaluation report, will engender curiosity and motivate people to help one another learn. In what ways does your plan enable learners to develop their identities, discover their limitations and explore their potential? In reviewing your work after a session or a project, ask how the community of learners has evolved in response to the encounter. Revisit and revise your goals periodically to ensure that you remain on track. You will learn from experience what contributes to reaching your goals, what detracts and what is missing from your plan.

Set goals for yourself as a learner as well as a teacher and facilitator of learning for others. What else would you like to learn about the content of your curriculum? What would you like to learn about the participants, about yourself and about your potential to enable others to learn? Prepare your curriculum as a guide for inquiry and understanding, including open questions that are not always designed to lead to exact answers. The questions learners adopt along the way are as important as the answers they receive; both will be important elements of how they will continue to pursue knowledge in the future.

CONTENT: CHALLENGE-BASED LEARNING

If you want to introduce participants to something new, construct a bridge of ideas stretching from the familiar to the unfamiliar via their interests and experiences. Begin to make your way to new ideas by first meeting learners where they are, starting with something they already understand. Then introduce something related. Help them see the connections and move on to an area they are likely to want to explore.

As learners take on greater responsibility in their projects they gain the ability to adopt and defend moral positions, and they develop a tolerance for ambiguity as reflected in ethical dilemmas. Each scenario provides genuine opportunities to cultivate skills for learning, coping and conflict resolution. Challenge-based learning prepares participants to face progressively more difficult responsibilities, to understand themselves as they come to understand one another and to resolve problems they encounter along the way.

Construct effective experiential frameworks by producing scenarios that offer authentic challenges with room for spontaneous interaction. Whether the medium is a ropes course, a mock trial or a product design session, activities begin as structured play and evolve into thoughtful collaborations. Whether participants are competing or helping friends to overcome a fear of heights, challenging a Supreme Court decision or engineering the next technical solution to a problem most people did not even realize they had, participants engage in their objectives not as spectators, but as actors and decision makers.

METHODS: THE WELL-FRAMED OPEN SPACE

The way space is used in a learning environment defines what sort of learning can happen there in much the same way that the design and utilization of physical structures determines what sort of activities can happen in various buildings. A bridge can traverse a river, but it would not be a good place to set up a movie theater; a skyscraper provides a great deal office space in a crowded urban setting, but it could not accommodate a baseball park. Educators frame learning spaces with ideas, materials, curricula and, most of all, the methods they employ during the encounter.

A lecturer, for example, divides a room into the small space from where the audience is addressed and the rest of the room, where people sit quietly to learn through largely passive engagement, if they are engaged at all. A question can temporarily reorient the dynamic to some extent, but the relationship remains essentially the same. Even if you are actively thinking, inspired and motivated—all potentially meaningful internal processes—you are still sitting quietly, listening to the presenter. In some cases a single source disseminating information can be a appropriate format to employ, but it is not necessarily the best model, and it is rarely if ever the only option. Given how commonly we see learners ignoring or resisting teachers, it is safe to say that unidirectional teaching is overused.

Experiential educators frame active, engaged learning spaces where learners become co-producers of their own meaningful experiences. Sharing the responsibility for learning brings down the divide between teacher and pupil. There are times when it is important to be a presenter and other times when it is more effective to be a listener or a learning companion. A well-framed, open and responsive space provides support and structure while allowing for the development of unscripted possibilities. Participants explore their potential as they learn, establish relationships and build community. Through their participation they join in the process of defining the framework. They share the responsibility as well as the credit for the success of their learning.

You can use the following rubric for planning an activity. Then return to it afterward to compare your intentions to the outcomes of the actual encounter. Reflect back on your role as a facilitator. Note the ways that you were responsive to the contributions of the participants and what else you would like to incorporate in the future. Using the rubric begins as a very deliberate exercise and becomes second nature over time.

Reflective Planning Rubric	(A) Inspiring Goals *Affective learning focuses on attitudes and emotions. What will the learner feel?*	(B) Meaningful Content *Cognitive learning focuses on knowledge acquisition. What will the learner know?*	(C) Engaging Methods *Behavioral learning focuses on active experience. What will the learner do?*
(1) Before an Encounter: *How does your plan provide for possibilities of self-discovery?*			
(2) During an Encounter: *How will your methods enable you to be attentive to needs and the contributions of the participants?*			
(3) After an Encounter: *How were you responsive to the participants? How will you respond to their input going forward?*			

THREE STAGES: OBSERVE, ASSESS, ADDRESS

These three stages provide a skeletal framework for transforming a workplace into a learning community of practice. While the principles can be explained through words on a page, the real value of reflective practice can only be discovered through experience. Many details and directions emerge though collaboration with a facilitator and peers, but you can take these ideas and engage in a self-guided process of trial and error to detect issues and assumptions worthy of closer examination.

STAGE I: OBSERVE

Study your surroundings as though you are a first-time visitor observing unfamiliar behavior. Suspend your natural tendency to rely on what you already know. Imagine you are an anthropologist or a travel writer who knows little or nothing about what you are seeing. Your job is to prepare a report for people who want to understand the intricacies of the culture you are observing. There is always more in our environment than we have attention to notice or time to process, so take this opportunity to adopt a fresh perspective.

Filter out the "noise" of your assumptions and become attentive to the "signals" that raise questions you may have ignored in the past. In order to become curious, sharp and attentive to details, you have to awaken your intuition. Pay close attention to anything that seems out of place or out of step. The feeling that something is not quite right can be a portal to a new awareness. Follow those leads toward deeper understanding.

The elements that determine the efficacy of teamwork become apparent differently in various contexts, but the core issues are quite similar across settings. Each of the following three elements—hierarchy, cooperation and diversity—characterizes an essential aspect of the way people function in groups. Taken together, they provide a tool you can use to assess the condition of any social organization. This approach can enable you to closely observe the significance of phenomena you may see on a regular basis, but which you investigate only rarely, if ever.

Hierarchy—There are explicit and implicit hierarchies, each of which can at times support and at other times inhibit the work of your team. In some instances a lot of energy is devoted to managing relationships without discussing them in a forthright manner. Perhaps one or more people are dissatisfied with their roles in the group. The dissatisfaction may be along formal lines of seniority or job titles, or it may have to do with issues such as gender, humor, cliques within the group or the manner in which the value of various individuals' contributions are recognized.

Cooperation—Everyone agrees that team members should cooperate, yet we do not always work effectively together. Sometimes cooperation means *separation:* "Live and let live." Doing what needs to be done without getting in each other's way is an efficient form of cooperation, but it can also lead to alienation between members of a team. There are times when people work better in close *collaboration,* but it can also be inefficient and in some cases ineffective. Your team may have a lot to accomplish in a limited period of time, and dividing responsibilities may be necessary. There are also instances of subtle or obvious *competition* among people who are cooperating, which may or may not be desirable. It could be designed into the structure of your team to promote productivity, or it could breed antagonism in the group dynamic.

Diversity—It is an objective fact that we do not all fit into the same categories recognized by our society. But whether we tolerate diversity or celebrate it, and how we set limits to what we can accept, is up to us to define though the policies we set, and even more so through our behavior toward each other. Some elements of diversity are *accepted,* even if not preferred. Other elements are highly valued, actively *embraced,* even worn as a badge of honor. Yet other elements of difference are *rejected,* either to protect the community or to protect the privileges of the powerful.

STAGE II: ASSESS

Having become an observant participant as you continue to play your active role in the group, you are carefully assessing the interactions among the participants and between the groups in your workplace. Consider how your team is dealing with hierarchy, cooperation and diversity. Use the results of your assessment to answer the following questions:

- How does the organizational structure of your team benefit the group?
- How are the elements of *separation, collaboration* and *competition* functioning?
- How are people listening and ensuring that everyone's voice is being heard? Is your environment actually as open and welcoming as it is said to be? Are the desired limits to diversity clearly communicated, and are subtle instances of discrimination or abuse dealt with effectively?
- What styles of leadership are present?
- Are there any indications of creativity, innovation or resistance to change?
- What is contributing to the success of your team, and what is diverting resources from achieving goals?

STAGE III: ADDRESS THE ISSUE

When you identify something worth addressing, formulate your question in terms of a worthwhile challenge that your team will want to resolve together. Bring the issue up for discussion. Simply having a transparent conversation about the issue is an important step in the right direction. Antagonistic exchanges, however, can motivate people to withdraw from an encounter, so focus on getting and keeping everyone on the same side of the issue.

As you discover and begin to investigate previously unacknowledged difficulties, it may seem that you are causing the problems simply by looking for them. This is a result of denying the presence of problematic issues. It is actually a good sign, because recognizing a problem is a necessary precondition to resolving the issue. Generate collaborative ideas and decide together when and how to divide responsibilities, taking into consideration how you can cooperate most effectively without imposing changes that are likely to alienate members of the group.

The idea of "moving people beyond their comfort zones" is often seen as a strategy to promote change, but it is more likely to shut down a willingness to take chances. People tend to prefer the comfort of familiar situations, even unpleasant ones, to the discomfort of not being able to predict what is likely to happen, as reflected in the expression "Better the devil you know (than the devil you don't)." On the one hand, enabling people to be comfortable, supported and valued encourages them to take chances. On the other hand, making a decision within a group offers safety in numbers, even when the direction itself is foolish or even dangerous.

The way to avoid the pitfalls of either pushing people out of their comfort zones or adopting self-defeating decisions is to investigate assumptions. Moving carefully through safe spaces as you work toward effective solutions enables people to expand their comfort zones through calculated risk. (The role of an experienced facilitator can be critically important in creating a safe space for effective learning, even among professionals.) Take this opportunity to clarify common goals as you decide together about a process for implementing an intervention.

IN CONCLUSION… THERE IS NOTHING NEW UNDER THE SUN

We are all emerging always—through our setbacks and disappointments as well as through our joys and our successes—usually rather slowly, and occasionally by a profound leap. The goal of reflective practice is to solve current problems without leaving matters worse than you found them and to move forward in a manner that averts future difficulties rather than putting obstacles in your path. Once you become aware of the signs that indicate your unsustainable assumptions, you can learn to interpret patterns of dysfunction. Then you can repair the elements or replace the systems that are not working. There is an undefined space between the impossible and the inevitable. This is where our viable visions have the potential to become practical realities, where our efforts can make a difference. Experience teaches us that some of our intentions do in fact bear fruit.

Committed learners seek out, recognize and supersede their limitations, and dedicated educators search for ways to enable others to become increasingly aware of their potential to become. If these ideas resonate with your sense of purpose, then interpret them through the lens of your experience. Adopt them, adapt them and make them your own. Search for ways that your work can help you animate that thin, still voice emanating as a faint whisper from within your spirit. Listen carefully to your intuition. Develop the insight to doubt your unfounded assumptions. Examine your experience for genuine meaning. When you are able express mutual aspirations clearly, your voice will reverberate in ways that help others to listen more carefully to one another and to themselves.

PRACTICAL REFLECTION ACTIVITIES AND EXERCISES FOR EXPERIENTIAL LEARNING AND PROFESSIONAL GROWTH

Richard D. Solomon, Ph.D.

"What exactly is repentance or *t'shuvah*? Repentance involves forsaking sins and removing such thoughts from one's way of thinking and resolving firmly never to do it again, as it is written, 'Let the wicked man forsake his way and the unrighteous man his thoughts, and let them return to the Eternal.'" (*Yishavahu* 55:7).

Maimonides on the Laws of Repentance in *Mishneh Torah-Hilkhot Teshuvah Halakhah* 2:2

Although Maimonides expressed the importance of reflection in repentance (*t'shuvah*) during the Days of Awe, *Yamin Noraim*, the major secular theoretical roots for reflection, can be found in the work of John Dewey and David A. Kolb. Accordingly, it was John Dewey who asserted, "We do not learn from experience…we learn from reflecting on experience." Moreover, it was David A. Kolb who first described the four-stage cycle of experiential learning that is listed below.

- **Stage One: Concrete Experience.** The learner experiences the original event.
- **Stage Two: Reflective Observation.** The learner cogitates on the meaning of the original experience.
- **Stage Three: Abstract Conceptualization.** The learner gains a more sophisticated understanding of the meaning of the original experience, which in turn informs the next stage in the cycle, active experimentation.
- **Stage Four: Active Experimentation.** Given an enhanced and more nuanced understanding of the experience through abstract conceptualization, the learner tries different ways to re-create or actively experiment with the original learning experience. These active experimentations, in turn, lead to new concrete experiences.

In addition to the theoretical work on reflection from Dewey and Kolb, there is significant research supporting the efficacy of reflection or "think time" for both learning and professional development.

For example, studies by Rowe (1972), Casteel and Stahl (1973), Tobin (1987) and others demonstrate a positive correlation between providing learners with reflection time and these outcomes:

- the length and correctness of student responses to questions posed by the teacher or another student.
- increase in the number of learners responding to a question.
- reduction in the number of learners who pass or don't answer a question.
- improved academic achievement.

We also have substantial evidence indicating that when teachers include reflection or "think time" during instruction, these positive changes in their own teaching behaviors also occur:

- Their questioning strategies tend to be more varied and flexible.
- They decrease the quantity and increase the quality and variety of their questions.

- They ask additional questions that require more complex information processing and higher-level thinking on the part of learners.

Regarding the research on the efficacy of teacher reflection on professional growth [Smylie and Conyers (1991), Osterman and Kottamp (2004). Quigley and Kuhne (1997), Valli (1997)], we have evidence that teachers

- develop a deeper understanding of their teaching.
- better assess their professional growth.
- develop more informed decision-making skills about their teaching.
- become more proactive and confident in their instructional practices.

In addition to the research on the efficacy of reflection on formal learning and professional development, Donald Schön (1967, 1985, 1991) has provided educators with an appreciation of how "reflection-in-action" enhances all aspects of experiential learning. More specifically, there is an expanding literature base on how reflection and reflection activities deepen and extend learning in informal education [Kolb (1988), Nadler et al. (1992), Priest et al. (1992), Deer, Richardson et al. (2001), Boud et al. (1985), University of Wisconsin Extension Service (2007 and 2011–12), Sugerman et al. (2000)].

HOLY TIME AND SPACE

Before we share specific reflection activities that can be incorporated into Jewish formal (i.e., religious school classroom, lecture hall, adult education class at the synagogue, etc.) and informal settings (i.e., camp, group activity location, trip to Israel or other important Jewish sites), let's discuss two important Jewish constructs, holy time (*zman kadosh*) and holy space (*makom kadosh*).

As a people we distinguish ourselves by establishing both holy time (*zman kadosh*) and holy space (*makom kadosh*) through the following activities:

- daily prayers (i.e., waking up in the morning, before and after meals, etc.)
- weekly blessings (i.e., lighting the Shabbat candles, lighting the havdalah candle, smelling the spices, etc.)
- seasonal prayers (i.e., lighting candles for Rosh Hashanah, Yom Kippur, Hanukkah, etc.)
- celebrating the cyclical events in our lives (i.e., *brit milah, b'nai mitzvah, kiddushin,* etc.)
- experiencing the precious moments of living (e.g., reciting the *Sheheheyanu* prayer at the *Kotel*)
- supporting those who need healing (i.e., saying the *Mishabeirakh* prayer)
- honoring those we have lost (i.e., reciting the *Kaddish* prayer)

These Jewish prayers, blessings, meditations and reflections transform that which is secular and profane—time and space—into something sacred and holy. These prayers, blessings, meditations and reflections are not relegated to nor conducted solely within the synagogue's sanctuary or the Jewish classroom. In fact, these acts of sanctification take place in the home, at camp, on local Jewish field trips and during excursions to Israel.

As Jewish educators, camp counselors, youth group leaders and tour guides we can embed these acts of sanctification into both formal and informal learning settings. In addition to these prayers and blessings below you will find a list and description of reflection activities that educators can implement before, during or at the end of an experiential learning event inside or outside your classroom.

Note: When we use the term "group leader' we are referring to a Jewish youth leader, a camp counselor in charge of a bunk with an assistant counselor, unit head, assistant head counselor, head counselor, camp director, tour guide, docent or any other person occupying a position of leadership in an informal Jewish setting.

1. SENTENCE COMPLETIONS

The educator states or records a sentence fragment such as:

- (reflection at the beginning of the activity) From this experience I hope to...
- (reflection during the activity) Right now I am thinking or feeling...
- (reflection at the end of the activity) Two things I learned from today's experience are...

2. THINK-PAIR-SHARE

The educator asks the participants to think about some aspect of what they are about to do, what they are doing or what they have just experienced.

Example: When I say the word *tzedakah,* what does that mean to you?

Participants are given time to reflect on the question posed and perhaps record their thoughts on the topic.

The educator places the learners in reflection pairs in which they discuss their individual thoughts.

At a designated time determined by the educator, each participant can share with the group:

1. what he or she was thinking.
2. what his or her reflection partner was thinking.
3. a synthesis of what the reflection partners were thinking.
4. a new thought/
5. the opportunity to say "I pass on this question."

3. COMMUNITY ROUND ROBIN

Each member of the experiential learning community is given some think time, perhaps thirty seconds, to reflect upon some topic determined by the teacher, group leader or member of the group; each person is given an opportunity to share a thought with the members of the experiential learning community. If members have a similar thought, they can say it in their own words.

4. DISCUSSION WHIP

The educator of the experiential group invites selected members of the learning community to share their thoughts or feelings in a few words. Accordingly, the educator might say, "as I point to you, tell us in a few sentences what you are thinking or feeling right now."

5. YOU'RE THE EDUCATOR

The educator of an experiential group poses a question to the learning community. After allowing for some "think time" for group reflection, the educator selects one member of the learning community to share his or her thoughts. After stating his/her reflections that person selects the next person to speak. Participants always have the right to pass or not share their thoughts.

6. DISCUSSION BALL

The educator poses a question to the learning community. After providing for some "think time" the group leader invites participants who wish to share their thoughts to raise their hands. The educator tosses a discussion ball (i.e., Nerf ball, Koosh ball, balloon ball, etc.) to one of the participants who wants to voice his or her reflections on the topic. After sharing his or her thoughts the speaker selects the next person to talk by stating the name of the person and gently tossing the discussion ball to him or her.

7. THE NUMBERS PROCEDURE

The educator poses a question to the experiential learning community. After providing for some "think time" the educator invites participants who wish to share their thoughts to raise their hands. The educator gives each participant who wants to speak a number, saying, for example, "You're number one, you're number two, you are number three," etc. These numbers determine the order for speaking to the members of the group.

8. REFLECTION PAIRS, TRIADS OR QUADS

Before, during or at the end of an experiential learning event the educator creates thinking or reflection pairs, triads or quads to engage in reflection time.

9. DYADIC ENCOUNTER

Dyadic Encounter is a specific paired reflection activity that follows these steps.

1. The educator places learners in reflection dyads (groups of two). Alternative: group members may select their own reflection partners.

2. Reflection dyads determine who completes sentence #1 first. Let us call you A and your reflection partner B. Let us assume that your partner, B, wants to go first. Remember, however, that B or A may pass at any time during the paired reflection activity.

3. B verbally completes the first sentence.

4. A may probe B or complete sentence 1. B may probe A's statement.

5. A completes sentence 2.

6. B may probe A or complete sentence 2.

7. The procedure continues until the dyad completes the nine unfinished sentences or the educator ends the activity.

8. If you want to modify the activity, start with any number or make up your own sentence starters.

---

1. My name is...
2. I live...
3. At the present time, I serve as…
4. The reason I am here is...
5. To me experiential learning means…
6. The mission of our school or organization is...
8. One thing I hope to do with our school or organization is...
9. One day I hope to…

---

10. HIDDEN AGENDA EXERCISE

A relationship activity designed to help a group surface its hidden agenda items

1. The educator explains that some members of the group may have hidden agenda items that are important to them and that are not being addressed. If these hidden agenda items are not surfaced and resolved, they can undermine the cohesion and productivity of the group. The educator then invites each member to record a concern on a piece of paper without including his or her name.

NOTE: Group members are not required to record a concern but must write something on the paper (e.g., "I pass") to protect the anonymity of those who would be sharing their concerns with the members of the class/group.

2. The educator collects all the members' papers and places them in a paper bag or hat.

3. The educator selects one of the written concerns from the paper bag and reads it to herself, and if she judges the concern to be appropriate for group discussion, she then reads it to the group.

   NOTE: Assuming the educator is responsible for justifying what takes place in a group, she has the right to decide which concerns to air with the group.

4. After reading the concern, the educator facilitates a problem-solving process that includes these steps:

   a. Determining the nature, intensity and pervasiveness of the problem.

   b. Generating alternatives.

   c. Selecting the most practical and effective alternative(s).

   d. Implementing a strategy to address the problem.

   e. Monitoring the strategy.

   f. Modifying and evaluating the strategy.

WHAT DO WE MEAN BY REFLECTION FOR PERSONAL AND PROFESSIONAL GROWTH?

Reflection for personal and professional growth refers to the dedicated time an experiential educator uses to cogitate upon his or her professional practices. There are two types of personal professional reflection activities:

1. Internal or self-reflection activities.

2. External, peer or collegial activities—reflection exercises that are implemented with fellow educators to improve professional practice. These external reflection activities can be done on site or online. Sometimes these cadres for collegial reflection are referred to as communities of practice or CoPs.

When educators assign time for personal and professional reflection the anticipated outcomes include (this is not a complete list):

1. To plan for instruction.

2. To modify instruction during a learning activity/program.

3. To assess the outcomes of the learning activity/program.

4. To plan an individual program for professional growth.

5. To problem-solve professional issues with colleagues.

6. To acquire new and more effective ways to facilitate learning.

7. To acquire new and more effective ways to mentor and supervise others.

Now let's identify several reflection practices that educators can use before or after an experiential learning event.

Note: All of the following internal and external reflection activities are fairly widespread in formal learning environments where good reflection is encouraged. We invite all experiential educators—those in formal and informal settings—to consider using these reflection activities to improve their professional practices.

SEVEN INTERNAL REFLECTION ACTIVITIES FOR PERSONAL AND PROFESSIONAL GROWTH

1. THE EIAG JOURNAL

The EIAG Journal is an internal reflection exercise that invites the professional to systematically think about an event (E) that occurred before, during or after an experiential learning experience. An explanation of the I, A and G follows:

E = Event or Experience: What event or experience happened today that was significant?

I = Identify what happened: What did you see or do?

A = Analyze: What were thinking and feeling at the time?

What do you think others were thinking and feeling?

G = Generalize:

What does this event or experience tell you about yourself as an educator?

What does this event or experience tell you about the participants in the experiential learning event?

What does this event or experience tell you about facilitating learning and leading groups?

What does this event tell you about experiential learning?

Other thoughts?

2. THE REFLECTION JOURNAL

Briefly record something you learned today that you want to remember in the future.

Record something new, if anything, that you learned about yourself today.

Record something new you learned about your learners today.

Record something new you learned about facilitating learning today.

Additional thoughts?

3. THE PROFESSIONAL REFLECTION LOG SAMPLE

Definition: A professional reflection log provides the educator with the opportunity to systematically think about (a) the educational decisions he/she made before and during the experiential activity or program; (b) the effectiveness of those decisions; (c) what to do in the future.

DATE	INTERVENTION	WHAT HAPPENED?	WHY DID IT HAPPEN?	PERSONAL LEARNING	WHAT'S NEXT?
10/10	Think-Pair-Share (TPS)	Learners responded well to the procedure. They spent too much time off task.	They liked the think time and opportunity to compare answers. They were not sure what to do and how long each phase of TPS would take.	Remember to clearly define the task and give specific time limits for TPS.	Ask Rabbi Keller how he prepares his learners for TPS. Try TPS with...
10/18	Time-Out	Eric sat in back of the room/hall in the time-out seat and seemed very upset with me.	He didn't like being singled out for misbehavior.	Time-out may create more problems than I anticipated. Perhaps I should ask the student/participant to tell me when he's ready to return to his seat. Maybe I should ask him to write down what he was doing, what rule he broke, and how he plans to modify his behavior.	Create a time-out form that a student/ participant must complete before returning to his/her seat.

4. SAMPLE FORMAT FOR AN INDIVIDUAL PROFESSIONAL DEVELOPMENT PLAN (IPDP)[1]·

Name:	Date:
Position:	School:

What is/are my goal/s for professional growth this year

How do my goals relate to the goals of my program?

How will I know that I have achieved my goals? What data will I use to determine if I have reached my goals?

How will this IPDP impact my learners?

Which of the professional development options/strategies/techniques listed in the boxes below will I use?

Collaborative Options	**Independent Options**
_____ Committee or task force participation	_____ Analyze audio/video tapes
_____ Delivery of workshops/courses	_____ Delivery of workshops/courses
_____ Development of instructional materials	_____ Development of instructional materials
_____ Discussion/study groups	_____ Experimentation or action
_____ Experimentation or action research	_____ Research within the program
_____ Networking group	_____ Professional visits
_____ New curriculum development	_____ Review of professional literature
_____ Participation in professional exchange program	_____ Staff development (course participation)
_____ Peer coaching	_____ Writing a reflective journal
_____ Professional visits	_____ Other (be specific)
_____ Team facilitation	
_____ Peer observation	
_____ Other (be specific)	

What material or human resources will you need to achieve your goal(s)?

How will you know that you are achieving your goal(s)? What evidence will there be to support your progress?

Experiential Educator: _____
Signature

Approved by: _____
Signature

5. END-OF-WEEK REFLECTION JOURNAL

> These significant events occurred this week:
>
> From these events I realize that …
>
> Here is an area that I must learn more about …
>
> This week I am very pleased that …
>
> Additional thoughts

---

[1] This IPDP is adapted from one used by the Montgomery County (MD) Public Schools.

6. LEARNER GOALS PLANNING FORMAT

Here are three major goals/learning outcomes I want my learners to achieve this coming year:
The major goals/learning outcomes of my program are:
How do my goals/learning outcomes for my learners and the goals/learning outcomes of my program connect?

7. REFLECTION ON THE PAST YEAR FORMAT

As I reflect upon my experience as a educator last year and I am about to begin a new year, I want to remember …
My best experience was …   This was because …
My worst experience was …   This was because …
This year I want to focus my learning on …
By the end of the year I hope to say to myself…

THE POWER OF EXTERNAL OR COLLEGIAL REFLECTION

Before we share several external reflection formats and practices, consider what Arthur L. Costa and Bena Kallick (April 2000) have written about the power of collegial reflection:

"The act of externalizing our internal voices and listening to the self-statements of our colleagues provides educators with an opportunity to:

1. Amplify the meaning of their work through the insight of others.
2. Apply meaning beyond the situation in which it was learned.
3. Make a commitment to modifications, plans and experimentation.
4. Document learning and provide a rich base of shared knowledge."

SEVEN EXTERNAL OR COLLEGIAL REFLECTION ACTIVITIES FOR PROFESSIONAL OR PERSONAL GROWTH

1. THINK-ALOUDS

Think-Alouds are the external expressions through speech or writing of one's internal reflections. Mentors or group leaders need to regularly model sharing their Think-Alouds with their mentees, and mentees need to be encouraged to give voice or put into writing their internal verbalizations. Through the use of Think-Alouds you enable the mentor and the mentee to understand and appreciate how novice, beginning and expert educators make professional decisions.

2. NOVICE EDUCATOR SELF-ASSESSMENT INVENTORY (LIPTON ET AL., 2001)

Key: On each line (____) in the boxes below, record the number 1, 2 or 3:

　　1 = I need assistance in this area right now.

　　2 = I think I have a handle on this, but I'd like to talk to someone with more experience.

　　3 = I feel comfortable about this right now

Information about Policies and Procedures	Resource Information
_____Educator evaluation system	_____Organizing/setting up my learning environment
_____Paperwork and deadlines	_____Accessing materials and resources in the facility or learning environment
_____Expectations of the supervisor	_____Arranging field trips
_____Expectations of my colleagues	_____Using the library and media resources
_____Communicating with parents	_____Working with special services
Working with Learners	**Time Management**
_____Establishing learning environment routines	_____Organizing my day/week
_____Motivating resistant learners	_____Learning activity/program or event planning
_____Maintaining participant discipline	_____Following the daily/weekly schedule
_____Differentiating learning for individual learners	_____Attending meetings
_____Implementing the curriculum	_____Supervising extracurricular activities
_____Evaluating learner progress	_____Opportunities for professional development
	_____Maintaining personal/professional balance

Here are other areas in which I'd like to receive some assistance:

_____

_____

_____

_____

_____

_____

_____

3. STRATEGIC QUESTIONS A MENTOR OR SUPERVISOR CAN POSE TO ACTIVATE AND EXPAND MENTEE THINKING DURING A PROFESSIONAL CONVERSATION

L. Lipton, B. Wellman and C. Humbard (2001) provide some helpful advice to mentors/supervisors about the strategic questions they might pose to their mentees. In particular, they argue that well-designed mentor questions can evoke two different kinds of thinking in their mentees:

　　1. Thinking that activates prior knowledge and engages the mentee.

　　2. Thinking that is expansive and invites the mentee to explores options.

The charts below identify sample questions from each of the above categories before and after facilitating a learning activity/program.

SAMPLE STRATEGIC QUESTIONS A MENTOR OR SUPERVISOR CAN POSE TO A MENTEE PRIOR TO IMPLEMENTING AN EXPERIENTIAL LEARNING ACTIVITY (LIPTON ET AL., 2001)

Sample questions that activate prior knowledge and engage the mentee	Sample questions that are expansive and help the mentee explore options
1. What are some of your current questions or concerns about this program/experiential learning activity?	1. How does this experiential learning activity relate to enduring Jewish knowledge?
2. What essential questions are you going to ask during the experiential learning activity?	2. Are there other essential questions that can be incorporated into this experiential learning activity?
3. What evidence will your learners demonstrate to prove that they understand your objective for the experiential learning activity?	3. Are there other assessments you can use for this experiential learning activity?
4. What assessments will you use for this experiential learning activity?	4. Are there other methods of engaging learners that you might use for this experiential learning activity?
5. Does your lesson meet the needs of ...?	5. Given this opportunity to think through plans for today's learning activity, what are some specific actions you intend to take to ensure success? [numbering has gone wonky here—see below]
6. Why did you choose to use _____ as the method for this experiential learning activity?	6. As you reflect on your plan for today's learning activity, what are some of the things that come to mind?
7. How do you plan on handling ... if he disrupts the class?	7. What are some of the differences between what you have planned and what we have discussed today?

SAMPLE STRATEGIC QUESTIONS A MENTOR OR SUPERVISOR CAN POSE TO A MENTEE AFTER IMPLEMENTING AN EXPERIENTIAL LEARNING ACTIVITY (LIPTON ET AL., 2001)

Sample questions that activate prior knowledge and engage the mentee	Sample questions that are expansive and help the mentee explore options
1. Now that the experiential learning activity is over, what, if any, are some of your questions or concerns about today's learning activity?	1. How did this experiential learning activity relate to enduring Jewish knowledge?
2. How satisfied are you that your learners were able to respond to the essential questions that you posed during the learning activity?	2. Are there other essential questions that could have been incorporated into this experiential learning activity?
3. How satisfied are you with the assessments you used for this learning activity?	3. What other assessments could you have used for this experiential learning activity?
4. Did your experiential learning activity meet the needs of ...?	4. Upon reflection, are there other methods that you should have used for this experiential learning activity?
5. Would you say ___ was an effective method of facilitating this experiential learning activity? Please explain your thinking.	5. Given this opportunity to think through today's experiential learning activity, what are some specific actions you intend to take in future?
6. How well did you handle ___ when he disrupted the experiential learning activity?	6. As you reflect on today's experiential learning activity, what are some of the things that come to mind?
7. What did you like most and least about today's experiential learning activity?	7. What have you learned from today's post conference?
	8. What other methods can you use next time to handle ___ when he disrupts the class/experiential learning activity?

4. GUIDELINES FOR WEEKLY PROFESSIONAL CONVERSATIONS AMONG MENTOR, PRE-SERVICE AND IN-SERVICE EDUCATORS (ROGERS AND BABINSKI, 2002)

• Make meetings voluntary and invitational. • Survey the staff for interests. • Begin on time. • Post an agenda. • Take minutes and distribute them to the entire staff. • Read and discuss professional articles and books.	• Have a specific curricular focus. • Encourage a knowledgeable educator to facilitate the conversations. • Request that the supervisor attend as a learner and equal group member. • Allow time for the sharing of ideas.

5. NEW EDUCATOR GROUP PROBLEM-SOLVING PROTOCOL (ROGERS AND BABINSKI, 2002)

Steps	Description	Minutes
1	Each educator talks briefly about a problem recently encountered or shares a success story.	15
2	Educators whose problems were discussed at the last meeting provide a follow-up report.	20–30
3	Two or three educators volunteer to very briefly present a problem to the group.	2
4	The group engages in problem solving with the presenting educator.	20–30 min. each person
5	The facilitator asks the participants to write a brief evaluation of the meeting.	5–10

6. THE TUNING PROTOCOL DEVELOPED BY JOSEPH MCDONALD AND DAVID ALLEN (IN T. BLYTHE ET AL., 2002)

Steps	Tuning Protocol Agenda	Minutes
1	Introduction: Facilitator briefly introduces protocol goals guidelines and schedule Colleagues briefly introduce themselves	10
2	Educator Presentation: Educator describes the context for learner work (e.g., writing, music, video, pictures, etc.) Educator poses a focus question to colleagues for their feedback Colleagues listen	20
3	Clarifying questions: Colleagues ask clarifying questions only (no feedback is given at this time)	5
4	Examination of learner work samples Samples of original/photocopied learner work are presented Video clips of presentation may also be presented	15
5	Reflection on feedback to be shared Colleagues silently pause to reflect upon the feedback they would like to share with the educator	2–3
6	Colleagues share feedback [is this numbering okay?] Colleagues share positive, negative and corrective feedback, and the educator listens Facilitator may remind colleagues of the educator's focus question (Step 2)	5
7	Educator reflection Educator responds to the feedback shared by his or her colleagues Facilitator may intervene to focus, clarify, etc. Colleagues listen	15
8	Debriefing Facilitator leads a discussion on the tuning experience: What was learned? What was helpful? What concerns were raised? Etc.	10

7. REFLECTION QUESTIONS TO GUIDE THE EXAMINATION OF LEARNER WORK (IN T. BLYTHE ET AL., 2002)

Question Focus	Sample Questions
Quality of learner work	What is the quality of this work?
	Is the work good enough for this age group?
	What standard should we use to judge this work?
	To what extent does this work meet or fail to meet that standard?
Educator's professional practice	What does this work indicate about the educator's professional practice?
	How might this experiential learning activity be improved?
	What other experiential practices might elevate the quality of this type of student work?
Learner's understanding	What does this work reveal about the learner's understanding of the topic or the assignment?
Learner's growth	What do these samples of participant work reveal about the learner's growth over time?
	What else might the educator do to support the growth of this learner?
Learner's intent	What does this work reveal about the learner's focus and interest in the subject?
	What parts of the experiential learning activity required the most and least effort from the learner?

Note: Below please find three reflection questions for the reader of this chapter to consider:

1. What would it take for the above internal and external reflection exercises to be implemented throughout all "good" learning environments?
2. What are some of the challenges that would prevent implementation?
3. How can these challenges be addressed in your learning environment?

CONCLUSION

In this chapter we have described some of the theoretical work (i.e., Dewey and Kolb) and research (i.e., Rowe, Castell and Stahl, Valli, Schön, Nadler et al., Priest et al., Deer Richardson et al., Boud et al., University of Wisconsin Extension Service, Sugerman et al.) supporting the use of reflection practices for both experiential learning, and the personal and professional growth of formal and informal experiential educators.

We then described how two Jewish constructs, sacred time (*zman kadosh*) and sacred space (*makom kadosh*), can be integrated within both formal (i.e., religious school classroom, lecture hall, adult education class at the synagogue, etc.) and informal (i.e., camps, group activity locations, Jewish sites, trips to Israel, etc.) Jewish educational settings.

Subsequently we listed, defined and explained ten reflection activities that can be implemented at the beginning, during and at the end of an experiential learning event.

In the last portion of the chapter we identified and explained seven internal (i.e., self-reflection) and seven external or collegial reflection exercises that are designed to promote personal and professional growth.

To deepen and enhance student learning and professional practices experience in and of itself does not improve performance. It is the time we dedicate and devote to reflect upon our experiences that makes the difference.

End note: In the Torah the importance of reflection is discussed in *Chesbon Hanefesh*. It is also specifically discussed in reference to educators undergoing consistent self-evaluation in *Klalei HaḤinuch*

Ve'Hahadrakha. In particular, see the Fifth Principle: The Educators Deliberate Reflection in Choosing Educational Approaches and Methods. This is the link for the Fifth Principle: http://tinyurl.com/6q9h97a

REFERENCES

Argyris, C. and D. Schön (1974). *Theory in Practice: Increasing Professional Effectiveness* San Francisco: Jossey-Bass.

Argyris, C. and D. Schön (1996). *Organizational Learning II: Theory, Method and Practice.* Reading, MA: Addison Wesley.

Argyris, C. and D. Schön (1978). *Organizational Learning: A Theory of Action Perspective.* Reading, MA: Addison Wesley.

Atwood, V.A. and W.W. Wilen (March, 1991). "Wait Time and Effective Social Studies Instruction: What Can Research in Science Education Tell Us?" *Social Education* 55.

Blythe, T., D. Allen and B. S. Powell (2002). *Looking Together at Student Work,* second edition. NY: Teachers College Press.

Bolton. G. (2005). *Reflective Practice: Writing and Professional Development.* London: Sage.

Boud, D., R. Keogh and D. Walker (1985). *Reflection: Turning Experience into Learning.* NY: Routleldge Farmer.

Boud, D. et al. (eds.) (1985). *Reflection: Turning Experience into Learning,* London: Kogan.

Brookfield, S. D. (1995). *Becoming a Critically Reflective Teacher.* San Francisco: Jossey-Bass.

Canning, C. (1991). "What Teachers Say about Reflection." *Educational Leadership* 48 (6), 18–21.

Casteel, J.D. and R.J. Stahl (1973). *The Social Science Observation Record: Theoretical Construct and Pilot Studies.* Gainesville, FL: P.K. Yonge Laboratory School.

Copeland, W.D., C. Birmingham, E. De La Cruz and B. Lewin (1993). "The Reflective Practitioner in Teaching: Toward a Research Agenda. *Teaching and Teacher Education 9,* 347–359.

Costa, A. and R.J. Garmston (2002). *Cognitive Coaching: A Foundation for Renaissance Schools,* second edition. Norwood, MA: Christopher-Gordon.

Costa, A.L. and B. Kallick (April, 2000). "Getting into the Habit of Reflection." *Educational Leadership* 57(5), 61–62.

Deer Richardson, L. and M. Wolfe (2001). *Principles and ractices of Informal Learning: Learning through Life.* NY: Routleldge Farmer.

Dewey, J. (1933). *How We Think.* Buffalo, NY: Prometheus Books. (Original work published in 1910.)

Eraut, M. (1994). *Developing Professional Knowledge and Competence.* London: Falmer.

Evans, C. (1991). "Support for Teachers Studying Their Own Work. *Educational Leadership* 48(6).

Farrell, T. S. C. (2004). *Reflective Practice in Action.* Thousand Oaks, CA: Corwin Press.

Finger, M. and J.M. Asún (2000). *Adult Education at the Crossroads: Learning Our Way Out.* London: Zed Books.

Glickman, C. D. (2002). *Leadership for Learning: How to Help Teachers Succeed.* Alexandria, VA: Association for Supervision and Curriculum Development.

Hutchins, R. M. (1970). *The Learning Society.* Harmondsworth: Penguin.

Killion, J.P and G.R. Todnem (1991). "A Process for Personal Theory Building." *Educational Leadership* 48,6, 14–16.

Kolb, D.A. (1984). *Experiential Learning: Experience as the Source of Learning and Development.* Englewood Cliffs, NJ: Prentice-Hall.

Lipman, M. (1991). *Thinking in Education.* Cambridge: Cambridge University Press.

Lipton, L. and B. Wellman with C. Humbard (2001*). Mentoring Matters: A Practical Guide to Learning-focused Relationships.* Sherman, CT: Mira Via LLC.

Lyman, F. T., Jr. (1987). "The Think Trix: A Classroom Tool for Thinking in Response to Reading. In J.D. Coley (ed.), *Reading: Issues and Practices,* 1987 Yearbook of the State of Maryland International Reading Association Council.

Sparkes-Langer, G.M. and A.B. Colton (1991). "Synthesis of Research on Teachers' Reflective Thinking." *Educational Leadership* 48(6).

Nadler, R. S. and J.L. Luckner (1992). *Processing the Adventure Experience.* Iowa: Kendall Hunt.

Newman, S. (1999) *Philosophy and Teacher Education: A Reinterpretation of Donald A. Schön's Epistemology of Reflective Practice.* London: Avebury.

Osterman, K.F. and R.B. Kottamp (2004). *Reflective Practice for Educators.* Thousand Oaks, CA: Corwin Press.

Pakman, M. (2000). "Thematic Foreword, Reflective Practices: The Legacy of Donald Schön," *Cybernetics and Human Knowing* 7, (2–3), 5–8.

Priest, S. and M. Naismith (1992). "A Model of Debriefing Experiences." *The Journal of Adventure Education and Outdoor Leadership* 10(3), 20–22.

Quigley, A. and G.W. Kuhne (1997). *Creating Practical Knowledge through Action Research: Posing Problems, Solving Problems and Improving Daily Practice.* San Francisco: Jossey-Bass.

Ranson, S. (1998). "Lineages of the Learning Society" in S. Ranson (ed.), *Inside the Learning Society.* London: Cassell.

Richards, J. C. and Lockhart, C. (1994). *Reflective Teaching.* New York: Cambridge University Press.

Richardson, V. (1990). "The Evolution of Reflective Teaching and Teacher Education" in Clift, R. T., Houston, W. R., and Pugach, M. C. (eds.), *Encouraging Reflective Practice in Education: An Analysis of Issues and Programs.* New York: Teachers College Press.

Rogers, D.L. and L.M. Babinski (2002). *From Isolation to Conversation: Supporting New Teachers' Development.* Albany, NY: State University of New York Press.

Rowe, M.B. (1972). "Wait-time and Rewards as Instructional Variable: Their Influence in Language, Logic and Fate Control." Paper presented at the National Association for Research in Science Teaching, Chicago, IL.

Rowe, M.B. (Spring, 1987). "Wait Time: Slowing Down May Be a Way of Speeding Up." *American Educators* 11, 38–43, 47.

Russell, T. and Munby, H. (1991). "Reframing: The Role of Experience in Developing Teachers' Professional Knowledge" in D. A. Schön (ed.), *The Reflective Turn: Case Studies in and on Educational Practice.* New York: Teachers Press, Columbia University.

Schön, D. (1983). *The Reflective Practitioner: How Professionals Think in Action.* London: Temple Smith.

Schön, D. A. (1967). *Invention and the Evolution of Ideas.* London: Tavistock (first published in 1963 as *Displacement of Concepts*).

Schön, D. A. (1967). *Technology and Change: The New Heraclitus.* Oxford: Pergamon.

Schön, D. A. (1985). *The Design Studio: An Exploration of Its Traditions and Potentials.* London : RIBA Publications for RIBA Building Industry Trust.

Schön, D. A. (1991). *The Reflective Turn: Case Studies In and On Educational Practice,* New York: Teachers Press, Columbia University.

Smith, M. K. (1994). *Local Education.* Buckingham: Open University Press.

Smylie, M.A. and J.G. Conyers (1991). "Changing Conceptions of Teaching Influence the Future of Staff Development." *Journal of Staff Development* 12 (1), 12–16.

Solomon, R.D. and E.C. Solomon (2009). *Toolbox for Teachers and Mentors: Moving Madrichim to Mentor Teachers and Beyond.* Tucson, AZ: Wheatmark Publishers.

Solomon, R.D., N. Davidson and E.C. Solomon (2003). *Mentoring Teachers in a Professional Learning Community: Participant's Guide.* Columbia, MD: National Institute for Relationship Training, Inc.

Solomon, R.D. and N. Davidson (2009). *Encouraging Skillful, Critical and Creative Thinking: Participant's Guide.* Tucson, AZ: Fourth R Consulting.

Stahl, Robert J. (1990). *Using "Think-time" Behaviors to Promote Students' Information Processing, Learning, and On-task Participation: An Instructional Module.* Tempe, AZ: Arizona State University, 1990.

Sugerman, D.A., K.L. Doherty, D.E. Garvey and M.A. Gass (2000). *Reflective Learning Theory and Practice.* Dubuque, IA: Kendall/Hunt Publishing Company.

Tobin, Kenneth (Spring, 1987). "The Role of Wait Time in Higher Cognitive Level Earning. *Review of Educational Research* 57.

University of Wisconsin Extension Service (2007). *Reflection Activity Ideas for Community Service and Service Learning Projects.* http://tinyurl.com/87wqh9y (Retrieved January 16, 2012).

University of Wisconsin Extension Service (2011–2012). *Buffalo County 4-H Countywide Service Learning Project.*nhttp://tinyurl.com/7rsd6ns (Retrieved January 16, 2012).

Usher, R. *et al.* (1997). *Adult Education and the Postmodern Challenge.* London: Routledge.

Valli, L. (1997). "Listening to Other Voices: A Description of Teacher Reflection in the United States. *Peabody Journal of Education* 72(1).

Wellington, B. (1991) "The Promise of Reflective Practice." *Educational Leadership* 48(6).

COACHING AND MENTORING
IN EXPERIENTIAL JEWISH EDUCATION

Clare Goldwater

Although the concepts and even the practices of both coaching and mentoring have been around for a long time (the definition of mentoring, after all, comes from the character of Mentor in *The Odyssey*), the widespread contemporary application of both coaching and mentoring is relatively new. Coaching in particular is a rapidly growing field that is finding application in an enormous number of industries and professional domains and is developing its own field of literature, professional training and accreditation.[1] The juxtaposition of coaching and mentoring with experiential Jewish education is particularly new. Certainly it is significant that this chapter has been commissioned, and it speaks to the future of the field of Jewish education rather than serving as a description of the past or even the present.

This chapter will primarily serve to bring the fields (coaching and mentoring on one hand and experiential Jewish education on the other) into dialogue with each other for the purpose of illuminating and strengthening the field of experiential Jewish education. There is a great deal in common between the fields, and it could be claimed that experiential Jewish educators have always functioned, in some form, as coaches and mentors. This is partly true, and as we examine some of the key concepts of coaching and mentoring we will find much that is familiar to the field of experiential Jewish education, at least when it is done well by thoughtful and effective educators. At the same time it is our claim that it is helpful to expose these similarities, as well as any differences that might appear, as a way of helping experiential Jewish education become more reflective, enriched by the richness of external domains and thus more effective and powerful than it already is. Our understanding of the field of informal education is continually enriched by influences from other fields (psychology, group theory and educational philosophy, for example), and we assume this will be the case here, too.

DEFINITIONS

The terms "coaching" and "mentoring" are used in many different ways to refer to a variety of roles. Sometimes they are used synonymously, even though they are quite distinct. And yet there are some significant similarities. This "slippery-ness" is compounded by the expansion of coaching in the past decade or two and the lack of regulation of either term. Unlike the term "doctor", for instance, anyone can call himself or herself a coach or mentor and go looking for clients. Nevertheless, for the sake of clarity and accuracy it is important to have a clear definition of both coaching and mentoring and to distinguish them from related roles and professions.

> One of the clearest ways to think about what coaching is borrows from the coaching model that is highly familiar: the sports coach. Whether we are talking about basketball players or executives or Jewish educators, the coach plays a supporting role that helps the individual (athlete or not) become a more effective player. The actual "work" is always done by the player

---

[1] For a 2012 comprehensive report on the size and scope of coaching on a global level, see *http://www.coachfederation.org/coachingstudy2012/*. The International Coach Federation (ICF) has seen its membership across 34 countries rise from 2,000 in 1999 to 13,000 (with nearly two thirds in North America) in 2007.
In the U.S. a 2008 survey of over 1,000 executives and managers, commissioned by the American Management Association, found that 52% of North American companies use coaching, and over half of these are using coaching more now than in the past. Almost 40% of respondents whose companies do not use coaching expect they will begin instituting coaching programs in the future (American Management Association). A 2004 *Harvard Business Review* article reports that "annual spending on coaching in the United States is estimated at roughly $1 billion" (Sherman and Freas).

on the court or the field, or in the camp or school, but the coach plays a significant role in supporting, motivating, teaching techniques and skills and providing a perspective from the sidelines that builds the capacity of the player to play at his or her full potential. In many ways, a leadership or executive coach is very similar to the sports coach.

Another way to define the role, away from the sports context, comes from the International Coach Federation (ICF), an international organization that trains and accredits (non-sports) coaches and advocates for coaching through research and public education. For the ICF coaching is "partnering with clients in a thought-provoking and creative process that inspires them to maximize their personal and professional potential."[2] This definition highlights some of the key elements. Coaching is a relational process between two people; it is designed to lead to growth or change on the part of the "client"; it results in enhanced capacity for success, either professional or personal. Further nuances in the definition of coach come from James Flaherty, a leading coach and trainer of coaches. He argues that the goal of coaching is to lead the client to long-term excellent performance (according to the terms of his or her professional role), along with the ability to self-correct that performance and be self-generative over time, such that the long-term need for coaching disappears and the client is able to function independently and more effectively in the future.

Mentoring shares many of the characteristics of coaching but has traditionally been distinguished from it by less formality, more fluid boundaries and a greater level of intimacy in the relationship. The Merriam-Webster dictionary simply defines it as "to serve as trusted counselor or guide,"[3] and in contrast to the definitions of coaching given above, it isn't necessarily designed to lead to the same kind of outcome-driven professional enhancement that is the goal of coaching. Where coaching is usually a formal relationship with goals, measurable outcomes and a fixed time frame, mentoring tends to be more informal and may continue over the course of many years. And whereas mentoring provides for the mentor to share his or her experience as a guide for the mentee, coaching does not assume that the coach's own experience has a role in the process. In addition, while coaching has developed into a professional field bolstered by its own professional associations, credentials, literature and a strong application in the corporate world, mentoring remains less formalized and is most often found in youth and educational work.

For all their differences, though, coaching and mentoring are both processes leading to learning and growth that take place primarily through conversation in the context of a supportive and confidential relationship. And they can both be creative, enjoyable and powerfully transformative for the individuals involved.[4]

In the Jewish community, just as in the nonprofit world in general, coaching and mentoring have become much more prevalent in the past decade.[5] It has become commonplace in professional development fellowships, as well as social entrepreneurship programs, to offer various forms of coaching and mentoring. As a result there are many roles for "coaches" and "mentors" to take in the arenas of organizational change and innovation, leadership development and academic study. The terms "coaching" and "mentoring" are often used interchangeably, and there is not much awareness of the nuances between them, nor in the differences in style, approach and credentials of practitioners. While I think that there needs to be more clarity and care applied to the use of the terms "mentor" and "coach" in general, for the purposes of this chapter I will continue to use them largely synonymously. The reason is that for the purposes of the field of experiential Jewish education, the differences between coaching and mentoring as they are found today in the broader world are largely irrelevant, and we will gain more by looking carefully at what these

---

[2] The International Coach Federation, www.coachfederation.org.

[3] http://www.merriam-webster.com/dictionary/mentor.

[4] These characteristics are also true, of course, of therapy. The distinction that coaches usually make between therapy and coaching, however, is that therapy focuses on the past, and coaching focuses on the future. Additionally, therapy assumes some kind of problem or dysfunction on the part of the client that needs to be "fixed", while coaching makes no such assumptions and treats the client as healthy and functional. The overlap that still exists between these fields is a source of some tension between practitioners of coaching and therapy.

5 There is no data on the prevalence of coaching in the nonprofit world in general, although 54% of foundations report that they have funded coaching for their grantees. For more information on coaching in nonprofits see *www.geofunders.org*, the work of the Evelyn and Walter Haas, Jr., Fund and the W.K. Kellogg Foundation. In the Jewish world there is no clear data on the prevalence of coaching. However, anecdotal evidence and an informal survey of a wide variety of professional training programs and fellowships show the presence of coaching/mentoring on a systematic level. This is probably the result of the external influences of the nonprofit and philanthropy arenas on the Jewish community and the growing numbers of professionals who have experienced coaching education themselves.

practices have in common and considering them together as a foil with which to interrogate experiential Jewish education.

COACHING, MENTORING AND EXPERIENTIAL EDUCATION

For much of the rest of this chapter we will look at a series of concepts that have resonance in both experiential Jewish education and the fields of coaching and mentoring. We will examine how the understanding of each of these concepts outside the Jewish world can serve to illuminate what goes on inside it and how Jewish educators can learn from wisdom outside their own field. The concepts we will consider are:

- The Mind-Body-Emotions Triad
- The Power of the Body
- Authenticity
- Dialogue and the Tools of Communication
- Reflection
- Leadership

THE MIND-BODY-EMOTIONS TRIAD

Coaching and experiential education share a concern for the whole person who is undergoing the learning process. Both disciplines exist in some part as reactions against the mind-focused culture that we live in, either in the formal educational world, which tends to privilege cognitive skills and learning, and in the business arena, where the rational mind is dominant over emotions and the power of the body. Both fields, then, engage with all elements of a person's being: the mind, the body *and* the emotions. And this triad plays a key role in how the learning or educational process is structured.

In experiential education it is commonplace to consider the three domains of mind, heart and body, otherwise known as the cognitive, affective and behavioral realms. Effective experiential educators build their outcomes by considering the following three questions: What do I want the student to know? To feel? And to do? And they look for congruence and balance among these three elements.

In coaching the triad is similar, except that the domain of the cognitive is focused on language rather than knowledge and information, reflecting the fact that coaching is concerned primarily with structure and not content. It is the interaction of the three domains of language (including internal and external conversations), body and emotions (including moods) that results in the way that each of us exists in the world. The role of coaching, then, is to help a client shift any or all of these domains in order to help the client see the world with a new perspective. This results in new actions and new outcomes. The hope, of course, is that change is in the direction of greater professional effectiveness.

Although the basic triad exists as a theoretical construct in both fields, coaching theory adds an interesting and useful element. As Chalmers Brothers says in his book about language ,which is very influential in the coaching world:

> Most of us already have an intuitive understanding of the connections which exist among our language, our moods/emotions, and our physical bodies. We have felt these firsthand, in a variety of situations. What may be unique about this particular way of looking is the claim that each of these three aspects may be used as the starting point, the "lever" for change and for designing something different. Each may be used to purposefully impact and influence... the other two.
>
> We claim that each of these three—our body, our mood/emotional state, and our language—can be a domain of design. That is, we can purposefully invent new conversations, knowing that over time they will have the effect of influencing or designing a new mood. We

can purposefully do something different with our body, knowing that, over time, this will produce different interpretations, different conversations, different available moodspaces ... This model has the advantage of explicitly providing three different domains of design, three different causal elements for use in creating new results in our lives.[6]

In other words, the triad is useful for more than just describing the learner or thinking about outcomes. It is also a way of thinking about educational interventions. If I intervene to shift the student's language, then he or she can develop new emotional responses. Similarly, if I intervene by offering new physical opportunities, the student's cognitive abilities also expand to take new possibilities into account. This approach could be very useful to experiential Jewish education. Although kids at camp are pushed to their physical limits in the lake, on the climbing wall or on camping trips, there is rarely an intention to create growth in their ability to think in new ways. Similarly, how exciting it could be to help students learn a new language (Hebrew or Yiddish, for instance) and then intentionally foster the emotional growth that comes with the new sense of belonging and connection that language and cultural acquisition provides.

At the same time as both coaching and experiential Jewish education utilize the triad of body, mind and language/mind and are interested in congruence between the realms, the fields are also focused particularly on the role played by the body as a powerful and deliberate corrective to our Western post-industrial society, which has underprivileged the body for many decades. We will, therefore, deal separately with the ways that the fields specifically relate to the power of the body.

THE POWER OF THE BODY

It may be a truism to say that human beings are embodied beings, but it is no less significant for that. Indeed, our whole experience of the world is fundamentally filtered through what our bodies allow us to do and see, even though this awareness has diminished in the Western world. Learning, then, in any form must also include this understanding and take it into account.

In coaching there is a growing emphasis on the body as a corrective to the modern world of (middle-class) work, in which one's body tends to be seen as a rather unimportant vessel for the really important part—the brain. Coaches understand that the body is a crucial part of an individual's being and that it needs to be part of the coaching process. Not only are our habits, emotions and patterns embedded in our bodies, they also play a crucial role in helping us learn. When a coach engages with a client, he or she consciously coaches that person's body as well as his or her mind. The coach might help the client become a more active observer of his or her own body, using the body as a source of clues about habits, responses, emotions and values. Clients are encouraged to ask themselves: Where am I experiencing this feeling in my body? Where does this habit show up physically? Coaches also make use of breathing exercises, helping clients use the discipline of conscious breathing to lower stress and become more mindful. There are also coaches who are influenced by many types of body-focused techniques to help clients internalize and embody new habits and lessons.[7]

Jewish education is both similar to and different from the coaching and mentoring domains. On one hand there is a similar recognition that successful learning depends on integrating the body with the mind, and that educative experiences often need to contain physical experience. For examples we need look no further than the physical components crucial to the power of camping and travel education. It is absolutely crucial to the educational process that children at a camp are given physical challenges through swimming and kayaking. And Israel trips include rappelling, hiking and lots of sensual stimulation (just think of the smells, music and extreme exhaustion), not purely because these things are attractive selling points, but also because of the ability they have to trigger powerful learning experiences through and on the body.[8]

---

6 Brothers, C. (2005), *Language and the Pursuit of Happiness*. Naples: New Possibilities Press.

7 See particularly Richard Strozzi Heckler, Jon Kabat-Zinn and many yoga practitioners.

8 Kirshenblatt-Gimblett, B, (2002). "Learning from Ethnography: Reflections on the Nature and Efficacy of Youth Tours to Israel." In B. Chazan (ed.), *The Israel Experience: Studies in Jewish Identity and Youth Culture*. The Andrea and Charles Bronfman Philanthropies.

At the same time Jewish education is often less intentional about using the physical as a genuine and valuable part of the education. Rather, the physical is an add-on, or an element that is not seen as a true part of the *Jewish* education. Here again Jewish education can learn from the coaching domain and start to recognize that true learning must include an element of the physical and take into account the learner's body. One wonders what Jewish education would look like if educators deliberately integrated the physical into an educational program and maximized their own skills in this area. There are many Jewish educators who themselves do yoga or other body practices, and in some programs for educators that have a more spiritual focus, they are able to integrate the physical and the cognitive (and the spiritual). But in most mainstream educational settings this is rare. Yet, if they deliberately integrated some of these practices into their education in thoughtful ways, the results could be extremely creative and powerful.

AUTHENTICITY

Authenticity is a complex concept that appears in many fields, including philosophy, education and psychology. It is notoriously slippery to define; and so rather than enter into a discussion of its different possible meanings, we use it here simply to refer to the genuineness of the educator, the way in which he or she is a living model of the values that he or she professes to hold. Is this person "genuine" to the extent that he or she upholds and expresses his or her values? This is important because we assume that the learner is learning as much, if not more, from the educator (or coach) than from any subject matter or external content, and therefore *who* that person is becomes crucial to the learning or growth process.

In coaching "authenticity" refers to the achieved self-understanding and integrity of the coach, who brings his or her whole self to the coaching relationship and offers him- or herself as a model of someone who has found growth through self-reflection, successfully integrating his or her values and beliefs into a meaningful life. Within the domain of coaching there is a great deal of emphasis given to the personal values and integrity of the coach. Training programs spend considerable time helping coaches develop their own clarity of purpose, become conscious of their motivations and ensure that they are deliberately and positively expressing their values in the world. For example, one book written by coaching leaders from a well-known training program is divided into three sections: "Being," "Doing" and "Using." The authors write, "Coaches have a professional obligation to aspire to become masters of their own discipline and to engage in continual self-development. Our becoming reflects our being. Our being informs our doing. The tools and techniques we use are an extension of our being. *Being* is the cornerstone."[9]

Jewish educators similarly ascribe great power to the educator's authentic or "holistic" personality.[10] A classic example of this is the traditional youth movement *madrich*, whose primary role is as *dugma ishit* (role model) and who is expected to be a living exemplar of the ideology of the movement. There are many more examples in all areas of Jewish education, and the Jewish community has been highly influenced by the work of those outside the Jewish community, such as Parker Palmer and his lesson that "We teach who we are."[11]

One of the things that coaching offers Jewish educators in this regard is the importance of the authentic role model continuing a personal journey of growth and self-reflection. Though one may have achieved a certain level of self-understanding and personal integrity, there is no sense of rest or stasis. Coach training programs and continuing education courses are full of workshops on how to continue to learn, to refine one's values and self-understanding and to model that ongoing growth for the client.[12] Jewish education would benefit from the challenge to educators to continually re-examine their own commitments and consciously inhabit their own personal journeys in order to model the process of journeying and growth for their students/*hannikhim*.

---

9 Stroul, N. and C.M. Wahl (2008). "On Becoming a Leadership Coach." In C. Wahl, C. Scriber and B. Bloomfield (eds.), *On Becoming a Leadership Coach: A Holistic Approach to Coaching Excellence*, Palgrave Macmillan.

10 Barry Chazan refers to the power of the "holistic educator" in "Definition of Informal Jewish Education."

11 Palmer, P. J. (1998). *The Courage to Teach: Exploring the Inner Landscape of a Teacher's Life*. San Francisco: Jossey-Bass, chapter 1.

DIALOGUE AND THE TOOLS OF COMMUNICATION

Coaching and mentoring are primarily relationship-based processes that rely almost totally on dialogue and the tools of communication. Similarly, experiential Jewish education relies heavily on the power of a conversation (between educator and learner, or facilitated within a group of learners) to create learning opportunities. Both fields assume that the interchange of spoken thoughts and ideas builds connection, sparks new insights and creates educative experiences. Dialogue is composed of two elements, listening and speaking, both of which play a significant role in coaching and in experiential Jewish education.

Listening is an extremely powerful tool, and the opportunity to be really listened to, with full attention and without judgment, is all too rare in contemporary society. Doctors, clergy, therapists and, of course, coaches often find themselves "just" listening, providing this crucial service to those they work with. And indeed, the skills of active listening are relevant and part of the training in many fields.

Active listening skills are the cornerstone of the coach's toolkit. Coaches listen for their client's stories, the (often unconscious) patterns that appear in speech, and for the things that are not said. One coach training manual speaks of three levels of listening, starting with the first level, in which the coach is primarily aware of him or herself rather than the client; progressing to the next level, where attention is focused sharply on the client; and continuing to the highest level, at which the coach's intuition and senses are actively hearing what the client is expressing through tone, posture and the spaces between the words.[13] The highest level is described in almost spiritual terms and reaches a level of empathy and connection that is reminiscent of Buber's I–Thou relationship. Good listening is aided by the practice of asking effective questions that function as openings for more conversation and as gateways to new insights.

If active listening is one half of communication, the other half is the judicious use of speech. And much of coaching tends to focus on helping clients improve their communication skills and the way they use speech acts such as requests, declarations and agreements. These are skills for life in general, not just work, and coaching focuses on honing the forms and structure of speech rather than the content.

In Jewish education, listening is similarly a crucial part of relationship building. Bunk counselors listen to the stories that their _hannikhim_ tell; teachers listen to what their students are really asking; and all good educators listen carefully and ask open and non-judgmental questions in order to help their students gain new insights. Some practitioners use these skills intuitively, but for many it takes experience and practice to really use them well. In order to raise the level of communication skills, Jewish education could learn from the clear and systematic methods used by coaching to train for these skills. Jewish education training programs could and should focus more explicitly on these skills, which are assumed to be obvious but are often not so simply acquired. I have seen enthusiastic and well-meaning Jewish educators close down educational moments, dominate conversations unnecessarily and misuse powerful speech opportunities. On the other hand, better training would allow Jewish educators to see what they are already trying to do as deliberate and intentional educative practices, as valuable tools to use judiciously. And they would strengthen their own practice by honing those skills continually and by recognizing and learning from those who are experts in these skills.

REFLECTION

With the notion of reflection we turn to the principle shared by coaching and experiential Jewish education that learning is about far more than acquiring new skills or techniques for more effective time management or communication, or becoming familiar with dates and personalities relevant to Jewish holidays and history. Rather, learning includes a component of personal introspection through which the learner takes information acquired during the educational process and integrates it into his or her previous experiences, values and commitments.

---

[13] Whitworth, L., K. Kimsey-House, H. Kimsey-House and P. Sandahl (2007). _Co-active Coaching: New Skills for Coaching People toward Success_, Chapter 3.

This element of personal reflection is a crucial part of the coaching process. Although conscious reflection is usually found throughout the coaching engagement, it typically forms the bulk of the work following the goal-setting phase. At this point, once the client has defined the goals and objectives of the coaching, he or she is encouraged to look inside at habits, beliefs and thought processes that drive behavior, and also outside to see how these habits and beliefs make their way into the world and impact others. Coaching is a highly pragmatic discipline. Clients are not asked to reflect on their own habits and behaviors in terms of "good" or "bad," but rather to find new insights when they pay attention to whether these habits and behaviors are working for them. Coaches ask their clients to notice the things that they do and feel automatically. When clients share what they have noticed, they are asked, "How is this working for you?" and "How is this behavior serving you and your goals?" It is through activities and questions like these that reflection is done. It is often the bulk of the work of coaching, and it can be the most powerful part of the work.

In Jewish education, reflection plays a role that is similarly crucial, but with different emphases. David Kolb's cycle of experiential learning has taught Jewish educators that real learning is not achieved unless there is an intentional space for reflection on the experience that has taken place, allowing the student to process the experience and integrate it with the learning from previous experiences.[14] If this happens at all, it usually takes place in a group, and through facilitated group discussion it is assumed that the reflection takes place.

Coaching teaches us that reflection happens, and can be extremely powerful, through ongoing encouragement to simply pay new attention to what is around us and what is habitual. It also reminds us that reflection is fundamentally an individual process, and that even though the group can be very helpful to spur the reflective process, there are many additional opportunities to maximize individual reflection beyond the specific "reflection session" in the schedule. Jewish educators could intentionally incorporate reflective questions into their conversations with their students, and through doing this they would significantly strengthen the stage of reflection within learning overall. Examples of effective reflective questions include "What is behind that opinion/expectation/belief?" "What can you learn from this experience?" "What are your emotions or body telling you?" and "You sound frustrated/excited/angry/engaged, etc. What is behind that feeling?"

LEADERSHIP

The rhetoric of leadership is all around us, especially in learning situations, which often aim to nurture the learner's leadership capacity or prepare him or her for a leadership position. In coaching this is particularly true. Coaching draws heavily on the literature of leadership, particularly business and corporate leadership; and the goal of coaching is often explicitly framed in terms of helping clients become leaders or improve their leadership capacity. One well-respected coach training program explicitly defines its field as "Leadership Coaching" to distinguish its focus from the more typical "Executive Coaching," highlighting the distinction between management and leadership. As coaching has become more widespread in the corporate world, and is used much less as a remedial tool than it used to be, many coaches work exclusively with corporate leaders and those who aspire to leadership roles. And so, in addition to the focus on management skills (communication issues, time management and prioritization, supervision etc.), coaching often involves helping clients to develop their vision and purpose, to express and articulate it effectively and particularly to maximize their leadership presence.

Leadership in experiential Jewish education takes many forms appropriate to the institutions involved. There are numerous "leadership development" programs for both adults and teens that utilize the tools of experiential education—powerful cohort experiences, trips (often to Israel) and retreats—in order to develop skills, transfer knowledge and help the participants develop their own Jewish commitments.

---

[14] Kolb, D. A. (1984) *Experiential Learning*. Englewood Cliffs, NJ.: Prentice Hall.

Although some of the skills for corporate leadership are not directly relevant to the world of nonprofit Jewish organizations, the focus that coaches often place on leadership vision and presence are useful and transfer into the Jewish arena. And experiential Jewish educators could certainly gain from being reminded that a key part of leadership is the passion and purpose that must underpin any leadership role. Too few graduates of Jewish leadership development programs can articulate their own visions for Jewish life and for their organizations or movements. And leadership presence, which focuses on using one's body to express leadership behaviors, could also be a valuable addition to the training of Jewish leaders. Just as in the corporate world, some leaders intuitively model exemplary behaviors and skills, and others can benefit from the help that a coach or educator/*madrikh* can bring to become more effective.

WHERE COACHING AND EXPERIENTIAL JEWISH EDUCATION DIVERGE

Each of the concepts that we have discussed so far in this chapter is shared by the fields of experiential Jewish education and coaching. And in each case we find a similar pattern: Despite differences of focus and style, there are some valuable lessons that the field of experiential Jewish education can learn from the world of coaching.

It would be remiss, however, to leave this discussion without also paying some attention to places where these two fields are very different, do not overlap or might even be mutually exclusive.

The first place where coaching and experiential Jewish education diverge is in terms of content and educational agenda. We have already noted several times that coaching focuses on structure and process for learning, not on content. Jewish education, of course, whether experiential or not, is concerned, among other things, with transmitting specific content—texts, language, beliefs, values, practices, etc. And although coaching is a set of techniques or a methodology into which any specific professional content can be introduced, there is possible conflict here. As we have already noted, coaching is driven by the needs and interests of the person being coached, while experiential Jewish education, however sensitive to the needs of the student, is fundamentally committed to that person's learning in a certain direction. Educators, by definition, have an agenda for their students and want them to grow, as defined by the ideology or educational vision of the educating organization. This provides a place for potential divergence between the open goals of coaching and the more directive goals of education.

The role of the community or group is another area where there is divergence between coaching and experiential Jewish education. Coaching is almost always done one-on-one and is based on the coach building a confidential individual relationship with a client. Even though there is a growing field of group coaching, in which a coach will work with a team, that format privileges the relationship between the coach and the team leader. Experiential Jewish education, however, is very group-focused. Much learning is designed to happen in the group, through the power of the group and the peer relationships. While I have tried to demonstrate that many coaching principles can be implemented even in groups (effective use of communication and the focus on the body, for example), it is nevertheless important to recognize that group learning and the power of community-building are not part of the field of coaching.

CONCLUSION

What is to be learned from coaching by the field of experiential Jewish education? First and foremost, as I have demonstrated above, and notwithstanding the divergences that exist, the field of coaching offers Jewish educators a set of techniques and an approach to personal growth that has enormous application in the field of Jewish education. Should Jewish educators aspire to become more like coaches? Well, that probably depends on the educators and their individual skills, as well as the needs of their organizational frameworks. What I would argue, however, is that it is worthwhile for Jewish educators to recognize and hone their coaching skills. As the twenty-first century gives more focus to the individual "consumer" and less to the group, these skills will be more and more necessary for Jewish educators wishing to impact their students.

In addition, perhaps the most important lesson can be gained by seeing the domain of coaching, as a whole, as a model for the professionalization and expansion that many of us aspire to in the world of experiential Jewish education. Coaching has evolved from an informal set of techniques practiced by a few disorganized practitioners into a growing field that has successfully won recognition and is now commonplace in the corporate world. A growing body of literature, research, training opportunities and professional regulations support coaches and their work. This evolution of the field can teach the world of experiential Jewish education that a more intentional and professional approach, including literature, research and greater professionalism, can help the field become more effective, more widespread and more respected. And that, of course, is what this whole book is about. Coaching offers a model of what can be attained and what has to be done to get there.

SECTION 3:
WHERE IS EXPERIENTIAL JEWISH EDUCATION

SHABBAT IN THE SANDBOX: EARLY CHILDHOOD AS THE AUTHENTIC BEGINNING OF EXPERIENTIAL EDUCATION?

Lisa Samick

Twenty-two years ago Robert Fulghum published the poem "All I Really Need to Know I Learned in Kindergarten." With a few tweaks this sentiment could easily be applied to this new compilation about experiential Jewish education. "All you really need to know about informal education, you learned in preschool."

Step into a high-quality early childhood classroom and you come face to face with a natural laboratory of experiential learning. By its nature early childhood education (ECE) is experiential in terms of both context and content. From the setup of the room to the activities contained within each area, young children are asked to explore, to ask questions, to take social and educational risks and to find their way through learning by engaging all of their senses and interacting with the world around them.

> Eighty-five children ages two to six are sitting on the floor under dimmed lights. Candles are flickering off to the side; the smell of fresh-baked challah wafts through the air. At the front of the room a man strums the guitar, and eighty-five voices join together in a gorgeous, albeit off-key, rendition of *Bim Bam*, or the *Dinosaur Shabbat* song, or *Chicken in the Pot*.

Whatever the song, the experience involves every aspect of the child. They are clapping their hands and stomping their feet, singing from the depths of their souls and feeling a part of their school community. Back in the classroom the children return to a beautifully set table with their own specially made placemats and *kippot*. The Shabbat parents for that week join them to bless the children and to welcome Shabbat in the classroom. Later, in dramatic play, children recreate their own Shabbat scene using a wooden challah and a stuffed Torah. In the sand table they uncover a wooden havdalah candle and spice box, a plastic Torah scroll, laminated pictures of Kiddush wine and Shabbat candlesticks. In the library corner the bookshelf features gorgeous picture books depicting Shabbat scenes and stories. The components of Shabbat are woven into their play so seamlessly that the two are inextricable, and the *kavannah* and traditions remain with them long after the preschool day ends.

HOW YOUNG CHILDREN LEARN

By nature of how young children learn, early childhood education is authentically experiential education. Intuitively we understand that toddlers and preschoolers learn by doing. Starting in earliest infancy they make meaning of the world through their senses—looking around, then grasping and next tasting. They use these experiences to inform their interactions with the world, and as that experience expands, so does their understanding of what is going on around them.

Research in early childhood education reinforces this notion about child development. The work of Piaget (1958, 1963), Montessori (1964), Erikson (1950) and other child development theorists and researchers (Elkind, 1986; Kamii, 1985) has demonstrated that learning is a complex process that results from the interaction of children's thinking and their experience in the external world. In *From Neurons to Neighborhoods* (2000) Shonkoff and Phillips sum up the research on early childhood development in a list of ten core concepts. While going into each would be beyond the scope of this chapter, two seem particularly relevant: "(1) Human development is shaped by dynamic and continuous interaction between biology and experience." And "(4) Children are active participants in their own development, reflecting the intrinsic human drive to explore and master one's environment" (pp. 3–4). Both of these concepts are critical to the success of an early childhood experience—and to informal education with any age group.

Several of the theorists mentioned above and others have developed systems or taxonomies for organizing how we understand that "interaction between biology and experience" and the "mastery of environment". While there are, of course, discrepancies between them, Dewey and Piaget perhaps provide us with the broadest insights into how we can better understand why the model of informal education so closely mirrors early childhood education.

Piaget believed that children go through stages of development in a predictable sequence. Between each stage is a period of cognitive restructuring or dissonance during which the child is momentarily off balance as he or she works to master the next stage. This "in between" is called active learning and can be defined as the direct and immediate experiencing of people, objects, ideas and events (Hohmann and Weikart 1995). In that process children begin to make sense of the world by "learning concepts, forming ideas and creating a system of symbols and abstractions through moving, listening, feeling and manipulating" (Hohmann and Weikart, p. 16). The onus for forwarding learning, according to Piaget, is on the child but supported by the adults in his/her life. In his mind it is critical for children to struggle through the unknown—to experiment, fail and try again—as they find answers and master new skills.

Similarly John Dewey, whose work is seen as foundational not only in the field of early childhood education, but also in experiential education, wrote extensively about children's involvement in their own active quest for new learning and ideas. He placed continuity and interaction as the two fundamental criteria for quality of experience. (Much of Dewey's writing deals with the processes of learning as experienced by young children, but particularly *The Child and the Curriculum* [1912] is relevant for further exploration.) Dewey's call for education that extends the lived experiences of the learner serves as a backdrop for much of the current work in Reggio Emilia and in Developmentally Appropriate Practice[1], two of the more prevalent philosophies in ECE today. Capitalizing on these lived experiences is the bread and butter of making early childhood education work and of creating meaningful informal educational experiences.

These understandings about how children develop and learn have given way to the curricular theorists and practitioners upon whose work much of the focus of the quality programming that exists in the field today is based. Whether the roots of a curriculum can be traced back to Dewey, Piaget, Montessori, Vygotsky or some combination thereof, all place the active child at the center of the story. Children who are vigorously engaged in their play are capturing lifelong lessons and skills that serve as the building blocks for future learning. Placing the active child at the center of the inquiry, providing hands-on experiences and opportunities to make and test hypotheses, gives children the chance to construct their own learning and to better internalize the results.

CHILD, TEACHER, ENVIRONMENT

In order to accomplish all that quality early childhood education sets out to do, the field employs three central components that are critical to success. The first, the active child, provides us with the apex and the focus. But equally important are the environment and the teacher. Excellent early childhood classrooms are set up with a deliberateness and purpose that allows the learner to navigate independently. Play areas are clearly defined and stocked with a variety of age-appropriate materials. Children are able to choose their own materials and explore what to do with them. Given a bin of interlocking rings, one student may begin to make a necklace, another begins to sort and classify them by size and by color and

---

[1] The origins of the term Developmentally Appropriate Practice are not clear; however it gained recognition when the National Association for the Education of Young Children (NAEYC) published a position paper promoting teaching practices that varied or adapted classroom practices to reflect the age, ability, interests and experiences of the children in the classroom. It has since been revised several times, most recently in 2009 and is an accepted part of the vernacular of quality early childhood education.

a third takes the links to use them representationally in the dramatic play area, creating a story with each of the links as a character. Each student is furthering his/her own knowledge and experience in math or art or literacy. There is no one directing their discovery; it comes naturally as they actively explore the materials.

The role of the teacher is critical to facilitating this kind of educative process. The teacher is responsible for the creation and maintenance of the space, as is mentioned above, but also for serving as a guide, mentor and role model. Piaget describes the teacher's directive as to arouse curiosity and stimulate activity, while Dewey defines it as the protector of "the spirit of inquiry" (1933, p. 34). Whatever the descriptive language, the teacher has the difficult but incredible job of bringing learning to life and of maximizing each child's inherent desire to learn.

> At the art table in a four-year-old classroom, six children are busy utilizing the various materials on the table—fabric, foam shapes, colored tape, paper, crayons, etc. A teacher sits at the table with the children, engaging them in conversation as they work. Each child's masterpiece is very different and, at first glance, seems haphazard. But upon closer examination you see that the teacher is paying careful attention to what each child is creating and asking questions that further the work. "Sarah, that looks so interesting. What can you tell me about the shapes that you used?" As Sarah describes her art and her process, the teacher is able to scaffold her geometric language. The teacher asks why she made certain choices about which shapes, which colors to use, and Sarah's response describes her process and begins to build the muscles of critical thinking.

This kind of careful questioning requires skilled teachers to be keen observers and copious note-takers. Given that the focus is for the children to learn through their own experiences and discoveries, there is little direct instruction happening in the classroom; instead adults in the classroom serve as supporters of the children's development. They do not tell children what to learn or how to learn it, but they empower children to pose questions and find answers. Teachers are purposefully listening to and participating in conversations held over the lunch table or during sensory play. These dialogues often give insight into children's lives and give the teacher the opportunity to plan learning experiences in the classroom that are based on their lived experiences outside of school.

This engagement bridges the gap between the ECE student's cognitive ability to really think critically about his or her own learning and the vitality of that component in the educative process. Reflection happens in several ways in the classroom—through conversations, questions and group discussions, teachers are able to lead children in making connections in and out of the classroom. Using this relational model situates teachers as guides in this process (relating back to Piaget's concept of teaching)—but equally critical to the success of ECE is the reflection of teachers themselves. Excellent teachers are going through a constant process of reflection—about each child's work, about their own practice and about the functioning of the classroom.

As role models, teachers set the example of acceptable behaviors in the classroom, of cultural norms and of what it means to be engaged in learning. Skilled early childhood teachers are learning with and from the children as much as the children are learning with and from them; they show a passion for learning that is passed on to their students.

In a Jewish early childhood classroom there is the added layer of cultural relativity—and teachers serve as a resource as well as an example of how Judaism is incorporated in life. When a teacher uses Hebrew words or Jewish traditions as part of the normal lexicon of the classroom, he/she is creating a familiarity and a comfort with these concepts that extends well beyond the preschool day.

EARLY CHILDHOOD EDUCATION SETS THE STAGE FOR JEWISH LIFE

During these "preschool" years children are exploding in all domains of learning (physical, social/emotional, cognitive, etc.). Yet the work of these children—their day-to-day agenda—is called play. Through experiments with cuisenaire rods, water and measuring cups, feathers and sand, preschool children begin to learn the concepts of length, volume and weight. Through working with paintbrushes, cutting with scissors and molding clay, children begin to exercise the muscles they will need for writing. And through cooking, literature, music, holiday celebration and values-based experiences, children in Jewish early childhood centers come to acquire the building blocks they will need for a Jewish future. While each of these activities is valuable in the development of the child, they are simultaneously setting the stage for future experiences and skills.

> In a three-year-old classroom the teacher begins circle time (called *ma'agal* in Hebrew) with attendance. She notes aloud that Jenna is absent for the second day in a row, and she asks Emma—whose classroom job this week is *bikkur ḥolim* (visiting the sick)—to choose three friends to go with her to the office to call Jenna at home. The children wish Jenna *refuah shlemah* (quick recovery) over the phone, tell her all about the progress of the hermit crab in their classroom and let her know that they can't wait for her to return to school as soon as she is better.

This practice serves many purposes in a Jewish early childhood classroom. Introducing the concept of *bikkur ḥolim* in this way—and giving it that language—provides the children with a concrete and manageable way to understand that they have a role to play in making the sick child feel better. The "well" children are empowered to take some action in the care and health of the members of the classroom; the "sick" child is reminded that her community awaits her and that somehow they are not complete until she is back with them. Extending this mitzvah, as the children get older, to visiting a nursing home or performing at a hospital becomes more meaningful by building these Jewish competencies while in preschool.

In the Jewish early childhood classroom, teachers have the opportunity to provide materials and experiences that bring Judaism—its holidays, traditions and rituals—to life. Each is seamlessly incorporated into the emerging curriculum through music, movement, stories, prayer and food. In our Shabbat example from the beginning of the chapter, one can see how the children's exposure to objects and concepts allows them to make sense of them and to utilize them in their play. This familiarity leads to mastery of the rituals, and by definition, their repetition each week or each year creates lasting memories and paves the way for ongoing Jewish engagement.

> In music class the children are singing a song about the names of the colors in Hebrew. Back in the classroom, at the easel a few hours later, four-year-old Nate and five-year-old Alexander are discussing their work. "I used *kachol* (blue) first and then added red. When you mix them together it makes *sagol* (purple)!"

This ability to speak in "Hebr-ish" demonstrates how a child is able to integrate his or her "Jewish self" with the daily work. Increasing Jewish literacy allows children to experiment with the traditions, customs and language and make them a part of their lives.

Of course, as they are just three or four years old, there is another critical component of Jewish early childhood Education that must be addressed. At no other time during the child's life are his/her parents more involved with school than in early childhood. Excellent ECE programs look at the relationship between home and school as fundamental to their success. Engaging parents in the classroom routines and rituals, as well as providing educational experiences geared toward parents, should be seen as part and parcel of the work we do with young children. This responsibility, often overlooked by teachers and administrators, is critical to fulfilling the Jewish potential of an early childhood program. For the vast majority of parents particularly in Reform, Conservative and non-affiliated schools—the Jewish preschool classroom is their first sustained interaction with the organized Jewish community since they became bar/bat mitzvah (if that). Perhaps they had a Jewish wedding, perhaps their child was named or circumcised in a synagogue, but never before have they been so open or exposed to ongoing Jewish education as parents. By empowering them to be active in their child's Jewish education, we are re-engaging them with formal Jewish learning. Programs like "How to Celebrate Purim at Home" or "Your Shabbat Table" offer parents a non-judgmental, family-centered approach to their own learning; through "Tot *Kabbalat Shabbat*" or a "Model Seder" we create opportunities for parents to have Jewish experiences that are age-appropriate for their child, in effect modeling Jewish behaviors that could be replicated (or transformed) at home.

As the children come home from school carrying their challah, singing songs they learned about Tu B'shevat or asking to perform the Shabbat blessings at home, parents are often confronted for the first time with deciding what their Jewish home life will be. This does not by any means require the school to dictate or prescribe home behaviors. In fact, the opposite is true—within that tension between what happens in the classroom and what may or may not be happening at home is the space for conversation and exploration for these parents to define for themselves what "Jewish" will look like in their home.

But by actively participating in that dialogue—providing resources, ideas, discussion groups and support—Jewish early childhood programs have an incredible and unique opportunity to guide families as they move forward on their Jewish journeys.

CONCLUSION

Informal Jewish education is fundamentally about building a lasting Jewish identity. It should not mean short-term or incidental, but rather should consist of accessible interactions with real life experiences at a developmentally appropriate level. That *is* early childhood education. Judaism is not a "read about it" kind of religion; the traditions and the culture beg for hands-on encounters—to light the candles, to drink the wine, to taste the challah. It is a naturally multi-sensory engagement, and developmentally, that is enormously powerful with young children.

However, that identity cannot exist in a vacuum; it must have context in a child's life, and, to have longevity, must be meaningful for that child and within that child's community. Jewish early childhood education is qualitatively good for children. On its own it expands children's experience with heritage, tradition and peoplehood and engenders positive associations with Judaism and Jewish learning. In and of itself, there is value in that experience for children. However, when it is viewed as a holistic experience for the child and for the child's family, participation in a quality Jewish early childhood program gives context to the larger Jewish world and to their place in it. Families are able to explore—together and as parents and children separately—how Jewish life will be lived in their homes.

While the tools and themes that have been discussed here are essentially geared toward young children, the concepts and methodology are applicable in any informal educational setting. Take away the sand table and the math manipulatives and you are left with pedagogy for education that works. Children (and adults) learn by doing. There is an ancient Chinese proverb that says, "I hear and I forget, I see and I remember, I do and I understand." This should be a mantra for Jewish education everywhere.

REFERENCES

Dewey, J. (1933). *How We Think: a Restatement of the Relation of Reflective Thinking to the Educative Process.* Boston, MA: DC and Heath Company.

Elkind, D. (1986). *Formal Education and Early Childhood Education: An Essential Difference.* Phi Delta Kappan, 631–636.

Erikson, E.H. (1950). *Childhood and Society.* New York: Norton.

Hohmann, M. and D.P. Weikart (1995). *Educating Young Children.* Ypsilanti, MI: High/Scope Press.

Kamii, C.K. (1985). *Young Children Reinvent Arithmetic.* New York: Teachers College Press.

Lindsay, A. and A. Ewert (1999). "Learning at the Edge: Can Experiential Education Contribute to Educational Reform?" *Journal of Experiential Education* 22(1), 12–19.

Miller, E. and J. Almon (2009). *Crisis in the Kindergarten: Why Children Need to Play in School*. College Park, MD: Alliance for Childhood.

Montessori, M. (1964). *The Montessori Method*. New York: Schocken Books.

NAEYC. "Questions about Developmentally Appropriate Practice." *Teaching Young Children*. 2(2), 22–24.

Piaget, J. (1963). *The Origins of Intelligence in Children*. New York: WW Norton & Company.

Piaget, J. and B. Inhelder (1958). *The Growth of Logical Thinking from Childhood to Adolescence: An Essay on the Construction of Formal Operational Structures*. New York: Basic Books.

Shonkoff, J.P. and D.A. Phillips (eds.) (2000). *Neurons to Neighborhoods: The Science of Early Childhood Development*. Washington: National Academy Press.

Torkington, K. (1996). "The Rationale for Experiential/Participatory Learning." *Working Papers in Early Childhood Development* 16. The Hague, Netherlands: Bernard Van Leer Foundation.

Yerkes, R. (1988). "What about the Young Child?" *Journal of Experiential Education*. 11:2, 21–25.

COMING OF AGE IN JEWISH LIFE:
GENDER, COMMUNITY AND RESILIENCE

Deborah Meyer

For most Jewish teens today, becoming bar or bat mitzvah is less a bridge from Jewish childhood to Jewish adulthood than an exit ramp out of Jewish life altogether. While some 80% of Jewish teens today become b'nai mitzvah, the majority see the ritual as a graduation from Jewish life. By their senior year of high school, only a fraction of Jewish teens participate in Jewish education, and fewer still find their way back to Jewish community as adults. Research conducted by my organization, Moving Traditions,[1] and others paints a clear picture. By age thirteen the majority of girls and boys describe Jewish programming as preachy, boring and adult-centered rather than adolescent-centered. Girls continue to participate through high school in slightly higher numbers than boys, but they are only marginally less dissatisfied than boys with what is being offered to them. The Jewish community is losing an alarmingly large portion of the young adults who could sustain it in the future. And Jewish teens are missing out on the tremendous spiritual and cultural resource Jewish communal life could provide them on their journey to adulthood.

Too often declining Jewish teen involvement is seen in terms of numbers, as a matter of retention or marketing. I contend, however, that this understanding of the issue is itself part of the problem. We need to go deeper; we need to craft experiential education programs that provide teens with what they need. Both the content and format of post-b'nai mitzvah education must reflect a thorough understanding of teens' interests and challenges at this transitional time in their lives, as well as manifest a rich understanding of what Judaism in particular can offer teens to meet their needs.

Crafting educational programs that appeal to adolescents is a challenge for adults precisely because adolescence itself is such a challenge for teens. The challenge of adolescence can be summed up in one word: gender.

Adolescence marks the onset of significant biological changes to children's bodies and minds—changes that will make them into men and women. Just as becoming b'nai mitzvah attaches Jewish spiritual and communal significance to the process of growing up, so the concept of gender describes the broad social and cultural significance of the transition to adulthood. Sex is biologically determined, but gender is socially constructed. It is a series of cultural, social and personal norms and expectations that help structure young men's and women's sense of who they are and what life choices are open to them. Thus gender defines and clarifies, but it also constrains and limits. From family, peers, the media, teen culture, the internet and society at large, teen boys and girls get strong, often conflicting gender messages that encode social values and judgments on their minds and bodies. When they enter adolescence teens

---

[1] Moving Traditions promotes a Judaism that inspires people to work for an inclusive and just world. By asking "What does it mean to be a woman?" and "What does it mean to be a man?" the organization champions an experiential educational approach that connects teens' character development to building a Jewish community in which both women and men experience spiritual, intellectual and moral growth.

A *Slingshot* guide "Standard Bearer," Moving Traditions' professional development, program certification training and curricular materials prepare Jewish educators—well over a thousand so far—to challenge and inspire preteen and teenage girls and boys through its single-gender programs that engage them in Jewish life after becoming b'nai mitzvah. These programs, *Rosh Hodesh: It's a Girl Thing!* and *Shevet Achim: The Brotherhood*, empower thousands of Jewish girls and boys each year to navigate the challenges of becoming women and men in American society, while inspiring them to find meaning in and connect to Jewish community. Girls from sixth to twelfth grades meet monthly in intimate *Rosh Hodesh* gatherings operated by over two hundred Jewish organizations, some for up to seven years. In *Shevet Achim*, starting in eighth grade, teen boys explore what it means to be a Jewish man and a mensch in groups now being operated by sixty of the organizations that offer *Rosh Hodesh* groups.

quickly grasp that gender consists of a complex set of rules, and that questioning or resisting these rules can be a risky proposition.

What teens need, then, are safe environments in which they can convene to freely explore and question what it means to become gendered adults, and well-trained, self-aware adults to help guide them in their collective explorations. This experiential education model recognizes that teens tend to individuate from their parents and to develop strong, meaningful relationships with their peers. It also recognizes that at this stage in their lives teens want and need to be actively engaged and to take a degree of responsibility for their own education.

The field of Positive Youth Development, or PYD, is based on these insights. PYD research shows that successful teen programs build on a framework of specific assets that cultivate emotional health and resilience, helping teens resist risky behaviors such as substance abuse and unsafe sexual activity, and adopt positive behaviors such as healthy friendships and academic achievement. Resilience enables a person to handle the inevitable challenges of life with strength and flexibility; the assets described in PYD literature all contribute to teens developing the coping mechanisms that facilitate their resilience.

In this chapter I will outline the four factors that I believe are essential in creating Jewish experiential programming that effectively helps teens come of age as healthy, engaged Jewish adults. These four factors are derived from a larger set of forty PYD assets identified by the Search Institute[2] and interpreted through the prism of my experience in the *Habonim Dror* youth movement and as co-creator with many talented colleagues of Moving Traditions' programs. They include:

- **An Exploration of Gender** that provides teen girls and boys with a lens through which to read culture that cultivates their inner resources to question and resist the simplistic, negative and sometimes violent cultural messages and influences relating to gender;

- **An Application of Jewish Values to Teens' Concerns** that enables teens to apply Jewish ethics, values and rituals to the challenges they face each day, including at school, with friends and at home;

- **The Cultivation of a Supportive Peer Community** in which teens can safely pose questions, express themselves, develop and maintain vital relationships and experience Jewish community as an alternative culture that is a source of joy and meaning; and

- **The Enlightened Guidance of Adult Mentors** who are able to facilitate teens' collective exploration of Judaism and gender, helping individual teen boys and girls to form a cohesive cohort from which they each derive strength and resilience as they progress through adolescence to adulthood.

The first two factors define the content of the programming. The second two factors define the structure. We know from research that programs embodying these factors do in fact lead to deeply satisfying experiences and resilient youth. We also know from practice that teens enjoy and will continue to participate in this kind of Jewish experiential education when it is offered. In the following pages I will provide examples of how this model can be put into practice and how it can inspire teens to find meaning—and make meaning—in Jewish life.

Consider the following scenario:

> Ten fourteen-year old girls are gathered on a cloth decorated with their names in Hebrew and English, seated in a circle around snacks and a candle lit for *Rosh Hodesh*, the new moon. They are engaged in a heated discussion of Rachel and Leah, biblical sisters who are often understood to compete for the love of the same man, their husband Jacob. Emma complains that "Girls are always supposed to be jealous of each other" and says she wonders if the sisters "maybe liked being able to stay in the same family." Jenny says, "Maybe they hate having to share, but they can't tell each other because they don't want to hurt each other's feelings." Their leader Liz notes that this kind of imagining is at the heart of midrash, or Torah interpretation, and invites each girl to write her own midrash centered on the story of Rachel and

---

[2] For a complete list of the Search Institute's forty assets, visit the website, www.search-institute.org/content/40-developmental-assets-adolescents-ages-12-18.

Leah. "Think about what it would be like to be Leah or Rachel. What would be difficult? What would you like? How could you tell each other what you really feel in a way that benefits you and the other person? Have you ever experienced anything that in some way is like the story of Leah and Rachel?"

In their *Rosh Hodesh: It's a Girl Thing!* group, Emma and her friends begin with a critical exploration of gender: They use their analytic faculties to notice a negative cultural message about what it means to behave as a girl. "Girls are always supposed to be jealous of each other." They then use Jewish knowledge and values to interrogate this message, relate it to their daily lives and creatively "push back" against it. They first determine their own individual ideas and feelings and then share them in the context of the supportive peer community offered by their *Rosh Hodesh* group. The entire enterprise is facilitated by a trained adult mentor who encourages them to reflect, ask questions and actively collaborate in creating their own alternative narratives as part of a community.

Over the past ten years this scenario has played out in countless variations across the United States as more than eleven thousand girls—and more recently, several hundred boys—have participated in groups facilitated by Moving Traditions–trained mentors and supported by loving, concerned Jewish communities. Jewish teens have learned valuable lessons from their experiences in these groups, and we can learn equally valuable lessons from them.

EXPLORING GENDER

As in the scenario above, the Jewish tradition of interrogating a text can be applied to help teens sift through the innumerable gender messages they receive each day from American culture so they can craft and make decisions about their own healthy self-concept, values and worldview.

American culture's definitions of masculinity and femininity can limit teen boys' and girls' expectations about how to behave and what they can expect out of their future. Popular culture geared toward teenage boys often promotes a masculine norm that is sexually predatory, physically aggressive and emotionally impoverished. Popular culture geared toward teenage girls often promotes a feminine norm that is over-achieving, highly sexualized and intensely competitive with other girls and women for the attention of boys and men. This binary understanding of gender makes it difficult for boys and girls to figure out who they are, to display their hearts and to speak their truth. This disassociation undermines resilience. It makes it more difficult to form healthy attachments. The impact on teen boys and girls makes it imperative to address restrictive gender norms and to open up for them the whole spectrum of human behavior so that they can each reach their full human potential.

The pressure to conform to expectations around gender during adolescence is apparent in nearly every aspect of teens' lives. What to wear, what to do on the weekend, what to post in social networks, how to behave in school and how to act at parties are all connected to ideas about being feminine and masculine. Gender norms are both pervasive and largely unexamined, which makes it vitally important to help adolescents learn to read, filter and actively choose among the gender messages they receive from the culture in which they live.[3] Jewish teens navigate what it means to be identified as a "Jewish girl" or "Jewish guy" in a multicultural and multifaith world.

At first glance, resisting the dominant point of view may sound antithetical to what it means to be an adolescent. Teenage girls and boys seem to long for nothing more than to fit in and be accepted. Yet teens resist expectations put on them by parents, teachers and other authorities. They embrace and often take pleasure in skeptical attitudes about advertising and mass media. This inherent resistance can be harnessed and used to help teens stay connected to themselves, to a supportive peer group and to the Jewish community.

---

[3] It is also important for adults who work with adolescents to be aware of and welcoming to the sexual orientation and gender identities of teens, whether straight, gay, lesbian, bisexual, transgender or questioning, as well as to be aware of and welcoming to the range of families that teens come from, with parents and grandparents who could be single or partnered, straight, gay, lesbian, bisexual or transgender.

The key is to provide teens with the skills to read culture and to interrogate the world around them. A significant body of research, along with Moving Traditions' considerable experience, clearly demonstrates that the most effective and powerful place to focus these skills is in the area of gender, because it is a primary source of both deep confusion and keen interest for teens. Despite what some may think, exploring masculinity matters to boys as much as exploring femininity matters to girls. The literature shows it, and Moving Traditions' research and program experience confirms it.

For teens today, the world looks very different than it did for past generations. Unfettered access to all aspects of secular life through social and geographic integration and through technology present this generation with more opportunities than any other in American Jewish life, which in turn shapes teens' expectations of and their participation in Jewish life. No longer held back by the anti-Semitism that restricted their grandparents, Jewish teens today do not need Jewish programming to provide them with outlets for academic, social or cultural fulfillment. With technology, teens are able to explore a much wider world, one defined by media and social networking. They are exposed to more data than teens at any time in human history—with images and information from their friends, their friends' friends and total strangers—often carrying extreme and conflicting messages about gender. From their homes to school halls to porn sites to music videos, the idea of what it means to be male and female can be highly confusing.

Teens need the support of adults who have themselves developed an analysis of American culture and its gender norms and who will be comfortable helping teens develop their own critique and what they each think it means to be male and female.

APPLYING JEWISH VALUES

When we connect Jewish values and ethics to the internal, deeply personal struggles Jewish girls and boys face, they come to see Judaism as deeply relevant to their lives. In the process they see their lives as more fundamentally Jewish, and adolescence as a path along which they will become not only men and women, but the Jewish men and Jewish women they want to be. Placing the questions "What does it mean to be a woman?" "What does it mean to be a man?" and "What does it mean to be a mensch?" at the heart of the discussion enables teen girls and boys to talk about the life issues that really matter to them.

Very rarely does Jewish education address the issues that teens see as intrinsically connected to their coming of age as young women or men. This is likely due to the persistence of the idea that Jewish education involves imparting a store of knowledge rather than creatively and dialogically engaging teens with the richness of resources and values Judaism has to offer. Yet there is a wealth of material in the Torah that can be brought to bear on the challenges teens face each day, especially when we define Jewish teachings to include all that was revealed at Sinai—from the five books through the Jewish feminist and queer writings of the twentieth and twenty-first centuries.

Friendship, intimacy, competition, power, sexuality—every issue that concerns teens is addressed in the Torah and struggled with by Jewish thinkers through the ages, including in the story of Rachel and Leah. From *shalom bayit*, a peaceful household, to *tzedek*, righting and healing injustice, when teens consider and apply Jewish values to their lives they experience Jewish community as being the location of support, guidance and meaning-making.

Yet in most cases teens drop out of Jewish life before they have the opportunity to take part in discussions except at a pediatric level. By offering teens sophisticated and nuanced material, we honor them and engage them.

CULTIVATING A JEWISH PEER COMMUNITY

Jewish community can help teen girls and boys defy the dictates of our dominant culture even as they appropriate certain aspects of it. Jews have been doing this for centuries, since ancient times. By combining Jewish values and a gender critique we can help girls and boys of this generation resist negative aspects of popular culture from within a frame of an alternate culture: Jewish teen community.

Most Jewish experiential educators and most parents recognize that above all, teens value the company of their peers. If their friends are planning to attend an event, they are much more likely to want to go as well. However, peer community is more than simply enjoyable for teens. The peer group is an essential arena for healthy teen development, as articulated in the work of Vivian Center Seltzer, among others, where teens compare and measure themselves against those of the same age, and where shifting roles help teens develop and mature.

What better grouping from among which to make meaning than the *minyan*, the sacred Jewish building block of ten people that constitutes the foundation for prayer? An effective Jewish teen community can be created in small groups of ten, with the help of adult mentors, where teens contribute to establishing emotionally safe space within which to take up issues that they care about deeply. To create a space that is their own, teens should be engaged from the beginning in setting group rules and norms. To have a space that is truly safe, and to learn how to create this kind of space for themselves as they grow, each participant should feel responsible for maintaining a safe space for everyone else across differences of denomination, sexual orientation, socioeconomic background, maturity level and so forth. The experience should tap into girls' and boys' souls. It should encourage reflection, exploration and self-acceptance, allowing the teens to build a sense of individual identity while working together to foster their connections to one another and to Jewish life.

A sense of mutual responsibility and obligation is central to Judaism—and again is reflected in our responsibility as adults to help form a *minyan*. It is only with one another that we can form a satisfying and sacred community. Through this experience teens will deeply appreciate the value of community, and they will learn how to create community for themselves when they are adults.

MENTORING TEEN GROUPS

Adult mentors are essential to the creation of intimate and safe community, and they provide critical benefit to teens' lives in and of themselves. Being able to turn to adults who are not parents—and who are connected to a community of meaning, such as the Jewish community—is a critical asset identified by the Positive Youth Development field, among others. How nourishing to have multiple healthy role models for teens to turn to.

A central goal of the kind of teen Jewish community I am describing is to make it possible for girls and boys to explore issues they rarely have the opportunity to reflect on elsewhere in their lives. The power of such an experience comes from the adult mentor's ability to genuinely connect with and understand teens, and from his or her expertise in creating spaces that allow this type of conversation to occur. Authenticity is paramount; when experiential educators possess it they instill confidence and are able to build trust and comfort. Similarly, when educators feel secure in who they are and in their skills, teens will feel confident that the group is in good hands.

The key is in raising questions—but not in offering solutions. Teens' ears are sharply attuned to adult expectations. If they sense that they are being asked to provide the "correct" answer, they will tune out and drop away. In addition, adults must be wary of attacking teens' culture per se. Inviting teens to be critical thinkers is one thing; mounting a wholesale attack against teens' music, dress, and manner of speech is another. To truly build teens' resistance and their belief that Judaism has meaning, adult mentors themselves must learn to sit with complicated questions and to trust teens and the questioning process.

It is essential to select as experiential educators those adult mentors who see gender as socially created and variable, who understand the complex dynamics of masculinity and femininity and who are not sexist in their world-view and demeanor. A male facilitator who values introspection, self-expression and relational interaction—and who can model respect for girls and women as an integral part of Jewish manhood—will have a powerful, positive impact on boys' learning and development. A female leader who values truth-telling above "being nice" and who enjoys girls' energy and excitement will have a powerful, positive impact on girls' learning and development. It is also essential that adult mentors be welcoming to and comfortable with boys' and girls' varying sexual and gender identities.

Few Jewish educators have had the opportunity to explore gender and Jewish values themselves, let alone consider how to support a teen community that takes up these issues. As teens are given the opportunity to explore the challenges of their daily lives, issues may arise that feel personally challenging or which the adult mentor has difficulty addressing. For all of these reasons, training and ongoing coaching are essential to prepare and support a successful adult mentor.

Moreover, this sort of programmatic approach will be most successful when everyone involved—clergy, education directors, heads of school, parents and experiential educators—supports the goal of helping teen girls and teen boys grow into self-aware Jewish women and men comfortable exploring both their religion and their gender along the spectrum of feminine and masculine behavior.

RESILIENCE: THE GOAL AND THE GIFT

By applying a gender lens and Jewish values to teens' developmental challenges within the context of an intimate and mutually supportive peer community, and with the guidance of a well-trained adult mentor, teens can take up the issues of their daily lives that they care about most. In the process they will experience Jewish community as a place to make meaning and a source of strength amidst the challenges they face.

As eighteen-year-old Mimi once told a roomful of adults:

> My boyfriend a few years ago had threatened to kill himself if I broke up with him. It was a very threatening situation for a girl at any age—and being fifteen and a freshman in high school made it difficult to go to anyone for help. My *Rosh Hodesh* group helped me figure out what to do about the situation.
>
> If I could give advice to Jewish educators, I would tell them to do what we do in *Rosh Hodesh*: It's a Girl Thing: weave Jewish teachings and ritual into the issues and challenges of teens' lives—as girls and as boys. Having Jewish learning that helped me with a personal problem is what really made Jewish community meaningful for me. Most Jewish programs focus on prayer—or bowling—but good programs like *Rosh Hodesh* really focus on our lives and the kind of problems we teens all go through. I come from a really warm Jewish family, but I still needed to experience Judaism in a way that is important to me personally. Connecting Jewish teaching and rituals with the kind of problems we teens all go through is what makes me and my friends feel like we want to be Jewish. I think that is the secret to showing teens how meaningful Jewish life can be.

What I am here calling resilience, we often call empowerment. Either term will suffice, but I believe the concept of resilience more accurately captures the importance of facing situations like the one Mimi describes—situations in which teens find themselves feeling vulnerable, afraid, uncertain and anything but powerful. If they have resilience, they can cope effectively and creatively with these situations, acknowledging their fears and vulnerabilities and drawing on inner resources to make healthy choices for themselves and in their dealings with their peers. This resilience grows out of an experience of connecting to oneself, drawing on a gender critique of the world and a set of Jewish values that allows each teen to discern what he or she believes and needs, with the support of a peer community and an adult mentor.

In order to help teen girls and boys come of age as resilient and Jewish women and men, the Jewish community needs to find a way to stay in relationship to teens. The fact that b'nai mitzvah comes in a liminal period, the age when most children are entering adolescence, provides the Jewish community with a now largely missed opportunity to accompany teens on their journey. One of the keys is helping teens wrestle with their core questions about gender and identity. How are they invited each day by the world around them to "perform gender"? What does it mean to become a man or woman? What does it mean to be successful? Care for children? Work for a living? Experience a satisfying sexual life? Be connected to other Jews? Make the world a better place?

In connecting meaningfully with Jewish teenage boys and girls we enact two of Judaism's most important imperatives: *talmud torah*, critical learning, and *rodef tzedek*, pursuing justice. We do so not by dictating to teens, but by inviting them to help create a Jewish community that serves their purposes and is centered on their interests. By helping teens resist the parts of our American culture that devalue what it means to be male and female, we engage them in healing the world with us—demonstrating that as we pursue justice we are made stronger and more resilient.

The post-bar and bat mitzvah years are a critical opportunity to make a difference in the lives of teens and help them come of age as Jewish men and women. If we make the gender issues that teens care about most the focus of Jewish offerings post-b'nai mitzvah, Jewish educators will give teens an experience that will keep them engaged throughout high school and will lead to life-long connection to Jewish community. When we create experiential educational offerings that help teen girls and boys navigate the choppy waters of adolescence by drawing on a gender critique and Jewish values within a safe and enjoyable peer community, we will strengthen their resilience and their Jewish identity—and we will strengthen our Jewish future.

EXPERIENTIAL EDUCATION AND JEWISH EMERGING ADULTS

Scott Aaron & Josh Feigelson

Young Jewish adults don't join institutions. Or at least that's the conventional wisdom. In general this perception has been perceived as a crisis demanding a muscular institutional response variously described as "bold," "innovative," "transformative" or some other catchword. Alternatively, it has been understood as an opportunity for "reinvention," "experimentation" or post-institutional creative ventures in new modes of Jewish life. The former view leads to programs like Birthright Israel, in which major institutional players invest in a massive effort to connect young Jews to Jewish life. The latter leads to acclamation for independent *minyanim,* Moishe Houses and other forms of Jewish engagement perceived as "innovative" or non- or anti-institutional.

Young adulthood is a time when Jewish adults tend to disaffiliate from institutions, and that reality frequently provokes some panic on the part of Jewish institutions. But it is imperative to remember two things: First, institutional affiliation declines for *all* young adults, not just Jews. It's not necessarily the case that Jewish life or Jewish institutions aren't compelling for young Jews; churches, civic organizations and most other voluntary institutions also serve and engage people on either side of emerging adulthood much more than they do emerging adults.

Second, this is not a recent phenomenon (either the lack of affiliation or the communal panic). "In every age the elders of the tribe raise their hands to heaven in horror at the defections and deviltry of the young, but somehow Jewish culture survives the fierce assaults of the young iconoclasts of Israel who, once their fury of revolt is spent, cherish the wisdom and carry on the work of their forebears." This was written by a Brooklyn College professor in 1955 (Glicksberg, 1955).

Let us step out of the institutional/anti-institutional dichotomy for a moment and ask a slightly different question: What can a theory of experiential Jewish education contribute to our understanding of emerging Jewish adulthood? Formal institutional thinking is rooted in the preservation of the form or institution, and education in this context is understood as the process of acculturating young people into an institutional order and way of life. A formal institutional approach to emerging adulthood tends to ask questions like:

- How can we get young Jews to meet each other, marry each other and raise Jewish children?
- How can we get young Jews to join our synagogues?
- How can we get young Jewish adults to love Israel and advocate for it on campus?
- How can we get young Jews to donate to our communal institutions?

All of these questions presume an importance to the institution: synagogue, Israel, Jewish communal organization, etc. They assume that young people need to be assimilated into Jewish institutions (rather than assimilating into non–Jewish ones). [1] They are ultimately centered on the institution, animated by the question "How can we ensure institutional survival?"

Experiential education begins with a different question: What are the needs of the learner? What are the human developmental tasks at his or her stage of life? And how can we create, alter or sustain an

---

[1] Consider Hillel's motto from the 1990s: "Maximize the number of Jews doing Jewish with other Jews."

environment that supports the healthy development of the learner in response to these needs and tasks? This is the approach we take in this chapter.

We first review some of the basic features of emerging adulthood, the developmental stage now recognized by many social psychologists as the period between ages eighteen and twenty-eight. Due to space limitations, we will not conduct a comprehensive review of Jewish programs for emerging adults. Instead, in the second half of the chapter we will reflect on some of the salient features of engagement vis-à-vis experiential education with emerging Jewish adults in the current landscape that we think bear particular attention and unpacking.

HUMAN DEVELOPMENT

A classic section of Jewish text, *Mishnah Avot* 5:21, explains Judaism's ancient understanding of human development:

> He (Yehuda ben Tema) used to say: At five years old [one is fit] for the [study of] Scripture, at ten years for [the study of] Mishnah, at thirteen for [the fulfilling of] the commandments, at fifteen for the Talmud, at eighteen for the bridal canopy, at twenty for pursuing [a career], at thirty for full authority, at forty for [wise] discernment, at fifty for [the ability to give] counsel, at sixty to be an elder, at seventy for gray hairs, at eighty for special strength, at ninety for a bent back, and at a hundred a man is as one that has [already] died and passed away and ceased from the world.

This text, some twenty centuries old at least, looks at the life span of a human being from a specific world view. The text assumes that one reaches adulthood in the eyes of the community at thirteen years of age, begins a family by eighteen and has established a career by twenty. Knowledge is assumed to be a province of youth, wisdom that of the aged, and one who lives to eighty is seen as having lived beyond expectation.

Our understanding of human development today assumes a much different life path for the modern person in the developed world. Knowledge and wisdom are intertwined. Formal education is the full-time activity of a student until at least age eighteen and commonly until age twenty-two, but learning is generally accepted as a lifelong endeavor. Careers are not started in earnest until the completion of education, and neither is marriage, although it is ever common for that to be postponed until the solid establishment of a career as well. Today one can live vibrantly for ninety or more years, under ideal conditions, and work almost as long. Should one live past one hundred years of age, with proper care one can still have a good quality of life and health.

In short, life spans are longer because modern life allows for a multiplicity of factors that extend the stages of life into longer segments than our ancestors could understand. The extension of those stages has gradually increased over time on pace with the technological development of a society. So, for instance, as the Industrial Revolution mechanized farm work and brought urban factory work to cities, children needed to extend their time in school in order to develop more sophisticated skills for the work force. Whereas in the eighteenth century a child with what we think of today as an elementary education could gain enough learning to enter the work force full-time as a teenager, by the end of the nineteenth century children needed to increase their knowledge base to a high school level. The twentieth century brought a need to extend education to college for the best jobs, and in the twenty-first century that need is increasingly becoming extended to graduate or professional school.

EMERGING ADULTHOOD: A NEW STAGE OF HUMAN DEVELOPMENT

All of this has resulted in an awareness of an arc of time called emerging adulthood. Emerging adulthood is a segment of developmental psychology, a field that evolved over the last century to track the cognitive, emotional and moral growth of the human mind. Emerging adulthood theoreticians have specifically focused on the developmental stage of the ages of eighteen to twenty-eight. Notable theories that frame developmental psychology are those of Erik Erikson, Lawrence Kohlberg, William Perry and Sharon Daloz Parks, among others. Erikson (1902–1994) composed an eight-stage theory of human development from infancy to late adulthood that marks the acquisition of important life skills such as trust, moral understanding and self-perception. Kohlberg's (1927–1987) six stages of moral development expanded upon those of Jean Piaget's (1896–1980) stage theory of cognitive development. Kohlberg's theory holds that each stage brings moral skills that increase in sophistication with each successive stage. In both Erikson's and Kohlberg's theories these skills have to evolve in their appropriate stages, or healthy human development can be delayed or even derailed. Perry (1913–1998) brought a systemic understanding of how a concept of right and wrong becomes increasingly layered and nuanced as people develop cognitively, and Daloz-Parks expands upon James Fowler's theory of faith development to the young adult population (Parks, 2000).

In 2000 a refined theory of development for this age group was introduced by Dr. Jeffrey Jensen Arnett of Clark University, who coined the term "emerging adulthood" and explained that

> having left the dependency of childhood and adolescence, and having not yet entered the enduring responsibilities that are normative in adulthood, emerging adults often explore a variety of possible life directions in love, work and worldviews (Arnett).

Arnett has determined that emerging adults are delaying traditional life experiences that accompany full adult independence, such as marriage, childbearing, home acquisition and membership in religious and cultural institutions, and he has observed a number of trends in this age group. Emerging adults are more transient than previous generations, and this transience is leading to less personal interest in affiliation with mainstream communal institutions such as houses of worship, social/fraternal organizations and political parties. Some of the most noteworthy aspects of emerging adulthood are:

a. Emerging adults seek personal meaning for their lives.

b. They seek a spiritual understanding of the world but are reluctant to be bound by a religious system.

c. Emerging adults seek intensive, intimate social relationships with a diverse range of peoples, and they challenge broad moral assumptions and large cultural and political institutions.

d. They mark time differently, such as in academic cycles or number of hours expected of them to complete an assignment, and they are unwilling to make long-term commitments beyond finishing school.

In short, the longer path to maturation of today's emerging adults is marked by more intensive social and personal experimentation, change and risk than previous generations, with an emphasis on short-term impact rather than long-term consequences.

WHERE IS HOME?

The most basic developmental task of emerging adulthood is the successful transition from home of origin to a self-authored home. For 80% of American Jews this begins with the journey out of home to university (Ukeles, Miller and Beck, 2006) and continues through the career- and relationship-defining time of the twenties. It likely involves multiple jobs, multiple romantic relationships, multiple places of living and stints back in higher education. Increasingly, particularly in today's economic climate, it may also involve a return to the emerging adult's home of origin. Emerging adulthood culminates in "settling down," a series of major commitments by which a new home is established: identification of and commitment to a career; commitment to another person through marriage; commitment to a place through purchase or long-term rental of a house or apartment; and ultimately commitment to children.

Before and after emerging adulthood, while home is a relatively stable concept, affiliation with Jewish institutions—camps, schools, synagogues and federations—is a strong possibility. Institutional life responds well to physical rootedness, and the years surrounding emerging adulthood tend to involve less uprooting than the multiple dorm rooms and apartments of the emerging adult years. To begin to understand how experiential education can inform our approach to emerging Jewish adults, we have to appreciate the basic embodied experience going on for them: This is a time of tremendous upheaval.

New York Times columnist David Brooks memorably referred to these years as "The Odyssey Years" in a 2007 column (Brooks, 2007). This is a useful term, because the physical odyssey of emerging adulthood is braided with a psychological odyssey as well. The question of "Where is home?" is not simply a physical question but a cognitive, emotional and spiritual question as well: Who will be in my home? Who will my partner be? What work will we do outside the home? What will be the values of our home? How do I understand my responsibility for those inside my home and family and those outside them? These are some of what Sharon Daloz Parks refers to as the big questions of emerging adulthood. Our understanding of experiential education for emerging adults must begin with them.

When approached with these questions in mind, the behavioral patterns of emerging adults suggest less that our institutional models are failing them than that we are expecting the wrong things. If the major issue on an emerging adult's mind is "Where is home?" then living in a house with a bunch of other Jews, trying out forms of Jewish living and experimenting with various visions of what home could look like—as a small but significant number of emerging adults have done through Moishe House, *AVODAH*, Israel experiences or less formally—starts to make a lot of sense. If this is a time of developing one's sense of spirituality and Jewish values, then an emerging Jewish adult may well prefer an independent *minyan*—a prayer community not affiliated with a synagogue or movement—populated by people in the same developmental boat, rather than going to a synagogue designed for people—both children and older adults—who are more rooted in a sense of home and intimate relationships, who are at a radically different place in their lives.

Successful organizational responses to Jewish emerging adulthood have realized that engaging emerging Jewish adults requires asking the right questions—the big questions that animate their lives. That is, they have used the assumptions and methodologies of experiential education.

EXPERIENTIAL EDUCATION EXPERIENCES IN EMERGING JEWISH ADULTHOOD

Formally speaking, we find quite a bit of experiential education for emerging Jewish adults. Between high school and college we have gap-year programs and yeshiva or seminary experiences in Israel. In 2008 one estimate put the number of American gap-year participants as high as six thousand (Soudry, 2008). When they arrive on campus many will be exposed to informal Jewish education through Hillel, Chabad or other campus organizations, either through traditional channels or through the increasingly sophisticated engagement strategies the organizations employ to reach unaffiliated Jewish students. Some will become active in Israel–related activities and young leadership programs through AIPAC or J-Street. Some will become involved in Challah for Hunger or other social justice work, including participating in an alternative break experience in the Third World or an area of need within the U.S., such as the ongoing efforts to rebuild New Orleans after Hurricane Katrina. Some may study, do service-learning or internship programs in Israel through MASA.[2] Below we will take up the case of the university in greater detail.

Particularly in the late teen and early twenties years, one of the most significant forms of experiential education is actually serving as an educator, as many emerging Jewish adults serve on summer camp staff and/or teach in supplementary school. As noted in one recent study, the effect of being a teacher, of taking responsibility for the education of others, has powerful effects in the development of an emerging adult's identity (Johnson, 2009). Through these experiences the emerging adult is ushered into one of the chief frames of adulthood, holding the educational future of younger people in his or her hands. To teach in these settings requires content mastery, which often leads to research and cognitive learning.

---

[2] It is estimated by MASA that as of 2008 two thousand American Jewish students a year study for a semester or longer at an Israeli university out of the estimated twenty thousand American Jewish students who study abroad each year. "Masa Fosters University Ties," Masa Israel Journey. Available at: http://www.masaisrael.org/Masa/English/News+and+Events/MASA+Fosters+Univ+Ties.htm, December 15 2011.

But beyond this a young adult serving as a camp counselor or Hebrew school teacher brings the same desire for authenticity and distaste for hypocrisy that informs the rest of his or her life to the teaching experience: The young person wants to be an authentic Jew in front of the younger charges. This leads to a significant affective dimension for emerging adults in the experience of serving as an informal educator, one that successful camp directors have known for decades: If you want summer camp to be successful, your focus should be not on the campers, but on the counselors.

After graduation we find yet more sites of experiential Jewish education for emerging adults: post-college programs in Israel, both for study and work; service-learning internship programs like AVODAH; formal and informal group living arrangements, as in Moishe House or the more widespread phenomenon of Jewish roommates living together and making Shabbat meals with one another. Emerging Jewish adults may join independent *minyanim* or attend retreats or events through young leadership programs. They may join a Jewish organization when they return to campus for graduate or professional school.

As serious dating and marriage become more pronounced features of their lives, emerging adults may find themselves engaging in formal study about Judaism with a non–Jewish boyfriend or girlfriend. As they prepare for family life they may have more substantive informal conversations with friends and romantic partners about Jewish values and their envisioned Jewish home life. And as they plan a wedding and make a home, they often engage Jewish life in a significant way.

And somewhere between eighteen and twenty-six, if they haven't already gone on an organized, peer-oriented trip, they may go to Israel for ten days courtesy of Taglit-Birthright Israel. They may extend their stay in Israel to study or travel some more around the country, and many returnees participate in the Birthright Israel Next programs in their communities as a means of transitioning into adult Jewish communal life.

The picture of experiential education for emerging Jewish adults is thus one of multiple, highly variegated opportunities. Indeed, of the items we've listed here, most are classically definable as experiential or informal experiences. They often involve travel. Some of them depend on group living arrangements. Some are focused on the educational experience of becoming a teacher, whether in camp or in school. Jewish education for emerging adults is overwhelmingly experiential education.[3]

In the remaining sections of this chapter we bring attention to two particular areas that, in our view, call for some particularly creative thinking in light of the phenomenon of emerging adulthood. They are the two most pervasive experiences for emerging Jewish adults, the things we can assume virtually all of them do: go to college and use the internet.

THE UNIVERSITY

We are now in the fifth generation of disproportionately high college attendance among American Jews. In 1968 Yitz Greenberg memorably quipped that the effect of the outsize representation of Jews on campus meant that "if college sneezes, the Jewish community catches pneumonia" (Greenberg, 1968). As we consider emerging Jewish adulthood, we need to pay attention to the university experience as an undergraduate, as a young alum and in the return to campus for graduate and professional education.

As institutional affiliation drops for emerging Jewish adults, the university becomes the dominant institutional force in their lives. For starters, this is a financial reality: Next to the purchase of a home, college is the single biggest personal investment most emerging adults will make, and it forms the biggest source of pre-mortgage debt they will incur. And it is a social reality: The social networks formed at college often prove formative for life in one's twenties, leading to professional and personal connections, roommates and friends in new cities, and access to alumni communities. While research needs to be done to confirm this speculation, we can reasonably conjecture that for most emerging Jewish adults, the largest Facebook network of which they are a part is their university network. So the university experience

---

[3] This also leaves aside the widespread availability of and participation in Jewish Studies courses on college campuses, which are more classically formal education.

needs to be taken into account when considering emerging Jewish adulthood. How does the university experience shape attitudes, values, dispositions and behaviors among emerging Jewish adults?

In the last two decades the Jewish community has witnessed a dramatic increased investment in Jewish life on campus through the co-curricular arms of Hillels, Chabad houses and other Orthodox outreach organizations; the curricular vehicle of Jewish studies programs; and most significantly, Taglit-Birthright Israel. Some of these developments reflect shifts toward best practices in experiential education. In place of formal classes (which many students can take for credit through Jewish Studies programs), immersion experiences, including Birthright and Alternative Student Breaks, and service-learning initiatives such as Challah for Hunger have become a centerpiece of the engagement strategies of both Hillel and Chabad. Hillel's Senior Jewish Educator initiative has piloted a new role for Jewish educators on campus, moving away from traditional rabbinic functions of supervising ritual observance and embracing an educational methodology built on peer-to-peer engagement and student-directed Jewish learning within a student's social network. And Hillel's Ask Big Questions initiative is creating frameworks for communal learning and reflection that are simultaneously rich in substance, highly accessible and learner-driven. All of these developments reflect a richer understanding of the contemporary landscape of emerging adulthood and best practices in experiential education.

Yet more can be done. Most of the Jewish campus institutions focus their energies on the traditional undergraduate experience. But one of the realities of emerging adulthood is that young adults are making major identity choices and life commitments at a later age. A key indicator of this is when people get married: Between 1950 and 2011 the median age of first marriage in the United States rose from 22.8 to 28.7 for men, and from 20.3 to 26.5 for women (Taylor et al., 2011). Likewise, college students do not graduate expecting to commit to a job or career, as evidenced by another statistic: According to the U.S. Bureau of Labor Statistics, between ages 18 and 42 the average late baby boomer held 10.8 jobs (Bureau of Labor Statistics, 2012).

This demographic backdrop has important implications for the communal conversation about emerging Jewish adulthood. If the undergraduate experience is no longer immediately followed by marriage and steady career, but rather by years of continued searching, probing and testing of identities and commitments, does the continued focus of traditional campus organizations on the undergraduate experience make sense? Are there other interventions that might be considered? For instance, could Hillel envision as a core part of its work facilitating continued Jewish experience for young alumni? As successful as AVODAH and Moishe House have been, they still reach only a fraction of the emerging adult Jewish population. Could the Jewish community think about ways in which the strongest institutional identity of emerging adulthood—the university identity—can be leveraged for greater Jewish engagement? We would argue that the advent of emerging adulthood as a real life stage for most Jews calls for a significant reassessment of the traditional model and creative reimagining of communal interventions.

TECHNOLOGY

A second significant area that demands our attention is the ways in which emerging adults interface with the world by means of technological devices. Mobile technology and the internet play a role in all life stages. While emerging adults may generally be thought of as particularly attuned to technological changes, the truth is that the fastest-growing demographic on Facebook is over age fifty-five, and children and adolescents are significantly shaped by their engagements with mobile and digital technologies. So as we consider how technology functions, or could function, in the experiential education of emerging Jewish adults, our focus is not on the false premise that "This generation is technologically savvy" (in any case, we're discussing the life stage of emerging adulthood, not the generation of Millennials that happens to currently occupy that life stage), but rather on understanding how technology functions in its life.

In doing so we are drawn back to some of the developmental observations we outlined earlier. Mobile and digital technology form an important component in the achievement of the developmental tasks of finding romantic relationships and life partners, maintaining peer networks and finding and doing meaningful work in the world. In ways we can intuit but still don't yet fully understand, the mediated experience is impacting the very idea of home, which is so central to the emerging adult years. What does it mean that I can carry my culture with me on a laptop or cell phone wherever I go? What does it mean that I can be connected with anyone, anywhere, whenever I travel? What does the cultural norm of photographing and video recording my experiences mean as I try to assemble a coherent sense of myself? What does the rise of social networking mean for dating and romantic relationships?

These questions are deeper than much of the communal discourse on technology and emerging Jewish adults today. If we are to take the lessons of experiential education seriously, we have to think not just about the effects of digital technology as pedagogy or technique, but also about the more significant ways in which these technologies are shaping the experiences of the learners themselves. The question can't simply be "How can we use digital media to engage the next generation?" We have to start where our students—emerging adults—are, and that demands that we ask "How do developments in technology change what it means to be an emerging adult?"

CONCLUSION

The current era of Jewish history is one of great social flux unlike any previous period in Jewish history; the phenomenon of emerging adulthood is central to understanding it. Jewish emerging adults are exploring and sampling Jewish adult life through experiential education venues. They are testing out living in Jewish homes, holding down Jewishly significant part-time jobs, experimenting with personally meaningful religious observances, sampling life and belief in Israel and probing both actual and virtual Jewish social networks. Jewish emerging adults are interacting with Jewish life and community not through the plethora of world events occurring around them and beyond their control, as their ancestors did, living as tolerated strangers in foreign lands, but by their own control in a country where they feel secure, integrated and at home.

Experiential education presents these emerging adult Jews with the means to develop their Jewish identities and commitments on their own terms and to deepen them when and where they find it meaningful to do so. Just as one life experience is not universally processed in the same way by everyone, so Jewish life experiences are not universally meaningful to every Jewish emerging adult. But data tells us that they can and will seek more experiences until they find ones that are significant to them, so long as they keep having quality Jewish experiences while they search.

The challenge for the Jewish community is thus to go deep in understanding the big questions of emerging adulthood: Who am I? Where do I come from? Where am I going? Who will be my partners? What will be my legacy? These questions are the ones that define this period. Engaging emerging adults is not simply a matter of making new programs or funding new initiatives to "draw them in." As Hillel has learned, and as the rest of the community is beginning to realize, success in engaging emerging adults requires understanding the big questions that animate their lives and creating accessible opportunities for them to explore those questions through the richness of Jewish tradition.

WORKS CITED

"Masa Fosters University Ties." *Masa Israel Journey*. December 15 2011. <http://www.masaisrael.org/Masa/English/News+and+Events/MASA+Fosters+Univ+Ties.htm>.

Arnett, J. J. "Emerging Adulthood: A Theory of Development from the Late Teens through the Twenties." *American Psychologist* 55.5 (2000): 469–80.

Brooks, D. "The Odyssey Years." *The New York Times,* October 9, 2007 2007.

Bureau of Labor Statistics, U.S. Department of Labor. "Youngest Boomers: 10.8 Jobs from Ages 18–42." *The Editor's Desk,* December 6 2012. <http://www.bls.gov/opub/ted/2008/jun/wk5/art01.htm>.

Erikson, E. *Childhood and Society.* New York: W.W. Norton & Co.,1993.

Fowler, J. W. *Stages of Faith: The Psychology of Human Development and the Quest for Meaning,* first ed. San Francisco: Harper & Row, 1981.

Glicksberg, C.I. "College Youth and the Future of Judaism." *Judaism* 4 (1955): 42.

Greenberg, I. "Jewish Survival and the College Campus." *Judaism* 17.3 (1968): 259–81.

Johnson, S. "Emerging Adults as Camp Counselors." *Fourth Conference on Emerging Adulthood.* Society for the Study of Emerging Adulthood, 2009.

Kohlberg, L. *Essays on Moral Development,* first ed. San Francisco: Harper & Row, 1981.

Parks, S. D. *Big Questions, Worthy Dreams: Mentoring Young Adults in Their Search for Meaning, Purpose and Faith.* San Francisco: Jossey-Bass, 2000.

Perry, W.G. *Forms of Intellectual and Ethical Development in the College Years: A Scheme.* New York: Holt, Rinehart and Winston, 1970.

Soudry, C. "'Gap Year' Entices Seniors to Live in Israel before College." *Los Angeles Jewish Journal,* February 29, 2008.

Taylor, P. et al. *New Marriages Down 5% from 2009 to 2010: Barely Half of U.S. Adults Are Married—a Record Low.* Washington: Pew Research Center, 2011.

Ukeles, J. B., R. Miller, and P. Beck. *Young Jewish Adults in the United States Today.* American Jewish Committee, 2006.

HEART, HEAD, HANDS:
LEARNING JEWISH SERVICE LEARNING FROM MOSES

Rabbi Brent Chaim Spodek

The Jewish tradition has inspired thousands of change agents, people who saw the world not as it was but as it could be and agitated to achieve that vision. From the prophet Amos calling for justice to roll like a mighty river straight through to Rabbi Abraham Joshua Heschel marching for civil rights in Selma, Jews have fostered hope for what the world could be and have worked to achieve that vision.

But there is no change agent in the Jewish tradition as powerful and effective as Moses. He was effective both in the Pharaoh's halls of power and in the streets where the Hebrew masses needed to be mobilized. He was revolutionary when circumstances warranted it, and he was a patient nation-builder when circumstances warranted it. He knew how to be a humble servant of the Holy One when circumstances warranted it and a confident teacher before his charges when circumstances warranted it.

Moses is the paradigmatic Jewish change agent. At a moment when interest in Jewish service-learning (JSL) is booming, when major funders and schools are talking about training change agents, it's worth examining the life of Moses to see what the old master might teach today's change agents.[1]

Moses' excellence as a leader was grounded in three traits that are essential for anyone hoping to effectively change the world. He was sensitive to the surrounding world, which is the work of the heart; he sought to comprehend the surrounding world, which is the work of the mind; and he worked to respond effectively to the surrounding world, which is the work of the hands. Moses needed each of these traits in order to liberate the Hebrews, and those developing JSL programs to train tomorrow's Jewish change agents should make sure that each of these aspects is developed. For each of these three traits we will look at its role in Moses' leadership, investigate what that trait might look like in the lives of JSL participants and discuss how program designers and educators might inculcate that trait.

The first and easiest trait for Jewish service-learning programs to inculcate is sensitivity. Before any leader can be effective, she must be sensitive to her surroundings, aware of things that are not immediately obvious. In the biblical tale Moses encountered God for the first time at a bush that burned but was not consumed.[2] In the minds of some, this was the sort of life-changing theophany that religious people pray for. However, the Ramban, one of the most important of the medieval Jewish mystics, suggests that the miracle was not that the bush was on fire but not consumed; the miracle was that Moses *noticed* that the bush was on fire yet was not consumed, for indeed, noticing can be miraculous. How closely must a person watch a bush on fire to realize that its branches are not consumed? Moses was a man exquisitely attuned to his surroundings.

Flaming bushes may be few and far between in our world, but there are many things that we see every day yet fail to notice because we don't look closely enough. By and large, those who grow our food, clean our

---

[1] For a sense of the growth of this field, see "Jewish Service Learning: What Is and What Could Be" (2008). *http://www.nathancummings.org/jewish/Jewish_Service_Learning.pdf* and Volunteering + Values: A REPAIR THE WORLD Report on Jewish Young Adults (2011). *http://werepair.org/cms/wp-content/uploads/2011/06/volunteering_+_values_full_report.pdf.*

[2] Exodus 3:1.

homes and care for our elderly are invisible. By and large, the world's 2.6 billion[3] chronically underfed people are invisible. Can we learn to look closely enough to see what is really happening in our world?

For those who hope to foster the next generation of change agents, service-learning programs can be an unparalleled way to sensitize students and to open their hearts. There are many of different ways that a JSL program can foster this sensitivity. For instance, every city in the world has a working class that tends to the needs of the moneyed class. While cities proudly present their Fifth Avenues and Rodeo Drives, the places where the serving class lives are often hidden from view. Most participants in Jewish service learning programs come from relatively privileged backgrounds and are likely not aware of backgrounds other than their own. They most likely enjoy the casual social privilege that comes with white skin, the unspoken assumption that they will finish high school and college, and they likely have no idea what life is like for people who work (or hope to work) in menial jobs, who cannot count on access to food, water or medicine or who endure oppression. JSL programs can find ways to appropriately and respectfully partner with local organizations that can bring participants to the parts of cities that are kept from view. Students whose eyes are sensitized by high-quality JSL programs will be able to come back to their regular surroundings and see things a little differently. For instance, students who live in apartment buildings, particularly in New York, might try to enter their own buildings through the service entrance and reflect on what their building shows to people who enter through the back door and people who enter through the front. Students might come to question why separate entrances need to be maintained at all. Effective JSL programs will be more concerned with inculcating in students the habit of questioning the world they inhabit than they will be with particular answers.

In the Ramban's telling of the tale, all those time that Moses walked past the bush before he finally noticed the Divine, he had no idea he was even missing a crucial piece of information. So, too, most participants in service-learning programs don't have any way of recognizing that they don't have any idea how the other half lives. Jewish service-learning programs can and should sensitize participants to the oppression and suffering that is hidden from them.

For Moses and for participants in service learning programs, comprehension follows sensitivity. Throughout the long haul of the exodus from Egypt Moses enjoyed unparalleled sensitivity to the Divine. Nevertheless, the relationship between Moses and God was always one of a student with a teacher. At the very beginning of their relationship Moses hid his face from God, and some commentators understand that to be because a student should not look brazenly into the face of his teacher.[4] Late in the game, after the splitting of the Sea of Reeds, after the building of the Tabernacle, after even the giving of the commandments, Moses intuited that what he had seen and experienced was but a small part of a larger whole. "Teach me Your ways,"[5] Moses said to God. He didn't need more miracles; he needed more *comprehension*.

Just as Moses needed to understand how the world worked in order to act in it, participants in JSL programs need to understand that the suffering they see is always part of a larger whole. Moses didn't change the world by simply working to alleviate the suffering of a few Israelites; he worked to change the system that oppressed them. It can be very difficult for service-learning participants to understand the invisible forces that shape the world around them. The Cold War policies that shaped Latin America seem like ancient history, and urban planning and economic policy can be fantastically dull. However, it is essential that JSL programs foster understanding of the systems they hope to change. The Rambam teaches that the root of human evil is lack of knowledge.[6] We simply cannot do good in the world if we don't understand how it works.

---

[3] 2.6 billion people worldwide live on less than two dollars a day. See World Bank Press Release, "New Data Show 1.4 Billion Live on Less than US$1.25 A Day, But Progress Against Poverty Remains Strong." September 16, 2008. *http://www.worldbank.org/en/news/2008/09/16/new-data-show-14-billion-live-less-us125-day-progress-against-poverty-remains-strong*

[4] *Bechor Shor* to Exodus 3:6.

[5] Exodus 33:13.

[6] *Guide to the Perplexed*, Chapter III:11.

Theorists of justice education refer to a "critical consciousness" in which participants can see that injustice on a large scale is never simply an accident but invariably the result of particular policies promoted or opposed by people with power.[7] Even on a rudimentary level, participants can be shown that the people in the country or town to which they are traveling don't just happen to be poor; there is something that led to their impoverishment. Perhaps a factory closed, or perhaps a road was routed in a way that was disadvantageous for some people. Perhaps zoning, tax or other policies shaped the environment in ways that are not immediately obvious. Before a JSL program, students can research the place that they are going to, even if it is their own town. Where does money in the town come from? What is the income distribution? How many people from different racial backgrounds are in the town? Beyond student research, any local college, whether in America or overseas, is likely to have someone in the economics, political science or sociology department who can explain some of the forces at play in a community. Good JSL programs will seek out these teachers or, if appropriate, empower students to invite them to come and speak.

The willingness to teach these difficult topics is part of what separates quality Jewish service-learning from ritual theater in which the "natives" play the victims and the Jewish participants play the heroes. Jewish American college students may be mediocre bricklayers and peanut-butter-sandwich makers, but if we teach them how, they can be excellent informed citizens who hold governments and corporations accountable for the effects they have on people.

Of course, comprehension is only as good as what you do with it. The best Jewish service learning programs develop hearts and minds and also help participants meaningfully respond to what they encounter. Again we turn to Moses, who did not free the Israelites until he acquired that skill. Before God charged him with leading the Israelites to freedom, Moses jumped in three times to save the powerless suffering at the hands of the mighty. When Moses first left Pharaoh's house he saw an Egyptian beating a Hebrew worker and killed the aggressor. The very next day he rescued one Hebrew from another who was preparing to assault him, and in a third instinctive act of justice Moses rescued shepherd girls who had been chased away from a well.[8] For a God who demands that the wretched and the needy be saved from the hand of the wicked, Moses looked like a promising ally. But while Moses had an instinct for justice, he didn't have a method. His behavior, while powerful and inspiring, was also impulsive, violent and ultimately inadequate. There was a whole Egyptian system that allowed the innocent to be beaten, but Moses didn't see or understand that—he saved individuals, not a people, by simply acting on rash impulse. Moses was a momentary hero, so fixated on the injustice in front of him that he could not see deeper into what caused and sustained injustice. But while Moses could only see the wrongs immediately in front of him, the Omniscient One could see deeper and taught Moses to understand the structures that caused this suffering. God took Moses, this young man of sentiment, and enrolled him in a brutal course in politics, economics and power with Pharaoh as his unwitting teaching assistant. Moses made a name for himself with his sentimental outbursts of passion, but he didn't make a difference until he had a teacher and a plan for affecting the power structures. Moses began his career as an unskilled volunteer, full of instinct and sentiment. At first he wasn't terribly effective, but as he learned to use his heart, his head and his hands, he ultimately changed the world.

JSL programs often seem to be built with the assumption that the work that the participants do in the field—making sandwiches, building latrines, clearing fields—will repair the world. But unskilled volunteers, no matter how well meaning, rarely solve difficult problems. Participants feel great when they grab shovels and pickaxes and pose for Facebook pictures, but real change is rarely photogenic. Real change takes not only sensitivity and comprehension but fortitude and skill. We know this well from other realms of life. If you're having heart palpitations, you don't want to hear that the fourth graders, motivated by *tikkun olam,* are coming to "make a difference." And if you are trying to improve your life in Guatemala, New Orleans' Lower Ninth Ward or Newburgh, NY, you take no solace from knowing that

---

[7] Cipolle, S.B. (2010). *Service Learning and Social Justice: Engaging Students in Social Change,* Chapter 4. New York, NY: Rowman & Littlefield Publishers, Inc.
[8] These three stories appear one after the other in Exodus 2:10–17.

well-intentioned volunteers who "want to make a difference" are coming; you need help from someone who knows what s/he is doing.

JSL programs can be more powerful if they build mechanisms for effective action into programs from the beginning. For most participants in JSL programs effective action will take the form of philanthropy and advocacy, both of which are easily incorporated into program design. For instance, participants in any JSL program could be required to know the name and phone number of their U.S. Representative and what committees he or she serves on. As part of the preparation for a JSL experience, participants could contact the Representative's office and set up a meeting to discuss what they have learned in the field and to ask what the Representative is doing on these issues. Similarly, participants could commit in the field to fundraising for a partner organization and begin thinking together about what information they would need in order to honestly represent the organization to their friends and families. These components need to be thought of in advance and built into the fabric of the program from orientation; otherwise, when participants return from the "high" of the experience to everyday life, these "supplemental" activities will be lost in the shuffle. However, it is precisely with these supplemental activities that participants can make the greatest difference. A JSL program that does not take the challenge of building effective advocacy or fundraising into their program runs the risk of becoming another empty Jewish ritual, heavy on stagecraft but drained of meaning. Service programs that do not make a material difference in the lives of the people they hope to serve are not service programs; they are photo ops designed to meet the narrative and photographic needs of American Jews.

At all three levels—sensitivity, comprehension and response—Moses came to see beyond his own need to play the hero and turned outward to meet the needs of others. In so doing he truly did change the word. JSL can and should be the place where Jews learn to be faithful inheritors of the mature Moses, people who live lives oriented to the needs of other humans.

Over the course of his life Moses grew in his sensitivity, his comprehension and his efficacy. He was and is the paradigm for what it means to be an effective agent for changing the world. Jewish service learning programs *can* make a difference in the lives of participants and the lives of people they aspire to serve. These programs can help students to develop hearts that are more sensitive to the needs of others, heads that understand the systems that lead to suffering and hands that are engaged in effective work.

IMAGINATION AND IMMERSION: JEWISH IDENTITY AND EXPERIENTIAL JEWISH EDUCATION IN VIRTUAL WORLDS

Deborah Price Nagler

Virtual worlds offer exceptional opportunities to spur imagination and cultivate immersion in the pages of Jewish history, custom and thought. This chapter will discuss the nature and function of virtual learning environments as well as their potential contribution to Jewish experiential education.

Imagine: It is hot. You are hungry and thirsty. You are walking in a wilderness, rocky and barren. The only sound is the shuffling of feet on loose gravel and the moaning of the masses around you as you walk toward the unknown. Only a miracle can save you…

IN THOSE DAYS AT THIS TIME

In every generation, according to Talmud *Pesaḥim* 116b, a person must see himself as participating in the Exodus from Egypt. We are to imagine that we were there. On Passover we engage the sense of taste to relive the bitterness of slavery and the poor taste of bread prepared in the haste of departure. On Sukkot we inhabit temporary dwellings in order to immerse ourselves in the history of wandering and appreciate the consequence of shelter. Taste and imagine. Sit here and imagine. To retell the story we must recreate elements of the experience. To accomplish this we employ imagination and immersion.

Imagination and immersion, two basic elements of experiential education, are among the most ancient tools for connecting Judaism's newest generation with its oldest in the continuing story of the Jewish people. John Dewey described the functions of imagination and immersion in *Experience and Education* (1937). Chazan (2003) summarized his theory as understanding people as "active centers of impulse… (who) learn best when they are actively rather than passively engaged in experiencing an idea or an event. Such experiencing is rooted in the interaction of the idea or event with the person's life and with a continuum of ideas that enables the experience to contribute to ongoing personal growth." Thus the essence of imagination and immersion in Jewish experiential education is to create meaning through a first-person connection with our national narrative and to develop the sense of "being there" rather than just learning about.

THE MEANING OF EXPERIENCE IN A VIRTUAL WORLD

One of the greatest educational opportunities of the digital era is the virtual world or Virtual Learning Environment (VLE). The VLE can be best described as a 3-D, online, immersive simulation that can be used to recreate physical settings in either a realistic or a stylized manner. The VLE is a three-dimensional canvas with limitless possibilities. Rather than simply observing a picture, the learner enters the picture, interacts with it and communicates with the other learners who are simultaneously experiencing the virtual surroundings.

The VLE has an outstanding capacity for the engagement of visual, auditory and kinesthetic modalities as well as a strong social component. In addition to moving and static, 3-D images, voice communication and musical soundtrack are easily incorporated into the simulation. The participant can move through the simulation in a variety of ways, manipulate the surroundings and acquire objects for immediate or later use. These qualities make it a natural venue for experiential education.

Each learner has an individual VLE presence in the form of an avatar. The avatar is a graphic depiction or facsimile representing the computer user. The appearance of the avatar can be customized in accordance with the desires of the user and/or in alignment with the features of the environment. For example, a VLE that teaches about Rashi and Jewish life in the middle ages might provide avatars and costumes in keeping with that time period.

AVATAR EXAMPLE TAKEN FROM HIDDEN CITIES KRAKOW 2011 ©SIMNIK.COM

The role of the avatar, however, is much more than window dressing. Combined with the communication tools of the VLE, the avatar is the key to social connection in this environment. As described by Damer, avatars "represent the real time embodiment of people in cyberspace and the fundamental avenue to meaningful community and a sense of place and memory" (Mason, 2011). This idea closely echoes Chazan's (2003) assertions that social interaction and dialogue are essential components of informal/experiential education. The "dynamic interactive process between student and educator, student and student, student and text, and student and tradition" as described by Chazan finds an amenable setting in the VLE.

The VLE can simultaneously accommodate any number of users and their avatars. For this reason it is also known as a Multi-user Virtual Environment or MUVE (Kapp and O'Driscoll, 2010). In the MUVE the learners, through their avatars, can do more than just connect and communicate; they also create and collaborate. Individuals or groups may "build" or create objects within a VLE. For example, parallel to Passover preparation in the "real world," learners might be asked to enter a room and select appropriate objects to set the table for a seder. The avatars can then be seated around the table to discuss their choices, the order of the seder, relevant texts (these can be shared on virtual screens) and so forth.

VIRTUAL SEDER TABLE CREATED BY ARIELLA DAVID IN THE SL JEWISH NEIGHBORHOOD

VIRTUAL WORLDS VERSUS VIDEO GAMES

For those as yet unfamiliar with the VLE or MUVE, this may appear to be similar to the description of a video game. It is true that the MUVE shares some of the characteristics of massively multiplayer video games (MMORPG). Both employ avatars, offer real-time communication, engage the participant in an interactive platform and provide for continuity of the environment and its digital assets. However, what differentiates the MUVE from a video game is the fact that the MUVE is a plastic environment—a digital canvas or stage that supports building and creation as well as social interaction. Activity in a virtual world is most often open-ended. The MMORPG has a specific narrative, defined avatar characterizations, rules and achievement levels. The MUVE can be used as a framework for games, role-play and simulation, but these are only a few of its possible applications.

A number of other terms have been used to describe various forms of virtual worlds, including metaverse, cyber or synthetic worlds and virtual immersive environments. This proliferation of names is likely a product of the infancy of the medium and the ongoing discovery of new uses for it. The terms VLE and MUVE will be used in this chapter, as both connote the essential communication and collaboration functions that are relevant for experiential education.

The best news for those interested in the MUVE is that development costs are minimal in comparison to video games. While the average cost of video game development may range from $18–28 million (Crosley, 2010), a MUVE pilot project can be constructed for under $25,000 (Kapp and Driscoll, p. 258). In fact, the biggest budgetary considerations in using an MUVE for experiential education are the costs of the computer hardware, internet service, server costs (Second Life, for example, charges a leasing fee) and occasional debugging by an IT expert. This field continues to change and develop such that potential users may anticipate the availability of more OpenSource options and even tablet access in the foreseeable future (Wagner, January 2010).

VIRTUAL WORLD PLATFORMS

Second Life, ActiveWorlds, Open Sim, Protoshere, OLIVE and Unity are among the many online platforms used to host and create MUVE. With more than 750,000 residents, Second Life, developed by Linden Labs, is the best-known and most popular virtual world. Second Life has a virtual economy that is backed by real currency; offers users the ability to lease and build on virtual land; and has an extensive marketplace for a wide variety of user-crafted virtual artifacts or, Prims, including clothing, furniture, buildings and landscaping. These pre-designed Prims make the task of designing an environment very accessible for the novice builder.

Over seven hundred educational programs have found a home in Second Life (SecondLife.com) to date. It is a dynamic distance-learning platform with multiple options for sharing and collaboration. Among the learning activities that Second Life offers are building, presentations and discussions; historical recreations; simulations and role-playing; multimedia and games design; and language learning practice (Linden Labs, 2011).

One reason that Second Life is an effective tool for experiential Jewish education is that learners cannot take a passive role. In a Second Life session consistent, active participation is maintained, because "if you walk away from your computer, or discontinue using your keyboard or mouse for a few minutes, your avatar slumps forward—asleep—and everyone else in the virtual space can visibly see that you're not paying attention" (Linden Lab, 2011). Particularly where team play is required, students tend to encourage one another and insist on attention to the task at hand.

One example of use of Second Life as a venue for experiential learning can be found on the website of the United States Holocaust Memorial Museum. In 2008 the Museum, in collaboration with Global Kids, created a Second Life simulation entitled "Witnessing History: *Kristallnacht*—the November 1938 Pogroms." Upon entering this simulation the participant assumes the role of an investigative journalist. The entry point is a 1930s pressroom with pictures, notes and eyewitness accounts covering its walls. The "journalist" is then whisked back into history to visit a German street where burning synagogues, anti-Semitic graffiti and breaking windows recreate the events of *Kristallnacht*. Moving through the simulation, the participant hears an audio narration that includes recordings of eyewitness accounts of *Kristallnacht*. The success of this MUVE can be gauged in the feedback from hundreds of participants who report that they found it to be an "emotional experience," "moving," "powerful" and "memorable" (Kapp and O'Driscoll 2010, p. 150).

A SCENE FROM THE U.S. HOLOCAUST MEMORIAL MUSEUM'S "WITNESSING HISTORY: KRISTALLNACHT"

VIRTUAL WORLD DESIGN AND EXPERIENTIAL LEARNING

Learning is not automatic in a MUVE. An educational experience in a MUVE, like any educational endeavor in the "real world," must be carefully planned and constructed in order to deliver the best results. The best results are achieved when design principles like those of Kapp and O'Driscoll (2010),are observed.

Recommended guidelines for planning Jewish experiential education in an MUVE setting:

- MUVE-based programs should be instructionally grounded, flowing from learning objectives. Do not use the technology for the sake of technology. Make sure that you know what you want to achieve.

- The needs and capacity of learners should be at the center of the plan. Do not underestimate the need to teach participants how to use this medium. Allow time for a learning curve and offer orientation activities that ease the learners into active participation.

- Context is key in using a virtual world. "Make it creative, memorable and meaningful" (p.199). The greatest asset of this environment is its immersive quality. Therefore, carefully consider the objects and scenery you wish to include so as not to overwhelm or confuse the learners. Over time the learners may be inspired to enhance the setting with their own creations.

- Learning in an MUVE should be discovery-driven. "MUVEs can provide students with authentic, situated learning experiences characteristic of ... inquiry-based instruction" (Clarke-Midura and Dede, 2010, p. 318).

- Learning in an MUVE should be activity-oriented. While it is possible to recreate a frontal classroom experience in a virtual world, this is not experiential education any more than it would be in a face-to-face classroom. Challenging the learner to move, explore, build and interact with the environment generates more value and engagement.

- The presence of multiple learners in the environment should be purposeful. Learning tasks in a MUVE should be designed with collaboration in mind.

- Students should be provided with opportunities to show the consequences of learning by way of demonstrating skills and acquired knowledge.

- During and after the MUVE-based program there should be opportunities for reflective synthesis of individual experiences and the program as a whole.

- Most important, the educator has a pivotal role in the implementation of successful programs in a MUVE. Guide, coach, observer, role model and referee are just a few of the potential roles of the group leader or teacher.

Here, too, program design, as part of the ADDIE Model for Instructional Design, is an iterative process. It should be tested and tweaked numerous times before final implementation.

Keep in mind that it takes a village to create an experiential education project in a virtual world. Kapp and O'Driscoll suggest that the design team include an instructional designer/curriculum developer, subject matter specialist, designer/builder, scripter/programmer, IT specialist representing the school or institution and a representative of the participating population (p. 210). In truth, any worthwhile program, whether in real or virtual space, requires thoughtful design and collaborative implementation. Programs in a MUVE are only bit more complicated because they necessitate the building of a "virtual set" before the program can begin.

As a final note about the overall design of a MUVE, the issue of student security must be addressed. In this, as with other online tools where there is social interaction, there is the potential for abuse. It is prudent to take a number of precautions. First, the MUVE can be set up as a closed environment accepting registered participants only. In this way the unwanted or unexpected appearance of strangers is avoided. (Currently there are about one million users registered for Second Life.) Second, all participants should be required to read and sign a code of conduct. Group leaders should monitor participation in the MUVE, including the use of the chat box. Violations must be addressed appropriately, in the name of both creating a positive learning community and fostering digital citizenship.

LEARNING ACTIVITIES IN VIRTUAL WORLDS

The MUVE provides four key areas of learner activity that can be used in experiential education programs: agency, exploration, connectedness and experience (Kapp and O'Driscoll, 2010). The following section will define these activities and provide examples of their application in Jewish experiential education.

Agency is the empowerment of the learner through the creation of a persona in the form of an avatar. The form and dress of the avatar can be customized in a way that reflects the personality of the learner and the context of learning. The learner animates the avatar, moves it through the virtual world and determines its interaction with the world and other avatars.

Avatar customization can be part of the learning event. Period clothing can be used as a discussion trigger in a historical simulation or role-play game. Students can research and build a character profile, then act out scenarios within the context of the MUVE. In Hidden Cities: Krakow, an MUVE developed by the Center for Educational Technology in Israel and Simnik.com, the avatars are designed to represent different segments of the Jewish population in pre–WWII Poland. Differing political and religious affiliations are reflected in the clothing, hats, hairstyles and accessories of the characters.

In the Krakow simulation, which is now being piloted in a number of Israeli schools, the avatars also have pre-assigned gathering points. For example, the Revisionists meet at well-worn tables in a café on the Nowy Square, while the _Hareidim_ gather in a book-lined _Beit Midrash_ near the Remuh synagogue. These environments are designed to create a backdrop for character development. Participants are either directed to interact based on detailed program notes or given brief instructions and then left to their own imaginations.

Machinima is video that has been filmed in a virtual world. This is another tool that can be used for creative and inexpensive learning activities. Through their avatars the students are actors on the stage set of whatever VLE they are using or have created. Once filmed and edited, scenes from role-play, simulations or scripted interaction can be replayed as trigger films or discussion material or simply posted as a video record of accomplishment.

Exploration describes the activities that require interaction with the virtual environment. A few examples of exploration are guided tours, conceptual orienteering and scavenger hunts.

In the guided tour the learner follows a prescribed path through a landscape. For example, students might be taken on a guided tour of a simulated _mikveh_. They can take a "dip" in the _mikveh_ by clicking on a button, peek behind the walls at the water collection system and have a "virtual conversation" with the _mikveh_ attendant.

Conceptual orienteering is an approach in which ideas are shown as concrete and explorable objects and spaces. For example, in a conceptual VLE built to teach about _Minha_, the afternoon prayer service, the learner might begin in an area composed of artistic representations of the Shema. He/she would progress through rooms or spaces reflecting the content of the _Amidah_, and the journey would end with the _Alenu_. Along the way the learner would engage with the environment by using animation triggers to simulate the "choreography" of prayer, examining pictures and artifacts that represent the content of prayers, listening to examples of prayer melodies and solving puzzles that reinforce prayer vocabulary. Such an experience is not meant to replace participation in a prayer service. Rather it offers a creative alternative to more traditional classroom instruction.

The scavenger hunt is another opportunity for exploration. Here the learner is tasked with finding locations and artifacts within the VLE. Explanatory note cards can be attached to 3-D artifacts. These artifacts can be collected by the learner and placed in an inventory file where they can be used for other learning activities. As an example, a VLE might be created to represent Israel. A number of historical personalities have been placed in various locations in the VLE. As the students navigate through the VLE they interact with these non-player characters and receive clues that will lead them to various collectable 3-D objects. This kind of program can simultaneously teach geography, history, culture and more.

Connectedness is at the heart of the MUVE. It is essentially a social environment. Embedded within the MUVE are social networking tools for voice and text chat, messaging and creating a social network of "friends". These communication tools make the MUVE an excellent environment for distance learning and collaboration.

In Hidden Cities: Krakow, for example, interactive posters positioned around the simulation are actually micro-blogs that offer students the opportunity to voice their opinions and react to the ideas of other students.

Virtual worlds can be used to educate and engage groups of any size, from two to two thousand. Spaces can be designed for small work groups to meet and work collaboratively. Stadium-style seating and larger arenas can be used for many different kinds of concerts, shows and presentations.

Timeless Jerusalem, a program developed by Timeless Cities, Inc., is an example of a MUVE that was used to bring together teens from the United States and Israel to discuss issues related to Jewish people-hood. In a MUVE modeled to look like Jerusalem in the time of the Second Temple the students debated, conversed and even celebrated *Yom ha-Atzmaut* with a virtual dance party. The American participants reported feeling "connected with Israelis and Israel as a whole as well as with the other student in the class" (BJE-NY/SAJE, 12/2009, par. 2).

Experience that is immersive and interactive is a valuable feature of the MUVE. The VLE can be used to create a learning path to a skill by demonstrating procedures. For example, animations and illustrations can demonstrate the proper way to light candles on Hanukkah, how to build a sukkah, how to hang a mezuzah and so forth.

In this creative environment 3-D artifacts can be rendered in any size desired. Students might climb inside and explore a giant shofar or fly high above a model of the Old City of Jerusalem to observe other landmarks in relation to the *Kotel*. They might scale a virtual Masada or float in the Dead Sea. These kinds of immersive experiences are not meant to replace the real thing; rather they are intended to stimulate interest and further exploration on the part of the student.

SLOODLE, the Simulation Linked Object Oriented Learning Environment, is an open-source product that creates a bridge between work in Second Life and Moodle (a free web application used to produce modular internet-based courses). A number of "game show"-type tools have been created for use in Second Life. "Jeopardy" and other types of quiz shows offer another kind of experience that can be incorporated into a VLE.

ASSESSMENT OF JEWISH EXPERIENTIAL EDUCATION IN VIRTUAL WORLDS

In large measure, assessment of learning in an MUVE is not unlike its counterpart in face-to-face experiential education. Program evaluations may target any or all of the following goals:
- Provide information about the effectiveness of the program
- Identify weaknesses and propose improvements
- Inform decision-making
- Assist in the clarification of options for future action (Rosov and Isaacs 2008)

The types of data collected in an MUVE program might include:
- Attitudinal changes
- Behavioral changes
- Measurable increase in skill or knowledge

- Desirability of the activity and degree to which participation influences other choices for the student

USABILITY OF THE MUVE

Because the MUVE is a platform of action, it lends itself to observation. Teachers or group leaders can easily see who is involved and what form that involvement takes. Student contributions by way of character research for role-play, student-built artifacts and performance-based accomplishments are easily observable and even recorded. In addition, the chat box and inventory provide a record of student interactions and artifact acquisition. Finally, as suggested above, reflective synthesis should be ongoing throughout the program. This kind of reflection is also important as a feature of the "exit ramp"—a summative session where students are brought together to analyze the experience and share their feelings and observations.

However, as Smith (2006) points out, there are a number of problems in trying to measure impact and drawing larger conclusions from experiential education program evaluations. Among these are the possibilities that there are multiple influences on behavior, that there might be an unmeasurable ripple effect from a particular serendipitous interpersonal interaction, that it is not always possible to gather accurate evidence to show the trajectory of behavioral change and that the problem of longitudinal measurement makes it impossible to know in advance exactly how long it might take for change to manifest and exactly what form that change might take.

With this caveat it is still important to gather data, particularly in the infancy of this educational medium, in order to prove and improve its use.

THE CASE FOR JEWISH EXPERIENTIAL EDUCATION IN VIRTUAL WORLDS

Virtual worlds cannot replace face-to-face, real-life experience. However, there are a number of compelling reasons and circumstances that appear to support the use of MUVE in Jewish experiential education.

The first reason is the wow factor. Students perceive learning in an MUVE as fun. It is estimated that 97% of teens play video games (Lenhart, September 2008). These students feel at home in an avatar-mediated environment and are attracted by work in a digital environment. Another explanation is that "Fun is the act of mastering a problem mentally" (Kostner 2005). Virtual learning environments are replete with opportunities to explore and solve problems that engage the learner. Students engaged in a MUVE tend to display higher levels of motivation and interest. Should we care that our students are having fun while learning? Absolutely! Brain research has shown that positive emotion engages multiple areas of the brain and results in greater retention of information (Jensen 2008).

In addition, the MUVE is an excellent vehicle for developing twenty-first-century skills. Collaboration, problem solving and digital literacy are just a few of the skills that can be cultivated in a VLE context. Transformational play is another of offerings of this medium. In transformational play the player becomes "a protagonist who uses the knowledge, skills and concepts embedded in curricular content to make sense of a fictional situation and make choices that transform that situation" (Barab, Gresalfi and Arici 2009). In this way students can learn how to analyze and address "real world" problems in a fictional and virtual setting. This approach is particularly well suited for values-based learning, as exemplified in the MUVE-based Quest Atlantis program.

There are also several practical reasons for employing a MUVE. In programs serving participants in multiple locations, the MUVE has a great cost advantage over face-to-face meetings. Similarly, if groups in different time zones wish to participate in asynchronous activities, all of the students will have the opportunity to participate in the same learning activities. The MUVE can mimic "real world" experience without the cost and offer the learners opportunities to do things that they might not do in real life.

The MUVE is an exciting new frontier for Jewish experiential education, but as with any digital tool, it is important to know what you want to achieve. Technology should not be used for the sake of using technology, but in furtherance of specific goals. All stakeholders—decision makers, educators and students—should understand why this is the application of choice.

THE CHALLENGES OF THE PRESENT

Virtual worlds in Jewish education are a work in progress. A few were developed and subsequently abandoned. A few new ones are now under construction and still need to prove themselves. Because this medium is in its infancy, beta testing and a certain amount of trial and error are to be expected.

For schools or institutions interested in developing a MUVE, capacity is an important consideration. The availability of appropriate computer hardware, a high-speed internet connection and institutional firewalls are all considerations. Technical glitches can and do happen. Access to technical support is a must.

Building a MUVE is more complicated than might be expected. More than likely MUVE development will require an outside vendor. In any case, the environment will need to be tested and retested prior to use to make sure that there are no unexpected bugs.

Finally, in preparing a MUVE it is important to know your audience. Not every teen is technology savvy nor every adult a technology novice. Allow time for an orientation and for the participants to learn how to navigate and use the medium.

Millions of dollars have been invested in the development of platforms like Second Life, but they are not without their weaknesses. While it is hoped that someday these applications will be the equal of Facebook or YouTube, until then the best counsel is patience.

VIRTUAL WORLDS AND THE FUTURE OF EXPERIENTIAL JEWISH EDUCATION

When does Jewish history will become our story? When the learner can enter the pages of the text and see the world as a participant. When the imagination is engaged and the learner fully immersed in meaningful activity and problem solving. No digital medium has greater potential for bringing history alive than the virtual world. We can recreate pivotal moments in history and invite our students to step into the action. We can walk through in a virtual desert to better appreciate the journey of our ancestors. We can see and imagine. Sit and imagine. First person is a powerful perspective.

What better way to engage the emotions and intellect of twenty-first-century Jewish learners than to translate Jewish history, content and practice into a visually exciting, interactive and socially stimulating digital experience? Growing pains notwithstanding, virtual world platforms continue to develop and improve. In the not-too-distant future Jewish experiential education will find VLE a welcome and accessible partner.

REFERENCES

Aldrich, C. (2009). *The Complete Guide to Simulations and Serious Games: How the Most Valuable Content Will Be Created in the Age beyond Gutenberg to Google*. San Francisco, CA: Pfeiffer.

Aldrich, C. (2010). *Learning Online with Games, Simulation, and Virtual Worlds*. San Francisco: Jossey-Bass.

BJE-NY/SAJES. (12/2009). *Timeless Jerusalem Mini-pilot Report* [Report].

Barab, S.A., M. Gresalfi, M. and A. Arici (September 2009). "Why Educators Should Care about Games. *Educational Leadership* 67(1), 76–80. *Educational Leadership*. Alexandria, VA: ASCD.

Chazan, B. (2003), "The Philosophy of Informal Jewish Education" in *The Encyclopedia of Informal Education*. Retrieved from *www.infed.org/informaleducation/informal_jewish_education.htm*.

Clark-Midura, J. and Dede, C. (2010). "Assessment, technology and change." *ISTE Journal of Research in Technology Education* 42, 3, pp. 309–328.

Crossley, R. (January 11, 2010). "Study: Average Dev Costs as High as $28M." *Develop*, Intent Media. Retrieved from *http://www.develop-online.net/news/33625/Study-Average-dev-cost-as-high-as-28m*.

Dewey, J. (1938). *Experience and Education: The Kappa Delta Pi Lecture Series*. New York: Simon & Schuster, Inc.

Jensen, E. (2008). *Brain-based Learning: The New Paradigm of Teaching*. Thousand Oaks, CA: Corwin Press.

Kapp, K. and T. O'Driscoll (2010). *Learning in 3D*. San Francisco, CA: Pfeiffer.

Koster, R. (2005). *A Theory of Fun Game Design*. Scottsdale, AZ: Paraglyph Press.

Lenhart, A. (September 16, 2008). "New Pew Internet/MacArthur Report on Teens, Video Games and Civics." Pew Internet & American Life Project. Retrieved from *http://www.pewinternet.org/Commentary/2008/September/New-Pew-InternetMacArthur-Report-on-Teens-Video-Games-and-Civics.aspx*.

Linden Lab (2010). "Second Life Education: The Virtual Learning Advantage." Retrieved from *http://lecs-static-secondlife-com.s3.amazonaws.com/work/SL-Edu-Brochure-010411.pdf*.

Rosov, W.J. and L.W. Isaacs (2008). "Program Evaluation in Jewish Education." In. R.L. Goodman, P.A. Flexner and L.D. Bloomberg (eds.), *What We Now Know About Jewish Education: Perspectives on Research for Practice*. Los Angeles, CA: Torah Aura Productions.

M.K. Smith (2001, 2006). "Evaluation, Theory and Practice." Infed. Retrieved from *http://www.infed.org/biblio/b-eval.htm*.

United States Holocaust Memorial Museum (2008). "Witnessing History: *Kristallnacht*—The November 1938 Pogroms [simulation]. Retrieved from *http://www.ushmm.org/museum/exhibit/focus/kristallnacht/*.

Wagner, M. (January 29, 2010). "Apple iPad: Will It Run Second Life?" Message posted to Computerworld Blog. [Weblog]: *http://blogs.computerworld.com/15496/ipad second_life*.

NURTURING PLAY-MAKERS & ACTIVE INVESTIGATIVE AGENTS: SCHWARTZ TAG, GOOD VIDEO GAMES AND FUTURES OF JEWISH LEARNING

Rabbi Owen Gottlieb

MAY THE SCHWARTZ BE WITH YOU

I am a Reform rabbi who was never a camper at Jewish camp, yet many Jews attended my camp in northern New Jersey. I can't imagine camping anywhere other than Summer Super Stars; my years there were formative. It was a haven for children who loved learning and creativity. It stoked the fire of our curiosity and set us free to create, explore and learn with great teachers and counselors and build deep friendships. I often refer to it, with great affection, as "geek camp"—a gifted-and-talented day camp with college-level courses (project-based, with no homework) in the morning and afternoons of sports, computer programming and pool time. While in the 1980s this kind of experience for children was rare, the internet and digital media have opened up opportunities for similar exploration to all children with a net connection and some guidance from teachers who care. In the twenty-first century learning is increasingly a culture of designers and "makers" (see *http://makerfaire.com/*). Some of the educational gifts originating in gifted and talented programs have become available to anyone with a YouTube account, a Google group and the desire to share media with friends (or make friends by sharing media).

One particular experience during my time at Summer Super Stars—the creation of a game—shows the link between gifted education and learning in the digital age and demonstrates how we Jewish educators can best leverage the offerings of the digital age and the medium of the video game. The game was called Schwartz Tag. As in "The Schwartz," the stand-in for "The Force" in Mel Brooks' now-classic *Star Wars* parody, *Spaceballs*. My buddy Walter and I created a pool-based game using a waterlogged Nerf ball. Schwartz Tag incorporated the various rules of the pool at camp (no running on the deck, always be ready for a buddy check) and well as our desire for a friendly, compassionate, challenging, fun and funny game. No "pegging"—you had to touch the player with the ball still in your hand (though you could hide it or fake it with a teammate/partner). You had to say "Schwartz" upon the tag, or it didn't count. Within a week the entire camp was playing the game, and the pool became the home of constant tourneys of Schwartz Tag. We had a hit on our hands.

There was one morning class that just wasn't up to Summer Super Stars standards. Though we had courses in archeology, rocketry, botany, Renaissance art, creative problem solving and songwriting, somehow Walter and I had found ourselves stuck in "Computer Applications," using word processors and other programs. Unfortunately, this wasn't the afternoon computer lab where we created our own homemade programs in BASIC. This was "how to use software". Zzzzzzz. Without a creative outlet we would act out in class, joke around and get yelled at by the teacher until we could move on to the next class. One morning we were summoned to the office of the principal—the man no camper ever wanted to let down. Ken Bratspies was our hero. He ran the place we all loved. Walter and I were upset; we had pushed our class disruption too far. As we sat in Bratspies' office he said, "So I hear what the two of you have been up to." Oh, boy. Then he opened up his desk drawer. What was coming next? He revealed two blue ribbons. "These are Game Creation awards—everybody is playing Schwartz Tag. Good work!"

What role should Jewish educators take in the age of the mobile device and the ubiquitous digital game? What does the modern digital game mean for engagement of learners, and how might we and the learners we work with reflect on the experience of living Jewishly with digital media?

PLAY VS. DESIGN

At the outset it is important to distinguish the process of game *design,* and learning through design, from the process of game *play* and learning through play. From a player perspective we can learn about optimal educational practice from the best video games. Market forces and talented creators have come together over the last thirty or so years to create highly advanced environments for learning—domain-specific learning. For example, great video games demand hard work, have scaffolding to support the learning and optimize engagement. James Gee's work[1] stresses this aspect of games. Game *design* as a tool for learning is a mode that can allow for collaborative, situationally specific problem-solving projects involving critical thinking. Such projects can lead to high engagement. Once designers are in the process of design, their internal motivation to achieve their design goals can lead them to deepened curiosity and information seeking, such as research. Designers and project builders can follow their curiosity and creative drive with a teacher as guide. Design processes also lead to "artifact" production by learners. The term "artifact" refers to any product of a design process, be it a paper prototype, audio file, model or story. Seymour Papert's constructionism[2] is an example of learning theory that emphasizes learning through design and artifact creation.

GAMES AND EDUCATION: UP WHERE WE BELONG

How can an experiential approach to education, in combination with a games-based orientation, help us reach often-elusive educational goals? In many ways the study of games and game design bring us back to tenets of education that we have long known, including the benefits of self-directed learning and project-based work. The heightened levels of engagement and engrossment in digital games and the growing popularity of the digital game are leading us to look at the ways in which games (both digital and analog) could potentially bring us closer to our long-standing educational goals. Brigid Barron and her colleagues (1998) pointed out the benefits and challenges associated with implementing project-based learning (one of the key areas of experiential learning). Project-based learning requires changes in curriculum, instruction and assessment, and such change is no small feat.[3] What are some aspects of games, be it in play or in design, that connect to what we know about learning? And how might the zeitgeist of youth culture and gaming make it not only possible to implement change through an emphasis in experiential education, but an imperative to remain relevant in the lives of young Jewish learners? Can the ubiquity of games as the ascendant cultural medium give us the political and institutional will to make change?

Researchers who study games and simulations for learning often turn to Mihaly Csikszentmihalyi's theory of "flow"[4] when addressing issues of engagement. Roughly, flow is a state of high-focused engagement that can be generated in situations with high feedback, a sweet spot between bored and overly challenged. Examples include moments in sports that some describe as "in the zone." Another kind of zone, Vygotsky's Zone of Proximal Development,[5] is helpful when thinking about how a good game system models a good learning environment. The Zone of Proximal Development has to do with how a learner can manage problem solving with or without assistance or guidance. Good games keep learners at the outer edge of their competency and provide scaffolding (as-needed, just-in-time support) to reach the

[1] See for example Gee, J. P. (2007). *What Video Games Have to Teach Us About Learning and Literacy. Second Edition: Revised and Updated Edition.* Palgrave Macmillan.
[2] See for example Papert, S. A. (1993). *Mindstorms: Children, Computers, and Powerful Ideas* (2nd ed.). Basic Books. Harel, I. and S. Papert, (1991). *Constructionism.* Ablex Publishing. Out of print. The first chapter is available at http://www.papert.org/articles/SituatingConstructionism.html
[3] Barron, B. J. S., D.L. Schwartz, N.J. Vye, A. Moore, A. Petrosino, L. Zech, L.and J.D. Bransford (1998). "Doing with Understanding: Lessons from Research on Problem- and Project-Based Learning." *Journal of the Learning Sciences* 7(3), 271–311.
[4] Csikszentmihalyi, M. (1991). *Flow: The Psychology of Optimal Experience* (first ed.). New York: HarperPerennial.
[5] Vygotsky, L. S. (1978). *Mind in Society: The Development of Higher Psychological Processes* (14th ed.). Harvard University Press.

next level. Video games also have robust communities of practice,[6] usually online, in which players trade tricks, tips and experiences. They share a lexicon, compete, collaborate, mentor one another and learn more and more advanced approaches to the game together. They create fan videos, stories and fan fiction, meet at live events and organize charities, essentially creating their own "participatory" culture around the game.[7]

Back in 1998, just a few years prior to James Gee's work that helped set in motion the contemporary Games for Learning movement, Brigid Barron and her colleagues provided four principles of design for project-based learning These principles can lead to "doing with understanding" rather than "doing for the sake of doing." The principles are (page 273):

1. Learning-appropriate goals

2. Scaffolds that support both student and teacher learning

3. Frequent opportunities for formative assessment and revision

4. Social organizations that promote participation and result in a sense of agency.

It happens that these are principles found in good games. Good video games match the core mechanics (the specific actions a player performs repeatedly in a game to achieve results) to the overall learning goals of the game. For example, in Minecraft a player performs the key mechanics of breaking down objects into component parts and builds objects out of the component parts, teaching "mining" and "crafting." The mechanics embody the learning and are precisely appropriate. As mentioned above, good games scaffold learning and have robust communities of players sharing in participation and agency; for some, the scaffolding *is* the community. I learned the basics of Minecraft by watching a child-produced video demo on YouTube. Today, at venues like The Games for Change Festival, James Gee points out that games have embedded assessment (leveling up in a game). An additional parallel between games and Barron and colleagues' principles is that game companies and software companies iterate (frequently revise) their software. In fact, the essential process of game design is the "playtest," which is an iterative design and inquiry process of test, play; test, play.

GOOD GAMES AND RABBINIC LITERATURE

Note that I use the notion of the "good" game, which Gee uses in his germinal work on Games for Learning, *What Good Games Have to Teach Us about Learning and Literacy.*[8] Games are often found in Jewish formal and informal education. Many of these games (the best-known in Hebrew supplementary school is perhaps "Jewpardy") center around trivia or memorization. The kinds of games that Gee discusses are ethically complex video games, often with in-depth role-play and the ability to grow a character's skill and experience over time. How often do supplementary schools use role-play and collaborative team play in complex ethical cases? Where can we push the boundaries of game play in Jewish education to the level of complexity that youth already experience in their digital games and strategy board and card games, like Settlers of Catan and 7 Wonders? How can we relate lessons of Jewish texts to collaborative team play? Games are the ascendant medium of entertainment (the *New York Times* even features game reviews; it will not be long before they have their own section, as film does today).[9] Although perhaps not all Jewish educators have easy access to digital teaching tools yet, they do have access to settings that are ripe for game-based interactions. These interactions can be designed at locales ranging from supplementary school classrooms to camps. One genre of game interactions that Jewish educators have easy access to is "backyard" games like tag or the New Games of the 1970s (see the *New Games Book* and *More New Games*)[10]. The next step is to move these kinds of games into *good* games for Jewish learning. Luckily, rabbinic literature falls into the categories from which game systems draw their central elements. *Halakhic* (Jewish law) systems are rule-based systems, and games are built through rule-based systems. *Aggadah* (story) is our narrative tradition, and games often interweave narrative. So the sources for the games we play and use in Jewish education—and those we

[6] Regarding communities of practice, see Lave, J. and E. Wenger (1991). *Situated Learning: Legitimate Peripheral Participation* (first ed.). Cambridge University Press.

[7] See Jenkins, H. (2008). *Convergence Culture: Where Old and New Media Collide* (Revised.). NYU Press. (This is the book from which my organization ConverJent.org takes its name.)

[8] Gee, J. P. (2007). *What Video Games Have to Teach Us about Learning and Literacy. Second Edition: Revised and Updated Edition.* Palgrave Macmillan.

[9] See, for example, Schiesel, S. (2011, December 29). "Video Games Worth Waiting for in 2012." *The New York Times.* Retrieved from *http://www.nytimes.com/2011/12/30/arts/video-games/video-games-worth-waiting-for-in-2012.html.*

[10] Foundation, N. G. (1976). *New Games Book.* Main Street Books. Foundation, N. G. (1981). *More New Games.* Main Street Books.

encourage learners to design—should stand on a foundation of Jewish learning and Torah values. The translation of Jewish learning to games, which is challenging, is in many ways more natural than, say, translating that learning to literature or film. This is so because the plethora of rabbinic rule-based systems for ethics and conduct are ripe for game play and design. And so we have an opportunity to open up the world of Jewish interaction from ethics, laws and stories to the ways in which people relate to media today—through play and design. This requires Jewish educators to take the art, craft and skills of game design seriously, and that means developing literacy in games and game design.

ACTIVE INVESTIGATIVE AGENTS: RAISING THE BAR WITH ARGS, EPISTEMIC GAMES AND MORE

The Covenant Foundation has recently sponsored a digital mobile history game that is being designed at ConverJent, an organization that I founded. The foundation has also sponsored an upcoming early childhood Hebrew language game by Not-A-Box. I believe that the larger Jewish philanthropic community should and will eventually turn toward game-based learning. In the near future we can turn to the *analog* game for critical lessons. Jewish groups today can leverage live in-person play and game design for learning. The Jewish camp and classroom can use game environments to inject a level of depth or "thickness" of learning in Jewish subjects, paired with the increased levels of engagement that good design courses and good games bring forth.

In order to do this we will have to raise the standards of content knowledge while adopting a new philosophic stance in Jewish education. We can train our learners to become what I call "Active Investigative Agents" or AIAs. AIA's have a curiosity, interest and drive to uncover an answer, and they have a knowledge of and facility with tool sets that they will need to find answers. "AIA" can describe players in learning games such as those created by Sasha Barab,[11] David Shafer,[12] Jim Mathews and Kurt Squire[13] and their colleagues. Mathews and Squire refer to students becoming "active agents."[14] In these learning games players emulate practitioners of professional investigative disciplines, such as journalists, architects or scientific researchers. For Shaffer, players in his teams' games are playing toward becoming "professional." But the meaning of "professional" here is not "with a specific job" but rather as a personal who can extemporaneously solve problems in a discipline, someone who displays what Donald Schön refers to as "reflection in action."[15] Shaffer's "Epistemic Games" use practical-based games and simulations to train learners in discipline-based problem solving. In doing so they have found that they can train learners in the skills, knowledge, values, identity and epistemology of each discipline. I treat this topic and its implications for Jewish education at length elsewhere.[16] The term AIA can also describe an aspect of those learners who are involved in participatory culture—creating videos, blogs and zines based on their own interests. The additional stress on "investigation" both highlights the disciplinary focus of this learning approach and shifts the focus to the interest of the students. If we think about nurturing Jewish AIAs, we may be able to turn our thinking from the desire to impart knowledge, heritage and identity toward a desire to nurture intrinsic curiosity and interest in Jewish topics.

In order to explain and explore the two needs—depth of content and the nurturing of AIAs—let us consider for a moment the World of Warcraft wiki, which Jane McGonigal[17] often cites—the second largest wiki after Wikipedia (at current count 92,342 pages). The level of data available to and known by youth and adults playing World of Warcraft is staggering. The wiki is a community-generated compendium through which players share and develop skills in play of the online MMORPG—massively multiplayer online role-playing game. The youth playing games do so with extreme sophistication, and the depth of content knowledge amassed to develop expertise is vast. If youth today become experts in complex gaming system

[11] Barab, S. (2009). "Conceptual Play Spaces." *Handbook of Research on Effective Electronic Gaming in Education* (Vols. I–III, Vol. III, pp. 989–1009). Hershey, PA: IGI Global.

[12] Shaffer, D. W. (2006). *How Computer Games Help Children Learn* (first ed.). Palgrave Macmillan.

[13] Mathews, J. M. and K.D. Squire (2010). "Augmented Reality Gaming and Game Design as a New Literacy Practice." In K. Tyner (ed.), *Media Literacy: New Agendas in Communication* (pp. 209–232). University of Texas at Austin: Routledge.

[14] Ibid,, 220.

[15] See Schon, D. A. (1984). *The Reflective Practitioner: How Professionals Think in Action* (first ed.). Basic Books.Schon, D. A. (1990). *Educating the Reflective Practitioner: Toward a New Design for Teaching and Learning in the Professions* (first ed.). Jossey-Bass.

[16] For an in-depth discussion of this topic, see my forthcoming paper on Epistemic Games and Jewish Learning (to be presented at the Network for Research in Jewish Education, 2012).

[17] McGonigal, J. (2011). *Reality Is Broken: Why Games Make Us Better and How They Can Change the World.* Penguin Press HC.

environments, and the norm in play is to have ever-developing levels of expertise, then Jewish learning likewise must be both engaging and challenging—but it also must deliver the potential for *levels of expertise,* the means to achieve that expertise and, at the very core, an inherent impetus to develop said expertise.

FICTIVE ENVIRONMENTS AND MOBILIZING JEWISH WISDOM

First I will address this core impetus, motivational and engagement question, and then I will turn to the need to develop the identity and role of an AIA. With regard to motivation and engagement, I am not suggesting a digital badge system, popular in the current push to "gamify" education. But at some point learning must be applicable. What is the real-world application of deep Jewish knowledge? And how does it tie to the interest of a learner? The fast answer would be that perhaps Judaism is the answer to "how to live one's life"; and yet in the marketplace of many compelling ways to live one's life, for someone who has not grown up in an environment steeped in Judaism, what does this really mean? I would argue that wisdom is practical knowledge and that Judaism is a wisdom tradition. Games allow for expertise in-game, but an area in which games are often lacking is developing expertise outside the game world. In her work, Jane McGonigal[18] seeks to bridge the gap by having participants play games out in the real world and encouraging action in the real world using fictive narrative. Players in World Without Oil, one of many examples, simulated an oil crisis online and then carried that narrative into conservation action in the real world. These ARGs, or Alternate Reality Games, are a means by which the Jewish world could operationalize Jewish wisdom. By constructing a fictive environment with real-world tasks shared by players, learners could build expertise in simulations and then put Jewish values into action. First they would experiment and model Jewish wisdom-ways in the fictive malleable environment, then carry them into action in the "real world."

OPERATIONALIZING JEWISH WISDOM THROUGH GAME SYSTEMS

One area to which teaching Torah through game design is, in my opinion, particularly well suited is the transmitting of wisdom tradition. I have come to believe this through my teaching of Torah through Game Design at a Reform synagogue in Manhattan. Wisdom is often recognized when it is situationally applicable. A list of wisdom teachings can easily become meaningless, decontextualized and even hypocritical (as in Shakespeare's famous parody of wisdom in the devious Polonius' speech to his son Laertes in *Hamlet:* "Neither a borrower nor a lender be….To thine own self be true"). But games and game designers can generate flexible models of situational behavior. The standard role-playing game (the genre of Dungeons and Dragons) is an excellent example. A character is confronted by a situation must react, and depending on the reaction, the game can shift. So what if our learners design their own Torah games? Learners must learn Torah to design the game; designing the situations in which the various laws could apply, they become the teachers. The players must then apply various wisdom positions and ethical dilemmas that force a player to call upon wisdom. The uncertainty necessary in game play could be leveraged. Sometimes wisdom would not work, but over time it would show itself to be a valuable strategic move. Here is an example from Proverbs: "Do not withhold good from one who deserves it when you have the power to do it [for him]. Do not say to your fellow, 'Come back again; I'll give it to you tomorrow,' when you have it with you" *Prov. 3:27–28* (NJPS translation). Resource management is important in many games. Just as in life, we must use our resources wisely, whether they are money, time, food or accessing and calling upon our social networks. So what if a player had to manage his or her resources in order to level up (advance to the next stage of a game)? What would the consequences be if the player withheld "good"? What if that player's resources were running low and the person might get knocked out of the game? They would have to judge, as we do in life, when they have the power to share good with others and when they have to concentrate on self-care. Here is an example of how a game designer must weigh out and determine the logic underlying the game's system of consequences. Through this process

---

[18]In addition to McGonigal's *Reality is Broken* (2011), cited in previous note, see her TED talk: http://www.ted.com/talks/jane_mcgonigal_gaming_can_make_a_better_world.html.

a designer has to wrestle with and internalize the real-world application of wisdom, then teach it through the game to others. The process of designing a system, testing it, playing it and sharing it with others puts learners into a unique and potentially intense situational application of Jewish teaching.

THE ROLE OF THE EDUCATOR AND GAME LITERACY

As mentioned earlier, teaching using games requires a certain level of game literacy and game design literacy. Understanding the ways in which games are played and constructed (through elements such as "resources," described above) is a prerequisite for teaching with games. Jewish educators using games should have a familiarity with multiple genres, game mechanics and play styles. The first place for them to start is by playing a variety of good digital and analog games—prize-winning games, popular games—and to familiarize themselves with a number of platforms. Games alone are not an answer, but teachers who understand game systems may very well be a new answer for Jewish education. To be clear, in case that talk of video games raises the notion of technology over educator, educators are critical. For example, in the case of simulations David Shaffer writes: "Wandering around in a computer-rich environment without guidance is a bad way to learn. Learners are novices, and letting them work in a simulation without support leads to the very real human tendency to look for patterns and to develop creative but spurious generalizations."[19] Jewish digital games, now in their embryonic stages, may someday provide excellent scaffolding, allowing a player-learner to pursue and continue learning on his or her own; however, teachers will remain critical to the process of igniting interest in subject matter and in initiating the use of games to spark learning that can then reach beyond the classroom. Game literacy for teachers goes beyond learning design skills and genres. It also requires at least a rudimentary sense of the research trends in Games for Learning. One such trend involves role-play and discipline-relevant practices.[20] What happens when a player takes on a role or roles in a game? How might this affect the learner's identity or change the learner's perspective, values and skills?

A THOUGHT EXPERIMENT: BENEATH THE CITY OF DAVID

Imagine Jewish learners enter a game in which their role is that of a team of futuristic archaeologists with a variety of roles and skills that they can build over time. I'll call it Beneath the City of David.[21] There is a philologist decoding languages, a cranky senior archaeologist, the young graduate student and the technical genius using the latest sonar and carbon-dating equipment. They are presented with a dig site, maps and clues from known history, based on a real dig in Israel. Using software we can simulate the site and artifacts. Or we can build it with paper and papier-mâché. You choose. The fiction layer on top of the game involves a ticking clock. The team must solve and locate a number of complex archeological puzzles and piece history back together while remaining ethically true to their character (perhaps some characters are more scrupulous than others, and ethical choices must be played out). If the team can solve the puzzles in time and fit the pieces of a broken amulet back together in time, they will unlock the next level, increase their skills and move on to more complex problems. If they can't, as a team, complete the puzzles in time, the site will become unstable, and they will have to leave and try again. Along the way they uncover ancient teachings from Jewish wisdom texts with Torah-based clues to game play. They can share data over the web with other teams simultaneously working on the problem. They can post to a wiki and generate pages on the puzzles. The puzzles then reveal applications of Jewish wisdom teachings to the journey of the players. Part of the journey is training them to use simulated or actual tools used by Jewish archaeologists, historians, philologists and modelers. By the end of the process, not only have they learned the content of the puzzles and built bonds with their players, but they also know how to use new tools and technology, some of which are those used by professionals who investigate the questions of the Jewish past and present. They've even watched a video of an archaeologist in Jerusalem helping

---

[19] Shaffer, D.W. (2006). *How Computer Games Help Children Learn* (first edition.). Palgrave Macmillan, p. 68.

[20] See previous references to Barab, Gee and Shafer.

[21] Mathews and Squire (2010) briefly hypothesize about an archaeology game similar to one David Levy taught at Summer Super Stars in the early 1980s: "For example, instead of simply taking a tour of an archaeological site, students might investigate the site as a team of archaeologists who have been hired to research the site and produce a museum exhibit about the people who once lived there," p. 212.

differentiate game play and the story of the game from the actual daily tasks of a working archaeologist. Through such a game and simulations they become AIAs in Jewish Studies discipline-related practices.[22] They become more literate Jews, having faced puzzles simulating the work of Jewish researchers, and their play choices are informed by Jewish wisdom and ethical dilemmas. Those AIAs re-enter the "real world" as empowered, curious Jewish learners with twenty-first-century skills. The game has helped teach them how to think critically, work collaboratively access and use data to solve problems. This can translate to learning beyond the confines of the classroom, born out of a curiosity nurtured in play.

MEANING, RELEVANCE AND CURIOSITY

Jewish learning must have a meaning and relevance for learners. Games can create their own internal relevance, such as "solve the puzzle" or "compete," but games can also create dramatic simulations of events and issues already relevant to learners. These dramatic situations include wrestling with ethical dilemmas, deciding whether to stand up for what is right and feeling compelled to organize in one's community. Consider that a raiding party in World of Warcraft is a highly organized collaborative team with specialized skills, sharing a goal.

Games and game design can draw out or incite the personal taste of learners helping to determine on what path a Jewish AIA will travel. And given the intersecting nature of Jewish learning, those paths are connectable. Searching for an answer to a question on the origins of a classic midrash—from *Bereshit Rabbah* for example—can lead through Jewish history, Greek philosophy, questions of language and culture and cultural context. It can lead forward in time through the Talmud into re-interpretation. It can lead into the modern era, when modern midrash asks questions relevant to today's context by drawing on wisdom gathered over centuries past. Jewish civilization, like a time machine and refracting glass, can be approached from many angles—but all angles have investigation and curiosity in common. We as a people have struggled and wrestled with ideas, always asking deeper questions. While some of our communities still eschew questions of history and historicity, all Jewish communities can use games as models for, say, a mishnaic passage and its ethical implications.

Games are not *the only* solution. But they are *a kind* of potential solution to some of the key questions we face today in Jewish education. This is because at the core of a Jewish education for the century to come are questions of relevance, curiosity, passion and compassion. Jewish learning must help us find applications of the wisdom that has been handed down to us—help us live our lives better in ever more complex problem-solving situations, be they managing family concerns during a deepening economic downturn or facing the dilemmas in America brought about by inequality in health care. We need Jewish wisdom now more than ever, and we need to understand it in flexible, role-play–based environments. As our curiosity turns to everywhere but our Jewish heritage, we need to re-light the flame of curiosity into our past and the lessons accrued over thousands of years. We need to stoke our curiosity, because it is at the core of our passion for the joy of learning—a passion that has sustained us, along with our faith, through the darkest of times. And how can we continue to train in compassion? Only through practice and teamwork—and collaborative games and simulations are the perfect medium through which to rehearse working together. When we play games together we build strengthened social bonds between us. Jane McGonigal reminds us that we like people better after playing games with them, even after we lose to them, because play involves *trust*.[23]

At the heart of thinking about Jewish learning in the next decades is an "i" word. The "i" word we need to consider is "imagination"—how will we help fire up the imagination of Jewish learners? Games come from and help us practice our imagination, our "what if" mind. They help us envision other ways of being who we are deep down inside. Play archaeologist for a day. Or researcher. Or team leader. Perhaps a wizened elder. Can you imagine yourself there? Can you help learners imagine themselves there? And if you

---

[22]In my forthcoming paper on epistemic games (NRJE Conference, 2012) I discuss the gaming role of the Jewish "professional" as a learner who uses what Lee Shulman calls "signature pedagogies," such as the *d'var Torah* form, to solve game problems.
[23]See her TED talk: http://www.youtube.com/watch?v=dE1DuBesGYM.

were to imagine yourself in one of those roles, what would you do, where would you go, what questions would you ask? What games would you play? What game would you design? Let's invite one another to design the games of our Jewish future. What might Jewish Active Investigative Agents who grow up in the twenty-teens and twenties be curious about, be knowledgeable about in 2032 or 2046?

GAMES FOR TASTE DEVELOPMENT

What if there was a way of learning Jewishly like Summer Super Stars? I don't necessarily mean the camp environment. We have wonderful Jewish camps. What I'm referring to is a way of learning in which the young learner's creativity could be nurtured and channeled, where investigation of subjects and ideas was encouraged and supported in team- and artifact-generated projects—projects in which deep content knowledge was expected, but it was gained through inquiry-based learning.

Games-based design and learning may provide a way to shift the discussion from "What should an educated Jew know?" to "How does a learner develop a taste for Jewish learning and living?" What trips the curiosity switches that lead to passion for a subject and the seeking out of community? Great games most certainly do this in their own domains with *contextually meaningful problem solving* in *communities of practice* that naturally build around good games. In today's environment of participatory and game culture, perhaps now more than ever, it is our responsibility to channel our learners' creative energy in finding the fascinating questions, places and ideas in Jewish culture—and then guiding those learners in designing, playing, exploring and experiencing them.

REFERENCES

Barab, S. (2009). "Conceptual Play Spaces." *Handbook of Research on Effective Electronic Gaming in Education* (Vols. 1-III, Vol. III, pp. 989–1009). Hershey, PA: IGI Global.

Barron, B. J. S., D.L. Schwartz, N.J. Vye, A. Moore, A. Petrosino, L. Zech, J.D. Bransford, et al. (1998). "Doing with Understanding: Lessons from Research on Problem- and Project-Based Learning." *The Journal of the Learning Sciences*, 7(3/4), 271–311.

Csikszentmihalyi, M. (1990). *Flow: The Psychology of Optimal Experience* (1st ed.). New York: Harper & Row.

Foundation, N. G. (1976). *New Games Book*. New York: Main Street Books.

Foundation, N. G. (1981). *More New Games*. New York: Main Street Books.

Gee, J. P. (2007). *What Video Games Have to Teach Us About Learning and Literacy. Second Edition: Revised and Updated Edition* (2nd ed.). Hampshire, UK: Palgrave Macmillan.

Gottlieb, O. (2012). "Making Jewish Meaning in the Digital Age: The Promise of Computer Supported Epistemic Games." Conference Presentation. Network for Research in Jewish Education, June 10, 2012. Hebrew College, Newton Centre, MA.

Harel, I., and S. Papert (1991). *Constructionism*. New York: Ablex Publishing.

Jenkins, H. (2008). *Convergence Culture: Where Old and New Media Collide* (Revised). New York: NYU Press.

Lave, J., and E. Wenger (1991). *Situated Learning: Legitimate Peripheral Participation* (first ed.). Cambridge, UK: Cambridge University Press.

Mathews, J. M., and K.D. Squire (2010). "Augmented Reality Gaming and Game Design as a New Literacy Practice." *Media Literacy: New Agendas in Communication* (pp. 209–232). University of Texas at Austin: Routledge.

McGonigal, J. (2011). *Reality Is Broken: Why Games Make Us Better and How They Can Change the World*. New York: Penguin Press HC.

Papert, S. A. (1993). *Mindstorms: Children, Computers and Powerful Ideas* (second ed.). New York: Basic Books.

Schiesel, S. (2011, December 29). "Video Games Worth Waiting for in 2012." *The New York Times*. Retrieved from http://www.nytimes.com/2011/12/30/arts/video-games/video-games-worth-waiting-for-in-2012.html.

Schon, D. A. (1984). *The Reflective Practitioner: How Professionals Think in Action* (first ed.). New York: Basic Books.

Shaffer, D. W. (2006). *How Computer Games Help Children Learn* (first ed.). Hamshire, UK: Palgrave Macmillan.

Vygotsky, L. S. (1978). *Mind in Society: The Development of Higher Psychological Processes* (14th ed.). Cambridge, MA: Harvard University Press.

Jane McGonigal's TED talk reference in this chapter can be found at http://www.youtube.com/watch?v=dE1DuBesGYM

BEYOND MAGIC AND PROPHECY: THE NEXT DECADE FOR EXPERIENTIAL JEWISH EDUCATION

Dr. David Bryfman

Only once in my life was I ever a magician. I was a teenager asked to perform some magic at my cousin's birthday party. In the pre-internet era that it was, I raced to the local library and borrowed a book that would teach me all of the tricks that I needed in order to entertain a bunch of screaming kids for a couple of hours.

Clearly magic is far more than the few magic tricks that I was barely able to perform. Historically magic has been associated with the spiritual or the supernatural. Through a variety of techniques, including ceremonies, incantations and casting of spells, magicians professed to be able to come into contact with the supernatural or exert influence on the forces of nature. Although met with skepticism by many, magic is a long-held tradition in many cultures.

Today the term "magic" primarily conjures up images of incredible performances designed to captivate audiences. Most of us associate magic with the *oohs* and *ahs* of watching a rabbit being pulled out of a hat or a woman being sawed in half. Often inherent in these experiences is a certain inexplicability and an aura of mystique. In popular parlance we also hear people describing fantastic events as being "magical," such as "Disneyland was magic" or "that sporting act was sheer magic."

It has also become commonplace to hear participants describing the "magic of summer camp" or the "magical experience of Birthright Israel." And it is in this context that I have a bit of discomfort with the term "magic". Observers have at times utilized the term "magic" or similar labels to describe successful experiential Jewish education, because identifying its core characteristics has been frustrating to identify, too difficult to decipher or challenging to measure. Sometimes naysayers have used magic as a pejorative, juxtaposing it with a formal education that is seemingly more understandable and quantifiable and therefore taken more seriously. For many years it led to even respected researchers applying to experiential Jewish education the oft ill-used adage of "You'll know it when you see it," because describing the magic in a more sophisticated way seemed impossible.

And while I have no reason to doubt the inspiring and powerful qualities of these experiences, I do reject the concepts of illusion and mystery that are associated with the field.

What this book has uncovered is that experiential Jewish education may be considered magical, but only if that definition encompasses a deeper understanding of everything that goes into creating a truly magical experience. Real magic involves a deep-rooted ritualism, symbolism and language. Essentially there is nothing random or designed without intentionality in a magical performance. A good magician gives the impression that everything is easy, but in reality years of learning and practice have led to the creation of the performance. While there is always room for improvisation and spontaneity, these moments allowing for individual exhilaration are carefully timed and built into the overall experience.

And so it is in good experiential Jewish education. As in a good magic show, there is very little left to chance. Years of training and prior experience may give the impression that the experiential Jewish educator is able to facilitate with ease. Settings are designed to provide all-encompassing experiences that allow learners to enter states of "flow." And while outcomes are defined, in good experiential Jewish education there is also room to allow for the spontaneous to occur, but this is built on a presupposition that unanticipated outcomes are welcomed and even encouraged.

The term "magic" may be useful inasmuch as it describes a powerful reaction, but it should never be invoked to diminish the preparation needed to achieve these peak experiences. Having a more detailed theory and a more comprehensive language for experiential Jewish education, such as the one articulated throughout this book, helps us to better understand the field as more than just a "magical experience."

BEYOND THE MAGIC

As we move forward to further our understanding of experiential Jewish education we must also be thoughtful about what we have yet to fully comprehend. This book is a major step forward in compiling our current knowledge base for this nascent field, but what is yet to be uncovered?

Putting magic aside and stepping into the even more precarious world of prophecy, allow me to conclude with five predictions for the future of experiential Jewish education and a single hope to carry us forward.

RESEARCH

As Socrates understood, "The more I learn, the more I learn how little I know." Such is the case in this field, and if the current interest in experiential Jewish education is any indication, the next decade will bring with it even more research and literature. With new academic programs, more graduate students, more family foundations and more evaluators engaging in this domain of Jewish life, we can only expect to increasingly know more about this field. If pressed to consider what research is most necessary for the field to reach the next level of significance in the Jewish world, I would suggest two necessary areas—both of which, not surprisingly, had chapters devoted to them in this book.

- Developing an understanding of the metrics necessary to measure the outcomes of experiential Jewish education. This would naturally lead to the development of measurement instruments that could be applied across settings and offer a better understanding of the impact of experiential Jewish education.
- Developing the core characteristics of an experiential Jewish educator. At the very least, research to better understand the personnel in this field would greatly enhance the recruitment, retention and professional learning of experiential Jewish educators.

INVESTMENT

Increased interest and understanding will necessitate further investment and expansion of the field of experiential Jewish education. In the last decade Jewish federations, foundations and philanthropists have invested heavily in Israel travel (primarily through Birthright Israel), Jewish service-learning and Jewish summer camping. What will be the next settings of experiential Jewish education to receive major funding? As age cohorts that are known to influence long-term identity development, adolescents, young adults and young families will, I predict, continue to be beneficiaries of more resources. A bit of a bolder suggestion is that adults, and increasingly older adults and the aged, will also become more favored by funders in the coming years. Although not dealt with in this book, it is not a huge leap to see how the principles of experiential Jewish education could be applied effectively with an older population.

In terms of settings, based on current trends, allow me to suggest that funding will be allocated toward experiential Jewish education taking place outside of conventional Jewish institutions. We are currently seeing this transpire in investment in organizations like Moishe Houses and Jewish Student Connection; but I predict that investment will increasingly be made in ways of engaging people who do not have to become members or affiliate in conventional ways—for example, museums, the digital world and other public spaces.

INTEGRATION

In any given year a Jewish communal professional could attend any number of educational conferences. In 2011 a fairly strange thing happened. I and a few of my colleagues kept on running into each other at these conferences—for summer camps, congregational schools, day schools, Jewish Community Centers, at convenings by central agencies of educators and working with individuals synagogues and schools—presenting basically the same conceptual material regardless of the specific venue. It didn't matter so much if anyone had put the label of formal or informal on these settings, or that there were both novices and experienced educators in the room. What mattered was that the common philosophies, values and pedagogies were permeating the settings and that people were willing to learn from people outside their traditional domain. I predict that in the next decade—perhaps as a result of economic rationalization, but more importantly as a realization that the Jewish world will be better off if we combine our intellectual resources—we will see more cross-setting gatherings and conferences, a greater exchange of thinking between individuals involved in these settings and greater incentives to break down these silos and encourage collaborations across the community. This will lead to a spreading of experiential Jewish education, philosophically and pedagogically, across almost all aspects of Jewish communal life.

TECHNOLOGY

Sometimes in education the introduction of technology literally makes a world of difference; at other times it changes very little except the illusion of doing something different because it is new. Larry Cuban suggests that over time the introduction of information technologies such as televisions, video recorders and even computers has done little to increase academic achievement in classrooms.[1] But my prediction is not just that we will invest in more educational technology (which we will), but that this latest and next round of investment will reflect and enhance a new way of learning, much of which is compatible with core principles of experiential Jewish education. Creativity, collaboration, creative thinking and problem solving are all key principles of twenty-first-century learning, and all are reflected in various aspects of experiential Jewish education.

Moving forward, I foresee the further development of technology in the educational world that will enable learners to continue to challenge themselves and grow from their experiences in digital space. Despite the relatively minor forays to date in this arena, I predict that the next decade will see the Jewish world also invest in technology as a means to educate, and that principles of experiential Jewish education will be central to many of these endeavors.

PURPOSE OF EDUCATION

In many ways the following Chinese proverb encapsulates much of what experiential Jewish education aims to achieve. "Give a man a fish and you feed him for a day. Teach a man to fish and you feed him for a lifetime." For a long time, and still in many more places than not, education in general, and specifically Jewish education, has been about feeding people fish. In the spirit of Dewey, Rousseau, Lewin and others I invoke the notion that the educator whose primary task is to deliver nuggets of information to passive learners is not what learning should be about. As Freire would expand upon, all of this was done in order to subjugate the masses to perpetuate the society in which they lived. Although the underpinnings of progressive education were developed over a hundred years ago, unfortunately it has not spread far and wide—yet. Jewish education has followed a similar line of thinking for many years. Jewish education has long been about feeding our learners fish in the form of rituals, language, texts, etc., and believing they will grow up to become the type of Jews that we want them to be. My prediction, perhaps infused with an idealistic (or naïve) anticipation, is that we will see many more fishermen being cultivated in the Jewish world. My belief is that experiential Jewish education is a key vehicle to create future generations

---

[1] Cuban, Larry. (2001). *Oversold and Underused: Computers in the Classroom*. Cambridge: Harvard University Press, p. 133.

of Jews who, by learning with and from their teachers to feed themselves, will be empowered to provide meaningful Jewish experiences for themselves, their families and their communities.

AND THE HOPE

This book began with Molly Wernick describing the tremendous impact that Jewish summer camp and youth group involvement had made on her life. I encounter stories reflecting these themes almost every day. Each one of these stories is unique and indeed magical in the deepest sense of the word—powerful experiences created by inspiring educators that allowed for what Heschel termed "radical amazement" to emerge. My hope moving forward is that this book can further serve to catalyze and develop a world that allows even more individuals to experience, if not the magic, then the power and amazement of experiential Jewish education.

CITATIONS

Cuban, L. (2001). *Oversold and Underused: Computers in the Classroom.* Cambridge: Harvard University Press.

ABOUT THE AUTHORS

RABBI SCOTT AARON is the current Community Scholar at the Agency for Jewish Learning of Greater Pittsburgh, but he has been a Jewish experiential educator since his first Hillel internship at Hofstra University as a second-year rabbinical student. That experience motivated him to choose a career path in "informal Jewish education," as it was called back in the day, rather than as a federation director, which was his original post-rabbinical school plan. Scott credits a combination of Judaic Studies courses and a positive Hillel experience as an undergraduate at the University of Cincinnati with helping him to personally form a strong Jewish identity during his own emerging adulthood years. After working in Hillel for a number of years, Scott became the Director of Education at the Brandeis-Bardin Institute (now part of the American Jewish University) and was privileged to participate in the Institute for Informal Jewish Education at Brandeis University. This learning experience and his work at Brandeis-Bardin with college-age and post-college adults motivated Scott to pursue his Ph.D. in the philosophy of education, focusing his work on developing a theoretical model of how Jewish experiential education programs such as Birthright Israel and Alternative Spring Breaks impact the identity development of Jewish emerging adults. Scott is also honored to currently be an adjunct faculty member at the Hebrew-Union College-Jewish Institute of Religion, the Jewish Theological Seminary of America and the Spertus Institute of Jewish Studies, where he prepares and mentors graduate students in Jewish experiential education programs.

DAVID BRYFMAN is currently the Chief Learning Officer at The Jewish Education Project. Growing up in Melbourne, Australia, he was active in the Habonim Dror youth movement, which fundamentally shaped his interest in experiential Jewish education. Over his twenty-year career he has seen Jewish education from all sides: as a student (Machon Le Madrichei Chutz l'Aretz/Institute for Youth Leaders from Abroad, Pardes, Melton Senior Educator's Program), a teacher (Mt. Scopus College, Melbourne), a Hillel director (University of New South Wales), a teen program director (Central Agency for Jewish Education, St. Louis), a graduate student (Wexner Graduate Fellow Program) and a consultant (The iCenter). David has also taught experiential Jewish education and ethnography in multiple settings, including NYU and Hebrew College. He received his undergraduate degree from Melbourne University and his masters from Monash University, and he earned his Ph.D. from NYU. David lives in Brooklyn with his wife and two children.

BARRY CHAZAN is Director of the Master of Arts in Jewish Professional Studies Program and Professor of Jewish Education at Spertus. Dr. Chazan is an internationally acclaimed Jewish educator and a pioneer in the fields of informal Jewish education and Israel education who has taught at the *Hebrew University of Jerusalem* and at major universities in North America. He earned his Ed.D. at Teachers College, Columbia University, New York, and has served in important professional capacities with the *Melton Center for Jewish Education* at the Hebrew University, the *Jewish Community Centers Association* and *Birthright Israel*. He is the author of a range of books and articles that deal with moral development and education, philosophy of Jewish education, informal education and Israel and Jewish education.

JACOB CYTRYN is the Director of Camp Ramah in Wisconsin. A Wexner Graduate Fellow, he is an advanced Ph.D. student in Jewish Studies and Education at the Mandel Center for Studies in Jewish Education at Brandeis University. His identity as an informal educator and ponderer of informal education was honed at Tikvat Shalom congregation in Metairie, LA, B'nai Amoona USY in St. Louis, MO, the Kelly Writers House and Student Committee on Undergraduate Education at the University of Pennsylvania, the Abraham Joshua Heschel High School and—most importantly—his intellectual playground of more than twenty years, Camp Ramah in Wisconsin. His Ph.D. research attempts to document and theorize how learning happens in an informal educational setting like Camp Ramah in Wisconsin. He holds degrees from the University of Pennsylvania and the Jewish Theological Seminary.

ROBYN FAINTICH is the product of the big four: camp, Israel, youth group and service-learning. She has OSRUI, Alexander Muss High School in Israel, Panim el Panim, USY NFTY to thank for laying the foundation of her professional path. She has over sixteen years of Jewish communal professional experience in areas that include youth movements and community teen initiatives, early childhood education, congregational family education and adult education. In 2010 Robyn launched a Jewish education consulting firm, Jewish GPS, LLC, which serves clients including synagogues, national Jewish organizations, community institutions, central agencies and day schools. She serves as a consulting faculty member of Shevet: the Jewish Family Education Exchange. Robyn earned her B.A.

degree in Journalism at Drake University and a masters degree in Jewish Studies with a focus on Jewish education at the Siegal College of Judaic Studies. She is a graduate of the Jim Joseph Foundation Fellowship with Bar Ilan University's Lookstein Center, which trained Jewish leaders to facilitate online communities of practice. Robyn has completed coursework towards an Ed.D. in Jewish Education Leadership at Northeastern University and Hebrew College and is pursuing a 2013 graduation. When she isn't neck-deep in professional journal articles and research for school, Robyn can be found cheering wildly for the St. Louis Cardinals, kvelling over her nephews (Evan, eight, and Jack, six), playing with her two cats or relaxing on the deck of a cruise ship.

RABBI JOSH FEIGELSON is founder and Educational Director of Ask Big Questions, an initiative of Hillel to bring diverse groups of people together for conversations about questions that matter to everyone. Josh is a doctoral candidate in religious studies at Northwestern University, where he also served as Hillel campus rabbi for six years. His research focuses on the place of history and memory in American Jewish life, as well as the intersection of American Jewry and university life. Josh has been a leader in advancing understanding of emerging adulthood in Jewish education. He and his family live in Evanston, IL.

CLARE GOLDWATER is an educational consultant and leadership coach working with organizations and professionals to expand their potential. She works with emerging leaders and forward-thinking organizations to develop new projects, nurture innovation and create meaningful Jewish opportunities that will impact individuals, communities and ultimately the Jewish world. A native of London, England, who has lived in both Israel and the U.S., Clare got her start as a student activist, experiencing the power of youth leadership and experiential education. She then spent many years working as an experiential educator with more groups than she can remember, of all ages, nationalities, denominations and backgrounds. She is also an Israeli tour educator, and even though today she has largely put aside her hiking boots and maps and works inside with organizations, she remains committed to helping people understand and interpret their own (professional and personal) landscapes so that they can learn and grow. Clare has a B.A. from Oxford University and an M.A. in education from the Hebrew University in Jerusalem. She was a Jerusalem Fellow at the Mandel Institute for Leadership in Jerusalem and is also a licensed coach with a focus on leadership development. She lives in Jerusalem with her family.

RABBI OWEN GOTTLIEB is a Jim Joseph Fellow and Ph.D. candidate in Education and Jewish Studies at NYU. He specializes in digital media and games for learning. Owen is the founder and director of ConverJent: Seriously Fun Jewish Games for Learning (*www.converjent.org*) and a resident faculty member at Clal: The National Jewish Center for Learning and Leadership. Through ConverJent he develops games for Jewish learning and teaches "Torah through Game Design" at venues nationwide. Owen has taught modern dance and hip-hop in the Negev Desert in Israel, worked as a project manager and business strategist for internet software development and written screenplays and teleplays for Paramount and Universal. Owen's doctoral research centers on the design and use of place-based mobile Augmented Reality Games (ARGs) to teach Jewish history. He investigates digital culture and opportunities to use technology to enhance interest and lower barriers to learner curiosity in Jewish subject matter. Owen has worked for years in supplementary schools, teaching second, fifth and seventh grades. At Central Synagogue he taught modern Hebrew using an Israeli teen TV soap opera, and he taught "Torah through Game Design" for fifth grade at East End Temple. Owen is a member of the Central Conference of American Rabbis, the Writers Guild of America, West, the International Game Developers Association and The Guides Track of Torah Trek. He is a co-founder of the Brooklyn havurah Shir HaMaalot and is a proud alumnus of Summer Super Stars, where Schwartz Tag, the game described in this chapter, was developed.

DANIEL HELD is a doctoral candidate in education at the Jewish Theological Seminary and a Wexner/Davison Graduate Fellow. His dissertation focuses on the motivations and developing professional identity of early career experiential educators. Daniel coordinates the educators' track at Yeshivat Chovevei Torah, training rabbinical students for careers in formal and nonformal education and is a Senior Associate at Rosov Consulting. Prior to moving to New York Daniel served as the Director of Student Activities, responsible for a curriculum of Jewish experiential learning, at TanenbaumCHAT, Toronto's Jewish community high school, and as a senior member of the educational staff at Brandeis University's Office of High School Programs, where he was also a fellow in the Institute for Informal Jewish Education's Seminar on Jewish Experiential Learning. Daniel holds a B.A. (Hons.) in business, a B.Ed. in Jewish education and an M.A. in Jewish Studies from York University and has studied at Bar Ilan University and the Melton Center for Jewish Education at Hebrew University. Daniel has held a variety of lay leadership roles, including serving on the boards of Yeshivat Maharat, the Bathurst Jewish Community Centre, the Jewish Disaster Response Corps and Canadian Jewish Congress. He writes a monthly column on Jewish education for the *Canadian Jewish News*.

JEFFREY S. KRESS is Associate Professor of Jewish Education and academic director of the Experiential Learning Initiative at the William Davidson Graduate School of Jewish Education at the Jewish Theological Seminary. He is the author of the book *Development, Learning, and Community: Educating for Identity in Pluralistic Jewish High Schools* (Academic Studies Press, 2012) and, together with Drs. Bernard Novick and Maurice Elias, of the book *Building Learning Communities with Character: How to Integrate Academic, Social and Emotional Learning* (Association of Supervision and Curriculum Development, 2002). He is also the editor of *Growing Jewish Minds, Growing Jewish Hearts: Promoting Spiritual, Social and Emotional Growth in Jewish Education* (URJ Press, 2013). Dr. Kress wonders if his ongoing inquiry into experiential education grew from confusion resulting from his spending summers as a youth at a range of overnight camps, including Native American, Young Judea, Bnai Akiva and Ramah.

DEBORAH MEYER is the Founder and Executive Director of Moving Traditions, which promotes Jewish education that applies a gender lens and Jewish values to the daily challenges of preteens and teens. For more than twenty-five years Meyer has built women's and Jewish change-making organizations. When she was co-director of Kolot Meyer helped create *Rosh Hodesh: It's a Girl Thing!*, now a program of Moving Traditions that empowers thousands of girls each year to identify and resist gender restrictions. Under Meyer's direction Moving Traditions has launched *Shevet Achim: The Brotherhood* to do the same for teen boys. Meyer credits her Jewish identity, commitment to the youth leadership model and progressive politics to Habonim Dror Camp Moshava and the movement's year program in Israel as much as to her parents' Shabbat observance, freilach holiday celebrations and passionate dinner conversations. Meyer is grateful to the women's movement for her opportunities and to two slightly older Mosh *chanichot* (campers) for introducing her to feminism when she was twelve. The mother of two young women, Carla and Talia, Meyer has a master's degree in communications from Emerson College and enjoys speaking and writing about gender, leadership and Jewish community.

DEBORAH PRICE NAGLER, MAJE, EMDTMS, has had a multiple-decade career in Jewish education built on a foundation of experiential education. In 1972 she co-taught the Zion class, a program that featured nine monthly retreats and a six-week work-tour program for eighth graders. From that time forward elements of experiential education have been a leitmotif of her work, which included positions as religious and day school principal, bureau director, March of the Living Regional Director, and National Director of Education and Leadership for Hadassah. For Nagler the combination of Israel and experience are ideal. In 1996 she served as CAJE Havayot Chair, crafting ninety-five full- and half-day field experiences for 1,800 CAJE attendees. Nagler earned an M.S. in Education Media Design and Technology from Full Sail University in 2009 and has expanded her experiential toolkit to include virtual learning environments. As the director of Simnik.com she partnered with the BJELA and Congregation Adat Ariel to produce the first-of-its-kind 3-D digital learning experience Virtual Israel: Neve Tzedek. A second Virtual Israel environment is now under construction. Nagler enjoys sharing her digital experiential education knowledge in courses at Gratz College and Hebrew College. She is also the Instructional Designer/Manager for the HUC Online Cantorial Certification Program.

PROFESSOR JOSEPH REIMER has taught at Brandeis University since 1986 and directed the Hornstein Program and the Institute for Informal Jewish Education. He has written one book on moral development, another on synagogue education and many articles on experiential Jewish education. These interests trace back his first year as a counselor at Camp Ramah. There he discovered what it meant to invest in your campers. The pleasure of that experience planted this question: What can make that relationship significant for both sides? That summer David Zissenwine was his *rosh edah*. At the end of staff week David proposed, following John Dewey, to establish "camper democracy," with the campers organizing a camper council. But that last-minute idea did not work well. Still, Zissenwine made a connection. Joe had studied Dewey but never made a connection between philosophy and education. He thought philosophy dealt with ideas and education with practice. He believed in a dichotomy of ideas versus practice. Ramah pointed to an alternative of ideas shaping practice and practice informing ideas. The Ramah experience led to the Harvard Graduate School of Education, where Joe studied and worked closely with Lawrence Kohlberg. A guru in the field of moral development, Kohlberg believed fervently in testing his ideas in the cauldron of urban schools and even prisons. He sent Joe to study Israeli kibbutzim to learn how they do moral education. Joe returned convinced that living in vibrant communities offers an unparalleled opportunity to take responsibility for others and count on others to take responsibility for you. Years later Joe wondered if summer camps could remain one of the last opportunities for young people to experience directly what a vibrant community feels like. Sure, camp is also a business, but need the business side obscure the beauty of waking up early on a summer morning, hearing the call of the birds, seeing the sleeping children in their beds and slipping out to sing Halleluyah?

LISA SAMICK has been working in the field of experiential Jewish education for more than twenty years. Her specialization and doctoral work is in the field of Jewish early childhood, but she began her career working with teens and university students. Lisa's engagement with Jewish learning began as a participant in Young Judaea—year-round and summer programs—throughout her middle and high school years and culminated in her participation in a year-long Israel program after college. She has worked in formal and informal educational settings ever since. Lisa is currently the Director of Early Childhood Education at the Brooklyn Heights Synagogue and serves on a variety of leadership committees, including the Advisory Council for *Shalom Sesame* and the Jewish Early Childhood Association. Her most impressive contribution to Jewish early childhood education, however, is her two-year-old daughter Jenna.

SCOTT M. SOKOL is Professor of Psychology, Jewish Education and Jewish Music at Hebrew College and the Associate Dean for Academic Support. He was the first dean of the Jewish Music Institute, the founding director of both the Cantor-Educator Program and the Special Education Program at Hebrew College and the inaugural Korman Family Professor of Jewish Special Education. Prior academic posts included a dozen years as a research scientist and clinical neuropsychologist at Massachusetts General Hospital and a professor of neurology at Harvard Medical School. When not at Hebrew College Scott serves as a part-time cantor at Temple Beth Sholom of Framingham and a part-time rabbi at Temple Emanuel of Marlborough. In the cracks he maintains a small private practice as a pediatric neuropsychologist. A consummate underachiever, Scott had formal education including a B.A. in psychology from Brandeis University, M.A. and Ph.D. degrees in Cognitive Neuropsychology from the Johns Hopkins University, an MSM and Cantorial Investiture from the Jewish Theological Seminary of America and rabbinical ordination from the Rabbinical Seminary International. A former Fulbright Scholar, Wexner Fellow and recipient of a Young Psychologist Award from the American Psychological Association, Scott is a Diplomate of the American Academy of Pediatric Neuropsychology and Fellow of the Association for Psychological Science. Academic achievements aside, Scott credits much of his current life path to his many years at Camp Ramah, where he returned last summer after a long hiatus, dragging along his wife, Dr. Francene Reichel, and their two children, Benjamin and Samuel.

BRADLEY SOLMSEN grew up on the Upper East Side of Manhattan. After becoming bar mitzvah at Central Synagogue he tendered what he thought would be his final resignation from the Jewish community. However, his beloved all-boys (non-Jewish) summer camp closed unexpectedly, leaving him no choice but to travel to Israel for the summer on a program operated by NFTY in Israel. The relationships he formed with the rabbi who led the trip (Tom Weiner) and the land and people of Israel affected him deeply. Bradley first encountered experiential education at the New England prep school he attended as a boarding student. Fast forward to his decision to pursue a career in Jewish education through rabbinical school at the Hebrew Union College—Jewish Institute of Religion, with a master's degree from the Jewish Theological Seminary and a doctorate in Jewish Education from JTS along the way. Bradley served as the Director of the Office of High School Programs at Brandeis University and is currently the Director of Youth Engagement for the Union for Reform Judaism. Bradley is married to Aliza Kline and is the proud abba of Ela, Gila and Nomi.

DR. RICHARD D. SOLOMON'S involvement in experiential education began in 1957 when, at age fourteen, he was enlisted to serve as a day camp counselor for fourteen campers at Starlight Bungalow colony in Monticello, New York. He was given this unusual opportunity because the counselor who was originally hired for the job suddenly quit. Dr. Solomon has been utilizing experiential educational strategies from 1965 to the present time in public, private, Jewish and non-Jewish formal and informal settings. From 1986 to 2001 Richard was the associate coordinator and then coordinator of Professional Development Schools, a collaborative teacher training and mentoring program of the College of Education at the University of Maryland, College Park and ten Maryland secondary schools. After retiring from the University of Maryland Richard was invited to serve as an adjunct professor at Baltimore Hebrew University in Maryland (now Baltimore Hebrew Institute at Towson University) and Gratz College in Pennsylvania, teaching graduate courses in supervision and staff development, instruction and classroom management. At the present time Richard is focusing his professional work on the integration of web technology into Jewish education. Toward that end he has a blog, *http://richarddsolomonsblog.blogspot.com,* teaches courses for Jewish educators, *http://jewish-education.org/,* has a book, *Toolbox for Teachers and Mentors: Moving Madrichim to Mentor Teachers and Beyond* and, with his wife Elaine, writes the Tech Tuesday column for BabagaNewz.

BRENT CHAIM SPODEK is rabbi of the Beacon Hebrew Alliance, home to deep and creative Jewish life in the Hudson Valley. In recent years he has served as the Rabbi in Residence at American Jewish World Service and the Marshall T. Meyer Fellow at Congregation B'nai Jeshurun in New York. An experienced leader and creator of Jewish service-learning experiences, Rabbi Spodek teaches extensively about spiritual approaches to justice work, Judaism and human rights and other topics in a variety of settings. He holds rabbinic ordination and a masters degree in philosophy from the Jewish Theological Seminary, where he was the first recipient of the Neubauer Fellowship. Prior to entering the rabbinate he attended Wesleyan University and worked as a daily journalist in Durham, NC.

SHUKI TAYLOR is the Director of Jewish Service Learning and Experiential Jewish Education at Yeshiva University Center for the Jewish Future (CJF). Shuki was born in Israel to a South African mother and a British father. He is married to an Australian and currently resides in New York, working with North Americans. (All of these factors contribute to his somewhat strange accent.) His love for experiential Jewish education comes from experiencing it as a learner and then as an educator in all of these countries. In his roles at YU Shuki founded the Certificate Program in Experiential Jewish Education, the Innovators Circle and the Counterpoint Israel Initiatives and has overseen the growth of YU Service Learning Missions benefitting underprivileged communities worldwide. Previously Shuki worked at the Koby Mandell Foundation, where he founded and directed innovative and experiential therapy programs for Israeli teens affected by terror. Shuki completed the Hesder program at Yeshivat Har Eztion and studied education at Herzog College and scriptwriting at Ma'aleh School of Television, Film and the Arts. Shuki currently resides New York with his wife Natalie and their three children.

ABIGAIL UHRMAN is an advanced doctoral student in education and Jewish Studies at New York University. Abigail graduated summa cum laude, Phi Beta Kappa from the University of California, Los Angeles, with a major in history and a minor in education studies. Following graduation she spent two years as a fellow at the Drisha Institute of Jewish Education. Abigail then worked as a fifth grade teacher at the Solomon Schechter School of Manhattan and later as a literacy coach and new teacher mentor. Upon completing her coursework Abigail worked at the Steinhardt Foundation for Jewish Life and was an adjunct faculty member at NYU. Abigail is currently in her second year of a doctoral fellowship at the Davidson School at the Jewish Theological Seminary, focusing much of her time on the program in experiential learning and working with Professor Jeffrey Kress. A long-time Ramah-nik, Abigail is particularly grateful to the field of Jewish experiential education not only for many amazing summers as a camper and staff member but also for allowing her to meet her wonderful husband, Cantor Israel Gordan. Nearly twenty years later, they live In Huntington, New York with their two incredible children, Noa and Eli.

JOSHUA YARDEN, Ph.D., is a learner, writer and facilitator. He is a "practicing reflective" who helps people examine the nature of their experience and look for effective ways to move beyond the obstacles they face. He works with individuals, camps, schools, community organizations, central agencies and national initiatives in Israel and North America. Josh grew up in the Hashomer Hatza'ir Youth Movement and began developing experiential programming as a youth leader in the democratic utopian culture of Shomria camps, where adults were few and far between and adolescents were encouraged to envision, to create and to cope with their own challenges. After moving to Israel he was involved in kibbutz education, Jewish-Arab and religious-secular encounters as well as community administration and immigrant absorption. He is a graduate of the Jerusalem Institute for Youth Leaders from Abroad and holds a B.A. in Middle East Studies from McGill University, an M.A. in Judaic Studies from the University of Haifa and a Ph.D. in Education, Culture and Society from the University of Pennsylvania. Josh is the proud father of Yuval, Segev and Dotan, from whom he draws unfailing inspiration to lead a life of meaning, joy and integrity.

MARK S. YOUNG is the program coordinator of the Experiential Learning Initiative, a Jim Joseph Foundation–funded program within the William Davidson Graduate School of Jewish Education at The Jewish Theological Seminary. Mark has developed and helped launch Davidson's M.A. Program in Jewish Experiential Education. Mark also designed and manages Davidson's new professional development program, the Jewish Experiential Leadership Institute for JCC Professionals, coordinated in partnership with the JCC Association. Mark's journey in Jewish education began during his fourteen summers at the Mandel JCC's Camp Wise in Cleveland, Ohio, where he served for several years as song leader, Judaic director and staff-in-training director. The journey continued with experiences in Central Region United Synagogue Youth and song leading in various synagogues throughout the tri-state area. Mark then completed a B.S. in psychology and economics from McGill University in Montreal, Canada, and later an M.P.A. in Nonprofit Management and M.A. in Hebrew and Judaic Studies from New York University. Mark then worked as human resources and volunteer programs manager for New York City's 92nd Street Y, where he developed and expanded a volunteer community of adults who participated in multiple communal service projects. Mark lives in Hartsdale, New York, with his wife, Rabbi Mara Young, a congregational rabbi serving Woodlands Community Temple in White Plains, New York. Mark is also the current Board Chair of the Advancing Jewish Professionals of NYC, a local professional development group of the Jewish Communal Service Association

Index